PARIS IN THE CINEMA
Beyond the *Flâneur*

Locations, Characters, History

Edited by **Alastair Phillips and Ginette Vincendeau**

BLOOMSBURY ACADEMIC
LONDON • NEW YORK • OXFORD • NEW DELHI • SYDNEY

BLOOMSBURY ACADEMIC
Bloomsbury Publishing Plc
50 Bedford Square, London, WC1B 3DP, UK
1385 Broadway, New York, NY 10018, USA
29 Earlsfort Terrace, Dublin 2, Ireland

BLOOMSBURY, BLOOMSBURY ACADEMIC and the Diana logo
are trademarks of Bloomsbury Publishing Plc

First published by Palgrave Macmillan 2018
Reprinted by Bloomsbury Academic, 2024

Copyright © Introduction and editorial arrangement
© Alastair Phillips and Ginette Vincendeau 2018
Individual essays © their respective authors 2018

The authors has asserted their right under the Copyright,
Designs and Patents Act, 1988, to be identified as the author of this work.

All rights reserved. No part of this publication may be reproduced or transmitted in any form or by any means, electronic or mechanical, including photocopying, recording, or any information storage or retrieval system, without prior permission in writing from the publishers.

Bloomsbury Publishing Plc does not have any control over, or responsibility for, any third-party websites referred to or in this book. All internet addresses given in this book were correct at the time of going to press. The author and publisher regret any inconvenience caused if addresses have changed or sites have ceased to exist, but can accept no responsibility for any such changes.

A catalogue record for this book is available from the British Library.

A catalogue record for this book is available from the Library of Congress.

ISBN 978-1-84457-818-4 hardback
ISBN 978-1-84457-817-7 paperback

To find out more about our authors and books visit www.bloomsbury.com
and sign up for our newsletters.

PARIS IN THE CINEMA

Contents

Acknowledgements — vii

Beyond the *Flâneur*: An Introduction — 1
Alastair Phillips and Ginette Vincendeau

PART I: LOCATIONS
The Eiffel Tower: A Parisian Film Star — 17
Nicoleta Bazgan

Working-class Paris and Post-war Noir: *Les Portes de la nuit* — 26
Thomas Pillard

The *Caves* of Saint-Germain-des-Prés in 1950s French Cinema — 35
Sébastien Layerle

Paris in the Summer of 1959: *Le Signe du lion* — 45
Michel Marie

Truffaut's Apartments — 55
Hilary Radner and Alistair Fox

The New Wave Hotel — 66
Roland-François Lack

The Vanishing of Les Halles — 76
Catherine E. Clark

The Parisian *Banlieue* on Screen: So Close, Yet So Far — 87
Ginette Vincendeau

PART II: CHARACTERS
Maigret from across the Channel — 103
Charlotte Brunsdon

Parisian Cinephiles and the Mac-Mahon — 113
Leila Wimmer

Beyond the *Flâneuse*: The Uniqueness of *Cléo de 5 à 7* — 125
Jennifer Wallace

Amateur Filmmakers' Paris: Home Movies at the Forum des Images — 136
Roger Odin

The Concierge in Contemporary French Cinema — 146
Raphaëlle Moine

Parisian Lovers in the Contemporary Romcom — 156
Mary Harrod

The Enduring Glamour of the Parisienne — 166
Stephen Gundle

PART III: HISTORY
Charles Dickens's Two Cities — 179
Colin Jones

From Meryon to Ulmer's *Bluebeard*: A Baudelairian Iconography — 187
Jean-Loup Bourget

Site of Infamy: The Vel' d'Hiv in French Cinema — 196
Sandy Flitterman-Lewis

'Unremarkable Paris': Jacques Becker's Urban Everyday — 207
Alastair Phillips

Television and the Renewal of Paris: From Official Discourse to Social Criticism — 218
Hélène Jannière

Parisian Building Sites (1945–75): From Modernity to Abstraction — 230
Marie Gaimard and Marguerite Vappereau

The Mirror of a City: The 'Parisian Collection' of the Forum des Images — 242
Jean-Yves de Lépinay

PART IV: INTERVIEW
Filming Paris: An Interview with Jean-Pierre Jeunet — 257
Isabelle Vanderschelden

Contributors — 266
Select Bibliography — 271
Index — 278

Acknowledgements

First of all our warm thanks go to Irène Bessière, the former Head of the research programme *La Ville au cinéma* at the Fondation Maison des Sciences de l'Homme (FMSH), Paris, for welcoming our project on Paris as part of this programme with her customary generosity.

We also wish to acknowledge the support of Irène Bessière at FMSH, and Laurent Creton at the Université Sorbonne Nouvelle-Paris 3 (IRCAV), for their personal, professional and financial support for the conference 'Paris au cinéma: lieux, personnages, histoire. Au-delà du flâneur' which took place at the INHA, Paris, on 6–7 December 2012. Our thanks too to Clémence Allamand, Gabrielle Tremblay and Stéphanie Passe-Coutrin and their team, for their expert work on the design of the poster and the organisation of the conference. We are also grateful to all the participants in the conference, many of whom are contributors to this volume.

Our thanks also go to the following for their financial support regarding translation costs for this book: in the UK, the School of Arts and Humanities and Professor Rosalind Galt, Head of the Department of Film Studies at King's College London, and the Department of Film and Television Studies and the Humanities Research Centre at the University of Warwick; in France, the ANR (Agence Nationale de la Recherche) and the research project ANRCinépop50, and

Reconstructing the city: the film set for *Boulevard* (Julien Duvivier, 1960) with the Sacré-Cœur basilica in Montmartre in the background.

Professor Raphaëlle Moine for coordinating finance for some of the French translations. We are also grateful to the translator Peter Graham for his excellent work and, as usual, for going the extra mile.

At BFI/Palgrave, we wish to thank Jenny Burnell, Nicola Cattini, Sophia Contento, Philippa Hudson, Jenna Steventon, Vidya Venkiteshwaran Iyer and Cecily Wilson.

Vanessa Schwartz, Richard Abel, Dina Iordanova, Antoine de Baecque, Maryn Wilkinson and Tom Brown were very helpful at various stages in the preparation of this book.

The cover picture was sourced from Collection EYE Filmmuseum. Our thanks to Leontien Bout and Annette Schulz.

Last but not least, we wish to thank all our contributors for their excellent work; we are especially grateful to the filmmaker Jean-Pierre Jeunet for agreeing to be interviewed for the book, and to Isabelle Vanderschelden for conducting the interview.

Beyond the *Flâneur*: An Introduction

Alastair Phillips and Ginette Vincendeau

> A few years ago, I thought that you could no longer make films in Paris; I was wrong. Paris is constantly on the move and you could still shoot 500 or 5,000 films there.
>
> (Jacques Rivette)[1]

Paris is the cinematic city par excellence, and, in the spirit of Jacques Rivette's words above, it remains one of the most iconic, filmed cities in the world. It can boast of being the 'official' birthplace of the cinema, with the first public screening at the Grand Café, boulevard des Capucines, on 28 December 1895. From then on, the city's cinematic presence has been phenomenal, as documented both by the enormous collection of audiovisual material set in Paris collected by the Forum des Images (discussed in this book by Jean-Yves de Lépinay, Roger Odin and Catherine Clark) and by the centrality of films set in Paris in the historiography of French cinema. Paris's world record-breaking number of cinemas,[2] including its rich network of art cinemas, enshrines further its place as the capital of cinephilia (see Leila Wimmer's chapter).[3] Paris, importantly, also holds a special place within the development of studies of cinema and the city, as the location where, or about which, many of the seminal texts on urban modernity and post-modernity have been written, notably by Charles Baudelaire, Walter Benjamin, Guy Debord, Henri Lefèbvre, Michel de Certeau, Anne Friedberg, Janet Wolff, Elizabeth Wilson and Marc Augé.[4] Paris's status as a leading tourist destination must be added to this rich heritage, with all of these elements generating a seemingly endless flow of films and publications. The sheer quantity of screen representations of Paris defies any attempt at exhaustiveness and, as a journalist in *Le Monde* put it, 'each year, Paris, with its history, its monuments, its habits and customs, spawns a whole truck-load of books'.[5] How can we, nevertheless, justify adding one more volume to this plethora of texts?

The starting point for this project was a conference that we organised at the INHA in Paris on 6 and 7 December 2012, entitled 'Paris au cinéma: lieux, personnages, histoire. Au-delà du flâneur'.[6] The conference took place, appropriately, in the Galerie Colbert, one of the beautiful early 19th century covered passages celebrated by Walter Benjamin among others.[7] The conference itself was sparked off by our awareness of a striking paradox when it comes to writing on Paris in the cinema. On the one hand, there are numerous beautifully illustrated survey books, such as Gilles Nadeau and Jean Douchet's *Paris cinéma: une ville vue par le cinéma de 1895 à nos jours* (1997),

N. T. Binh's *Paris au cinéma: la vie rêvée de la capitale de Méliès à Amélie Poulain* (2003) or Marie-Christine Vincent and François de Saint-Exupéry's *Paris vu au cinéma* (2003). On the other hand, there is the wider scholarly field of 'cinema and the city' studies, in which the French capital, as mentioned above, has been established as the emblematic site of modernity with a repeated focus on Baudelaire and Benjamin's defining figure of the *flâneur*, and later its feminine companion, the *flâneuse*. Foundational as these texts and concepts are, our contention is that in between these two broad approaches, the actual representation of Paris – in its visual, aural and generic richness – remains strangely lacking. *Paris in the Cinema: Beyond the Flâneur* thus aims to retrieve, explore and celebrate this richness, building on, but also departing from, the familiar '*flâneur* paradigm'.

Before the *Flâneur*

The literature on Paris as a cinematic city remains surprisingly slim given the centrality of the French capital to the definition of French cinema. Within and beyond the previously mentioned illustrated anthologies by Douchet, and Binh and Nadeau, three main canonical strands of Parisian filmmaking dominate critical writing in the field: French cinema of the 1930s (with special attention to the legacy of poetic realism), Paris as imagined by Hollywood (exemplified by such films as *An American in Paris* [Vincente Minnelli, 1951]) and the French New Wave (typified by films such as Jean-Luc Godard's *A bout de souffle* [1960]).

Dudley Andrew's *Mists of Regret* (1995) remains the most detailed historical survey of the genesis of French poetic realism and its atmospheric iconography of Parisian working-class streets, nocturnal bars and cafés, canal banks and factories. Andrew's rigorous historical method argues for a grounded understanding of the aesthetic and cultural fields that produced such a distinctive way of picturing the capital and his work provides several seminal readings of major Paris films of the period such as *Sous les toits de Paris/Under the Roofs of Paris* (René Clair, 1930) *Le Crime de Monsieur Lange/The Crime of Monsieur Lange* (Jean Renoir, 1936) and *Le Jour se lève/Daybreak* (Marcel Carné, 1939). Alastair Phillips's *City of Darkness, City of Light. Emigré Filmmakers in Paris 1929–1939* (2004) builds on this work to survey the distinctive contribution of foreign filmmakers to the representation of the French

Shooting a street scene on the set of *Sous les toits de Paris/Under the Roofs of Paris* (René Clair, 1930).

capital during this key decade of its cinematic imaginary. Moving beyond the study of popular 'dark Paris', Phillips also considers the representation of the city in various 'lighter' films that engage with the long history of Parisian mass culture and spectacular entertainment. Both authors draw upon an important body of articles and publications by Ginette Vincendeau, whose unpublished PhD thesis on popular French cinema of the 1930s remains an essential resource for all scholars of the period.[8] Dudley Andrew and Steven Ungar's monumental *Popular Front Culture and the Poetics of Culture* (2005) remains the definitive study of the intertextual history of Parisian culture during the momentous period of the French Popular Front, while Kelley Conway's *Chanteuse in the City* (2004) surveys the rich interrelationship between song, performance and Parisian representation in several key films of the decade.[9] All these studies acknowledge the fact that Parisian films of the decade were largely, though not exclusively, studio-made and Sue Harris's detailed scrutiny of the work of French set designers of the decade,[10] building on earlier work by Léon Barsacq (1970), among others, makes a further intervention in the study of this key role in visualising the spaces of the French capital.

Of course, the majority Parisian representation of the Hollywood classical era was also studio-bound and much of the literature on the Paris-based films of Maurice Chevalier (e.g. *Innocents of Paris* [Richard Wallace, 1929]), Ernst Lubitsch (e.g. *Ninotchka* [1939]), Billy Wilder (e.g. *Sabrina* [1954]), Vincente Minnelli (e.g. *Gigi* [1958]) and Stanley Donen (e.g. *Funny Face* [1957]), directly or indirectly, acknowledges this legacy in terms of the construction of an Americanised ideal of the city. In addition to Antoine de Baecque's 2012 compendious anthology of articles edited for the catalogue of the exhibition of the same name, *Paris by Hollywood*, Vanessa Schwartz's *It's So French! Hollywood, Paris, and the Making of Cosmopolitan Film Culture* (2007) is the most comprehensive study to date on how Hollywood appropriated and visualised the spaces of the French capital as a privileged site of cultural alterity and desire.

As Jean Douchet has suggested, 'the street as seen by the New Wave reflected the aspirations of the young people who made it theirs. ... Paris was at their feet. It

The crew and cast of *Paris nous appartient/Paris Belongs to Us* (Jacques Rivette, 1961) filming the capital from the rooftops.

The poetry of the streets: Antoine (Antoine Bourseiller) and Cléo (Corinne Marchand) pass the Verlaine bus stop in *Cléo de 5 à 7/ Cleo from 5 to 7* (Agnès Varda, 1962).

was a place of unlimited possibility.'[11] In words that echo much critical writing on the New Wave's representation of the city, Douchet thus argues that 'there was no screen image that did not correspond to its real-life double. The real took precedence over fiction.'[12] As almost every survey text on the French New Wave suggests, this attention to 'the real' relates to a number of important determinants: the development of new portable and lighter-weight camera and sound-recording equipment, the growing prominence of French televisual reportage and ethnographic filmmaking and the influence of Italian neo-realism. But just as important was the development of Paris as a site of international travel and tourism, and André Malraux's project of the *ravalement* (renovation) of the city's principal monuments and public spaces which gave the city a much-needed 'makeover' in the aftermath of World War Two. The meeting of Paris and the New Wave cinema produced a plethora of canonical films featuring the streets of the city, even though in his influential study of the New Wave, Michel Marie points out that the limited number of locations we see in many films was determined by the filmmakers' own experience of city as filmgoers, not citizens[13] (in his chapter here, Marie examines one such film's exploration of the city streets, Eric Rohmer's *Le Signe du lion/The Sign of Leo* [1959–62]). As Roland-François Lack and Hilary Radner and Alistair Fox point out in this book, it is more or less a myth that this attention to 'the real' was solely devoted to an exterior view of real-life Paris locations. The New Wave was as much a cinema of apartments and hotels, they argue, as it was of streets and cars. In any case, as Charlotte Brunsdon also argues, while

> cinema seems so readily to render up the real and it is, in one sense, constituted through the production of spaces ... these cinematic spaces are [also] produced through the manipulation of other spaces and processes: editing, camera movement, sets, models, back-projection, paintings, refilming, computer-generated imagery and, occasionally, locations.[14]

Much of the work in this book seeks to recognise this productive tension.

The Figure of the *Flâneur*

The *flâneur*, as famously defined in Charles Baudelaire's 'The Painter of Modern Life' (1864), emerged as a quintessential figure of the new Paris engineered by Baron Georges-Eugène Haussmann.[15] As the Prefect of the Seine *département*, charged by Emperor Napoleon III to modernise the French capital, Haussmann led a vast series of public works involving the construction of parks, railway stations, civic amenities and illuminated avenues and boulevards that offered new resources, vistas and means of circulation for the growing population of the city. Baudelaire saw the *flâneur* as a uniquely mobile artistic figure capable of registering both 'the passing moment' of the modern Parisian experience and 'all the suggestions of eternity that it contains'.[16] 'Beauty', for the poet, had a dual nature. It was 'made up of an eternal, invariable element, whose quantity is excessively difficult to determine, and of a relative, circumstantial element, which will be, if you like, whether severally or all at once, the age, its fashions, its morals, its emotions'.[17] It was the duty of the contemporary Parisian artist – 'Observer, philosopher, *flâneur* – call him what you will'[18] – to depict the newly fugitive qualities of the city in ways that drew this fundamental connection between urban perception and the movement of the urban body in space and time.

The figure of the *flâneur* has been primarily important to the study of the cinematic city because Baudelaire's apprehension of the city was, in some senses, already 'cinematic'. It is through him that we discover an enduring parallel between the perception of the modern life of the city as a fact by the strolling urban citizen, and the perception on the part of the artist (and their intended audience) that modern life may be best represented in the form of a contingent sensory experience. Both notions appear to concern a broken and fragmented mode of vision capable of disrupting a pre-modern sense of the unity of space and time. In the case of the city walker, this was achieved by the relationship between the moving body and the Parisian street and its numerous attractions. In the case of the cinematic spectator that emerged at the end of the 19th century, this was achieved by means of the eventual mobility of the camera and the fragmentation of space and time through editing.[19]

Janet Wolff argues there was no such thing in Baudelaire's time as the *flâneuse* because 'such a character was rendered impossible because of the sexual divisions of the nineteenth century'.[20] She nonetheless points out several significant female role types that did circulate within the spaces (and texts) of Parisian modernity. These included 'the prostitute, the widow, the old lady, the lesbian, the murder victim, and the passing unknown woman',[21] and, interestingly, many of these later became incorporated, for better or worse, within films set in the French capital. Wolff's denial of the *flâneuse* has been challenged by numerous feminist scholars, including Elizabeth Wilson, who suggest that by the end of the 19th century (and thus the emergence of cinema), middle and lower-middle-class women *were* entering the urban public sphere as mobile agents either as shoppers, travellers, office workers and service-sector employees.[22] The figures, in turn, were represented in numerous novels, paintings and newspaper and magazine articles depicting the modernity of the Parisian everyday.

Baudelaire's language is full of references to speed, light and fleeting images that circulate largely within this emerging urban environment. This sense of impermanence and a subjectivity aligned with the idea of drifting and wandering imply an almost kinaesthetic sense of belonging to the modern world that still remains strikingly contemporary. As Ben Singer[23] and Tom Gunning[24] have pointed out in their influential work on the relations between modernity and the cinema, the qualities of ephemerality, display and surface, all of interest to the figure of the *flâneur*, are also fundamentally related to the nature of urban filmic reality that deals explicitly with texture, gesture and expression. Anke Gleber argues the same point in her influential study of the relationship between the figure of the *flâneur* and the development of cinema, stating that 'the figure of the [Parisian] flâneur is the precursor of a particular form of inquiry that seeks to read the history of culture from its public spaces'.[25]

This project of reading a culture from the representation of its public spaces has been a significant element of much formative scholarship on the cinematic city that takes the feature of a journey through the streets as a central narrative trope of the film in question.[26] It is for this reason, too, that the *flâneur* has endured as an emblem of the ways in which so many other artists and writers encounter Paris and reflect on 'the age, its fashions, its morals, its emotions'. From the Paris Surrealists such as Louis Aragon and Philippe Soupault to the modern-day romantic dramas of Richard Linklater, the French capital has been taken as the locus point of a certain kind of observant, aimless urban wandering. Seeing the city from the gaze of the passer-by has been central to the ways in which Paris has been constituted as a cultural (or touristic) myth, from the art of the Impressionists (especially Manet) to the Parisian street photography of Charles Marville, Eugène Atget, Brassaï and Robert Doisneau. These references, including related emblematic shots from the French New Wave, now form part of a contemporary pictorial shorthand for the French capital that circulates in brochures, posters, book covers, postcards and online media. In this sense, despite the continued growth and modernisation of the city, the early modern period and the related notion of Paris as 'the capital of the 19th century'[27] still remain a fundamental aspect of how we think about the visual image of the city today.

Beyond the *Flâneur*

As is evident from the above, the figures of the *flâneur* and the *flâneuse* constitute a core concept within cultural studies of the city, one that in some sense may appear all but exhausted if not clichéd. Our slightly provocative subtitle is however not meant to indicate a wholesale rejection. Researching this book and working with our contributors has confirmed both the ubiquity of the term – whether we like it or not – and our intuition that it was time to move 'beyond the *flâneur*'. This is partly because the deployment of the term has become akin to a *doxa*, and partly because the concept clearly needs revisiting, in terms of its historicity and applicability to the city, the need to nuance the notion of *flânerie* and what it entails, and the desire to offer more diverse, and more specific, points of view on both the city and its representation on screen.

Baudelaire's *flâneur*, as we have seen, is a deeply historical figure, a product of the Haussmannian 1860s. However, in the way it has been taken up by versions of theories of modernity and studies of the city, this historicity has too often been ignored, leaving aside distinctions of gender, social class, ethnicity and periodisation. This is a point developed in some detail in Keith Tester's anthology *The Flâneur*, which situates the figure within a range of historical and theoretical contexts.[28] What relationship can there be, for instance, between the 19th-century *flâneur* and the Parisian worker, the *banlieusard* or the tourist in the early 21st century? In trying to avoid an anachronistic, blanket application of the figure beyond its immediate historical timeframe, it is important to deal with a wider representation of men and women in the city. In this volume, Stephen Gundle, for example, discusses how the evolution of the myth of the Parisienne in the 20th century contributed to 'a revival of the city's associations with modernity and femininity' and how from the 1950s onwards, stars such as Brigitte Bardot and Catherine Deneuve brought the historical links between the city and fashion literally to the streets. Similarly, the young women in New Wave films are much less restricted in their movements, their occupation of public space and social identity than the historical *flâneuse*. As Jennifer Wallace points out, the heroine of *Cléo de 5 à 7*/*Cleo from 5 to 7* (Agnès Varda, 1962), despite being repeatedly linked to the figure, is not limited to a narrow definition of the *flâneuse*; she works in the city, goes to the cinema, orders drinks in cafés, walks the streets, meets a friend and travels widely through the city in taxis, a friend's car and public transport. Our concern has also been to move away from the distinctly bourgeois connotations of the historical *flâneur*, to encompass different strata of the Parisian population in terms of social class and topography – such as the inhabitants of the working-class north-eastern *quartiers* of the city (Thomas Pillard, Alastair Phillips), the *banlieusard(e)s* (Ginette Vincendeau), workers on building sites (Marie Gaimard and Marguerite Vappereau) and the concierge (Raphaëlle Moine) .

Young women reclaim the *banlieue* street in *Bande de filles*/*Girlhood* (Céline Sciamma, 2014).

The accent on the *flâneur* also means the dominance of late 19th-century Paris, and we felt a need to stretch this periodisation. Thus for instance in their chapters, Colin Jones and Jean-Loup Bourget turn their gaze towards earlier periods and iconographies (the French Revolution, Meryon's etchings). Closer to us, the extensive transformations of Paris in the 20th century have produced different urban vistas and different relations between the inhabitants and their environment, challenging the distanced and aestheticising gaze of the leisured *flâneur*. The building of new housing, the demolition and rebuilding of Les Halles (discussed by Catherine Clark and by Gaimard and Vappereau), and the extension of the suburbs (Vincendeau) have not only profoundly changed the urban landscape, but the way Parisians relate to and negotiate these spaces. In turn, the representation of these sites on film and television has altered (see Hélène Jannière's chapter, for example, about French television's shifting view of urban regeneration). In the post-war period, the ongoing modernisation of the city has also had an impact on the evolution and screen representation of specifically Parisian social types, such as the concierge (Moine), the Parisienne (Gundle), the cinemagoer (Wimmer), city lovers (Mary Harrod), women in the suburbs (Vincendeau) and 'ordinary' inner-city dwellers (Phillips). Such analyses enable us to observe how the inhabitants negotiate spatial and social relations to new buildings, how they cover distances within the city or between the city and suburbs, and even how they deal with the physical impediment of building sites (Gaimard and Vappereau).

In the same way as the *flâneur* has often been deployed as a universal, ahistorical figure, there has been a tendency to apply the term *flânerie* to any form of movement through the city, from simply walking from A to B, or anxiously searching for something or someone, to being in pursuit. In the process we lose the specific connotations of aimless wandering and aesthetic experience that the term carries.[29]

The concierge (Denise Clair, right) assisting the police (Jean Gabin, left) in *Maigret tend un piège/Maigret Sets a Trap* (Jean Delannoy, 1958).

It thus seemed important to distinguish between different types of mobility around the city: wandering, yes, but also the process of trying to reach a precise destination, going shopping, investigating a murder, going to work and so on – all forms of movement that are not adequately covered by the term *flânerie*. In their respective chapters, Marie on *Le Signe du lion* and Wallace on *Cléo*, explicitly challenge received opinion in this respect. But beyond these two chapters, the theme of urban mobility implicitly underlines many other chapters.

The impact of the concept of the *flâneur* on the conceptualisation of Paris has also been to privilege the street as *the* locus of urban modernity. While we do not deny the validity of this point, our aim in this book is to widen our vision of the city beyond the street. Landmarks play a key role in visual representations of the city, and our book inevitably examines some of the best-known Parisian iconic sites: the Eiffel Tower (Nicoleta Bazgan), Notre-Dame (Bourget), the Sacré-Coeur (Pillard), the banks of the Seine (Marie), and some unexpected ones, such as the city's demolition and building sites (Jannière, Gaimard and Vappereau). In her chapter, Sandy Flitterman-Lewis explores the changing representation of an *absent*, yet historically significant, landmark – the Vel' d'Hiv stadium where thousands of Jews were rounded up on 16–17 July 1942, in horrific conditions, before being deported (the stadium was demolished in 1959). More widely, the layout of the city, its *quartiers* and *arrondissements*, its rings of boulevards including the *périphérique* and the suburbs that lie beyond, its waterways, provide an inescapable topography that permeates every chapter of the book.

In our quest for a more detailed and embedded look at the city, we particularly sought to explore sites rarely discussed in relation to Paris on screen. These include a number of interior spaces such as hotel rooms (Lack), apartments (Radner & Fox), underground nightclubs (Sébastien Layerle), the concierge's *loge* (Moine), the Mac-Mahon cinema (Wimmer) and the screening rooms of the Forum des Images (de Lépinay).

One of the most productive avatars of the *flâneur* is the filmmaker and we are delighted that Isabelle Vanderschelden was able to interview Jean-Pierre Jeunet for this book, given the impact of his film *Le Fabuleux destin d'Amélie Poulain/Amélie* (2001) on contemporary perceptions of the city. Jeunet admits he made the film, on his return from Los Angeles, 'dazzled by the beauty of [his] city', but that he deliberately produced 'fake images of Paris in a postcard style'. Nevertheless, the massive international success of the film has meant, for instance, that tours of Montmartre where 'Amélie' resided are now available to tourists. Jeunet also pays tribute to earlier canonical Paris filmmakers such as Marcel Carné, whose film *Les Portes de la nuit/Gates of the Night* (1946) is examined here in detail by Pillard. Similarly, the previously mentioned centrality of Paris for the New Wave cinema means that several of its directors are discussed in

Amélie (Audrey Tautou) in front of an elevated Métro station in *Le Fabuleux destin d'Amélie Poulain/Amélie* (Jean-Pierre Jeunet, 2001).

this book: Eric Rohmer (Marie, Gaimard and Vappereau), François Truffaut (Radner and Fox), Jean-Luc Godard (Lack), Agnès Varda (Wallace) and others too, from mainstream figures like Maurice Tourneur (Gaimard and Vappereau) to auteurs such as Marco Ferreri (Clark). We have also included television: Brunsdon discusses British television's take on Georges Simenon's hero Inspector Maigret, and Jannière the way French television documentary filmmakers have approached the material transformation of the city. Roger Odin highlights a particularly neglected area by looking at how the fascinating collection of home movies about Paris in the Forum des Images yields 'a host of factual details about everyday life in Paris'. The Forum des Images itself, its origins, function and usage, is examined by de Lépinay, while its collection was also an important resource for Clark.

Our contributors themselves bring a variety of perspectives to bear on to this kaleidoscopic view of Paris, offering a combined vision that is interdisciplinary as well as international. In terms of experience and scholarly discipline, writers in the book hail from architecture, history, art, literature, film and television studies, film theory, filmmaking and archiving. We felt it was particularly important to give space to French (and Parisian) authors. If, as Jeunet argues, Parisians 'no longer pay attention' to the beauty of the city, they still nonetheless bring a detailed gaze to some of its more mundane vistas and characters, from the concierge to family meals to the building site.

Locations, Characters, History

While challenges to the centrality of the *flâneuse/flâneuse* constitute a continuous thread through this volume, the subtitle, 'Locations, Characters, History' hints at another key concern, one that acted as an organising principle for both the 2012 conference and for this book.

In the first part, *Locations*, the built fabric and the topography of the city and its environs are not simply envisaged as social décor but as 'actors', determining themes, genres, situations, social milieux and characters. The chapters thus range from landmarks (the Eiffel Tower) to specific areas (the north-east *arrondissements*, Saint-Germain-des-Prés, Les Halles, the banks of the Seine, the suburbs) and interior spaces (hotel rooms and apartments). The second section, *Characters*, examines a number of Parisian social and professional types (concierges, lovers, tramps, the Parisienne), fictional figures whose image is strongly linked to the city (Maigret, Cléo), and particular Parisian types, such as the amateur filmmaker and the avid cinephile, who engage in the city's cultural activities. In the *History* section we relate the topography of the city, its institutions and characters to history in a wider sense – politics (Revolutionary Paris, the German occupation), social history (the post-war 'everyday', the ongoing demolition and rebuilding of the city), and Parisian culture and the arts (Meryon's etchings and Hollywood cinema, the Forum des Images collection). We are of course aware that these divisions are to some extent arbitrary. Indeed, the interview with Jean-Pierre Jeunet that concludes the book makes this point forcefully as Jeunet's replies to Isabelle Vanderschelden show his equal interest in (cultural) history, locations and characters. Similarly, each chapter, beyond its immediate focus, also concerns the meeting of all three areas.

Conversely, in view of the overwhelming quantity of audiovisual representations of Paris that we point out at the beginning of this introduction, we aimed at selectivity. As a result, we inevitably left out a number of prominent and much-loved films set in and/or about the city. Fans of *Les Amants du Pont-Neuf/The Lovers on the Bridge* (Leos Carax, 1991), *J'ai pas sommeil/I Can't Sleep* (Claire Denis, 1994), *Chacun cherche son chat/When the Cat's Away* (Cédric Klapisch, 1996), *De battre mon coeur s'est arrêté/The Beat That My Heart Skipped* (Jacques Audiard, 2005), *Dans Paris* (Christophe Honoré, 2006), *Paris* (Cédric Klapisch, 2008), *35 rhums/35 Shots of Rum* (Claire Denis, 2008) and *Holy Motors* (Leos Carax, 2012), to name but a few, may be disappointed not to find analyses of these key Parisian film texts. These, however, are abundantly discussed elsewhere. The plethora of Paris films ensures that any critical approach, be it sexual, ethnic, cultural, philosophical or political, must intersect with discussions of the French capital. As we were putting the finishing touches to this volume, *Made in France* (Nicolas Boukhrief, 2015), *Bastille Day/The Take* (James Watkins, 2016) and *Nocturama* (Bertrand Bonello, 2016) came out, anticipating or documenting in their different genres the sinister rise of terrorism on the city streets. Time will tell whether this may, alas, become a new subgenre of Paris films. On a more joyous note, comedies such as *Midnight in Paris* (Woody Allen, 2011), *Le Week-End* (Roger Michell, 2013), *Quai d'Orsay/The French Minister* (Bertrand Tavernier, 2013) and *Victoria* (Justine Triet, 2016) display more classic and glamorous Parisian representational tropes. Likewise, books on the city's touristic, cinematic and gastronomic attractions, on the Métro, on fashion, and so on, continue to appear. We want our book to take its place within this ongoing conversation about the fascination of Paris, but also to intervene in the evolving theoretical paradigms that enable us to understand this unique city.

Reflecting on 'how the actual world of the city helps to contextualise his idiosyncratic representation of singular Parisian spaces and iconic characters', Jean-Pierre Jeunet puts his enduring fascination for the cinematic history of the capital down to how 'different intertextual influences [...] contribute to the construction of his personal signature'.[30] In this spirit, we invite the readers of this book to also engage in such historical, location specific and intertextual *flânerie* and hope they take as much pleasure in this Parisian journey as we did in assembling its trajectory.

Notes

1. Jacques Rivette, 'Les Rues de Paris, de nouveau', in Jean Douchet, Michel Boujut and Serge Daney, *Cités-Cinés* (Paris: Ramsay/La Villette, 1987), p. 328.
2. The *World Cities Culture Report* commissioned in 2012 by London mayor Boris Johnson indicates inner Paris's number of cinemas as 302, a much higher figure than all major cities surveyed. The CNC (Centre National du Cinéma et de l'Image Animée) in 2015 indicates the figure of 389. Available at: www.worldcitiescultureforum.com/assets/others/World_Cities_Culture_Report_2014_hires.pdf; www.cnc.fr/web/fr/geographie-du-cinema-en-2015-departements (accessed March 2016).
3. See also Dina Iordanova and Jean-Michel Frodon (eds), *Cinemas of Paris* (St Andrews: St Andrews Film Studies Publishing, 2015).

4. Charles Baudelaire, *The Painter of Modern Life and Other Essays* (London: Phaidon, 1995); Walter Benjamin, *Charles Baudelaire. A Lyric Poet in the Era of High Capitalism* (London and New York: Verso, 1997); Guy Debord, *The Society of the Spectacle* (New York: Zone Books, 1995); Henri Lefebvre, *Writings on Cities* (Cambridge, MA: Blackwell Publishers, 1996); Michel de Certeau, *The Practice of Everyday Life* (Berkeley: University of California Press, 1984); Anne Friedberg, *Window Shopping: Cinema and the Postmodern* (Berkeley: University of California Press, 1993); Janet Wolff, 'The Invisible *Flâneuse*. Women and the Literature of Modernity', in *Theory, Culture & Society*, vol. 2, no. 3 (1985), pp. 37–46; Elizabeth Wilson, *The Sphinx in the City: Urban Life, the Control of Disorder, and Women* (London: Virago, 1991); Marc Augé, *In the Metro* (Minneapolis: University of Minnesota Press, 2002).
5. Emmanuel de Roux, 'Traversées de Paris', *Le Monde* (9 December 2005), p. 4.
6. While working on this book, we have become aware of a PhD thesis in English and French literature researched and written at King's College London by Estelle Murail, entitled *Beyond the Flâneur. Walking, Passage and Crossing in London and Paris in the Nineteenth Century*. Available at: https://kclpure.kcl.ac.uk/portal/files/13145103/Studentthesis-Estelle_Murail_2014.pdf (accessed August 2017). The similarity in titles is entirely coincidental.
7. See Susan Buck-Morss, *The Dialetics of Seeing. Walter Benjamin and the Arcades Project* (Cambridge, MA: MIT Press, 1991).
8. Ginette Vincendeau, *French Cinema in the 1930s. Texts and Contexts of a Popular Entertainment Medium* (UEA: Unpublished PhD thesis, 1985).
9. For more on the intersection between musicality and Parisian visual representation, see Adrian Rifkin's influential study, *Street Noises. Parisian Pleasure 1900–1940* (Manchester: Manchester University Press, 1995).
10. Tim Bergfelder, Sue Harris and Sarah Street, *Film Architecture and the Transnational Imagination: Set Design in 1930s European Cinema* (Amsterdam: Amsterdam University Press, 2007).
11. Jean Douchet, *French New Wave* (New York: D.A.P., 1999), p. 123.
12. Ibid., p. 126.
13. Michel Marie, *The French New Wave: An Artistic School* (Malden, MA: Blackwell Publishing, 2003).
14. Charlotte Brunsdon, *London in Cinema. The Cinematic City since 1945* (London: BFI, 2007), p. 7.
15. Elizabeth Wilson points out the etymology of the term is vague, with perhaps the first published instance being an anonymous pamphlet that appeared in 1806. In this, 'M. Bonhomme spends most of his day simply looking at the urban spectacle … he is fascinated by the many new building works … and he passes the hours by shopping or window shopping, looking at books, new fashions … and novelties of all kinds.' See Elizabeth Wilson, *The Contradictions of Culture* (London: Sage Publications, 2001), p. 75.
16. Charles Baudelaire, 'The Painter of Modern Life', in *The Painter of Modern Life and Other Essays* (London: Phaidon, 1995), p. 5.
17. Ibid., p. 3.
18. Ibid., p. 4.
19. See also Leo Charney and Vanessa R. Schwartz (eds), *Cinema and the Invention of Modern Life* (Berkeley: University of California Press, 1995).
20. Wolff, 'The Invisible *Flâneuse*', p. 45.

21. Ibid., pp. 41–2.
22. Wilson, *The Contradictions of Culture*, pp. 81–4.
23. Ben Singer, *Melodrama and Modernity. Early Sensational Cinema and Its Contexts* (New York: Columbia University Press, 2001).
24. See, for example, Tom Gunning, 'From the Kaleidoscope to the X-ray: Urban Spectatorship, Poe, Benjamin, and *Traffic in Souls* (1913)', *Wide Angle*, vol. 19, no. 4 (October 1997), pp. 25–61.
25. Anke Gleber, *The Art of Taking a Walk* (Princeton, NJ: Princeton University Press, 1999).
26. See, for example, several of the essays in the following: David B. Clarke, *The Cinematic City* (London and New York: Routledge, 1997); Richard Koeck and Les Roberts, *The City and the Moving Image: Urban Projections* (Basingstoke: Palgrave Macmillan, 2010); Mark Shiel and Tony Fitzmaurice (eds), *Cinema and the City: Film and Urban Societies in a Global Context* (Oxford: Blackwell, 2001); Mark Shiel and Tony Fitzmaurice (eds), *Screening the City* (London and New York: Verso, 2003); and Andrew Webber and Emma Wilson (eds), *Cities in Transition* (London: Wallflower Press, 2008).
27. See David Harvey, *Paris, Capital of Modernity* (London and New York: Routledge, 2005) and Christopher Prendergast, *Paris and the Nineteenth Century* (Oxford: Blackwell, 1992).
28. Keith Tester, *The Flâneur* (London and New York: Routledge, 1994).
29. For such a deployment of the term, see Suzanne Liandrat-Guigues, 'Une moderne flânerie (*Le Signe du lion*),' in Patrick Louguet (ed.), *Rohmer ou le jeu des variations* (Paris: PUV, 2012), pp. 51–8.
30. See Isabelle Vanderschelden's interview with Jean-Pierre Jeunet in this volume.

Part I
LOCATIONS

The Eiffel Tower: A Parisian Film Star

Nicoleta Bazgan

For a world-renowned icon that has been filmed from all angles, the Eiffel Tower remains intriguingly opaque. It still exudes an enigmatic fascination, like a film star coming from the silent era. At first glance, the immobile Tower seems to be merely a clichéd image that offers a readily readable location. Yet, in a dynamic interaction with the on-screen cityscape and the cinematic audience, the Tower has constantly challenged the representation and experience of Parisian space. The monument's image has been actively marketed since the Eiffel Tower's debut at the 1889 Exposition Universelle when postcards were sold underneath its great spanning arches.[1] In its very first roles in newsreels, the towering landmark tested the limits of the camera. Its massive height led to the first vertical tracking shot in the history of cinema in the Lumière Brothers' *Panorama pendant l'ascension de la Tour Eiffel/Panorama during the Ascent of the Eiffel Tower* (1897–98) and redefined the tilt in Thomas Edison's *Panorama of the Eiffel Tower* (1900). As its image is now intimately connected to the history of cinema, the very presence of the landmark on screen might be considered a cinephilic gesture in itself.

Since the Tower's breakthrough role in René Clair's *Paris qui dort/The Crazy Ray* (1924), the monument's fame has grown through unforgettable performances and countless cameos. In a stunning range of films, the Parisian icon has, for example, been examined in the documentary *Paris 1900* (Nicole Védrès, 1948), revered in *Les Quatre cents coups/The 400 Blows* (François Truffaut, 1959), featured in the blockbuster *Taxi 2* (Gérard Krawczyk, 2000) and celebrated by Hollywood in *Funny Face* (Stanley Donen, 1957). Over the course of its long career, the Tower has therefore acquired all the characteristics of a French film star. It enjoys dual success in mainstream and *auteur* cinema, with regular appearances in Hollywood films. In the national industries of tourism, fashion and cosmetics, the glamorous monument embodies a sophisticated form of Frenchness.[2] On screen, numerous cameos define the Tower's star persona as a Parisian icon capable of invoking well-established facets of the city. In more complex roles, however, the landmark fully reveals its paradoxical nature. It acts as a protagonist but also takes the place of the camera itself. Notoriously ambivalent, its body is connected to both joyful celebration and deadly seduction. Through these constitutive paradoxes, rather like all major film stars, the Tower embodies a wide range of contradictions.

As an urban icon,[3] the Tower has been typecast in a 'perfect fit'[4] with its off-screen *image*. Roland Barthes explains its magnetism in the real cityscape as a 'pure – virtually empty – sign'.[5] In contrast, its appearances on screen, however brief, are already invested with meaning. Even in establishing shots, the Tower cannot be solely read as a metonymical monument. Instead, it becomes a site where different facets of Paris – the city of romantic love, the city of modernity, the touristic city – are shaped through

The Eiffel Tower's cameo as an urban icon in *Paris, je t'aime* (Olivier Assayas, et. al., 2006).

shifting meanings. The prologue of *Paris, je t'aime* (2006) shows a twinkling Tower at night, with fireworks that burst into a spectacular celebration, setting the audience ablaze with emotion. The gleaming beam and magical shimmer of the landmark recall that cinema, too, is light in movement. When the film title appears over this background, cinematic gaze and desire are aligned with the consumption of Paris, the city of romantic love. Although the iconic cameos of the Eiffel Tower have become a key part of its global mainstream appeal, this typecast role represents only one side of its intricate stardom.

Through its position as both protagonist and camera, the Eiffel Tower reveals a simultaneous sense of concrete presence and subjective perception in urban space. Taking the Tower's place, the camera as a material ghost can record the Parisian cityscape through a myriad point-of-view shots in all directions. In over-the-shoulder shots, the on-screen landmark 'cuts' the landscape using its open latticework as a frame and viewfinder. Through its architecture, the Tower merges inner and outer space, situating the visitor at once in its structure and elsewhere in the surrounding Parisian landscape, immersed in a multisensory experience. In the 15-minute short *La Tour/The Tower* (1928), René Clair conveys the transformative experience of a visit to the landmark. The monument's symmetrical latticework cuts kaleidoscopic slices in the Parisian landscape, displaying fragmentary ways of seeing. Pans, tilts and tracking shots frame a mobile cityscape. Close-ups of the Tower reveal the tactility of the iron filigrees through startling details. The concrete materiality of the edifice and the emotional immersion in the Parisian scenery fuse objective and subjective perception, changing the experience of the city.

As a star body, the Tower appears in different scales that emphasise its tactile qualities, from a lofty silhouette to a fetishised element such as a girder, pillar, arch, elevator, platform, staircase or filigree in a technique originating from photography.[6] At night, shimmering lights outline the landmark to display its electric glamour. The monument's tridimensional structure opens up a vertical labyrinth, while its platforms function as stages, mirroring the horizontal maze of the urban sprawl and public squares. Its architecture offers countless possibilities for actions to assert or contest the urban power grid.

The honourable Tower has been regularly filmed hosting official and festive events. The short newsreel *Lunch on the Eiffel Tower* (Topical Film Company, 1914), for example, records a sumptuous formal meal in the landmark's restaurant and an elevator descent showcasing the stunningly beautiful cityscape. In stark contrast, a British Pathé newsreel from 1912 shows Franz Reichelt testing a flying costume and jumping off the Tower to his death in front of the cameras, becoming, as François Truffaut puts it, 'without a doubt, the first victim of cinema'.[7] The Icarian hubris captured on screen highlights the morbid side of the monument where spectacle and danger coalesce. Since the first documentaries, the Tower's body has thus been deeply ambivalent, torn between sensational leisure and fatal magnetism.

Connected to the broader landscape, the Tower, through its constitutive paradoxes, taps into, and frequently unsettles, the main binaries that structure cities to produce multiple layers of social, cultural, economic and affective space. The interplay between the distance and proximity to the landmark, for instance, translates into social belonging and exclusion. Numerous films use windows with a view on the Eiffel Tower to indicate an affluent position in the city, from *La Règle du jeu/The Rules of the Game* (Jean Renoir, 1939) to *Le Dîner de cons/The Dinner Game* (Francis Veber, 1998). In *La Haine/Hate* (Mathieu Kassovitz, 1995), a character's failed attempt to 'switch off' the lights of the monument poignantly shows his marginalisation in social space.[8] In this role, the Parisian landmark actively exposes, and often problematises, the main binaries that produce urban space: centre/periphery, inclusion/exclusion, order/chaos and self/other. During its long career, the star landmark has therefore become a celluloid palimpsest where different social and cultural tensions are constantly reworked.

In more complex appearances, the Tower undermines the artificial divisions that filter the lived experience in urban space, thriving through the embodiment of perplexing contradictions. Three key performances of the Tower illustrate how its function as protagonist/camera and ambivalent body interact to disrupt conventional binaries, while establishing the main coordinates of its star appeal. In *Paris qui dort*, René Clair links the Tower's image to romantic love and deadly seduction, showing its tremendous visual power. In *Le Mystère de la Tour Eiffel/The Mystery of the Eiffel Tower* (Julien Duvivier, 1928), the landmark is screened as a site of playful adventures and uncanny danger, revealing a mysterious sonic space. Within the next decades, as film production moved into the studios, the Tower was mostly present on sets as a replica. Returning to location shooting, the French New Wave filmmakers established the icon as a coveted presence in art-house films and revitalised its image through roles displaying its timeless modernity, self-referential persona and everyday presence in the city. In particular, *Zazie dans le métro* (Louis Malle, 1960) shows how a visit to the monument becomes an inner journey and how films mediate the experience of the landmark, contributing to its affective impact.

A Dark-Bright Star Is Born

René Clair cast the Eiffel Tower in his first feature film, *Paris qui dort*, at a time, in 1923, when the Tower was a prominent subject in the Paris art world. Influenced by both avant-garde groups and the mainstream film industry in which he worked, the filmmaker, who saw cinema's main purpose as 'recording movement', directed a film with motion as a 'visual theme'.[9] In it, an old scientist paralyses the city with a crazy ray, a transparent reference to cinema itself.[10] Only Albert (Henri Rollan), the watchman of the Eiffel Tower, and five persons travelling in an airplane remain out of the ray's reach. All Paris belongs to them, but soon their absolute freedom becomes oppressive. When they receive a call for help from the scientist's niece, they hurry to reset the world in motion.

The film opens with the Tower's subjective viewpoint in an aerial vista screening the Seine, flickering in the sun, on which barges slowly advance underneath the arched bridges. An extreme-long shot of a majestic panorama follows, with a recognisable Arc de Triomphe in the frame. When the watchman wakes up the next day, he discovers a frozen city, shown through a dizzying tilt on the Champ de Mars. Disguised as Albert's point of view, the shot unexpectedly uncovers him at the bottom of the frame. The playful shift in perspective certainly serves to undermine fixed points of observation, in a contemporary change that reflects the modernist era. It also reminds us that the Eiffel Tower is, at all times, both camera and protagonist.

When Albert leaves the edifice, the camera vertically tracks his circular descent of a spiral staircase, thus reinforcing the symmetrical geometry of the frame. His active movements are intercut with tilts of the Tower's silhouette viewed from a distance. After several cuts, the camera forgets about the hero and begins to wander on the Tower's iron curves, fetishising its tactile latticework. A shot lingers on a platform to absorb the massive iron beams radiating in all directions. When Albert steps into the *mise-en-scène*, his presence comes as a surprise, since the Tower now occupies the spotlight. As the watchman gets off the west pillar, the spectator feels more connected to the bodily presence of the monument than to the protagonist.

In the second part of the film, the Tower becomes both a site of playful spatial practices and a fault line where the urban id erupts through aggressive and libidinal impulses. After using Paris as a playground, the six protagonists spend their days on the Tower. A fast tilt on a girder uncovers the bourgeois Parisian, the thief and the policeman playing cards. With the city landscape well below, Hesta (Madeleine Rodrigue), a woman of the world, and Albert flirt on the edge of the void. The pilot (Albert Préjean) is perched on top of one of the Tower's girders, isolated against the sky. In a playful stunt, he hangs upside down to light Albert's cigarette. But soon the ludic tone of spatial tricks and mundane delights on the verge of the abyss darkens into ennui. As the logical and productive order in the capital is suspended, irrational and destructive drives generate full chaos.

In striking shots, Hesta is shown isolated on the edge of a platform, her white lace dress billowing in the wind. Through a decadent gesture captured in a close-up, she throws pearls from the top of the world onto the frozen Parisian rooftops. These lyrical images establish a poignant tension between the eternal magnificence of the stone landscape and the transient beauty of the adorned female body. Rapid point-of-view shots show that the heroine, the only woman in sight, becomes the inaccessible object of unleashed male desire. Like mesmerised automatons, the men start chasing her in unison on the symmetrical staircases. Soon, the pursuit accelerates, degenerating into frenzied fights on the criss-crossing girders of the Tower. In a climax, the pilot steps off a platform, but the following shots show him hanging on a bar and climbing back up, oblivious of the magnificent Parisian vista unfurling behind him. The mimicry of death, however, is not enough to appease destructive drives. Only an unexpected message from the scientist's niece, promising the re-establishment of order, ends the turmoil.

At the end of the film, the scientist's niece and the watchman meet at the Tower, now the site of an erotic encounter. Their ascent alternates eyeline matches that frame the shifting Parisian vistas with interior shots in the elevator, where rays of light pierce the mobile latticework of the edifice. On the platform, the image of the couple kissing dissolves into the picturesque vista of the Palais du Trocadéro, in an amorous episode celebrating uplifting harmony and beauty. In its first main role, the Tower therefore embodies both unleashed desires and harmonious bliss, offering a complex view of the tensions that traverse the spaces where city dwellers move and live.

Femme Fatale and Iron Lady

In Julien Duvivier's *Le Mystère de la Tour Eiffel*, the Eiffel Tower is cast as a site of power struggles for spatial manipulation and conquest. In this dark thriller, Achilles Saturnin (Tramel), heir to an unexpected fortune, is chased by William Dewitt (Gaston Jacquet), the leader of a secret organisation named Ku-Klux-Eiffel. Threatened and kidnapped, Achilles barely escapes the villains' grip. A thrilling chase on the Tower plays a significant part in the film, ending with the death of the clan leader and the capture of his followers.

At the beginning of his career, Duvivier takes on the challenging task of visualising the sonic space of the Eiffel Tower in a silent film, forecasting his style defined by a 'virtuoso technique'.[11] The Tower's first appearance on screen occurs right after Dewitt decides to eliminate Achilles. Emerging from a fade to black, its arch appears on screen framing a view of the Palais du Trocadéro, from which the camera begins to scan the monument's soaring height. A close-up shot of a loudspeaker follows, on which the image of a female singer gradually appears, taking over the frame. The sound from the radio tower is visualised as a disembodied presence linking distinct private spaces through montage and superimposition. Next, a dissolve overlays the female singer onto the orchestra playing. A succession of five quick shots screening the radio equipment in the transmitter room of the Eiffel Tower follows. The camera briefly pans and tilts on the static massive structures to capture their material yet abstract presence, conveying a fearful fascination in front of the mechanical life of the machines. After a masked Ku-Klux-Eiffel member hijacks the waves of the radio broadcast in the transmitter room, the editing accelerates. To illustrate the general confusion, the agitated faces of the listeners in close-ups are rapidly intercut with fast pans from humans to the radio diffusers, an extreme close-up of the singer's mouth and a mysterious cypher. The relatively new radio technology – the first radio station on the Tower started broadcasting on 24 December 1921 – still generates fears about invisible forms of communication, materialised on screen in the secret code transmitted by the Ku-Klux-Eiffel. Belonging to the world of modern technologies as well, the Tower is cast in a progressive yet potentially malefic role that functions as a lightning conductor for societal anxieties.

The final chase sequence, innovative in its verticality, illustrates the Tower's capacity to function as an ambivalent body and site of both entrapment and play. For the leader and his gang, chased by the police and Achilles, the Tower becomes a multidimensional maze of steel pillars. Fast tilts on its structure illustrate the confrontation between the gang members and the police arriving at the lower levels. Static shots frame numerous policemen, dressed in identical uniforms, endlessly climbing steps on staircases in the symmetrical structures of the Tower. Disembodied viewpoints show plunging heights in unsettling angles and an increasingly remote landscape, where crowds seem like cosmopolitan ants. In elaborated compositions, the shadows of the Ku-Klux-Eiffel members are rendered visible on the Tower to illustrate their evil manipulations. At a higher level, shots showing Dewitt isolated while inside the skeletal arms of the Tower convey a strong sense of entrapment in a deadly iron web. The Parisian panorama, visible in sharp focus from the lower platforms, becomes gradually overexposed. When the villain almost reaches the top, the sky and cityscape merge in a white void, illustrating the impossibility of escape.

During the same chase, Achilles discovers a completely different space. The Tower protects the hero, as he hides behind iron pillars, dodging bullets. The gargantuan scale of the monument is conveyed in the long shots of the iron fretworks on which his body, comically minuscule, becomes visible. After the Ku-Klux-Eiffel members sabotage the elevators, Achilles climbs on the iron girders. To illustrate the protagonist's vertigo, Duvivier superimposes on his face the spinning crossbeams of the Tower and shifting landscapes. When long takes pan on or track Achilles's acrobatics, his physical experience and the tactility of the iron construction are emphasised as he steps onto the frames, grips the bars and balances his weight. His position is by no means one of mastery, but rather of improvisation. His movements on the Tower belong to the 'clever tricks of the weak', to the spatial tactics defined by Michel de Certeau as individual practices that creatively eschew normalised uses to create a space for themselves.[12] In this spirit, after defeating Dewitt, Achilles does not take the staircase, but slides down the elevator cables. Duvivier clearly shows how the Tower, popular object of the masses, offers its panoptic construction as a site of tactical improvisation. Before our eyes, the same space of the landmark shifts from deadly entrapment to protective play, from femme fatale to iron lady. The Tower's architecture, aptly chameleonic, remains an uncanny space where thrills and danger can coexist.

The Grounded Transcendence of a Film Star

In Louis Malle's third feature film, *Zazie dans le métro*, the terrible gamine Zazie (Catherine Demongeot) takes Paris by storm, running compulsively through the city during a two-day visit to her uncle Gabriel (Philippe Noiret). Malle's film perfectly illustrates the formula of French New Wave films 'to let young people loose in an old city',[13] while showcasing a visit to the Eiffel Tower that combines cinephilia and on-location shooting. Arriving at the landmark, Zazie, in a close-up, muses that she finds the city wonderful, displaying a rare smile. As she looks up, not one but nine point-of-view shots show the monument in different angles. The affectionate proliferation of the icon prompts her uncle Gabriel to ask why Paris is represented as a woman. His question introduces a key oscillation of the Tower between strict gender dichotomies: an obvious phallic symbol and industrial marvel, the landmark is yet perceived as feminine in its iconic appeal and grammatical usage. The Tower unsettles another opposition when Zazie interrogates Charles (Antoine Roblot), her uncle's friend, about the meaning of the word 'homosexual'. Their conversation is screened during a never-ending descent of a spiral staircase scanned through a vertical tracking shot, in a plunging high angle. Zazie's understanding of a homosexual as a man who wears perfume highlights the gap not only between words and meaning, but also between identity and practices. This sequence subtly links the discussion of identities that unsettle conventional binaries to a dizzying geography, revealing the Tower as a stage where performances of sexuality, and performances of identity in general, are rendered unstable.

With its iconic views, the monument constitutes a preferred site to subvert the topography of touristic Paris, a main theme also in Raymond Queneau's book adapted by Malle. When Zazie's uncle shows her the Panthéon, Les Invalides and the Métro, he points in arbitrary directions from the platform, with no eyeline match that follows. Inspired by the panoramic landscape, Gabriel goes into an oneiric overdrive. In a flow of surrealist unconsciousness, he recites an incomprehensible monologue, gradually drifting into a fictional space where iconic film sites and vistas, particularly from *Paris qui dort*, are revisited. In several poses shown in separate cuts, Gabriel adopts acrobatic postures on girders, teeters on the edge of the platform and climbs ladders that dissect the cityscape plummeting behind him. Like Clair's pilot, he grips a platform and jumps onto it, effortlessly, from the void below.

As Gabriel ascends the Tower, he charts his journey into more dense layers of oneiric space, confessing: 'All Paris is a dream, Zazie is a reverie, and all of this is a reverie within a dream.' The Tower here becomes a dream world, quoting famous cinematic moments. It comes as no surprise then that when Gabriel takes the elevator, he stands on its top, where the cameras for the original vertical tracking shot of the Lumière Brothers were mounted. A quick bird's-eye-view shot looking straight down on the elevator follows, visually comparing the geometry of the girders to a looking glass. Gabriel's journey, in which inner space cannot be securely separated from outer space, points out how the ascent of the Tower 'seize[s] the viewer

Imagination and reality collide on the Eiffel Tower in Louis Malle's *Zazie dans le métro* (1964).

viscerally', reminding us that 'we are not only looking, but also *feeling*'.[14] The movement through (meta)-cinematic space is therefore necessarily accompanied by emotion.

Descending from the elevator and its maelstrom of feelings, Gabriel encounters a bearded sea captain on one of the balconies formed by the spiral staircase. The juxtaposition in the composition of this scene brilliantly illustrates the surrealist tenet of the use of inner space to understand the material world. Gabriel joins the captain on the staircase, which is transformed into a ship's rail. Below, the Seine meanders past Haussmannian buildings seen as massive vessels from the Tower's high-angle view. As the spectator's gaze plummets into the urban sea underneath, a wave comes crashing on Gabriel and his maritime companion. Further up the landmark, freezing temperatures create a space for Arctic explorations, where humans wearing polar bear costumes shiver. This site is also a laboratory for unconventional tests, where colourful balloons are released and observed through a magnifying glass by an old scientist. Here, Malle comically subverts the scientific experiments, including meteorological observations and physical measurements, that are taking place on the Tower. Gabriel grabs one of the balloons and floats down to the real world, putting an end to his fantastic journey. Through this interlude on the Eiffel Tower, the filmmaker affectionately celebrates the monument's never-ending capacity to channel dreams and open up fictional spaces. The Eiffel Tower, massive marvel of engineering and vessel of impalpable reveries, attests to the impossibility of neatly separating reality and imagination in urban life.

Conclusion

In these three key performances, the Tower's function as protagonist/camera and its ambivalent body expose the tensions between love/death, play/danger and reality/dream, contributing to its transformative power and ambiguous charisma. Each filmmaker also highlights a strategic aspect of the Tower's multisensory appeal: its visual force (Clair), mysterious sounds (Duvivier) and affective impact (Malle). Even in more recent roles, the Tower continues to contest established perceptions and representations. In the documentary *Married to the Eiffel Tower* (Agnieszka Piotrowska, 2008), the landmark as an object of sexual desire renders porous the distinction between human/non-human, challenging notions of public desire and inanimate intimacy. More recently, in *Bande de filles/Girlhood* (Céline Sciamma, 2014), the icon appears as a decorative replica on a mini-golf course, suggesting that the city centre has become an emotionally remote simulacra for the inhabitants of the Parisian periphery. An ambiguous film star, the Tower thus still continues to jolt us out of the conventional ways of looking at Paris, moving beyond the recognisable urban grid to reveal the multiple uncanny experiences that the city offers.

Notes

1. See Naomi Schor, 'Cartes Postales': Representing Paris 1900', *Critical Inquiry*, Vol. 18, no. 2 (Winter 1992), pp. 188–244.
2. I employ several key aspects of French stardom as identified by Ginette Vincendeau in *Stars and Stardom in French Cinema* (London: Continuum, 2000), pp. 1–2, 31–40.

3. See Philip E. Ethington and Vanessa R. Schwartz, 'Introduction: An Atlas of the Urban Icons Project', *Urban History*, Vol. 33, no. 1 (2006), p. 13. The authors argue that the Eiffel Tower might be the first urban icon, developed through the productive linkage between modern urbanism and visual culture. See also Vanessa Schwartz, 'The Eiffel Tower'. Available at: http://journals.cambridge.org/fulltext_content/supplementary/urban_icons_companion/atlas/content/eiffel_tower.htm (accessed 11 October 2017).
4. For a definition of the 'perfect fit' between a star image and an on-screen role, see Richard Dyer, *Stars* (London: BFI, 1979), p. 145.
5. Roland Barthes, *The Eiffel Tower and Other Mythologies* (Berkeley and Los Angeles: University of California Press, 1997), p. 4.
6. See Lucien Hervé, *The Eiffel Tower* (New York: Princeton Architectural Press, 2003), p. 12. In the introduction of Lucien Hervé's collection of photographs, Barry Bergdoll notes that Henri Rivière used the technique of cropped views of the Eiffel Tower in its lithographic work *Thirty-six Views of the Eiffel Tower under Construction (1888–1902)*. Hervé developed this technique, rendering it famous through his photographs of the Eiffel Tower.
7. François Porcile, 'Parcours. Le Paris de François Truffaut'. Available at: http://collections.forumdes images.fr/CogniTellUI/faces/details.xhtml?id=P149 (accessed 7 September 2017). These are the words of François Truffaut's main character from *La Peau douce/The Soft Skin* (1964), in a scene cut from the final version.
8. The 'turning-off' the Eiffel Tower is a quote from Eric Rochant's *Un monde sans pitié/Love without Pity* (1989), in which a very different urban outcast, Hippo, who belongs to a growing privileged class of a disaffected youth, performs it.
9. René Clair, *Reflections on the Cinema* (London: William Kimber, 1953), pp. 57–8.
10. For an analysis of the parallels between the film camera and the 'crazy ray', see Annette Michelson, 'Dr. Crase and Mr. Clair', *October*, vol. 11 (Winter 1979), pp. 43–6.
11. Ginette Vincendeau, *Pépé le Moko* (London: BFI, 1998), p. 10.
12. Michel de Certeau, *The Practice of Everyday Life* (Berkeley and Los Angeles: University of California Press, 1984), p. 40.
13. James Tweedie, *The Age of New Waves: Art Cinema and the Staging of Globalization* (London: Oxford University Press, 2013), p. 54.
14. See Tom Gunning's remark on the Lumière tracking shot from the 1900 World Exposition in 'The Birth of Film Out of the Spirit of Modernity', in Ted Perry (ed.), *Masterpieces of Modernist Cinema* (Bloomington: Indiana University Press, 2006), p. 14.

Working-class Paris and Post-war Noir: *Les Portes de la nuit*

Thomas Pillard

Les Portes de la nuit/Gates of the Night (Marcel Carné, 1946) represents something of a paradox in the history of Paris on film: limited research exists on this famous work, which remains little known as a result. Indeed, while everyone knows that Alexandre Trauner's reconstruction of the Barbès elevated Métro station became very controversial for its allegedly outsize budget, issues related to the film's representation of the French capital, and more specifically of its north-eastern neighbourhoods, have not raised much interest to date.

Produced in 1946, *Les Portes de la nuit* ushered in 'dark realism', a style that was permeated with a sense of gloom and continued the pre-World War Two tradition of French film noir, in which Carné had been the central figure during the late 1930s.[1] The film takes place in the immediate aftermath of the Liberation, as its opening indicates. The voice-over of a narrator situates the action in time and space over images of the city:

> February 1945. The end of a winter day, the harsh and sad winter that followed the magnificent summer of the Liberation of Paris. The war is not over yet, but north of the city, everyday life resumes its course, with its simple joys, its grave difficulties, its woes, its dreadful secrets.

Prévert's script, despite its present-day context, looks to poetic realism. The film recounts the fatal ending of a night-long love encounter between Diego (Yves Montand), a hero of the Resistance, and Malou (Nathalie Nattier), a lonely young woman, after she leaves her lover, Georges (Pierre Brasseur), a bourgeois exiled in London during the Occupation. Quite logically, this nostalgic project seeks to bring back to life the main settings used in the narratives of the 1930s French film noir: the working-class neighbourhoods of Paris. The entire action unfolds in the vicinity of Barbès and La Villette; from the very beginning, the film immerses its audience in the north-eastern part of the city, long a traditional landscape for French cinema, from *Ménilmontant* (Dimitri Kirsanoff, 1926) to *Hôtel du Nord* (Marcel Carné, 1938).

While the film oscillates between tragic populism and socio-political commentary, its interest also lies in its mix of 'very French' images and a number of American traces: when Malou first appears, the *mise-en-scène* takes us outside the restaurant in La Villette where the characters are dining to show the arrival of 'a very beautiful American car coming to a rather sudden halt in front of the restaurant's door';[2] a few seconds later, we discover a young blond woman evoking the stereotype of a Hollywood icon inside the vehicle. This chapter will examine these juxtapositions between past and present, France and the USA, bringing together film analysis and historical perspective to shed light on them.

Images of 'Frenchness': An Artistic and Cultural Lineage

Marcel Carné was one of the filmmakers for whom the Occupation period represented an 'odd golden age', due to the ban on US films that lasted until the Liberation: for four years, French cinema thus benefited from an exceptionally favourable situation.[3] Since the two films made by Carné and Prévert during those years, *Les Visiteurs du soir* (1942) and *Les Enfants du paradis/Children of Paradise* (1945), have been construed as affirmations of 'the wartime brilliance of French cultural life',[4] one may wonder where *Les Portes de la nuit* stands with regard to the 'new crusade against Hollywood'[5] that marked French cinema in the immediate post-war period.

If, on the surface, the film's opening seems merely informative, it already provides the elements of an answer. Its function is in fact to proclaim a specifically French identity and to do so in several ways. The films begins with a long high-angle panning shot, left to right, which presents a succession of rooftops and buildings; the Butte Montmartre and the Sacré-Coeur appear in the distance. As the camera moves laterally and slightly downward, various sites epitomising the north-eastern part of the capital are also revealed: the boulevard de la Chapelle, the canal basin of La Villette, the La Villette rotunda and the elevated Métro station where the camera comes to a stop as a train enters the frame. In a single shot, *Les Portes de la nuit* manages to articulate a complex position in terms of identity and memory that follows a number of French traditions in photography, painting, literature and cinema and evokes a set of representations of Paris within a protean artistic ancestry that runs from the 1830s to the late 1930s.

A first set of references involves 19th-century photography and literature. Edward Baron Turk, describing the initial images of *Les Enfants du paradis*, wrote that they were 'the cinematic correlative of the *panorama*, a mode of perception that came to the fore in both literary and visual depictions of Paris in the mid-nineteenth century'.[6] *Les Enfants du paradis* begins with a backward tracking shot from a slightly high angle, presenting a panoramic point of view on the boulevard du Temple. Not only is the opening of *Les Portes de la nuit* reminiscent of this previous inaugural shot, it also fits

A view of the elevated Métro in *Les Portes de la nuit/Gates of the Night* (Marcel Carné, 1946).

Turk's description better insofar as Carné placed his camera much higher, choosing the top of a building as a vantage point. Furthermore, the shot does not proceed from a movement of the camera but out of a fixed position. The result is an image whose framing is as carefully crafted as that of a photograph, and a spectacular wide view of an urban topography stretching as far as the eye can see.

The selection of the panning shot over the tracking shot thus brings a photographic quality to the film's image. The feeling of contemplation before a photograph is reinforced by the absence of movement within the frame as well as the subject of the representation (Parisian rooftops and buildings). Carné adopts an old technique to present the 1946 spectator with a type of image which is itself dated and highly referential. The primary reference is 'old Paris' through the countless iconographic representations spawned by the emergence of the first photographic processes in the first half of the 19th century. The impetus came from daguerreotype artists, and all over Europe the 'views of Paris' soon became the ambassadors of a new art 'which was to change completely the vision of the world in the 19th century'.[7]

The invention of the daguerreotype by Louis-Jacques-Mandé Daguerre between 1838 and 1839 in France constituted an innovation whose impact was felt worldwide. As a result, a large number of views of Paris were produced, including many reproductions of Parisian rooftops and the expanse of the city as seen from the top of a building. As Shelley Rice points out, the most spectacular representations of this kind of landscape were undoubtedly panoramic views.[8] The beginning of *Les Portes de la nuit* thus cites both a French invention (the daguerreotype) and the multiple representations of the Parisian urban landscape that contributed to the international fame of the invention.

Yet the citation is not limited to the process perfected by Daguerre. In the history of photography in France, the period between 1840 and 1850 was marked by the growth of 'the large panoramic image' and the will on the part of photographers to record the visual identity of the old city before it disappeared. As Mary Warner Marien writes, photographers of the time 'often chose to picture the enduring monuments from the past with which the public customarily identified cities'.[9] A century later, Carné happened to mobilise a similar technique to film the La Villette rotunda. The monument was built at the end of the 18th century, and one of its particularities is that it survived the successive transformations of the area, from the demolition of the city toll in 1860 to the construction of the elevated Métro line at the turn of the 20th century, not to mention the destruction by fire during the Commune (1871), after which the rotunda was restored to its original state.[10]

The system of representation adopted for *Les Portes de la nuit* also echoes a *topos* in 19th-century literature, found for example 'in the closing moments of Balzac's *Le Père Goriot* (1834–35), in which the ambitious Rastignac surveys Paris from the heights of Père Lachaise cemetery and vows to conquer the capital'.[11] More pointedly, a correspondence of sorts may be established between the opening of Carné's film and the way in which Victor Hugo and other writers used this model of visualisation over a century earlier. In *Notre-Dame de Paris* (1831), Hugo points to a description of 1830 Paris to evoke the transformations affecting the Parisian landscape over a 350-year-long history and denounce the fact that 15th-century Paris is gradually vanishing.

The writer thus invites the reader 'to follow him in a back and forth movement between past and present'.[12]

From the inaugural shot, Les Portes de la nuit similarly lays claim to an immediate contemporaneity (Paris in 1945) while looking to the past. Here, the film obviously summons up the memory of French cinema in the 1930s: films as 'quintessentially French'[13] as Sous les toits de Paris/Under the Roofs of Paris (René Clair, 1930) and La Bandera (Julien Duvivier, 1935) begin in a similar manner, with an opening shot of Parisian rooftops. Les Portes de la nuit actually proceeds with a scene showing a group of people gathered in the street to sing together, as did the beginning of Sous les toits de Paris. The reference to Clair's work is notable due to its importance in French film history as well as its place in the career of Marcel Carné, who was Clair's assistant director on the film.

A Mythological Parisian Zone: The Fascination for La Chapelle

The film does not merely look to the 1930s or to the cinema. Between the first seconds showing the Butte Montmartre emerging in the light and the epilogue marking the return of the main character to the Barbès station, Les Portes de la nuit takes the viewer through different sites charged with history, and whose evocation is tied to the memory of artists and writers as significant as Emile Zola, Pierre Mac Orlan and Francis Carco.

To understand this, a return to the inaugural panning shot is necessary, this time with a focus on the spaces revealed by the camera. The vantage point chosen for the camera, the top of a building which a 1946 spectator familiar with Parisian geography would have easily situated at the level of the La Villette junction,[14] is telling; so is the fact that, in the opening of the film, the orientation of the camera is to the north of the city, allowing a glimpse of the recognisable shapes of the Sacré-Coeur; significant too is the fact that the camera then pans towards the east.

The horizontal movement of the camera spans a specific area of Paris, across the current 9th, 10th, 18th, 19th and 20th *arrondissements* of the French capital. A section of one of the rings of Parisian boulevards – where the Mur des Fermiers généraux[15] used to stand – runs through the area in question from west to east. This part of Paris includes the former villages of Montmartre, La Chapelle, La Villette and Ménilmontant as well as the Goutte-d'Or neighbourhood and railway stations Gare de l'Est and Gare du Nord. Its social and geographic makeup is the result of specific historical developments. Before the destruction of the 1791 Mur des Fermiers généraux and the expansion of Paris to the limits of the Thiers defensive wall in 1860, the northern part of this area situated between faubourg Saint-Martin and faubourg Poissonnière comprised undeveloped and deserted wasteland; its eastern part, around La Villette, was a budding industrial area and started to grow after 'the port was opened to trade in November 1826'.[16] As Louis Chevalier explains, at the time it already was a 'staunchly working-class area' where the crime rate was significant. Distinctly different from the more central neighbourhoods of the city, it was home to a large population on the margins of society (rag pickers, unemployed people, vagrants). Still, these 'eastern territories'[17] were essentially a *mythological zone* whose identity was tied to its multiple representations in the sphere of culture, and whose epicentre was undoubtedly the boulevard de la Chapelle shown in Carné's panning shot for several seconds.

The first representations that come to mind are pictorial. Jill Forbes notes that the first shot of *Les Portes de la nuit* revives the memory of Impressionist painting and works by the Ecole des Batignolles painters – Monet and Renoir for instance – who in the 1860s and 1870s were fond of the Montmartre neighbourhood and the north of Paris and owned apartments and/or studios there.[18] With the camera movement connecting Montmartre to the point where the canal Saint-Martin flows into the La Villette basin, the film evokes the great painters who called Montmartre home or often depicted the neighbourhood from the mid-19th century on. This allows *Les Portes de la nuit* to expand on the world represented in some Impressionist and post-Impressionist paintings: the works of Alfred Sisley and Maurice Utrillo on the canal Saint-Martin, the canal Saint-Denis and the boulevard de la Chapelle come to mind.[19]

The interest of the film for this geographic zone also relates it to a considerable literary tradition. From the early 1850s to the 1930s, the north-eastern part of the capital underwent successive transformations while paradoxically holding on to the same general identity. This persistence of the past is precisely what drew naturalist writers to this territory in the second half of the 19th century. In *L'Assommoir* (1876), Zola thus situates the hotel where Gervaise lives 'on the boulevard de la Chapelle, to the left of the Barrière Poissonnière'[20] and across from the imposing façade of Lariboisière hospital – the place chosen by Carné and Prévert 70 years later for the climax of their story, Malou's death.

By the start of the 20th century, a new generation of authors led by Mac Orlan and Carco made the territory their home. While naturalist novelists were 'strangers in Montmartre, visiting for the time needed for a novel […], their younger counterparts settled in the area, where they spent the most important years of their lives: their youth'.[21] Both Mac Orlan and Carco showed a particular fascination for the teeming world of La Chapelle once described by Zola, as exemplified in Carco's sole autobiographical novel, *La Rue* (1930). The entire action of the novel takes place between rue des Poissonniers and boulevard Barbès. Like *Les Portes de la nuit*, it begins on a winter evening with a moment of suspended contemplation: 'Rue des Poissonniers, across from the workshops of the Northern Railways. I stopped to consider the façade of a house.' The opening pages include detailed descriptions of the 'smoky landscape' that immediately caught his attention: 'Past the saw-tooth like roofs of the workshops, blinking lights appeared through a gaping space. I glimpsed the massive outlines of buildings which I could not locate anywhere.'[22] Similar descriptions follow in the novel, revealing a fascination for the neighbourhood in French literature. Carné's film shares such fascination while also turning it into a marker of national identity.

A Confrontation of Identities: 'Made in France' vs the 'American Model'

As these references show, heritage constitutes a particularly strong dimension of *Les Portes de la nuit*.[23] This is reinforced by the fact that the entire film takes place in the north-eastern part of Paris reconstructed in Trauner's sets: after the Barbès Métro station, the plot unfolds on the banks of the canal de l'Ourcq, the Pont de Crimée footbridge, the section of the railway tracks from Gare de l'Est situated beyond Porte de la Villette, and finally inside Lariboisière hospital – without ever leaving the area mapped out in the opening shot. Also of note is the film's emphasis on the rue de l'Evangile (Gospel Street), located between rue de la Chapelle and rue de Crimée, a street famous for its Calvary and which at the time ran by 'the huge gasometers behind the long stone wall parallel to the railway tracks'.[24] The street fascinated many French writers such as Alexandre Arnoux, Jules Romains and Marcel Aymé, who wrote a short story entitled *Rue de l'Evangile* in 1938.[25]

Diego (Yves Montand) and Malou (Nathalie Nattier) in the rue de l'Évangile set in *Les Portes de la nuit/Gates of the Night* (Marcel Carné, 1946).

While filming this space in a wide shot for the climax of *Les Portes de la nuit* when Georges shoots Malou as a powerless Diego looks on (she later dies in Lariboisière hospital), Carné tried to highlight the 'purely geometric' dimension of the street, which had deeply struck writers like Aymé.

By ostensibly highlighting these settings, the film seems to hold on to an album of representations long imprinted in the national collective memory. It mobilises what the historian Bronisław Baczko calls '*image-ideas* through which societies give themselves an identity'.[26] This 'compulsive' choice of location is all the more significant as the action of both *Jenny* (1937) and *Hôtel du Nord* was already set in the vicinity of the canal de l'Ourcq and canal Saint-Martin. The film's return to this heritage time and again heightens its own status as heritage, retrospectively emphasising how an intense Frenchness always defined the cinema of Carné. As it happens, this palpably nationally specific film attempts to confront the national past to traces of contemporary America. At the time, 'the wave of American goods and culture'[27] sweeping through France since the arrival of the GIs in the summer of 1944 already announced the wide-ranging process of Americanisation that was to mark the 1950s. *Les Portes de la nuit* features a number of allusions to Hollywood (Georges's car, Malou's first appearance) as well as to the USA as a foreign power: besides the soldiers seen in the first sequence on the Métro, a character is shown selling lamps at the Barbès station and may be heard shouting '*Libérator*, American model, made in France'.

In that regard, one should point out the extremely abrupt and violent arrival of the American car driven by Pierre Brasseur's character in a setting that connects *Les Portes de la nuit* so closely to the works of Zola, Carco and Aymé. The film as a whole, like its inaugural panning shot, is characterised by the slow pace typical of realist songs and populist novels, which usually take time to depict the social context and the atmosphere of the places where the fiction unfolds. This makes the sudden intrusion of the American car all the more startling in this Parisian environment and the relaxed atmosphere prevailing inside the restaurant – just before, sitting at a table with his friends, Montand's character was humming 'Les Feuilles mortes', the famous song written and composed for the film by Prévert and Joseph Kosma. Likewise, Malou's Hollywood-like appearance clashes so strongly with the conventions of French film noir that a critic from *La Revue du cinéma* expressed surprise at the sequence, writing that 'Fate raises the curtains of the bistrot and discovers a kind of fake movie star seated deep inside a black and silver automobile'.[28] Here, the critic refers to the symbolic figure of the tramp, played by Jean Vilar in the film, who introduces himself as 'Fate' and accordingly embodies the predetermination that hovers over the narrative. A *deus ex machina* of sorts, able to predict tragic developments, 'Fate' does raise the curtain of the restaurant at that point of the film and exclaims 'Voilà!' ('There!'). In so doing, he himself points to the strangeness of this foreign cultural presence as much as he casts it as disturbing and even sinister.

Conclusion

Les Portes de la nuit may be read as a document on the life of a working-class neighbourhood in north-eastern Paris, a snapshot taken in the immediate aftermath of World War Two before the advent of inevitable transformations tied to the Americanisation and modernisation of France. To some degree, Carné and Prévert's 'ethnographic' gesture is reminiscent of that of mid-19th-century photographers as they tried to record the identity of the old Paris for posterity before the onslaughts of Haussmann's urban modernisation completely destroyed it.

Still, this 'community film' is paradoxically disembodied, as it faithfully reproduces the architecture of a Parisian working-class neighbourhood without ever showing its inhabitants. Here, the sets almost always appear empty, in a striking contrast with 1930s films noirs such as *Coeur de lilas*/*Lilac* (Anatole Litvak, 1932), *Dans les rues*/*Song of the Streets* (Victor Trivas, 1933) or even *Le Jour se lève*/*Daybreak* (Marcel Carné, 1939). Here, urban spaces are symbolically deserted; the archetypal characters created by Prévert (the Hollywood icon, Fate, etc.) are in fact the only figures moving through them. Despite numerous shots of the most evocative places in the north-east of Paris, *Les Portes de la nuit* is characterised by the *absence* of the local population (with the exception of the crowd in the Métro station early on) and a refusal to show the colourful figures – *Apaches* (hoodlums), tramps, prostitutes – who made this working-class Paris so animated and lively in the populist literature and cinema of the 1930s. The phenomenon is all the more remarkable as Trauner's sets, though extremely 'realistic', explicitly appear as artificial, almost abstract 'film sets'. This has to do with their nostalgic or backward-looking aspect (the banks of the canal Saint-Martin), but also their monumental and symbolic dimension (Malou's assassination occurs in front of the large cross at the intersection of rue de l'Evangile and rue d'Aubervilliers), and the excessive insistence of the *mise-en-scène* on their geometry (the railway tracks).

This singularity is better understood when the nostalgic dimension of the film is put in perspective with the cultural memory it evokes – notably through the song and the sequence showing Montand humming 'Les Feuilles mortes' melancholically before the 'American' appearance of Malou causes the plot to veer towards tragedy. The tune enjoyed an exceptional fame and was covered by many artists in France, but also in the USA (by Nat King Cole, for instance), becoming a jazz standard. Still, Phil Powrie argues that in Les Portes de la nuit, it should be read as the end point to a certain use of popular song in French cinema: the chanson as a French tradition coming from the music hall, which Poetic Realism had frequently mobilised in its time to celebrate the imagined representation of a specifically French community (already) doomed to disappear in the face of contemporary upheavals linked to modernisation. The gradual but genuine disappearance of chanson as a form of expression for the community in post-war French cinema thus points to the acceleration of a process already under way in the 1930s and perceived as intractable even then: 'the disintegration of a specifically French community defined by distinctly French cultural forms (however much that sense of community might well have been no more than a utopian dream in the 1930s)'.[29] The film's attempt to give a new lease of life to a certain idea of Paris and working-class life in the city (an idea that may well have existed only in film and literature) is correlated to its disembodied world and the juxtaposition of French and American cultural referents. While deeply rooted in the present of the immediate post-war period, Les Portes de la nuit celebrates a world already vanishing, a world whose traces now seem so distant that it may take Zola's or Carco's novels to retrieve them. Simultaneously, Carné's film therefore suggests a point of equivalence between the Americanisation of French culture and the fading away of a 'national community' imagined as intrinsically French.

Translated from the French by Franck Le Gac.

Notes

1. For a study of post-war French film noir, see Thomas Pillard, Le Film noir français face aux bouleversements de la France d'après-guerre (1946–1960) (Nantes: Editions Joseph K., 2014).
2. Jacques Prévert, Les Portes de la nuit [1946], in Le Crime de Monsieur Lange/Les Portes de la nuit. Scénarios (Paris: Gallimard, 1998), p. 264.
3. François Garçon, 'Ce curieux âge d'or des cinéastes français', in Jean-Pierre Rioux (ed.), La Vie culturelle sous Vichy (Brussels: Complexe, 1990), pp. 293–313.
4. Edward Baron Turk, Marcel Carné and the Golden Age of French Cinema (Cambridge, MA: Harvard University Press, 1989), p. 263.
5. Garçon, 'Ce curieux âge d'or des cinéastes français', pp. 293–313.
6. Turk, Marcel Carné and the Golden Age of French Cinema, p. 229 [my emphasis].
7. Jean-Louis Bigourdan, '1839: les "vues de Paris" et l'introduction du daguerréotype en Europe', in Paris et le daguerréotype (Paris: Musée Carnavalet, 1992), p. 31.
8. Shelley Rice, 'Paris en daguerréotype', in Paris et le daguerréotype, p. 19.
9. Mary Warner Marien, Photography. A Cultural History (London: Laurence King Publishing, 2006 [first published 2002]), p. 57.
10. Jacques Hillairet, Connaissance du vieux Paris, vol. 1, Rive Droite (Paris: Editions Princesse, 1956), p. 333.
11. Turk, Marcel Carné and the Golden Age of French Cinema, p. 229.

12. Guillaume Le Gall, 'Paris, objet d'histoire', article accompanying the online exhibition on photographer Eugène Atget curated by the Bibliothèque Nationale de France in 2007. Available at: http://expositions.bnf.fr/atget/ (last accessed on 19 February 2015).
13. Dudley Andrew, *Mists of Regret. Culture and Sensibility in Classic French Film* (Princeton, NJ: Princeton University Press, 1995), p. 64.
14. Located in the 10th and 19th *arrondissements*, La Villette junction is now the place de la Bataille-de-Stalingrad, formerly known as place Stalingrad.
15. Built between 1784 and 1791, the Mur des Fermiers généraux acted as a toll [Translator's note].
16. Louis Chevalier, *Montmartre du plaisir et du crime* (Paris: Payot & Rivages, 1995 [first published 1980]), p. 71.
17. Ibid., p. 90.
18. Jill Forbes, *Les Enfants du paradis* (London: BFI, 1997), p. 28.
19. Alfred Sisley, *Vue du Canal St-Martin*, 1870; Maurice Utrillo, *Le Canal St-Denis*, 1906–08; Maurice Utrillo, *Le Mur rouge, Boulevard de la Chapelle à Montmartre*, 1910.
20. Emile Zola, *L'Assommoir* [1876], trans. Margaret Mauldon (Oxford: Oxford University Press, 2009 [this translation first published 1995]), p. 6.
21. Chevalier, *Montmartre du plaisir et du crime*, p. 217.
22. Francis Carco, *La Rue* [1930], in *Romans* (Paris: Robert Laffont, 2004), pp. 751–2.
23. In the sense of something worthy of being credited to the nation and preserved in collective memory. See André Chastel, 'The Notion of Patrimony', in Pierre Nora, David P. Jordan (eds), *Rethinking France: les lieux de mémoire, volume 3: Legacies*, trans. David P. Jordan (Chicago, IL: University of Chicago Press, 2009), pp. 1–46.
24. Prévert, *Les Portes de la nuit*, p. 356.
25. Marcel Aymé, *Rue de l'Evangile*, in *Derrière chez Martin* (Paris: Gallimard, 1994 [first published 1938]).
26. Bronisław Baczko, *Les Imaginaires sociaux* (Paris: Payot, 1984), p. 8.
27. André Kaspi, *La Libération de la France* (Paris: Perrin, 2004 [first published 1995]), p. 473.
28. *La Revue du cinéma*, no. 4 (1 January 1947) [my emphasis].
29. Phil Powrie, 'The Disintegration of Community: Popular Music in French Cinema 1945–Present', in Steve Cannon and Hugh Dauncey (eds), *Popular Music in France from Chanson to Techno. Culture, Identity and Society* (Aldershot: Ashgate Publishing, 2003), p. 106.

The *Caves* of Saint-Germain-des-Prés in 1950s French Cinema

Sébastien Layerle

In the aftermath of World War Two, Saint-Germain-des-Prés was the Parisian neighbourhood that probably best represented modernity. An ebullient intellectual and artistic life fuelled by various feats and legends soon made it famous in France and abroad. From the inauguration of Le Tabou jazz club in April 1947 to the so-called 'death-knell of the check shirt' in March 1950,[1] the 'cave dwellers' of the Left Bank had a strong feeling for cinema, but their film essays, shot on shoestring budgets in non- or semi-professional formats, have not gone down in history. Short films by Freddy Baume, Jean Soyeux or Jacques Baratier[2] are mostly forgotten today, as are the short touristic documentaries, mass-produced in the 1950s and presented as complements[3] to the feature film. Saint-Germain-des-Prés instead owes its filmic imaginary to sequences from *Rendez-vous de juillet/Rendezvous in July* (1949), with Maurice Ronet cast in the part of a trumpet player in Claude Luter's orchestra (he was dubbed by famous jazzman Rex Stewart). Jacques Becker's film, a romanticised chronicle of post-war Paris, captured the mindset of a young generation flocking to Left Bank cellars. A keen eye, the right tone and the ability 'to record some aspects of the era on film'[4] are especially present in how the atmosphere at the Caveau des Lorientais is conveyed, with the musicians and the band of bebop dancers 'Les Rats de cave' led by Jano Merry.

As the historian Pascale Goetschel has pointed out, '[p]laces of spectacle played a significant part in the construction of Parisian urban culture'. Not only did they contribute to the shaping of the image of Paris as the 'city of lights', they also helped the French capital extend its influence beyond its regional and national boundaries'.[5] In the 1950s, French cinema represented the variety of Parisian establishments offering live shows that had proliferated after World War Two by using different formulae for narration and *mise-en-scène* (crime stories, French-style musicals, 'chase comedies', and so on[6]). The cellars of Saint-Germain-des-Prés have a special place in the array of venues frequently shown on screen (music halls, cabarets, nightclubs). There were few direct representations on film and these repeated the clichés promulgated by the press, clichés that were criticised – with a hint of condescension – by Boris Vian in his *Manual of Saint-Germain-des-Prés*. The neighbourhood became one of the places to go to on a trip to Paris and soon became a fashionable location attracting tourists.[7] Over the length of a sequence, it was often depicted on film as an exotic 'elsewhere' (a subterranean world with its own 'primitive' mores, disorderly body language and cryptic words) where Existentialism was the rule and writer Jean-Paul Sartre the figure of reference. This chapter looks at three feature films that epitomise French entertainment films of the 1950s. André Berthomieu's *Pigalle-Saint-Germain-des-Prés* (1950), Marcello Pagliero's *La Rose rouge/The Red Rose* (1951) and Alfred Rode's *C'est la vie ... parisienne/It's the Paris Life* (1954) share the particularity of devoting a substantial amount of their setting and action to real or fictional cabarets and cellars, doing so in a parodic mode. A twofold relation to the image of Saint-Germain-des-Prés emerges out of the comparisons offered by these films, which make light of contemporary, yet already established stereotypes while taking part in the creation of an imaginary with which Left Bank Paris has long been associated. As Eric Dussault has noted, 'prior to 1960, the myth of Saint-Germain-des-Prés was forged by the media as well as by photography, cinema and literature. After 1960, a certain memory of the neighbourhood was written mostly by participants and witnesses of the era.'[8]

A Musical Journey: *Pigalle-Saint-Germain-des-Prés* (1950)

Produced and co-written by jazz band leader Ray Ventura in the wake of Jean Boyer's box-office success *Nous irons à Paris/We Will All Go to Paris* (1950) in which the band featured, *Pigalle-Saint-Germain-des-Prés* was André Berthomieu's 48th feature. A prolific director practising a cinema of entertainment, Berthomieu had started his career as a non-professional cabaret singer in the 1920s. This 'musical fantasy' focuses on Jacques Hélian's jazz orchestra as it inadvertently gets entangled in a police investigation. The group, swindled by the owner of a Pigalle nightclub who turns out to be a gangster, finds itself unemployed until a Saint-Germain cellar-bar, 'La Pivoine écarlate' ('The Scarlet Peony'), gives it a second lease of life. In their book *Paris au cinéma*, N. T. Binh and Franck Garbarz write that *Pigalle-Saint-Germain-des-Prés*, 'in its very title, significantly relates modernity to tradition'.[9] From one nightclub to the next, the film traces a typically Parisian journey, from a Right Bank then on the decline to a Left Bank bustling with life, as attested by this bit of dialogue:

> Oncle Jules (Paul Faivre): Pigalle is over, if you want my opinion.
> Gustave (Henri Genès): Well, people are still looking for a good time, aren't they?
> Oncle Jules: True, but they no longer go to Montmartre.
> Gustave: Where then?
> Jean-Pierre Francis (Gabriel Cattand): To Saint-Germain-des-Prés![10]

The plot of *Pigalle-Saint-Germain-des-Prés* does not develop around real entertainment venues; most settings were reconstructed in the studio, including the Saint-Germain-des-Prés abbatial church where the lovers (Jeanne Moreau and Gabriel Cattand) meet. Still, the script includes many allusions, slightly modified names and puns, as with the name of the cabaret-cellar 'The Scarlet Peony', a fictional transcription of *La Rose rouge*. According to Gilles Schlesser, 'the qualifier "rive gauche" was (quickly) placed next to the word "cabaret" to refer to spectacles with a strong cultural or even intellectual ambition'.[11] In the film, the 'spirit of Saint-Germain' is embodied by the character of Jean-Pierre Francis, the 'poet of cellars' and the author of *Sulfamides 313*, who contributes to the journal *The Scarlet Peony*, 'the mouthpiece of Neo-Nothingness, the new avant-garde movement'; and by musician and novelist 'Saxo', the already famous author of *J'irai baver dans votre bière* (*I Slobber in Your Beer*) – an obvious reference to Boris Vian's detective novel (published under his pseudonym Vernon Sullivan), *J'irai cracher sur vos tombes* (*I Spit on Your Graves*). Likewise, Serge Veber and André Hornez's dialogue contains many amusing aphorisms such as: 'Existentialism is the most beautiful invention of the century. Nobody has come up with anything better since the be-bop and the zip!' Or: 'Parisians have fun only in coal storage cellars. Existentialism is not a pit though, it's a mine!'[12] The picturesque crowd of the neighbourhood is depicted in broad outline (crew cuts and check shirts), especially in the scene where the cabaret is inaugurated with the original song 'A Saint-Germain-des-Prés':

> Here Ladies and Gentlemen, in Saint-Germain-des-Prés,
> Everyone pretty much looks alike,
> Unshaven, hair poorly cut, messy
> [...]
> Our fathers sang, 'Get up there and you'll see Montmartre',
> We get down, not up, and we see Jean-Paul Sartre ...

When the film was released in November 1950, *Cinémonde* was in complete agreement, offering the reader two versions of the synopsis, which writer Hervé de Peslouan revised and rewrote for the occasion in the style of Francis Carco (with a title redolent with gangster slang[13]), and Jean-Paul Sartre ('How sadly abject existence is'). In *L'Ecran français*, Édouard Berne commented on the colourful account of Left Bank cellars given by the film:

> Natives of Saint-Germain-des-Prés will perhaps call it a caricature ... But it would be bad form for them to complain about this cheerful idealised image, the most flattering there is (though not any less accurate for that)...[14]

The final sequence of the film fuses the two geographic 'circles' described by Gilles Schlesser, that of 'Montmartre-Pigalle, the historical birthplace of the Parisian cabaret of the 1900s', and that of 'Saint-Germain-des-Prés'.[15] The trendy nightclub 'La Vache à la cave',[16] in which the characters meet and where the plot is resolved, is introduced at once as 'the highest cellar in the world, on the first floor of the Eiffel Tower' and as 'an unlikely establishment for an international clientele'.[17] Its interior architecture represents an original synthesis between the music-hall theatre (with stalls and an orchestra) and the cabaret-cellar (ornamented with animal figures and featuring characteristic vaults). With this unlikely place in an ideal location, the film ends with a geographic recentring which, thanks to the panoramic view, combines the heart of Paris and its influence abroad. Indeed, Jacques Hélian's orchestra is promised a new career when an American impresario expresses interest.[18]

A Cabaret in the Limelight: *La Rose rouge* (1951)

Shot over the summer of 1950 from a script by journalist and writer Robert Scipion, *La Rose rouge* is the only identified fiction of the period whose entire plot takes place in an existing cabaret-cellar, La Rose rouge, situated in the rue de Rennes. Marcello Pagliero,

The Frères Jacques on stage in La Rose rouge (Marcello Pagliero, 1951).

who had just directed a short documentary on the neighbourhood (*Saint-Germain-des-Prés* [1949]), reportedly had the idea for the film as he attended a song recital by the Frères Jacques.[19] While the *quatuor* had done little work in film at that point, their song performances, available on records and broadcast on the radio, had already met with much success. Their fantasy and humour embodied the rejuvenation of the Left Bank, as Boris Vian wrote in his *Manual of Saint-Germain-des-Prés*: the Frères Jacques are 'beyond description – You have to see them. These four young singers have completely reinvented the genre [...]. With them, we can laugh without shame.'[20] The film honours the singers by placing them first in the credits and articulating its central plot around the group: due to a Swiss tour by the Frères Jacques, the art director of La Rose rouge (Yves Deniaud) scrambles to put a programme together to fill in the time until they return. On stage, as well as backstage, the Frères Jacques play their own parts and perform their most famous numbers ('La Gavotte des bâtons blancs', 'La Marche des footballeurs', 'Le Général Castagnetas'). They also appear in the audience made up as four Mexican generals looking for thrills in the neighbourhood's cellars. The cast additionally includes Nico Papatakis (a.k.a. Nico), the founder of the cabaret, and another 'in-house' artist, comedian and director Yves Robert (Yves Gérard in the film), noted for his stage adaptation of Raymond Queneau's *Exercises de style* (1949). In his biography of Queneau, Michel Lécureur writes that 'some sections from *Exercises de style* performed by Yves Robert and the Frères Jacques were originally to appear in [Marcello] Pagliero's film *La Rose rouge*, but the project failed due to the length of the *Exercises* and only the sets appear in the film'.[21]

The sole ambition of *La Rose rouge* was to present 'the programme of attractions of a famous cellar of Saint-Germain-des-Prés'.[22] As the credits run, a camera shooting from a truck records an itinerary across the streets of Paris, from Concorde to Notre-Dame. Further on, a bus of American tourists stops in front of the café Les Deux Magots. Their tour guide then gives a quick lecture:

> Saint-Germain-des-Prés, one of the oldest churches in Paris, first built in 1103, destroyed in 1280, rebuilt in 1329, the current centre of night life and the headquarters of Jean-Paul Sartre and Existentialists. Our 'Paris by Night' tour, 2,995 francs with champagne included, also includes a stop at Saint-Germain-des-Prés and its famous existentialist cellars. On to Napoleon's tomb! Come on, let's hurry, please!

After this sequence, shot outdoors and on location,[23] the bus enters the rue de Rennes reconstructed at the Epinay studios. Studio shooting allowed Pagliero to free himself from the confined space of the real cabaret and present each number and its surrounding activities. The camera keeps moving between stage and audience and follows characters roaming the corridors. As the film comes to a close, with characters escaping onto the roof of the building (from the cellar to the attic!), the set collapses on the comedians in a moment of confusion and cacophony, bringing theatre, stage and backstage area together on a single plane of action.

This circulation between spaces opens the possibility for the director to put to the test – with light-hearted detachment – the budding legitimacy of the Left Bank cabaret scene. One of the subplots involves a renowned actress, Evelyne Dorsay (Dora Doll), who made a name for herself with performances adapted from the literary classics such as *Anna Karenina* and *Manon Lescaut*. Dorsay scouts comedians at La Rose rouge to find the one who can play Don José in a film adaptation of *Carmen* that she is set to star in. Approaching the members of the company one by one, she already pictures herself in the part. At this point, a screen on which the credits and sequences of the planned film are projected literally appears in the frame. While these scenes suggest that the cabaret constitutes a pool of new performers which more established forms of spectacle such as cinema can tap into, they also hint at difficult transitions across domains. In the following exchange, for instance, Evelyne Dorsay's producer Matignon (Philippe Olive) is critical of the Left Bank cabaret phenomenon, which in his view is too Paris-centred:

Evelyne Dorsay: What do you call him?
Claire Claris (Barbara Laage): Yves Gérard. He is good, isn't he?
Evelyne Dorsay: Do you know him?
Claire Claris: A little bit ...
Evelyne Dorsay: I would like to meet him. That could be interesting ...
Matignon (Philippe Olive): My dear, are you serious?
Evelyne Dorsay: Well, do you know him well?
Claire Claris: Yes.
Evelyne Dorsay: You should ask him to come and have a drink. Yes, try to arrange something! This kind of warmth, of youth, of spontaneousness ...
Matignon: It won't work outside Paris!

Later on, an angry Yves Gérard complains about his flimsy part to the director and his scriptwriter (the real Marcello Pagliero and Robert Scipion, seated at a table in the nearby café, writing the scenario of the film we are watching). Unlike *Pigalle-Saint-Germain-des-Prés*, which had been a hit at the box office (3 million tickets sold overall), *La Rose rouge* drew only 550,000 spectators in the months following its release in February 1951.[24] The film is often considered a minor work, if not a potboiler, in Pagliero's atypical career as art critic, actor (in Roberto Rossellini's *Roma città aperta/Rome Open City* [1945]) and director (he was hailed for two social dramas, *Un homme marche dans la ville/A Man Walks in the City* in 1950 and *Les Amants de Bras-Mort/The Lovers of*

Bras-Mort in 1951). Still, with this entertaining film, Pagliero celebrated a neighbourhood of Paris to which he was personally attached.[25] In 1952, the filmmaker was to co-author an adaptation of Jean-Paul Sartre's *The Respectful Prostitute* with Charles Brabant.

From One Paris to Another: *C'est la vie ... parisienne* (1954)

Adapted from a script by Jacques Companeez, *C'est la vie ... parisienne* articulates two sentimental tales separated by time. In the Paris of 1906, social conventions and their different backgrounds stand in the way of the relationship between cabaret singer Cri-Cri Delagrange and Viscount de Barfleur. A half-century later, their respective grandchildren fall in love with each other but manage to leave prejudices behind and live their love freely. Reproducing the formula of Robert Siodmak's *La Vie parisienne* (1935), the film repeats a similar situation a few decades apart (both couples are played by the same actors, Claudine Dupuis and Philippe Lemaire), following a model of reverse symmetry: over time, the lineage of Cri-Cri Delagrange has become wealthier, while that of Viscount de Barfleur suffered a setback. Musically speaking, the film also brings together two iconic periods in the history of Parisian sites of spectacle: on the one hand, the Second Empire French cancan, the Belle Epoque café-concerts; on the other, post-World War Two cabarets and Saint-Germain-des-Prés cellars. The ellipsis between these two moments is bridged by a non-diegetic voice-over narration which brings up countless humorous details and addresses the audience:

> Yet time has passed, with hair turned white and orange blossom blown away. Be-bop has replaced the slow waltz and the aeroplane is now called an airplane. That's progress! [...] Paris is still Paris, as the song goes, but the Belle poque is over. As people keep repeating that times are tough, they end up believing it and the children of Paris, its future taxpayers, are already broke! If Cri-Cri knew the songs of her elder better, she would no doubt be singing 'On s'est rencontré, simplement' ['we met, quite simply'][26] at this very moment.

Director, producer and composer Alfred Rode had already made a series of musical films whose action took place in the world of show business (*Cargaison clandestine/Alarm in San Juano* [1947]; *Boîte de nuit/Hotbed of Sin* [1951]) and cinema (*Tourbillon* [1953]). In a way, *C'est la vie ... parisienne* was part of a Belle Epoque subgenre in post-war French film production, which Geneviève Sellier has already examined.[27] It also played into a certain propensity to nostalgia, as Catherine Gaston-Mathé has noted:

> The French projected their dreams of a golden age back onto the time period preceding the two World Wars. [...] Their yearning to escape and return to childhood pushed creators and spectators to turn to the Belle Époque, found in many films whose quality varied, depending on the talent and the ambition of the director.[28]

Shot for the most part at the Boulogne studios and using a new colour film process (Gévacolor) as a promotional tool, the film featured a postcard version of Paris, past and present. Chosen in reference to Jacques Offenbach's *opéra bouffe, La Vie parisienne* (1866), the title first appears to point to the logo of the fictional cabaret where Cri-Cri Delagrange tops the bill. More importantly, it serves as a rallying cry

Be-bop dancers and a jazz band in *C'est la vie ... parisienne* (Alfred Rode, 1954).

with which the Paris of partying and love is generally associated – a city where, across different eras, emotions always triumph in the end. In this setting, the visit to Saint-Germain-des-Prés is also reduced to a few specimens (the 'uniform' of the jazzman and his jeep, reminiscent of the amphibious car in *Rendez-vous de juillet*; the bohemian flat, its brass instruments and its African statues), to the intellectualism attached to the neighbourhood (the recitation of the poem 'The Aphonic Syllogism on its Suspension Bridge') and to its cellars bursting with life (be-bop dancers and band). These attributes led the film critic Jean-Louis Tallenay to comment following the film's release in June 1954: 'Many people unfortunately believe that such is Parisian life, especially abroad where the film will probably be exported as a genuine Parisian item ...'[29]

In Maurice de Canonge's film *Boum sur Paris/Rendezvous in Paris* (1954), the *mise-en-scène* of Juliette Gréco's and Mick Micheyl's singing performances ('Je hais les dimanches' and 'Rien, rien, jamais rien', respectively) suggests similar comparisons between the Paris of the Belle Epoque and that of the post-war period. One of the sequences in this 'chase comedy' takes place in a fictional cabaret, 'Le Pingoin'. Both performers are filmed on stage in a slight low-angle shot. Camera movements reveal a painted canvas behind them represents fragments of stylised, typically Parisian locations such as steps leading to a windmill, the front of a bar and a façade with the sign 'Commune libre'. With this *trompe l'œil* as a background, the sequence develops yet another symbolic encounter between the traditional neighbourhood of the Butte Montmartre and the contemporary neighbourhood of Saint-Germain, but also between the Paris of late 19th-century struggles and the existential, politically committed song of the Left Bank which took 'individuals out of the box in which they ... [were] confined and ... [gave] them a space of freedom', while singing 'of war, misery, despair [and] railing at politicians, priests and the military'.[30]

Conclusion

In the late 1950s, the venues – including the cabarets-cellars – that had prospered in the post-war period gradually lost their influence before finally fading away. As Jean Derens writes,

> The golden age of cabarets was drawing to a close. The audience was thinning out. With competition from radio, television, records, cars, second homes and the success of yé-yé songs rather than poetic, committed or rebellious songs, we were moving towards uniformity. [...] The spirit of Saint-Germain-des-Prés, which had been triumphant for 15 years, died in the early 1960s as another civilisation was beginning.[31]

With the sensation caused by the eruption of the New Wave in 1959, another Parisian topography emerged, one following 'a descriptive tendency that owes so much to documentary practice', as Michel Marie points out:

> One decisive New Wave action was to move away from studio-bound cinema. The New Wave thereby inscribed itself into a Rossellini-inspired gesture, following in the tradition of *Rome, Open City* (1945), *Paisan* (1946) and *Voyage in Italy* (1953). Rossellini had presented a radically different face of Italy by showing Rome's popular neighbourhoods, the landscapes of the highways, and the museums of Naples.[32]

In these new depictions of the French capital filmed on location, Saint-Germain-des-Prés did not feature prominently, unlike the iconic Right Bank (place de Clichy, the Champs-Elysées) or even Left Bank locations such as the Latin Quarter and Montparnasse. In 1965, the omnibus film *Paris vu par …/Six in Paris* still devoted one of its episodes to Saint-Germain-des-Prés. Named after the neighbourhood, Jean Douchet's short film proposes a new representation of it, one tuned into the present and inclined to demystify. The opening sequence repeats the perennial guided tour of Left Bank landmarks, but only to better mark its rejection of condescension. Frédéric Bas observes that

> After this travel brochure, the fiction uses a bachelor flat as its only setting, telling the story of how a young American woman buys into the narrative of the bohemian neighbourhood and is deceived as a consequence. The Saint-Germain-des-Prés of the 1960s is immediately presented as a place where appearances rule, its attraction for tourists and its bohemian identity often mere façades that enable all kinds of pretence and flirtation. There bohemians pass as bourgeois while the bourgeois like to act bohemian to seduce tourists.[33]

If Jean Douchet thus chooses in turn to 'play the game of the neighbourhood without restriction', it is not so much to celebrate its history and its mythologies as to reveal its flip side and its artificial dimension, thus 'revealing a certain truth'[34] in the process.

Translated from the French by Franck Le Gac.

Notes

1. 'L'Univers de Saint-Germain-des-Prés. Dessins et documents originaux de Jean Suyeux', special booklet produced for the 2009 edition of Boris Vian, *Manuel de Saint-Germain-des-Prés* (Paris: Librairie générale française/Le Livre de poche, 2009), p. 32. [Editors' note: this is not available in the 2005 English-language edition of Vian's book, quoted elsewhere – see note 20.]
2. 'Saint-Germain-des-Prés à l'écran', *Zeuxis*, no. 8 (Autumn 2002), p. 25.
3. Frédéric Hervé, 'Un Eros de celluloïd: l'érotisation cinématographique de Paris (1945–1975)', 'Eros parisien', *Genre, sexualité et société*, no. 10 (Autumn 2013), p. 11. Available at: http://gss.revues.org/3016 (accessed 8 September 2017).
4. Robert Chazal, 'Les Rendez-vous de juillet', *Cinéma amateur*, no. 128 (February 1950), p. 6.
5. Pascale Goetschel, 'Le Paris du spectacle vivant: entre stéréotypes et réalités, XIXe–XXe siècles', in Myriam Tsikounas (ed.), *Imaginaires urbains du Paris romantique à nos jours* (Paris: Le Manuscrit, 2011), p. 67.
6. Sébastien Layerle and Raphaëlle Moine (eds), *Voyez comme on chante! Films musicaux et cinéphilies populaires en France (1945–1958)*, *Théorème*, no. 20 (Paris: Presses de la Sorbonne Nouvelle, 2014).
7. It was also a place to go to for Hollywood musicals, as shown in a few sequences from Vincente Minnelli's *An American in Paris* (1951) and Stanley Donen's *Funny Face* (1957).
8. Eric Dussault, *L'Invention de Saint-Germain-des-Prés* (Paris: Vendémiaire, 2014), p. 18.
9. N. T. Binh and Franck Garbarz, *Paris au cinéma: la vie rêvée de la capitale de Méliès à Amélie Poulain* (Paris: Parigramme, 2003), p. 78.
10. The periodical *Cinémonde* assessed the situation in similar terms: 'Pigalle … The end of a rule … Parisians, visitors from other regions, foreigners themselves are somewhat skipping the famous neighbourhood that used to be a must-see for anyone going out on the town.' ['Pigalle … La fin d'un règne … Les Parisiens, les provinciaux, les étrangers eux-mêmes délaissent un peu le célèbre quartier sans lequel naguère, une « tournée des grands ducs » ne pouvait être complète.'] *Cinémonde*, no. 846 (23 October 1950), p. 7.
11. Gilles Schlesser, *Le Cabaret 'rive gauche'. De la Rose rouge au Bateau ivre (1946–1974)* (Paris: L'Archipel, 2006), p. 35.
12. 'Poursuite en musique de Pigalle à Saint-Germain des Prés', *Cinémonde*, no. 852 (4 December 1950), pp. 10–11.
13. Editors' note: the title, 'Les poulets sont à la moutarde' was a pun on the slang word *poulet* (chicken) for cop and the name of a chicken dish; Francis Carco (1886–1958) was a popular writer known for his depictions of the picturesque underworld of Paris.
14. *L'Ecran français*, no. 284 (20 December 1950), p. 16.
15. Schlesser, *Le Cabaret 'rive gauche'*, pp. 40–1.
16. 'The Cow in the Cellar', yet another play on a name: 'Le Boeuf sur le toit' – literally, 'The Ox on the Roof', a famous Right Bank cabaret.
17. Excerpts from the synopsis, Bibliothèque de la Cinémathèque Française, scenario collection, CN1608-B687.
18. In his 1953 film *Le Portrait de son père/His Father's Portrait*, André Berthomieu was to repeat the journey from Montmartre-Pigalle to Saint-Germain-des-Prés in a cab ride scene. 'Yes, everything happens in the cellars, it keeps the patrons cool!' the driver commented. In the cellar

'Le Pot aux roses', the provincial character played by Jean Richard was the incredulous witness of a be-bop dance and the recitation of an existentialist poem.
19. Pierre Chatelein, 'Quand Saint-Germain-des-Prés émigre à Epinay …', *L'Ecran français*, no. 265 (31 July 1950), p. 10.
20. Boris Vian, *The Manual of Saint-Germain-des-Prés* (New York: Rizzoli, 2005), p. 131. Published in French as *Le Manuel de Saint-Germain-des-Prés* (Paris: Chêne, 1974 [1951]).
21. From a booklet titled 'Raymond Queneau et le cinéma', quoted in Michel Lécureul, *Raymond Queneau: Biographie* (Paris: Les Belles Lettres, 2002), p. 384.
22. 'La Rose rouge', *Le Film français*, no. 334 (16 February 1951), p. 21.
23. The sequence, which almost stands alone in the film, spawns a recurring gag: an American tourist left behind on the church square tries to get to the Dôme des Invalides.
24. Simon Simsi, *Ciné-Passion. Le Guide chiffré du cinéma en France* (Paris: Dixit, 2012).
25. Jean A. Gili, 'Marcello Pagliero, cinéaste italo-français', *1895*, no. 10 (October 1991), p. 48.
26. Editors' note: an allusion to the famous 1905 song 'Fascination' (lyrics by Maurice de Féraudy, music by Fermo Marchetti), a Belle Epoque standard.
27. Geneviève Sellier, 'Les Films 'Belle Epoque' dans le cinéma d'après-guerre. Invisibilité d'un genre féminin', in Raphaëlle Moine (ed.), *Le Cinéma français face aux genres* (Paris: AFRHC, 2005) pp. 151–61.
28. Catherine Gaston-Mathé, *La Société française au miroir de son cinéma* (Condé-sur-Noireau: Arléa/Corlet, 1996), p. 162.
29. Jean-Louis Tallenay, 'Drôle de vie pour les Parisiens', *Télérama*, 13 June 1954. *C'est la vie … parisienne* attracted 1.4 million spectators overall in France.
30. Michel Trihoreau, *La Chanson de proximité. Caveaux, cabarets et autres petits lieux* (Paris: L'Harmattan, 2010), p. 87.
31. Jean Derens, in Geneviève Latour, *Le 'Cabaret-Théâtre' (1945–1965)* (Paris: Bibliothèque de la Ville de Paris, 1996), p. 6.
32. Michel Marie, *The French New Wave. An Artistic School*, trans. Richard Neupert (Malden, MA, and Oxford: Blackwell, 2003), p. 81.
33. Frédéric Bas, 'Saint-Germain-des-Prés', conference given at Forum des Images, 2012. Available at: http://collections.forumdesimages.fr (accessed 8 September 2017).
34. Jean Douchet, *L'Homme cinéma, entretiens avec Joël Magny* (Paris: Ecriture, 2013), p. 142.

Paris in the Summer of 1959: *Le Signe du lion*

Michel Marie

Up until the last few years, *Le Signe du lion/The Sign of Leo* (1959–62), the first feature-length film completed and released by Eric Rohmer, was not the subject of extensive study. It would seem to have been rediscovered in 2007, and even more comprehensively since 2012, as can be judged from a number of studies.[1] The place occupied by the film in Rohmer's oeuvre is rather unusual. It is an atypical work – one of those unfortunate films made at the beginning of the New Wave, along with Jacques Rivette's *Paris nous appartient/Paris Belongs to Us* (1961) and Jean-Daniel Pollet's *La Ligne de mire/Line of Sight* (1959–60), which was never released. It is fascinating to view it again today because of its almost documentary portrayal of the central districts of Paris, filmed during the summer of 1959.

Rohmer was the oldest of the group of film critics on *Cahiers du cinéma*[2] who became filmmakers and spearheaded the French New Wave. The first part of his career was blighted by a succession of failures. These included his first short as a director, *Journal d'un scélérat/Diary of a Scoundrel* (1949), co-scripted by Paul Gégauff, *Bérénice* (1954) and *La Sonate à Kreutzer/The Kreutzer Sonata* (1956), films that were either shown only to very restricted audiences or not released at all. All of them were shot on 16 mm using makeshift equipment. The worst of these failures was Rohmer's first feature film, *Les Petites filles modèles/Good Little Girls*, which was shot on 35mm in 1952. The visuals were completed, but as a result of the producer going bust, the soundtrack remained unfinished.[3]

In 1959, Rohmer, at nearly 30, was no longer a very young man. He had been co-editor-in-chief of *Cahiers du cinéma* since 1957 and took on a more prominent role after the death of André Bazin in 1958, of whom he was the spiritual heir. It was the success of Claude Chabrol's and François Truffaut's first full-length films that enabled Rohmer at last to shoot his first feature that had the benefit of rather more professional facilities. Indeed, it was Chabrol's production company, AJYM Films, which he had set up to produce his own first feature, *Le Beau Serge*, that produced *Le Signe du lion*. In the early summer of 1959, the time seemed ripe for a breakthrough by the 'Young Turks' of cinephilia. Chabrol had just released in quick succession *Le Beau Serge* (in February), then *Les Cousins* (in March), which was a box-office success; Truffaut took the 1959 Cannes Film Festival by storm with *Les Quatre cents coups/The 400 Blows*. The New Wave was well and truly launched.

Rohmer's First Completed Feature Film

Rohmer filmed *Le Signe du lion* in seven weeks during July and August of 1959. The shooting conditions were 'normal' or 'traditional'. He had two assistant directors, Jean-Charles Lagneau and Philippe Collin, and his cinematographer was an established professional, Nicolas Hayer,[4] who had three assistants, including Pierre Lhomme and Alain Levent, who both went on to enjoy successful careers in the 1960s. Only the music, composed by Louis Saguer, deliberately diverged from a traditional film score.[5] But that approach was justified by the subject of the film, which was about a violinist who has composed a sonata. Indeed, music plays a key role, particularly in the central section, where almost nothing is said. The cast included professional actors who later appeared in films by Jean-Luc Godard (Van Doude), Chabrol (Stéphane Audran), Jean-Pierre Melville (Paul Crauchet), Pierre Kast (Françoise Prévost) and even Howard Hawks (Michèle Girardon). Rohmer's only bold decision was to choose as his lead Jess Hahn, a former member of the US Marines who settled in France in 1949 and became an actor, specialising in supporting roles and gangster films because of his 'tough guy' physique.

What greatly hampered the career of *Le Signe du lion* was the lack of a distributor. Neither Chabrol the producer nor Rohmer the director had properly gauged the vital importance of a theatrical release. Distributors were put off by both the austerity of the film's theme and its long, very undramatic and quasi-documentary central section (to which I shall return), which was based on a misadventure experienced by Gégauff.[6] It took two years for the film to get shown in Paris, in May 1962, and then only in a single cinema, La Pagode. It was a box-office flop: it was seen by only 4,978 people on its first run, a figure that eventually totalled 14,073 in Paris after several years and 16,527 in the whole of France.[7] In other words, it represented a considerable loss for Chabrol's production company. By May 1962, the New Wave was losing its appeal in France. Distribution of *Le Signe du lion* was in the hands of an art-house cinema that could not afford to provide it with adequate publicity. Moreover, Hahn's physical appearance and manner did not square with the cinema's idea of good looks at the time. He did not possess the casual boxer's charm radiated by someone like Jean-Paul Belmondo, nor did he meet the traditional criteria of handsomeness like Gérard Blain, Jean-Claude Brialy or Gianni Esposito. He had nothing of the adolescent awkwardness of Jean-Pierre Léaud or the touching shyness of Charles Aznavour.

The main characteristic of *Le Signe du lion* is the classicism of its construction. There is no explicit modernity in its narrative style of the kind to be found, for example, in Alain Resnais's *Hiroshima mon amour* or Godard's *A bout de souffle/Breathless*, both of them made the same year, 1959. The narrative is linear and moves forward in a regular way. It is divided up into three parts, which comprise several rather arbitrary narrative surprises:

- The first part portrays a bohemian musician called Pierre Wesselrin (Hahn) who inherits a fortune from his aunt (the first surprise) and prematurely celebrates the event with friends. He is then disinherited in favour of a cousin and evicted from his flat (30 minutes).
- The second part describes the gradual disintegration of his personal life. It is August and all his friends have left Paris. His cousin dies in a road accident (the second narrative surprise – an accident of which only the spectator, and not the central character, is aware) (48 minutes).

Pierre (Jess Hahn), left, and his friend the tramp (Jean Le Poulain), in front of Notre-Dame cathedral in *Le Signe du lion* (Eric Rohmer, 1959–62).

- In the third part, by now in a state of utter destitution, our unfortunate musician meets a cheerful *clochard* (tramp) and discovers with him the world of down-and-outs. They perform a burlesque little musical act in front of café terraces in Saint-Germain-des-Prés. Pierre's friend Jean-François, who is a reporter on *Paris Match*, miraculously tracks Pierre down when he recognises the sonata he plays on the violin (the third twist in the plot – and its epilogue) (21 minutes).

As we can see, the first and third parts of the film are roughly the same length, but the second – and central – part is by far the longest. Not only that: it is strikingly slow-moving and repetitive as it charts Pierre's daily perambulations through the streets of central Paris, then his return from Nanterre, and further aimless walking.

What is however most unusual in Rohmer's approach is the way the time of shooting coincides with the unfolding of the story. They are both strictly chronological. So *Le Signe du lion* could be interpreted as a kind of manifesto of realist aesthetics as formulated by Bazin, to whom Rohmer pays tribute. The shooting followed the chronology of the story, from 22 June (as we see from the first inter-title) until 23 August (the end of the film). The dates are indicated by inter-titles or by the events depicted: 22 June, the evening of 13 July (the Bastille Day ball, held the night before), 30 July and 22 August. They mark very scrupulously the abrupt twists in the narrative. The film is punctuated by references to socio-political events that actually happened during the shooting in July and August of 1959. Jean-François, Pierre's journalist friend, reports on his trips for *Paris Match* to, among others, Hassi Messaoud in the Sahara (oil plants) and Moscow (President Nixon's visit). This series of assignments also explains why he is not in Paris.

But the way the dates of shooting and the dates in the film's narrative coincide is echoed by the dates that mark the beginning and end of the sign of Leo, from 23 July to 22

August, in the zodiac system. The film indicates that Pierre's birthday is on 2 August – in other words roughly halfway through the 'sign of Leo'. True, it took seven weeks of shooting to chronicle eight weeks of fictional narrative, but that remains only a minor discrepancy compared with the usual practice of shooting schedules. The sequences were systematically filmed in the order they occur in the film, starting with the arrival of the postman who wakes Pierre up on 22 July. The telegram brings news of the aunt's death and Pierre's inheritance, thus setting the narrative in motion. The central section, which describes how he is gradually marginalised after being thrown out of his hotel and running out of money, covers the days from 30 July to 2 August. It ends with him as a complete down-and-out.

This chronological authenticity, which is by no means the rule in mainstream film production, is paralleled by a spatial authenticity. The aesthetic approach adopted here is one of 'true representation'. It can be seen in the choice of locations and the filming of what is going on in actual streets and districts. The first part[8] ends in the early hours of the morning in Saint-Germain-des-Prés after the Bastille Day ball. We find Pierre sitting alone on a chair on which he has spent the night in front of the Royal Saint-Germain café. This first part of the film consists of a rather conventional portrayal of the bohemian lifestyle of Pierre and his group of friends. They move from apartments to hotel rooms, often by car, and spend some time on café terraces. The atmosphere is one of general euphoria. In this respect it is typical of the representation of young people in Saint-Germain-des-Prés as depicted in many films, from Jacques Becker's *Rendez-vous de juillet/Rendezvous in July* (1949) to Chabrol's *Les Cousins*.

Pierre: Much Less and Much More than a *Flâneur*

Everything changes after Pierre is thrown out of the Hôtel de Seine on 30 July. In less than three minutes, the upbeat story suddenly turns into a relentless nightmare. Pierre collects his last pieces of loose change and goes to sell his detective stories to a *bouquiniste* (open-air bookseller) by the Seine. It marks the start of his ordeal, in the course of which he tramps to and fro through the streets of the capital and occasionally bumps into old friends. He walks everywhere, in the Latin Quarter, on the banks of the Seine, and past a string of hotels and cafés. This long-drawn-out central section of the film, as already mentioned, lasts more than 48 minutes in all, or half the film's total running time. It is of course this long central section charting the wanderings of the central character that does not conform to the narrative conventions of traditional cinema in the late 1950s. Rohmer describes, day after day, the various stages in the process that causes Pierre to be marginalised. This central section has almost no dialogue, except for some trivial remarks by passers-by. Pierre walks solely through the central *arrondissements* of Paris (5th, 6th, 1st and 4th). The only time he leaves them is when he travels out to the suburb of Nanterre, which is the longest sequence within this section. It is the only time he takes the Métro.

In his scholarly and fascinating article 'The Sign of the Map, Cartographic Reading and *Le Signe du Lion*',[9] Roland-François Lack describes eight of Pierre's walks, which are punctuated by ellipses and dissolves – a succession of sequences which alternate between night and day, starting with his being thrown out of the Hôtel de Seine. Lack enumerates in detail the streets Pierre walks along, the types of buildings lining them and the names of cafés, thus reconstituting very meticulously his exact itinerary. In this way he reveals the documentary authenticity of the film, which can be used as a guide to most of the streets in the districts Pierre walks through. Rohmer here anticipates the obsessive topographical precision of his later work, as François Penz demonstrates.[10] His first walk in the central section begins with Pierre sleeping on a chair in the early hours of the morning outside the Royal Saint-Germain café. He wakes, gets up and walks along the boulevard Saint-Germain and the rue de Buci, passes the Café Mabillon and finds himself again at the Royal Saint-Germain. It is there that he meets his friend Philippe, who gives him 10,000 francs, worth roughly 100 euros in today's money. On his second walk, Pierre leaves the Hôtel de Seine and goes to sell his detective stories. On his third walk, he tries, unsuccessfully, to find a room at the Hôtel de Senlis in the rue Malebranche. He comes back towards the Pont des Arts. His fourth walk takes him to the place de l'Opéra, then he spends the night sleeping on a chair outside the Café de Flore back in Saint-Germain-des-Prés.

Pierre's fifth excursion is the most spectacular. In the course of it, he treks out to the rue des Carriers in Nanterre. He first takes the Métro as far as the Pont de Neuilly station, then walks from there to Nanterre. For the return journey, he has to walk back all the way along the avenue de la Grande-Armée because he inadvertently dropped his last Métro ticket when he earlier took a handkerchief out of his pocket. He walks almost 10 kilometres. This excursion occupies more than 12 minutes of the film and includes many moments where he sits down and eavesdrops on young women's conversations. This is Pierre's desperate final journey. In Nanterre, the job he had been offered by a friend at a café, which involved some smuggling scam, turns out to be pie in the sky. This is also the point where we see the first signs of physical exhaustion on Pierre's face: he looks haggard and has beads of sweat on his forehead. He takes off his jacket as he walks. The sun blazes down on him. He encounters a lot of strangers, mainly women but also young lovers, who chat animatedly with each other. Many of them are eating chocolate or biscuits, or quenching their thirst with soft drinks.

On his sixth walk, Pierre goes looking for food at Les Halles just as the market is packing up, then returns to the Hôtel du Pas-de-Calais, where Jean-François's girlfriend, Dominique, is staying. He tries, again without success, to pick up some of the things he had left in his flat on the quai des Grand-Augustins, and ends the day sitting in the square du Vert-Galant, on the tip of the Ile de la Cité. His seventh walk is located mainly in the area of Saint-Germain-des-Prés, Mabillon and boulevard Saint-Michel. It ends in front of the Lycée Saint-Louis. His eighth walk takes place on the embankment of the Seine, chiefly the quai de Montebello.

What is remarkable is the continuity of the action and the very precise topography of the places Pierre visits. Rohmer systematised this topographical precision in the first of his 'Moral Tales', *La Boulangère de Monceau/The Girl at the Monceau Bakery* (1963), at the Villiers crossroads, and in the rue de Lévis in the 17th *arrondissement*, but above all in 'Place de l'Etoile', his segment in the episode film *Paris vu par ...*/*Six in Paris* (1965). The latter may be regarded as the theoretical manifesto of 'Cinéma, art de l'espace' ('Cinema, the Art of Space') – the title of Rohmer's first published article, under the name of Maurice Schérer.[11] In *Le Signe du lion*, we meet the habitués of each district, anonymous passers-by and people sitting at café terraces. But the cheerful and carefree atmosphere of the first part of the film here gives way to indifference on the part of the people Pierre encounters. They quite literally do not see him. He is desperately lonely and invisible in the big city. All he can think of is how to find his friends, borrow some money from them and simply eat and find somewhere to put his head down. For this reason, I feel it does not make sense to describe, as many have done,[12] Pierre's perambulations through Paris as *flâneries*. Most French dictionaries define the verb *flâner* as 'to walk unhurriedly and aimlessly'. But in *Le Signe du lion* Pierre does not walk aimlessly: he has a very precise objective. He is both much less, and much more, than a *flâneur*, and in no way could he be described as such. He criss-crosses the streets of the 5th and 6th *arrondissements*, like a hunter in search of game or a beggar looking for money. In the course of doing so, he occasionally ends up going round in circles, like someone who is lost in a forest or desert. Losing one's way in a forest or desert is not at all the same thing as strolling. It is about trying to find a way out, getting out of a dead end, escaping from a maze and shaking off the predestination of the signs of the zodiac.

The process of Pierre's physical deterioration becomes more marked the more he walks. The actor himself begins to supplant the character he is playing. He is increasingly unwashed and unshaven, and his clothes are filthy. He is also increasingly solitary, to the point of no longer opening his mouth. Rohmer displays a very real cruelty in the way he describes the physical suffering and social misery of his central character. The framing of each shot emphasises the physical weakening of the actor's body. Day after day Jess Hahn had to comply with the exacting demands of his director. On screen we can see that he becomes increasingly dirty, unshaven, haggard and sweaty. He moves forward like a ghost. In a way, he is subjected to the torture of the most meticulous form of realism. Indeed, one wonders whether Hahn was deliberately starved so he could express hunger with the greatest possible authenticity.

Pierre's silence coincides with the appearance of a non-diegetic musical composition – the sonata that he is supposed to have composed. It can be heard during the opening credits, and recurs when Pierre is on his way back from Nanterre, after he has started walking up the avenue de la Grande-Armée. It accompanies his successive walks and recurs diegetically at the end of the film when Pierre plays it in the street, thanks to which his friend Jean-François, who has returned to Paris, finds him. Pierre's deterioration is described in a very meticulous, almost obsessive way: Rohmer spares us no detail as we see Pierre buying some Brie cheese, a tin of sardines, a baguette and some stain remover to get rid of an oily mark, before scavenging some discarded fruit at Les Halles and buying a final small piece of bread (6 francs, or roughly 0.10 euros). Finally, he tries to steal a packet of biscuits from the street market in the rue Mouffetard and later, fishes another packet out of the Seine.

His trek is characterised by several toings and froings and by a series of comings and goings between the street level and the flight of steps that takes Pierre down to the riverbanks. This scenography of Paris suggests a veritable 'descent into hell'. The flat at the beginning of the film is on the third floor. His room in the Hôtel de Seine is only two floors up. Pierre walks through streets and past café terraces, goes down into the basement of cafés to use the phone and, above all, walks down steps that take him to the banks of the Seine, normally a place where people go to relax, but in his case one where he is blinded by the sun and feels increasing pangs of hunger. On several occasions, the film shows close-ups of the surface of the Seine sparkling in the sun. In Pierre's eyes, the same images simply reflect *a contrario* the intensity of his despair which leads to him contemplating suicide by drowning, an allusion to Jean Renoir's *Boudu sauvé des eaux/Boudu Saved from Drowning* (1932), a film particularly admired by Rohmer, in which the hero, unlike Pierre, does actually jump into the river. *Le Signe du lion* is in a sense a dark and satanic version of Renoir's Dionysian fable, in which Boudu's immersion in the river is a form of resurrection, as he is rescued by a kind bookshop owner.

Pierre's decline reaches its peak when the sole of one of his shoes comes unstuck, following his long trek back from the suburbs. This brief and very revealing episode takes place on the Ile de la Cité. Pierre has dozed off under a tree in the square du Vert-Galant, on the western tip of the island. He wakes up and picks up a piece of paper in the (mistaken) belief that it might contain something to eat. Night falls. He goes into a crowded café on the boulevard Saint-Germain and asks the woman at the cash desk whether she has seen his friend Willy. He goes out, walks past the Café Mabillon and shuffles along the pavement to the nearby Lycée Saint-Louis. As he walks alongside its stone wall, he scrapes it with his fingertips, then, turning to face the wall, pushes against it. We next see him lying the following morning on the steps leading up to the *lycée*'s entrance, where he has been sleeping. He gets to his feet and goes back the way he came. His feet are shown in close-up. His sole comes unstuck. He rummages in a rubbish bin in search of something he can use to tie his shoe together. He goes down to the Seine and sits on a parapet. The heat of the sun is increasingly oppressive. He watches a flock of pigeons wheeling around Notre-Dame. He passes three noisily chatting Italian tourists. This is when Pierre pathetically fishes a floating packet of biscuits out of the water. The city's indifference to his plight is signified by the opacity of the walls he encounters. He is everywhere faced by stone and its hostility – stone that he wants to mark, to move, to destroy. At this point Pierre is the most radical anti-hero produced by the New Wave – a character plucked out of the darkest Italian neo-realism and arbitrarily plunged into the sunny, cheerful Paris of 1959.

Pierre (Jess Hahn) going down to the river in *Le Signe du lion* (Eric Rohmer, 1959–62).

Character's Purgatory – Filmmaker's Setbacks

By way of an epilogue, I would like to draw a parallel between the character of Wesselrin and the professional setbacks suffered by the renowned filmmaker-to-be: Rohmer was abruptly sacked from the editorial board of *Cahiers du cinéma*,[13] was unemployed for a time, then worked in educational television so as not to have to go back to a job as a teacher of French in some remote province, far from the cinephile and intellectual life of the capital. Rohmer managed to bounce back by setting up a production company with Barbet Schroeder, Les Films du Losange. While continuing to make films for educational television, he started directing the initial series of his 'Moral Tales' on 16 mm and without synchronous sound, first *La Boulangère de Monceau*, then *La Carrière de Suzanne/Suzanne's Career* (1963), which is set in the inner southern suburbs of Paris. He followed them up with two short films, *Nadja à Paris/Nadja in Paris* (1964) and 'Place de l'Etoile'. The whole film in which the latter appears, *Paris vu par ...*, was the first major production undertaken by Les Films du Losange; it can be seen as the second aesthetic manifesto of the New Wave.[14]

Mirroring the fate of his bohemian American musician, Rohmer's hitherto bumpy career suddenly looked up in 1966, when Les Films du Losange (Schroeder) and Rome Paris Films (Georges de Beauregard) co-produced Rohmer's third moral tale, *La Collectionneuse/The Collector*. This feature-length film could not have been more different from *Le Signe du lion*, just as Patrick Bauchau, the dandy in *La Collectionneuse*, has nothing in common with the rough diamond played by Hahn in *Le Signe du lion*. The banks of the Seine are replaced by the Côte d'Azur, narcissistic dandies and the devastating charm of the woman who 'collects' men, the curvaceous Haydée Politoff – all filmed in glorious colour by cinematographer Néstor Almendros. Rohmer's career could at last take off. Almost 50 at the time, he went on to direct more than 20 features which make up one of the most personal and original oeuvres of the New Wave. Major recognition came with *Ma nuit chez Maud/My Night with Maud* in 1969 and continued for a further 38 years up until his final film, *Les Amours d'Astrée et de Céladon/The Romance of Astrea and Celadon* (2007). Rohmer died in 2010. In the end, *Le Signe du lion* brought him luck and secured him international recognition. Rather like Pierre Wesselrin, Rohmer believed in his lucky star.

Translated from the French by Peter Graham.

Notes

1. Recent analyses include: Antoine de Baecque and Noël Herpe, *Eric Rohmer, biographie* (Paris: Stock, 2014), pp. 97–112; Nicolas Drouin, 'Forme filmique, labyrinthe urbain et temps circulaire dans *Le Signe du lion*', in Sylvie Robic and Laurence Schifano (eds), *Rohmer en perspectives* (Paris: Presses Universitaires de Paris Ouest, 2013), pp. 125–46; Fujita Jun, 'Poésie de l'argent dans *Le Signe du lion*', in Noël Herpe (ed.), *Rohmer et les autres* (Rennes: Presses Universitaires de Rennes, 2007); Roland-François Lack, 'The Sign of the Map, Cartographic Reading and *Le Signe du lion*', *Senses of Cinema*, April 2010. Available at: http://sensesofcinema.com/2010/feature-articles/the-sign-of-the-map-cartographic-reading-and-le-signe-du-lion/ (accessed 9 September 2017); Suzanne Liandrat-Guigues, 'Une moderne flânerie' (*Le Signe du lion*), in

Patrick Louguet (ed.), *Rohmer ou le jeu des variations* (Paris: PUV, 2012), pp. 51–8; Jacqueline Vergnault-Scieux, 'Le Paris de Rohmer, de Saint Germain des Prés à l'Etoile, naissance d'un regard', in Robic and Schifano (eds), *Rohmer en perspectives*, pp. 147–60.

2. Eric Rohmer (the pseudonym of Maurice Schérer) was born in 1920, Claude Chabrol, Jean-Luc Godard and Jacques Rivette in 1930, and François Truffaut in 1932.
3. François Thomas, 'Rohmer 1952: *les petites filles modèles*', *Cinéma 09* (Spring 2005), pp. 32–47.
4. Nicolas Hayer worked as cinematographer with eminent filmmakers such as Henri-Georges Clouzot, Jacques Becker, Jean Cocteau and Jean-Pierre Melville.
5. It is in fact the only film score composed in France by Louis Saguer, the pseudonym of Wolfgang Simoni, a German composer who emigrated to France in 1933.
6. Rohmer wrote the dialogue of the film, contrary to what is indicated on the credit titles. 'Gégauff's contribution was limited to listening to Rohmer's dialogue and approving it.' De Baecque and Herpe, *Eric Rohmer, biographie*, p. 97.
7. Simon Simsi, *Ciné-Passions. 7e art et industrie de 1945 à 2000* (Paris: Dixit, 2000), p. 488.
8. This corresponds to Chapters 1–5 of the DVD published by Les Films du Losange, which divides the film up into 14 chapters, conforming more or less to the way it is organised into sequences.
9. Lack, 'The Sign of the Map, Cartographic Reading and *Le Signe du lion*'.
10. François Penz, 'From Topographical Coherence to Creative Geography: Rohmer's *La Femme de l'aviateur/The Aviator's Wife* and Rivette's *Pont du Nord*', in Andrew Webber and Emma Wilson (eds), *Cities in Transition: The Moving Image and the Modern Metropolis* (London: Wallflower Press, 2008), pp. 123–40.
11. *La Revue du cinéma*, no. 14 (June 1948), pp. 3–14. He stresses the importance of the spatial parameter in film by pointing up Keaton's comic geometry and the spatial metaphysics that operates in Murnau's films, chiefly in 'his admirable – yet highly controversial – *Faust*'. This demonstrates how consistent Schérer/Rohmer's ideas were.
12. Liandrat-Guigues, in particular, argues: 'So, half an hour into the film, we see the start of Pierre Wesselrin's perambulations, which take up 35 of the following 50 minutes. It is here that the nub of the film unfolds – the part that lends it its most remarkable aspect of *flânerie*'; and [after Wesselrin's fifth journey (to Nanterre)], 'that thread is abandoned, since, as we shall see, the aim is now to represent the singular and highly modern experience denoted by the term *flânerie*' (p. 56). 'Une moderne flânerie (*Le Signe du lion*)', pp. 55–6.
13. Editors' note: Rohmer was evicted from his post as editor of *Cahiers du cinéma* in June 1963 following a dispute that placed him, as head of the 'classicists', in opposition to the 'moderns' led by Jacques Rivette. Rivette replaced Rohmer as editor until 1965.
14. See Michel Marie, *The French New Wave: An Artistic School* (Malden, MA: Blackwell Publishers, 2003), p. 84.

Truffaut's Apartments

Hilary Radner and Alistair Fox

In the English-speaking world, the word 'Paris' typically evokes a set of postcard views of city life, from its bistros to its monuments. While these have become the staple of many Hollywood films, with a trip to Paris one of the recurring narrative tropes that define the 'chick flick', Paris is also indelibly associated with French New Wave cinema, which has had an equally important influence on the public imagination since the 1960s, in terms of defining the essence of 'Frenchness' and offering a vision of city life defined by the apartment to several generations of spectators situated across the globe. Not inconsequentially, in recent times, an increasing number of Parisian apartments have been mobilised as holiday locales, in particular short-term rentals,[1] so that sophisticated tourists can enjoy the experience of the city in an authentic environment, putting increasing pressure on the market with regard to the needs of the city's permanent inhabitants. The apartment functions, then, as a sign of Paris, a dimension of the city routinely represented in French cinema.

New Wave Films and the Apartment

In its early, most vigorous and inventive phase, the French New Wave was inseparably connected to the Parisian apartment: one need only think of the prominent role it played in the setting of Jacques Rivette's first short film, *Le Coup du berger/ Checkmate* (1956), which was shot in the apartment of Claude Chabrol; or of the setting in François Truffaut's first short film, *Une visite* (1955), shot in Jacques Doniol-Valcroze's apartment. Later, as the young filmmakers began to attract attention, Truffaut himself commented in interviews on the importance of these apartments, especially the one belonging to Antoine Doinel's parents in *Les Quatre cents coups/The 400 Blows* (1959), and that in *La Peau douce/The Soft Skin* (1964).

The presence of the Parisian apartment in French New Wave films is such a striking phenomenon that one is prompted to ask the question, 'why?' Obviously, financial considerations had much to do with the choice of apartments as settings. As Truffaut underlines, he and his fellow filmmakers had so little money they had to economise to the utmost. Rivette's *Le Coup du berger*, for example, was shot 'in two weeks, with money spent only on the film stock, and with a borrowed camera, several actor friends'.[2] Similarly, Rivette's *Paris nous appartient/Paris Belongs to Us* (1961) 'was shot with nothing: several loans, some people who lent a bit of money, and an apartment, and film stock that came from another movie'.[3]

Truffaut suggested the multiple reasons for this phenomenon, when he was asked why he never shot anything in a studio and replied that it was not a matter of 'principle, but of both economic and aesthetic considerations':[4] 'I like to shoot on location because it's real. Studio doors don't close properly; I'm very attached to the truth of a door, the truth of a window, the truth of curtains.'[5] The economic advantages of this strategy are obvious enough; however, the aesthetic ones were more subtle, implying both psychological and sociological motivations. Some sense of this can be gleaned from Truffaut's remarks on *Les Quatre cents coups*. Significantly, Truffaut draws a parallel between his father as depicted in the film and the father he knew as a child, and the apartment depicted in the film and the apartments in which he had lived as a child – first at an apartment in the rue de Clignancourt (18th *arrondissement*) in 1942, then one in the rue Saint-Georges (9th *arrondissement*) in 1943, and finally in a second-floor apartment at 33 rue de Navarin (9th *arrondissement*) from January 1944:[6] 'There was a close physical resemblance between my father and the man who played him in the film. It was the same with the apartment in which we filmed. It was located in the same neighbourhood in which I had grown up.'[7] Here the director suggests that the verisimilitude imparted by setting his films in apartments rather than studio recreations served a thematic and affective function as well as a merely expedient one. As Truffaut went on to say: 'the film engages with everything that had not been acknowledged or talked about in our lives', and its apartment setting played an important part in communicating the feeling of what was at issue.[8] The relationship between what is shown about the apartment when used as a setting in these New Wave films and the emotional, psychological and sociological issues presented by the characters-in-action who inhabit them served a crucial function in defining these works. Truffaut's *La Peau douce*, produced at a hinge moment in the director's career and in the development of the New Wave itself, offers an especially striking example of the apartment and its instrumental role, to the point that it acquires, arguably, the status of another character, which it derives, at least in part, from the evolution of the Parisian apartment in its sociological contexts, developments that would have been very familiar to French audiences at the time of the film's release.

The rue de Navarin (9th *arrondissement*) today, in the Pigalle district (photograph by Alistair Fox).

Sociological Implications of the Parisian Apartment

In general, scholarly discussions of cinema and the city have focused on street life and the public arena of urban culture, with Walter Benjamin's *flâneur* as its primary exemplum.[9] Literary scholar Sharon Marcus notes that, in part because of the pervasive influence of Benjamin, the received view of 19th-century cities, Paris in particular, was based on a marked division of experience with regard to gender, which she summarises as follows: 'Men freely stroll the boulevards, mingling with the crowd and collecting impressions, but women enter the streets only at the risk of being taken for streetwalkers.'[10] Notwithstanding, as Marcus points out, the emergence of the multi-storied apartment building proved to be one of the most salient features of urban life in the 19th century, again particularly with regard to Paris. Marcus emphasises how, during that period, the apartment challenged what she calls an 'urban geography of gender' by 'dissolving the boundary between residential and collective space'.[11] The resulting spatial configurations and their development in the 20th century remain relatively unexplored with regard to the cinematic representation of Paris, in spite of the fact that this city 'in Walter Benjamin's formulation ... became a symbol of urban modernity'.[12]

One of the factors contributing to the proliferation of apartments was a housing shortage that had plagued Paris throughout the 19th and early 20th century, and which intensified during the post-World War Two period. While the Haussmann renovation project that continued from 1853 until 1927 had to a degree cleaned up Paris, it had not resolved the problem posed by the steady increase among the lower-income population. The new apartments that had continued to be built were often only within the grasp of the relatively wealthy bourgeoisie. The poor, however, were shunted off to various peripheral, suburban neighbourhoods, where they lived in frequently insalubrious conditions. The situation reached epic proportions in the wake of World War Two, exacerbated by the depredations of the war itself. In the late 1940s and 1950s, to address this situation, emphasis was placed on the construction of cheap housing on the outskirts of Paris, with significant consequences in terms of a lowering of quality. By the 1960s, concerns about housing and the social effects of overcrowding were reaching a crisis point, and contributed to the upheavals of 1968.[13] In this period, the term 'right to the city', coined by sociologist Henri Lefebvre, came to be a watchword among the Left.[14] As Lefebvre's slogan suggests, the mid-20th century proved an especially fraught period in terms of the evolution of the apartment as the primary dwelling place of the city's citizens – an emblem of urban life itself. Debates about housing and the perceived housing shortage have continued to this day, despite the fact that since the decade between 1950 and 1960 the population of Paris has actually decreased, with some increase in the 21st century.[15] What these debates point to is a widening of social divisions exacerbated by the evolving spatial dispositions of the city.

Subsequent to the Haussmann renovations, social class became commensurately associated with neighbourhood or *quartier*, a trend reinforced systematically throughout the 20th century, contrasting with earlier class demarcations, which had depended not so much upon the location of the *quartier*, but of the dwelling within a particular building, with the more expensive apartments located on the lower floors. In one interview, commenting on his film *Domicile conjugal/Bed and Board* (1970), Truffaut himself alludes to the reorganisation of Paris by nostalgically recalling his childhood in Pigalle, an area that had been unevenly developed:

> I grew up in Pigalle, where no social or political demarcations affected me because in that neighbourhood during the German Occupation, well ... everything was about love affairs. In these neighbourhoods, opulent apartment buildings exist side by side with poor houses and there are hotels of all different sorts. It is so mixed up that there is a veritable explosion. My love for this Pigalle quartier, and for the people who live there (and those who live off it), makes me think that although it might be normal to hate a society that pushes people to prostitution, theft, and fraud, well then, one also has to hate any society that will not tolerate them.[16]

In contrast to the social mingling Truffaut remembered from the 1940s, segregation by class according to differentiated neighbourhoods, which had become even more marked in subsequent decades as Paris moved into the 1960s, contributed to an intensification of the divisions between the affluent and the less affluent, those who had 'the right to the city', and those who did not. These delineations by neighbourhood, together with the architecture associated with each, are routinely used in French cinema to define character types already familiar to French and especially Parisian audiences. *La Peau douce* displays this function in a particularly striking way.

Bourgeois Domestic Urbanism and the Apartment in *La Peau douce*

Among Truffaut's films set in Paris, *La Peau douce* stands out as offering an almost ethnographic study of the bourgeois Parisian apartment of the time – in marked contradistinction to the more humble type of apartment he had depicted in *Les Quatre cents coups*, the setting of his childhood in a family that occupied a much lower social status than that which Truffaut had acquired by 1964. As C. Garson, commenting on *La Peau douce* for *L'Aurore*, observed: ' The New Wave has aged – the heroes who sat around in the "Flore" have changed their neighbourhood. They now live in Passy and are men who have arrived.'[17]

Truffaut's rise in status is conspicuously reflected in the apartment he chose as the setting for the domestic scenes involving his fictional avatar, Pierre Lachenay, with his wife Franca, and their daughter. The choice of this apartment for the *mise-en-scène* is not accidental, as it facilitates the representation of what Pamela Robertson Wojcik has described as 'the experience of domestic urbanism',[18] the defining characteristic of what she has labelled 'the apartment film'. This genre includes films like *Rear Window* (Alfred Hitchcock, 1954) and *Pillow Talk* (Michael Gordan, 1959), in which apartments were meticulously recreated on Hollywood sets. As in the case of the heroes of these American apartment films, the protagonist of *La Peau douce*, Pierre Lachenay (Jean Desailly), is shown to be having a mid-life crisis that is induced, in part, precisely by this experience of bourgeois domestic urbanism, which leaves him so emotionally unfulfilled that he enters into an affair with a flight attendant.

It is all the more significant, then, that Truffaut elected to shoot the film in his own apartment, which at that time he was sharing with his wife, Madeleine Morgenstern, at 11 rue du Conseiller Collignon in the 16th *arrondissement*, in the area known as

View of the rue du Conseiller Collignon, 16th *arrondissement*, in *La Peau douce/The Soft Skin* (François Truffaut, 1964).

Passy.[19] Madeleine Morgenstern has confessed that she herself was surprised when Truffaut decided to shoot the film in their apartment, admitting that it was not until she saw *La Peau douce* that she understood the significance of his choice: 'Probably he sensed that he was not going to stay in this apartment much longer. It was on seeing the film that I understood the state our marriage was in.'[20]

This choice signals the privileged position in Truffaut's corpus that *La Peau douce* occupies as 'an extremely personal film', especially given that Truffaut, like Lachenay, was unfaithful to his wife during the period when the film was made, and would experience the breakup of his own marriage shortly before it was released.[21] The place of *La Peau douce* in Truffaut's personal and social trajectory, therefore, makes it a particularly apt example of the use of the apartment as a cinematic device with a diagnostic purpose, given that it shows clearly the presence of the emotional and sociological implications that inevitably inflect the choice of this location for the *mise-en-scène* of a New Wave film, irrespective of any economic expediency involved. By setting the film in the apartment at rue du Conseiller Collignon, Truffaut was able to reveal the existence of a continuum between the private and public by representing an architectural intersection of the familial and the urban.

Truffaut's '*Embourgeoisement*' and the Waning of the New Wave

The Parisian apartments depicted in Truffaut's films about contemporary French life in this period, starting with *Les Quatre cents coups*, followed by *Tirez sur le pianiste/Shoot the Pianist* and, finally, *La Peau douce* mirror Truffaut's own social itinerary – from the modest cramped apartment of his youth, through the varied locales inhabited by Charlie (Charles Aznavour), whose bohemian lifestyle requires him to traverse a range of milieus, to, finally, the affluent bourgeois domestic interior of Pierre Lachenay in *La Peau douce*.

After his marriage on 29 October 1957 to Madeleine Morgenstern, daughter of one of France's most important film producers and distributors of the period, Truffaut took up residence in a sixth-floor three-room apartment on rue Saint-Ferdinand in the 17th *arrondissement*.[22] Antoine de Baecque and Serge Toubiana describe 'the building' as 'unexceptional, modern and impersonal, but the three-room apartment was comfortable, well laid out, and tastefully furnished'.[23] At the end of March 1960, a little over two years later, the Truffaut family moved into a five-room apartment on rue du Conseiller Collignon in the 16th *arrondissement*, marking François's new identity as a member of the bourgeoisie who ordered 'four or five suits twice a year' and 'solid-color shirts by the dozen, first from Ted Lapidus in 1959, and 1960, then from Pierre Cardin ...'.[24] De Baecque and Toubiana report that 'Truffaut agreed to this move reluctantly. Though his family was beginning to feel cramped in the rue Saint Ferdinand apartment, which was flooded with light, Truffaut liked it.'[25]

A significant point in this trajectory was the 1962 trial in which Roger Vadim, initially a sort of fellow-traveller in the New Wave movement, brought a libel suit against Truffaut over an article published in 1960. For de Baecque and Toubiana this trial, in which the judge found in favour of Vadim, 'marked the end of an era, the (ephemeral) reign of the young directors'.[26] The rue du Conseiller Collignon apartment, then, gives a visual form to the conclusion of the New Wave and the consequent significant change in the status of the directors associated with this artistic school. The new location and geography of these directors reflects the place of cinema in French culture as a medium that had gained purchase as an art form, with attendant legitimacy, but also increasingly served as an expression of an elitist rather than popular vision of society.

Thus, *L'Aurore*, cited above, was not alone in pointing to *La Peau douce* as yet another sign that the New Wave had waned. Even those who praised the film saw it as indicating that the moment of the New Wave had passed. Raymond Bellour and Jean Michaud described Truffaut in *Les Lettres françaises* as 'a filmmaker who no longer belongs to the New Wave, who is not yet of the old school, a filmmaker who is in-between the two'.[27] Georges Sadoul in the same publication saw the film as evidence that the director was evolving towards a certain 'neoclassicism'.[28] Paule Sengissen in *Télérama* points to the film as evidence of Truffaut's growing 'maturity of outlook'.[29] On a negative note, *France Observateur* prefaces its review with the title 'Ultra-Old-Fashioned', characterising the film's direction as harking back to 'twenty years before Kazan or Zurlini'.[30] The *Coopérateur de France* remarks that the film 'is very removed from this new blood'.[31] *Combat* sums it up as 'the film of an old young man who is settling down'.[32] Henry Chapier, for the same publication in an earlier issue, reporting from Cannes, compares Truffaut's description of his film to 'truisms of the sort that circulate around the good old bourgeoisie'.[33] Pierre Marcabru in *Arts* depicts the film as plagued by 'bourgeois conventions',[34] while *Le Figaro* referred to the director's '*embourgeoisement*'.[35]

The evolution of the New Wave and its solidification as part of the French cultural establishment occurred at a paradoxical period in France's history. On the one hand, the 1960s were located squarely in the middle of what is known as 'Les Trente Glorieuses', years of marked economic growth from 1945 to 1975. On the other, the social unrest that would lead to the upheavals of 1968 were already brewing. The use of the rue du Conseiller Collignon apartment in *La Peau douce* has a significant function within this film, in the displaying and playing out of the issues encapsulated in this paradox. To put it succinctly, the spatial disposition of the apartment announces both the protagonist's material success and his personal failures, his relative impotence within a particular vision of the city. Thus, the apartment, spacious and well laid out by Parisian standards, built in the 1930s under the influence of modernism, is filmed in such a way as to feel cramped, labyrinthine and emotionally stifling.

The Décor and Its Signification in *La Peau douce*

To show how central the bourgeois apartment in *La Peau douce* is to Truffaut's conception of his protagonist's predicament, one only need compare it to that inhabited by Antoine Doinel in *Les Quatre cents coups*, in which Antoine has no bedroom of his own, but has to sleep in the family's living area. In contrast, the floor plan of the apartment in the rue du Conseiller Collignon shows the influence of modernism on French architecture of the 1930s. The building permits for the three blocks and 25 apartments that comprise 11 rue du Conseiller Collignon were issued in 1929–30,[36] while the construction date is reported as 1933.[37] Eight floors in height, in terms of its architectural design and sparse ornamentation, it clearly partakes in what is now known as Style Moderne; however, certain details, such as the lift, echo the Belle Epoque style of earlier decades.

The apartment itself is simple, with a layout suggesting again the influence of modernism and the rise of the bourgeoisie as the primary market for new apartments in this period (the 1930s). The kitchen is small, with appliances conveniently placed so as to be manageable by a single woman. We note in one scene how double doors can be opened to link the kitchen to the dining area. Similarly, the sunken sitting room is united through a curved staircase with the dining area (the most obvious art deco detail) that in turns flows into the hall, evoking a vision of a common social space, while remaining within the bounds of conventionality. Finally, the bedroom opens directly onto the sitting room, separated by a screen that can be rolled up or down at will, again evoking the more forward-looking open-plan approach to space that was one of the hallmarks of French modernism.[38] A corridor from the dining area leads to a second bedroom and a study – and perhaps another bathroom. The bedroom includes an en-suite shower/bath, while the living room windows look onto the street. As such, the apartment is designed to accommodate a small family, with perhaps one servant who comes in on a daily basis – as is the case in the film. It is a far cry from the pre-World War Two affluence of the Marquis de la Chesnaye (Marcel Dalio) as represented by the lavish setting of his Paris residence in *La Règle du jeu*/*The Rules of the Game* (Jean Renoir, 1939), but also distinct from a working-class accommodation, characterised by crowding and a specific neighbourhood (as represented in *Les Quatre cents coups*).

The relative affluence of the rue du Conseiller Collignon apartment is emphasised through its décor, in particular the artworks that adorn its wall, such as the painting by Foujita that figures in one of the couple's exchanges;[39] however, the environment is not portrayed as enriching or embracing – every object seems to have its precise place in a *mise-en-scène* designed to proclaim the inhabitants' good taste. Only the study, with its piles of books and papers, and the child's room, littered with toys, counter the general sterility of the more public rooms, which seem overly tidy. Life seems always on view – a feeling underlined by the placement of the bedroom, with its window opening directly onto the living room area. For the couple to achieve privacy, a screen must be rolled up and in place – separating the two rooms, at least temporarily. The opening up of the apartment's floor plan, conceived as a means of breaking down class and gender divisions by modernist architects,[40] becomes an instrument of surveillance and control through which the woman of the house comes to dominate interior urban experience, as will be amply played out in the film itself.

Commenting on why the film lacks any moments of humour, Truffaut observed: 'The character played by Jean Desailly [i.e. Pierre Lachenay] finds himself cornered, the trap closes on him. No smile is possible.'[41] Contributing to this sense of a man trapped in a particular kind of life is the scene just before the moment at which Nicole (Françoise Dorléac), as the flight attendant, announces that she must end the affair, which had resulted in the initial separation of the married couple. In this scene, the film's protagonist, Pierre, describes the life and the apartment that he envisions for himself and his mistress or prospective second wife. The apartment seems to mirror spatially the one he has just left on rue du Conseiller Collignon – as does the life that it implies. Horrified, Nicole breaks off the relationship, while Pierre is left alone, disoriented, on the work site – his dream arrested before it even has a chance to materialise.

In fact, Truffaut would leave rue du Conseiller Collignon and eventually settle into another apartment on rue de Passy, only a few streets away, another five-room apartment. Anecdotally, Truffaut would return to rue du Conseiller Collignon a few weeks before his death. In the film, Pierre Lachenay's demise is more immediate – before he is able to reconcile with his wife, a course of action on which he decides, she shoots him as he awaits his midday meal in a restaurant. While Lachenay's death – highly emblematic in its symbolic suggestiveness – is definitive, in real life Truffaut, at the time he was making the movie, was neither able to escape that new position in which he found himself, nor resolve his ambivalence about it. In the short term, however, his ambivalence would be temporarily resolved when his marriage broke up and he and Madeleine divorced – even though it would resurface with a vengeance in the course of his later career and relationships, which are mirrored in those of the hero of *L'Homme qui aimait les femmes/The Man Who Loved Women* (1983), whom Truffaut described as 'the type of individual who is anxious, secret; who avoids conflicts while flying irresistibly from woman to woman, perhaps out of fear of becoming too attached, out of fear of according too much space to a unique feeling ... someone who is scared of love'.[42]

La Peau douce: A Fusion of the Personal, Political and Historical

As Anne Gillain has pointed out, the tensions that inspired the stories presented in Truffaut's films have their origins in his unresolved relationship with his mother, with whom he, like Bernard and Mathilde in one of his last films, *La Femme d'à côté/The Woman Next Door* (1981), could be 'neither with nor without'.[43] Unsurprisingly, then, the apartment turns out to be the domain of the woman, a space over which she exerts her control, evidenced in the *mise-en-scène* and her position as the mistress of the house, whose every word is a command to her housekeeper and child. In contrast, in the streets she is vulnerable, subjected to aggression that she must combat. In one of the most compelling scenes of the film, a middle-aged man stalks Franca as she runs an errand in her own neighbourhood, eventually propositioning her in an insistent and insulting manner. Uncharacteristically, for a Truffaldian woman, she counters with a tirade of verbal abuse and he skulks off, seemingly humiliated.

The city streets, with their promise of anonymity, offer the masculine subject the opportunity to release his latent aggressions against a feminine subject who appears all-controlling in the domestic environment. The identification of *flânerie* with masculine sexual aggression and harassments and the image of the *flâneur* as a masculine sexual predator challenge the more utopian interpretations that have predominated in the wake of Walter Benjamin. In contrast, the apartment may constitute a terrain for feminine empowerment through which she exercises dominance and control, and in this film becomes a stand-in for the mother with whom Truffaut was unable to reconcile while she lived.[44]

Conclusion

On the basis of Truffaut's use of the apartment in his *mise-en-scène*, it is clear that his choice of Parisian apartment settings, like those of other filmmakers during the initial phase of the French New Wave, was neither merely decorative, nor merely expedient. Instead, this choice illustrates how the treatment of space was used to articulate the emotional, psychological and sociological preoccupations that were closest to the heart of the filmmaker, and his choice of the specific style of dwelling at the particular time when each film was being made is far from being casual. His work in *La Peau douce* illuminates the complicated set of gendered and sociological relations that in French cinema characterise domestic urbanism generally in the post-World War Two environment as played out notably in the Parisian apartment *au cinéma*; however, it also documents a very personal itinerary. Although Truffaut may have voyaged far afield through the topics he chose and the characters he subsequently invented, in his own life he would never leave the environment of the 16th *arrondissement*. As a New Wave director he had arrived, and, whether he wanted it or not, there was no turning back.

Notes

1. ristretti, 'Paris – Chronologie – Français et Arabe'. Available at: http://ristretti-oliviacollection.blogspot.co.nz/2011/01/paris-chronologie-francais-et-arabe.html (accessed 22 November 2012).

2. Anne Gillain (ed.), *Le Cinéma selon François Truffaut* (Paris: Flammarion, 1988), p. 42. All passages quoted from this book are translated by Alistair Fox.
3. Ibid., p. 66.
4. Ibid., p. 223.
5. Sanche de Gramont, 'Life Style of Homo Cinematicus', in *François Truffaut: Interviews* (ed.) Ronald Bergan (Jackson: University Press of Mississippi, 2008), p. 41.
6. See Antoine de Baecque and Serge Toubiana, *Truffaut: A Biography* (New York: Alfred A. Knopf, 1999), p. 12.
7. Gillain, *Le Cinéma selon François Truffaut*, p. 33.
8. Ibid., p. 34.
9. A notable exception is Pamela Robertson Wojcik's *The Apartment Plot: Urban Living in American Film and Popular Culture, 1945 to 1975* (Durham, NC: Duke University Press, 2010), in which she considers a set of films for which the apartment serves as a significant narrative device. Wojcik's corpus focuses on Hollywood cinema and American television. See also Lee Wallace, *Lesbianism, Cinema and Space: The Sexual Life of Apartments* (New York: Routledge, 2008). See also Katherine Shonfield, *Walls Have Feelings: Architecture, Film and the City* (London and New York: Routledge, 2000).
10. Sharon Marcus, *Apartment Stories: City and Home in Nineteenth-Century Paris and London* (Berkeley and Los Angeles: University of California Press, 1999), p. 1.
11. Ibid., p. 3
12. Ibid., p. 5.
13. W. Brian Newsome, *French Urban Planning 1940–1968: The Construction and Deconstruction of an Authoritarian System* (New York: Peter Lang, 2009).
14. For an extended discussion of Lefebvre's views, see Henri Lefebvre, *Writings on Cities*, trans. and intro. Eleonore Kofman and Elizabeth Lebas (Cambridge, MA: Blackwell Publishers, 1996).
15. ristretti, 'Paris – Chronologie – Français et Arabe'.
16. Gillain, *Le Cinéma selon François Truffaut*, p. 273.
17. *L'Aurore*, 21 May 1964.
18. Wojcik, *The Apartment Plot*, p. 39.
19. de Baecque and Toubiana, *Truffaut*, p. 204.
20. Anne Diatkine, 'François Truffaut, du côté de chez Madeleine', *Libération*, 10 October 2014.
21. de Baecque and Toubiana, *Truffaut*, p. 207.
22. Ibid., p. 145.
23. Ibid., p. 120.
24. Ibid., pp. 144–5.
25. Ibid., p. 145.
26. Ibid., p. 188. The dispute arose when Truffaut published a vitriolic attack on Roger Vadim, who had been brought in to replace Jean Aurel as the director of *La Bride sur le cou/Please, Not Now!* in December 1960 against the latter's wishes. Vadim counter-attacked by suing Truffaut, which led to a highly publicised trial in January 1962, following which the judge found for Vadim and sentenced Truffaut to pay him 1 franc in damages.
27. *Les Lettres françaises*, 10 October 1963.
28. *Les Lettres françaises*, 14 May 1964.
29. *Télérama*, 7 June 1964.

30. *France Observateur*, 21 May 1964.
31. *Coopérateur de France*, 1 June 1964.
32. *Combat*, 5 May 1964.
33. *Combat*, 19 October 1963.
34. *Arts*, 27 May 1964.
35. de Baecque and Toubiana, *Truffaut*, p. 206.
36. 'Paris 1876–1939: les permis de construire'. Available at: http://parisenconstruction.blogspot.co.nz/ (accessed 22 November 2012).
37. MeilleursAgents.com. Available at: www.meilleursagents.com/prix-immobilier/m2/rue-du-conseiller-collignon-2273/11/ (accessed 22 November 2012).
38. Newsome, *French Urban Planning 1940–1968*, p. 36.
39. Leonard Tsuguharu Foujita (1886–1968) was a Japanese-born artist who lived in Montparnasse, moving in a circle that included Pablo Picasso and Henri Matisse. Foujita, in the words of his biographer Phyllis Birnbaum, painted works that 'stirred the French critics to rapture', while the high demand for his paintings, mainly of cats and female nudes, turned them into a social status symbol that reflected 'safe' good taste; see Phyllis Birnbaum, *Glory in a Line: A Life of Foujita – the Artist Caught between East and West* (New York: Faber and Faber, 2006).
40. Newsome, *French Urban Planning 1940–1968*, p. 36.
41. Gillain, *Le Cinéma selon François Truffaut*, p. 158.
42. Ibid., pp. 357–8.
43. Anne Gillain, *François Truffaut: le secret perdu* (Paris: Hatier, 1991). See also Hilary Radner, '*La Peau douce*: François Truffaut's Passionate Object', in Dudley Andrew and Anne Gillain (eds), *A Companion to François Truffaut* (Malden, MA: Wiley-Blackwell, 2013), pp. 469–88.
44. de Baecque and Toubiana, *Truffaut*, pp. 142, 282.

The New Wave Hotel

Roland-François Lack

The association of the French New Wave with the kind of movement through urban space that has been called *flânerie* is a familiar one. A defamiliarising strategy in this chapter, and in my research more broadly,[1] is to examine and occupy the spaces in which New Wave films come to rest, countering a general assumption that cinema is always about movement. The hotel is a peculiarly cinematic stopping place because, it has been argued, it is 'always already in motion', a 'ceaseless flux of reservations, occupations and vacancies'.[2] By fixing exactly the locations of Paris hotels in New Wave films and by looking closely at the contents of the rooms in those hotels, this chapter will try to resist the appeal of such mobility and fix its gaze firmly on its object, unmoved. The suggestion will be, finally, that the French New Wave is less a cinema of *flânerie* than it is a cinema of stasis; is as much a cinema of interiors as it is a cinema of the street.

What, cinematically, is particular about the New Wave's use of hotels? New Wave hotels are places of passage, temporary stopping places that signify transience and, in the end, mobility. In her study of cinematic *flânerie*, Suzanne Liandrat-Guigues defines the cinematographic image as 'passage',[3] and though she goes on to illustrate the point through New Wave films that follow characters as they walk in streets, fixing on their 'singular mobility', here we will be following the New Wave's characters into spaces where walking is restricted. In those spaces they talk, read, listen to music, eat, have sex, sleep, and so on. They also look out from those spaces onto the street. The emblematic shot of the New Wave hotel film is a view from a window.

The first shot of François Truffaut's 1962 short film *Antoine et Colette* pans from street level up past a cinema towards the upper storeys of a hotel.[4] The next shot is a closer view of a window on the second floor, and the third takes us into the room beyond the window, where we see Antoine Doinel (Jean-Pierre Léaud) waking for the day. A minute later he goes to the window and we are offered a view from inside the room over the city, complementing and expanding what was shown in the opening shot. The vis-à-vis of room and street reminds us that the novelty of New Wave cinema was not that it filmed in real exteriors but that it filmed in real interiors – cafés, shops, cinemas, dance halls, Métro carriages, apartments and, of course, hotels.

Antoine et Colette provides some useful illustrations of how hotels signify in New Wave cinema.[5] Of the 40 or more Paris hotels that feature in New Wave films, almost all are, like Doinel's, localisable, either from being named or from the distinctiveness of the vicinity. Hotels are landmarks in the topography of New Wave Paris. That topography is often articulated in a film through contrasts between different hotels, or between a hotel and a different type of place. In *Antoine et Colette* Doinel moves from the Modern-Hôtel, rue Forest (18th *arrondissement*) to the Hôtel de l'Europe, on the rue Lecluse (17th *arrondissement*), just two streets away. The room he moves into is of exactly the same type as the one he moves from, but the hotel is immediately opposite the building where Colette lives with her family. The first point of contrast is between the family's comfortable bourgeois apartment and Doinel's small, shabby room, but more significant is the contrast between the two hotel rooms: in moving to be nearer the object of his desire, Doinel exchanges an expansive view for a restricted one, a panorama over the boulevard de Clichy for an ordinary apartment building across a narrow street. The failure of his pursuit of Colette is intensified by the loss of the city as spectacle.

The boulevard de Clichy is Truffaut's territory, and a topographical intertext for the New Wave: to film there is to refer explicitly to Truffaut. He himself returns there in *Domicile conjugal/Bed and Board* (1970), showing Doinel once again looking out from a room at the Modern-Hôtel. That Truffaut places his character in a room one storey higher than the one he occupied in *Antoine et Colette* is a nice topographical refinement.

Several places in New Wave Paris were, in a similar way, territorially marked by Jean-Luc Godard in *A bout de souffle/Breathless* (1960). When, for example, the protagonist of Agnès Varda's *Cléo de 5 à 7/Cleo from 5 to 7* (1962) passes the junction of the rue Campagne-Première and the boulevard Raspail in the 14th *arrondissement*, or when, in Jacques Rozier's *Adieu Philippine* (1962), his characters walk down the boulevard des Italiens (9th *arrondissement*), both films prompt us to remember Godard's film. A more striking example concerns the hotel in *A bout de souffle*, memorialised in the title of Claude Ventura's 1993 documentary, *Chambre 12, Hôtel de Suède*. Ventura revisits the famous hotel that takes up 25 minutes of Godard's film but he doesn't mention that it had been revisited earlier, in 1962, by Jean-Louis Trintignant as Clément in Alain Cavalier's *Le Combat dans l'île*. Clément is looking for his wife, who had been staying at the Hôtel de Suède. Told that she is no longer there, he nonetheless – like Jean-Paul Belmondo in *A bout de souffle* – grabs the room key to see for himself. The room is number 12, the same as in *A bout de souffle*. The room over which Trintignant casts his gaze is empty not just of his wife's possessions but also of everything that had filled it when the occupant had been Jean Seberg's character, Patricia. By visiting an already emblematic New Wave hotel room, Cavalier incites an intertextual reading of his film as a New Wave film.

The Modern-Hôtel and the Hôtel de Suède are, I think, the only New Wave hotels to function as intertextual signposts *between* films. More common are the connections made within a film between different hotels, as in *Le Signe du lion/The Sign of Leo* (Eric Rohmer, 1959), whose protagonist moves from one Latin Quarter hotel to another and then to another, or when, in *L'Amour à la mer/Love at Sea* (Guy Gilles, 1963), we pass hotel after hotel along the boulevard de Rochechouart (18th *arrondissement*). These cheap hotels contrast collectively with higher-class establishments, a pattern reproduced in *A bout de souffle* when, in Patricia's room at the Hôtel de Suède, Michel quips that he always stays at the Claridge, and when, in Godard's *Alphaville* (1965), Lemmy Caution (Eddie Constantine) goes from the luxury of the Hôtel Scribe to the Hôtel de l'Orient, a squalid establishment in the 13th *arrondissement*. Less dramatic but still discernible is the difference between the one-star hotel where Nana is with her first client in *Vivre sa vie/My Life to Live* (Godard, 1962) and the two-star hotel where she is put to work by her pimp.

Room 12 at the Hôtel de Suède is *the* New Wave hotel room, but there is no New Wave hotel film, no film situated in and centred on a specific hotel, in the manner of Godard's later *Détective* (1985) or of several films from the Swiss New Wave, where the setting itself becomes the subject.[6] The hotel film typically presents its location as an internally articulated space, and its characteristic elements are all there in the 30 minutes that *Alphaville* spends at the Hôtel Scribe – entrance, lobby, reception desk, dining room, bar, telephone exchange, lift, corridors, hotel room and view from the room's window; doorman, manager, desk clerks, bellboys, lift attendants, maids, guests – but of course *Alphaville* is a film about something other than hotels.

Elements of a New Wave discourse on hotels could be assembled from the contrasts of place and type already mentioned, and from occasional passages of explicit comment. In *L'Amour à la mer* Guy Gilles remembers the misery of earlier days in Paris:

> Because I was poor I lived in depressing rooms in sordid hotels that all looked alike, rooms that sometimes I shared with boys in the same situation as me. Sometimes we slept four in a room, but that wasn't a record. For us it was temporary but once, in the same hotel as me at Barbès, there was a family of North Africans who had been living there, all six, for ten years.

All other North Africans in New Wave cinema live in *bidonvilles*, not hotels – see *Les Lâches vivent d'espoir/My Baby is Black!* (Claude Bernard-Aubert, 1961) or *L'Amour existe* (Maurice Pialat, 1960). The latter makes a joke about the contrast between the two kinds of domicile, showing a sign that reads 'Hôtel Floride' affixed to a makeshift shack.

New Wave hotels accommodate a different class of foreigner. In a key hotel sequence of *Paris nous appartient/Paris Belongs to Us* (Jacques Rivette, 1961), a character describes the Finnish, Hungarian and German migrants who live in his hotel;[7] he himself is American, like most of the foreigners in New Wave hotels.[8] The most assiduous frequenter of hotels in New Wave cinema is the protagonist of *Le Signe du lion*. Played by Jess Hahn, an expatriate American with a German name, Pierre Wesselrin's nationality is obscure. He boasts that 'I am everything, American, Austrian, Swiss …', and on the registration card he completes at the Hôtel de Senlis he gives his name as Peter Winter, his place of birth as Vienna and his nationality as French. He illustrates well one narrative function of the hotel in New Wave cinema, as a locus for the displaced.

The long-term residents of New Wave hotels tend to be either workers or students. The students are all in the 5th or 6th *arrondissements*: Patricia at the Hôtel de Suède (*A bout de souffle*), Katherine at the Hôtel du Pas de Calais, rue des Saint Pères (Jean Douchet's 'Saint-Germain-des-Prés' in *Paris vu par …/Six in Paris* [1965]), Cathy

Union-Hôtel, 17 rue des Canettes, *Paris nous appartient/Paris Belongs to Us* (Jacques Rivette, 1961).

at the Hôtel Bossuet, rue de Grenelle (*Le Signe du lion*), Bertrand at the Hôtel de l'Observatoire, boulevard Saint Michel (Rohmer's *La Carrière de Suzanne/Suzanne's Career* [1963]). The workers are spread around Paris, like Antoine Doinel near the place de Clichy (*Antoine et Colette*) or later in Montmartre (Truffaut's *Baisers volés/Stolen Kisses* [1968]), the journalist Jean-François near the Champs-Elysées (*Le Signe du lion*) and Léon the dishwasher on the rue Saint-Denis (Jean-Daniel Pollet's 'Rue Saint-Denis in *Paris vu par* …). There are two unemployed women who live precariously in cheap hotels – in Marcel Hanoun's *Une simple histoire/A Simple Story* (1959) and Jean Eustache's *Du côté de Robinson/Robinson's Place* (1963); neither lives in the Latin Quarter or Saint-Germain-des-Prés.

Residence in a New Wave hotel is associated with the character's narrative situation. Since at least the 1930s the Paris hotel film as a genre has engaged with the hotel not only as residence but also as place of work. The New Wave, however, tells no stories about the workers in its hotels, with the exception of Doinel in *Baisers volés*, employed as a night clerk at the Hôtel Alsina in Montmartre, and then the story we are told is of how he loses this job. We occasionally see receptionists, concierges and cleaners in New Wave hotels, but the type of labour most frequently represented in these places, and to which narratives are attached, is prostitution.

The briefest instance is in Truffaut's *Jules et Jim* (1962), where the narrator relates that Jules, in search of a woman, had frequented 'professionals' without finding satisfaction. The mention is accompanied by a shot of a ceramic sign that reads 'HOTEL' and archive footage of a prostitute's leg. Prostitution plays a more substantial role in the Doinel films, from the 12-year-old Antoine's story in *Les Quatre cents coups/The 400 Blows* (1959) about waiting for a prostitute at a hotel on the rue Saint-Denis to Antoine's retelling of the same story 20 years later in *L'Amour en fuite/Love on the Run* (Truffaut, 1979), the last film of the series. That last film also retells Antoine's visit to a hotel for prostitution in *Baisers volés* (supposedly near the boulevard de Clichy but actually just off the rue Cardinet in the 17th *arrondissement*).

Young Antoine had been told that he would find prostitutes in the rue Saint-Denis area, a truth confirmed by grown men in later New Wave films: Emile, in *Une femme est une femme/A Woman Is a Woman* Godard, 1961), quotes Plato to a prostitute in her room on the rue Sainte-Foy;[9] Claude, in *Janine* (Pialat, 1962), falls in love with the woman he visits at a hotel in the vicinity; Léon, in 'Rue Saint-Denis', brings a prostitute to his hotel room on that street – though by making a hotel on the rue Saint-Denis the home of the client rather than of the prostitute, Pollet's film inverts the cliché.[10]

Through Anna Karina as Nana, *Vivre sa vie* gives the New Wave's most detailed account of prostitution in hotels, above all in its eighth tableau, with 'les hôtels' included among the headings and in the voice-over's quotation of a 1959 study of prostitution in France: 'The sheets are not usually changed between two occupancies, only the bathroom towels. In some hotels the beds have no blankets, only a bottom sheet.' Aside from a brief glimpse of prostitutes standing outside a hotel on the rue Saint-Denis, *Vivre sa vie* avoids the clichéd location.[11] The hotel in which were filmed the accompanying illustrations of Nana's daily routine was on the boulevard de Grenelle, near the Eiffel Tower, and was not actually a *hôtel de passe*, an establishment used

The Eiffel Elysée in *Vivre sa vie/My Life to Live* (Jean-Luc Godard, 1962).

for prostitution. The owners of hotels that did serve that purpose had refused to allow their premises to be filmed, for fear of scaring away clients.[12] Nonetheless, the hotel we see has an air of authenticity, not least when compared to the setting for Karina's role as a prostitute in the New Wave parody *Dragées au poivre/Sweet and Sour* (Jacques Baratier 1963), where the rue Saint-Denis hotel is, inside and out, a studio set.

Seven of Godard's New Wave Paris films feature prostitution, four of them in hotels. Two of these contrast prostitution in luxury and lower-class hotels. Matching *Alphaville*'s contrast between the Hôtel Scribe and the Hôtel de l'Orient, *Deux ou trois choses que je sais d'elle/Two or Three Things I Know about Her* (1967) shows prostitution in first a one-star then a five-star hotel. We don't see the exterior of the former but a bad joke told by the client indicates what class of hotel it is.[13] Godard's last New Wave film featuring hotel-set prostitution is 'Anticipation', his contribution to the sketch film *Le Plus vieux métier du monde/The Oldest Profession* (1967). 'Anticipation' is set and filmed at the Hilton Orly, a four-star hotel near the airport.

This airport setting recalls Godard's earlier visit to Orly in *Une femme mariée/A Married Woman* (1964), that time using the Air Hotel, a more modest establishment within the terminal building. This brings us to a third narrative function of the New Wave hotel, after home and workplace: as place of adulterous assignation. Three films in particular present this activity in great detail. The 10-minute sequence at a hotel in Versailles[14] that opens Louis Malle's *Le Feu follet/The Fire Within* (1963) is matched by the even longer sequence that closes *Une femme mariée*. Between these, Truffaut's *La Peau douce/The Soft Skin* (1964) conducts its affairs in five different hotels, in the New Wave's most complicated articulation of hotel topography. Tom Conley describes the topography of *La Peau douce* as one of 'connections, displacements and deviations'.[15] Not one of the film's five hotels is exactly what it seems; each is in some way displaced. The first is a composite of the Hotel Tivoli in Lisbon, seen from the exterior, with interiors filmed in Paris, at the Hôtel Lutetia on the boulevard Raspail.[16] The second is first presented in an advertisement: 'Résidence La Parisienne, 6 rue Bouffemont', but the address of this high-class *hôtel de passe* is a fiction – the street on which the couple park is the avenue Foch, near the Arc de Triomphe, and the exterior we see in the next shot is somewhere else (unidentified). The third and fourth are supposed to be hotels in Reims. On the way there the couple consult the Michelin guide and run through possible hotels, firstly the Grand Hôtel, which doesn't exist, then the Lion d'Or, which does, then the Hôtel Michelet, which doesn't. When they arrive at this last hotel, what we see is the Hôtel Michelet in Paris, on the rue de Vaugirard, near the place de l'Odéon, and when the man goes to the Grand Hôtel, what we see is the Hôtel Trianon Palace at Versailles. The fifth hotel, renamed La Colinière in memory of Jean Renoir's *La Règle du jeu/Rules of the Game* (1939), is actually the Hôtel des Saisons at Vironvay in Normandy.

One narrative function rarely served by the New Wave hotel is tourism. In *A bout de souffle* Michel complains that the hotels are full of 'ces cons de touristes', but we hardly ever see those 'stupid tourists' in New Wave hotels. In 'L'Homme qui vendit la tour Eiffel', Claude Chabrol's contribution to *Les Plus belles escroqueries du monde/The World's Most Beautiful Swindlers* (1964), the stupid German who has come to buy the Eiffel Tower resides in a 'discreet hotel' nearby. To finalise the deal he has to go to a more luxurious hotel that is ostensibly in Paris but actually is the Hôtel Trianon Palace at Versailles – the same hotel that Truffaut situates in Reims that same year.[17]

The real New Wave tourists are the filmmakers themselves, exploring the hotel-topography of Paris and surrounding region in search of stopping places for their itinerant characters. Narrative needs determine whether they book into a palace, a fleapit or somewhere in between. A classification of New Wave hotels according to degree of luxury might have been a simpler alternative, from the five-star George V in *Deux ou trois choses que je sais d'elle* to the no-star Regina Hotel in *L'Amour à la mer*.

The groupings would not be the same as with narrative function, chiefly because of the ubiquity of prostitution, present in every class of New Wave hotel. A further alternative might have been to mark the locations of these hotels on the map of New Wave Paris, reinforcing the concentrations around Pigalle, the Latin Quarter and the rue Saint-Denis that correspond more or less to narrative function.

I said at the beginning of this piece that the novelty of the New Wave is in its interiors. The New Wave interior is a cinematically singular space, tellingly exemplified by the New Wave hotel room, though the hotel room shares features with the multi-roomed apartment and the one-room garret. *A bout de souffle* features homes of each type: Patricia's hotel room, Liliane's 'chambre de bonne' and the Swedish model's apartment-cum-studio. In each type of space the restless mobility of characters has as correlative the restless mobility of the camera, enabled by the New Wave's technical characteristics: lightweight camera, minimal crew, basic augmentation of available light, post-synchronisation. Room 12 at the Hôtel de Suède is the *locus classicus* of the small-space construction. Larger spaces allow for more complex compositions, with cameras tracking down corridors or between rooms, and montage enabling play between subdivisions of the space. The best example of this is room 344, Lemmy Caution's room at the Hôtel Scribe, in *Alphaville*.

A further particularity of these New Wave spaces is confined to the longer-term residences and, as far as hotel rooms are concerned, to those at the lower end of the scale. In *L'Amour à la mer*, Guy Gilles describes how he would make his tawdry hotel room liveable 'with books, a few records and some photographs that I fixed to the wall each time'. What we see, when he says this, is a room transformed into an intertextual space by the accumulation of images, more than 20 of them, including photographs of Rimbaud and Marilyn Monroe, a poster of a Greek kouros and a postcard of a painting by Braque. These images are motifs thematised within the film, but Gilles has also put on the wall a painting of his mother, an object that reappears in the apartment of a different character in his next film, *Au pan coupé/Wall Engravings* (1968), inflecting the intertextual through personal association.

Pictures on the walls of higher-class New Wave hotel rooms are rare. There is none at the Palais d'Orsay in *Tirez sur le pianiste/Shoot the Pianist* (Truffaut, 1960), none at the Hôtel du Palais in *Le Feu follet*, none at the Scribe in *Alphaville*. A print of an 18th-century seascape by Joseph Vernet on the wall at the George V is hard to connect to the themes of *Deux ou trois choses que je sais d'elle*, and Vernet is not one of Godard's known enthusiasms, so we can say that it is a function of realist set décor rather than the inscription of a personalised or thematised intertextuality. On the other hand, Chagall's *Le Cirque* (1956) on the wall at the Air Hotel in *Une femme mariée*, if its subject is hard to thematise, does match a taste elsewhere in Godard for this artist.

What we don't see in the higher-class hotel rooms are images pinned to the wall, the personalisation of the space by its occupant. In *Paris nous appartient* Philip's room is decorated with more than twenty of his own drawings and a photograph of Antonin Artaud; his neighbour Birgitta's room is decorated with photographs of herself. In Godard's short film *Charlotte et son Jules/Charlotte and Her Boyfriend* (1960), the boyfriend's room at the Unic-Hôtel, rue de Rennes, is decorated with photographs of Charlotte – that is, of Anne Colette, Godard's partner at the time. This is character-centred décor, with a twist. The same is true of Antoine Doinel's room in *Antoine et Colette*: as a music lover he has record covers pinned to the wall, and as a Balzacian he has a photograph of Rodin's Balzac. However, his poster of himself, unfeasibly based on a scene from *Les Quatre cents coups*, is décor that moves beyond character into the intertextual space of the Doinel cycle.

Patricia's room at the Hôtel de Suède is, unsurprisingly, the most heavily personalised New Wave hotel room. The walls are covered with posters and postcards of paintings by Fragonard, Degas, Renoir, Klee and Picasso, alongside a photograph of Jean Seberg by her husband François Moreuil. Like the photographs of Anne Colette in *Charlotte et son Jules*, this predates the shoot and is, effectively, the insertion into the fiction of the actor's reality. The fashion shots of Birgitta in *Paris nous appartient* are in the first place photographs of the actress, Birgitta Juslin, and secondly photographs of the character ('Birgitta'). In the two other homes shown in *A bout de souffle*, Liliane's 'chambre de bonne' and the Swedish model's apartment, the walls are similarly decorated with photographs from the preceding career of each actress, alongside postcards of paintings in the former case, and actual paintings in the latter.[18]

A photograph of the actress who plays the room's occupant remains readable as character-centred décor, even if it personalises the space beyond the confines of character. The other images that decorate the room are more detached from the occupant. Patricia is shown putting up a poster of a Renoir painting in her bathroom, and though her admiration of the painter is in character, the personal investment in Renoir – and in Fragonard, Degas, Klee and Picasso – is not Patricia's but Godard's. These are his references, exhibits from an imaginary museum installed across his work, with a privileged place of exposition on the walls of apartments and hotel rooms. Truffaut, Rivette, Rohmer, Chabrol, Varda, Eustache and others form similar habits in the New Wave period, producing a set of individualised representations that are peculiar to and characteristic of the New Wave. These *musées imaginaires* illustrate forcefully the point that the New Wave is as much a cinema of interiors as it is a cinema of the street.[19]

Focusing on the New Wave's interiors rather than its exteriors would be a good strategy for taking our sense of New Wave cinema 'beyond the *flâneur*', if the New Wave *flâneur* were not just a myth; there is only one genuine *flâneur* or *flâneuse* in New Wave Paris, and that is Nadine in Jean Rouch's *La Punition/The Punishment* (1962).[20] At one point, very briefly, the neon sign of a hotel can be seen ahead of Nadine as she continues her nightwalking, but she doesn't stop there. This essay has been an attempt to engage with the hotel's particular significance for the New Wave's mobile subjects, enough of whom stop at, work in or reside in hotels for these to warrant such close attention. Other constituent parts of the hotel should also be examined as cinematic spaces. Some of these, like neon signage or the registration desk, are hotel specific, inviting comparative analysis with those elements in other hotel-heavy corpuses.[21] Other parts connect with other types of space within the New Wave corpus. There will, I hope, be work done on New Wave corridors, on New Wave lifts and New Wave staircases; on New Wave windows and New Wave balconies; on New Wave bedrooms.[22] The stopping place examined here, in this chapter, is just a starting point.

Notes

1. See Roland-François Lack, 'The Cine-Tourist's Map of New Wave Paris', in François Penz and Richard Koeck (eds), *Cinematic Urban Geographies* (London: Palgrave, 2017) and also my work on New Wave locations at The Cine-Tourist website. Available at: www.thecinetourist.net/new-wave-paris.html.
2. David B. Clarke, Valerie Crawford Pfannhauser and Marcus A. Doel, 'Checking In', in David B. Clarke, Valerie Crawford Pfannhauser and Marcus A. Doel (eds), *Moving Pictures/Stopping Places* (Lanham, MD: Lexington Books, 2009), p. 3.
3. Suzanne Liandrat-Guigues, *Modernes flâneries du cinéma* (Saint Vincent de Mercuze: De l'incidence, 2009), p. 11.
4. 'Antoine et Colette' is François Truffaut's contribution to the sketch film *L'Amour à vingt ans/ Love at Twenty* (1962), and the second of the five films that make up the Antoine Doinel cycle, starring Jean-Pierre Léaud.
5. I apply the broadest possible definition of what makes a New Wave film, with a timeframe from the mid-1950s to the late 1960s that includes filmmakers from five distinct groupings: 1.) former *Cahiers du cinéma* critics; 2.) the Left Bank group; 3.) the *cinéma-véritistes*; 4.) the unaffiliated, making a first film in the New Wave period and in a New Wave style; 5.) those filmmakers with independently established reputations who make New Wave or para-New Wave films in this period. On this basis I have constituted a corpus of about a hundred films in which Paris is a location.

6. See Roland-François Lack, 'The Swiss Hotel Film', in Clarke *et al.* (eds), *Moving Pictures/Stopping Places*, pp. 143–82.
7. The Union-Hôtel, 17 rue des Canettes, in the 6th *arrondissement*.
8. Patricia in *A bout de souffle*, Lemmy Caution and Harry Dickson in *Alphaville*, Katherine in 'Saint-Germain-des-Prés', Paula Nelson in *Made in U.S.A* (Godard, 1966), John Bogus in *Deux ou trois choses que je sais d'elle*.
9. This room is not presented as a hotel room. The chief contribution of *Une femme est une femme* to the New Wave hotel corpus is the blue neon sign reading 'HOTEL' just outside the protagonists' apartment window. Both apartment and sign are studio constructions.
10. Pialat's hotel is somewhere near Strasbourg-Saint-Denis Métro station; Pollet's is the Hôtel du Grand Saint-Denis at 289 rue Saint-Denis, 2nd *arrondissement*.
11. The Hôtel du Croissant d'Argent at 47 rue Saint-Denis. The other hotels in *Vivre sa vie* are the Hôtel de Monaco, 10 rue du Débarcadère, 17th *arrondissement*, and the Eiffel Elysée at 5 boulevard de Grenelle, 15th *arrondissement*.
12. Alain Bergala, *Godard au travail* (Paris: Cahiers du cinéma, 2006), p. 109.
13. 'Is this hotel reserved for Jews? – Why? – Because it's only got one star.' The shots preceding this sequence imply that the hotel is somewhere near the avenue Mac-Mahon.
14. The Hôtel du Palais, place du Maréchal Lyautey. A later sequence of Malle's film shows the Hôtel du Quai Voltaire, in the 7th *arrondissement*.
15. Tom Conley, 'A Psychogeography of Silky Cinephilia', in Dudley Andrew and Ann Gillain (eds), *A Companion to François Truffaut* (Malden, MA: Wiley-Blackwell, 2013*)*, p. 458.
16. For an exterior view of this hotel, see Jean Rouch's *Petit à petit/Little by Little* (1971).
17. I don't think Chabrol and Truffaut were aware that in 1913 this hotel had served as the 'Royal Palace Hotel' in the first of Louis Feuillade's *Fantômas* films released in 1913.
18. At least some of these paintings are by Godard himself.
19. To visit some of these imaginary museums, see The Ciné-Tourist website.
20. Despite many claims to the contrary, whatever Cléo does as she walks the streets of Paris, it is not *flânerie*. The protagonist of *La Vie à l'envers/Life Upside Down* (Alain Jessua, 1964) might have a claim to being the New Wave's one *flâneur*, if he weren't clinically insane. [Editors' note: See Jennifer Wallace's chapter in this volume for a discussion of Cléo as a *flâneuse*.]
21. See, for example, Jann Matlock's seminal study of the registration desk in American cinema: 'Vacancies: Hotels, Reception Desks and Identity in American Cinema 1929–1964', in Clarke *et al.* (eds), *Moving Pictures/Stopping Places*, pp. 73–142.The key reception desk moments in New Wave cinema are in *Le Signe du lion*, *A bout de souffle*, *Le Combat dans l'île*, *La Vie à l'envers*, *La Peau douce*, *Alphaville*, *La Chinoise* (Godard, 1967) and *Baisers volés*.
22. Editors' note: see Hilary Radner and Alistair Fox's chapter in this volume, devoted to the representation of the apartment in Truffaut's work.

The Vanishing of Les Halles[1]

Catherine E. Clark

In the summer of 1973, as Parisians left the city on holiday, two groups breathed a sigh of relief. The first, well documented and acknowledged by contemporary critics and historians since, were the workers employed in demolishing and rebuilding Paris for the future. These teams had infamously taken advantage of the summer holidays two years earlier in order to begin the controversial operation of destroying the Baltard pavilions at Les Halles in what the news magazine *L'Express* had called 'the dirty tricks of August'.[2] In 1973 the ever-expanding *trou des Halles*, or 'pit of Les Halles', as the construction site became known, proved a playground for members of the second group, who have been almost entirely overlooked by scholars: the production team of Marco Ferreri who shot *Touche pas à la femme blanche/Don't Touch the White Woman!* (1974) in and around the site that summer. This chapter reads *Touche pas à la femme blanche* in the context of its spectacular production in the ruins of Paris's former central food markets to explore how its juxtaposition of the past and the present commented on and took part not just in the destruction and reconstruction of Paris in the 1960s and 1970s, but also in the media spectacle that accompanied it.

Touche pas à la femme blanche seems at first to have very little to do with Paris in 1973. It is a comic restaging of Custer's Last Stand, or the Battle of the Little Bighorn. The battle, fought in 1876 in what is now Montana, was a rare victory for a coalition of Native American tribes – the Lakota, the Northern Cheyenne and the Arapaho – and a slaughter for the American soldiers, notably Lieutenant Colonel George Armstrong Custer and the 700 men of his 7th US Cavalry division. The film reunited the four stars of Ferreri's 1973 hit *La Grande bouffe*, filmed in the Parisian suburbs. He cast Marcello Mastroianni as George Armstrong Custer, Michel Piccoli as Buffalo Bill, Philippe Noiret as Custer's direct superior General Terry and Ugo Tognazzi as Mitch, Custer's Native American informant. Mastroianni's then wife Catherine Deneuve joined them as Custer's love interest and the object, referenced in the title, off-limits to Native Americans. Alain Cuny interpreted the role of Sitting Bull, and Serge Reggiani played a 'mad' Native American seer. Philippe Noiret would look back on the filming as a lark with friends.[3] Ferreri's project in gathering his cast, however, was not a simple reunion. The film builds on contemporary cinematic trends – absurdist comedy, post-1968 social and political critique, and utopian imaginings – to stage a radical commentary on the forces at work in contemporary Paris.[4] Through a story of the American West, it criticises both the removal of the working classes from central Paris and the influence of American cultural imperialism embodied in the replacement of the food markets with a US-style shopping centre.

In the early 1970s, the destruction of Les Halles was one of the most controversial of the urbanisation projects transforming the French capital. At times it seemed like the whole city was under construction as workers built towering housing blocks in the outer *arrondissements*, a ring highway and expressways along the Seine.[5] A journalist writing in *Le Monde* quipped in August 1973: 'worksites are overrunning the entire city. [...] One can hardly walk 500 metres without encountering a red and white barrier in one's path.'[6] On the Right Bank, Les Halles, known as *le ventre de Paris* or 'the belly of Paris' and immortalised in Emile Zola's 1873 novel of the same name, had housed markets since the 10th century. During the latter half of the 19th century, it underwent major renovations, which included the construction of 12 soaring iron and glass pavilions designed by architect Victor Baltard. By the early 1970s, they were a familiar sight – often the seat of a criminal underworld – in both French and American films.[7]

But by the mid-20th century the markets (with the traffic they entailed) had come to seem too large for the centre of Paris.[8] In 1969, the city moved them to a new, larger site in the southern suburb of Rungis. Over the next two years, their former pavilions would shelter a variety of community-based artistic and cultural performances and activities before succumbing to the wrecking ball in 1971. In the summer of 1973, the destruction was almost complete. The site's west end still contained several pavilions, while the east side was the growing pit that would house the central exchange for Paris's regional rail system and the subterranean shopping centre. Workers were also destroying blocks of houses around the edges to make way for office buildings. Further east, they enlarged the markets' former car park into the future site of the Pompidou Centre. City officials' decision to move the markets, destroy the pavilions and replace them with a shopping centre would, both for activists at the time and historians since, come to represent the worst of the top-down urban planning that was slowly removing the working classes from Paris's centre.[9] By setting his film in the demolition site, Marco Ferreri confronted these issues head on.

At the same time, *Touche pas à la femme blanche* suggests the generative possibilities of urban destruction, which, after all, made this cinematic production in the heart of a major western capital possible.[10] The very idea for the film grew out of what was happening at Les Halles. Ferreri explained that he was inspired by the 'houses that were being blown up'.[11] Years later Ugo Tognazzi recalled a phone call from Ferreri about making a film at Les Halles, in 'the hole'.[12] Shot almost entirely in the demolition site and the surrounding neighbourhood, the film depended on the situation created by the excavation of more than 30 acres of urban implantation. Demolition opened up space in an otherwise dense neighbourhood to host what must have been dozens of extras and horses (some even trailing foals) as well as a crew of 15.[13] It ensured that locals were accustomed to disrupted traffic flows and crowds of spectators. The growing pit had, since the very beginning, become a mediated spectacle documented by official photographers and film crews, television reporters and photojournalists, as well as amateur photographers.[14] There have been very few other times in Parisian history when the city centre could have accommodated hundreds of actors dressed as US cavalrymen and Native Americans.[15]

Ferreri did very little to transform modern Paris into the 19th-century American West. He had worked, one reviewer noted, 'without concern for anachronisms in the set, the costumes, [or] the action'.[16] Even though Ferreri could not control the people, buildings, piles of debris, businesses, pedestrians, shopkeepers and onlookers who appear throughout the film, their presence is far from unintentional. An account of the filming listed 'all of the spectators watching the shooting and the construction site' as part of Ferreri's team.[17] The juxtapositions of past and present make the film absurd – even funny. Passengers with luggage carts pass the two US cavalrymen sent to meet Custer at the Gare de Lyon. A woman in a red sweater turns to watch Custer on horseback trotting past parked cars. The critic for *Le Canard enchaîné* dubbed the film 'not great' but did appreciate these anachronisms, which created 'all of the film's appeal'.[18] But they also work to translate a 19th-century story into a critique of the contemporary world. The 19th-century soldiers and politicians chat unselfconsciously with a college sweatshirt-wearing 'anthropologist' (an undercover CIA agent) who follows them around eating tortilla chips. The violence they will use against the Native Americans, we understand, is not random but sanctioned by the highest levels of government. Custer's punishment of his men, gathered at the Fontaine des Innocents, for the piles of faeces they have left, becomes a criticism of the debris from the Baltard pavilions that dominate the site. Mitch's wife runs a small shop that sells cowboy boots and Native American crafts, not unlike the art galleries and second-hand shops that moved into the neighbourhood after the markets left.[19] Ferreri actively cultivated these incidental anachronisms to comment on the transformation of Les Halles.

The removal of the markets and renovation of Les Halles thus becomes the first of *Touche pas à la femme blanche*'s many critical targets.[20] At the time, Marco Ferreri explained his choice of settings: 'in the Far West as well, everything was destroyed to make way for something more efficient'.[21] With this film, he argues that progress and efficiency demand great human costs. During the early 1900s, the Parisian lower classes were often referred to as *les Apaches*, or Apaches.[22] Few Parisians would have been likely to miss the parallel, remarked upon in almost every contemporary review of the film, between the removal of Native Americans from the pit of Les Halles and the removal of workers, prostitutes and the homeless from the markets that once stood there. Jean-Louis Bory, film critic for *Le Nouvel Observateur*, read 'the destruction of Les Halles [as] an episode in the colonisation of Paris, from which one chases the natives towards reservations in the suburbs'.[23] A journalist writing in *Le Monde* explained that by 1973 the homeless no longer lived at Les Halles: they had 'emigrated ahead of the pneumatic drills'.[24] By placing the story of 'Indian removal' at the centre of Paris, the film criticises the destruction of the capital's social fabric.

The question of who should occupy Les Halles drives the plot of *Touche pas à la femme blanche*. The film opens with a discussion about the Native Americans among four American 'economists', investors and officials. Integration has failed, they declare, and the Native Americans are ruining the economy and society itself. With only scant resistance from the head of Native American affairs, they decide that 'the interest of progress demands the application of a, let's say, definitive, solution'. The film thus draws a parallel between the genocide of European Jews during the Holocaust and that of the Native Americans, committed in the name of the efficiency that Ferreri saw at work at Les Halles.²⁵ General Terry and Custer are called in to help carry out this operation. But the two have a more immediate problem: the Native American occupation of the pit of Les Halles. Tribes from as far away as Mexico are leaving their reservations for 'the great pit of the Black Hills', which belongs to the railroad company. As Sitting Bull and the other Native Americans insist to Custer and Terry, they have left the reservations not necessarily to wage war (although they will) but because they are starving. Critics at the time would only see the pit as a desolate place of mass killing: '[the] pit [...] reminds Ferreri of the circuses of gladiators, the stadiums and the velodromes where the police lock up their prisoners, and finally the fields of honour [*champs clos*] where all the soldiers of the world die'.²⁶ But this vast emptiness that fills the screen in repeated panoramic shots framed by the remaining pavilions and the Eglise Saint-Eustache functions in the narrative as a place of bounty, shelter and sustenance. It is a refuge from the state-sanctioned poverty of the reservations. Even though the markets are gone from Les Halles, their function endures to provide shelter and food to the deceived and persecuted Native Americans.

The pit's evolution at Les Halles determined the very shape of the film as Ferreri and his team improvised around the destructions.²⁷ Pneumatic drills accompany Custer's review of his regiment at the Fontaine des Innocents. Soldiers gallop their mounts up piles of detritus, and Native Americans take refuge behind great broken slabs of concrete. In one early scene, Custer and Terry watch with awe as a wrecking

On the set of *Touche pas à la femme blanche/Don't Touch the White Woman!* (Marco Ferreri, 1974): the pit of Les Halles occupied by Native Americans and framed by the Eglise Saint-Eustache as well as one of the remaining pavilions.

ball destroys a building. Terry, entranced, bobs his head in rhythm with its swing. Custer reverently says 'boom' at each hit, declaring with admiration, 'now *that's* progress'. Custer was, after all, as the reviewer for *Libération* described him, one of these 'capitalists [who are] always ready to crush a people in order to lay railroad tracks'.[28] He who sought to commit genocide in the name of progress thus pays the ultimate compliment to those who destroyed the Baltard pavilions in order to lay their own regional rail lines.

The team of *Touche pas à la femme blanche* would end up participating in the destruction of Les Halles. When asked if working in the middle of a demolition site bothered him, Ferreri responded: 'It's rather the film shoot that bothers the clearing ... The workers, Algerians, Portuguese, etc. often stop pickaxing to watch us'.[29] Twice, the filmmakers and the demolition workers even switched places as Ferreri, his crew and actors took on the active role of destroying the pavilions. The first time occurs early in the film, when several soldiers on horseback corral a group of Native American women and children into the base of the site's smokestack, declaring ominously, 'now we're going to play a game'. According to the newsletter of Les Halles, the workers helped the filmmakers prepare the scene that follows. As the whole neighbourhood gathered to watch on the morning of 8 June, they replaced some of its bricks with wood, used a pneumatic drill on its foundation and soaked the whole thing in petrol. The filmmakers then yelled out instructions to the crowd on the ground and the gawkers 'at windows, balconies, [and] roofs', not to move for 15 minutes after the chimney fell.[30] They only had one chance at this shot. The structure was set on fire, and it worked perfectly. The chimney falls in the very middle of the frame, kicking up a cloud of dust and sending bricks skipping along the ground. Here, Custer's men murder a group of Native Americans with the aid of an improvised crematorium at the same time that they reduce a piece of the old markets to rubble.

One of the Baltard pavilions themselves becomes a target for cannon practice in the second scene that merges the destruction of Les Halles and the production of *Touche pas à la femme blanche*. Although Custer refused to use cannons during battle, General Terry and Buffalo Bill want to demonstrate the latest in 'scientific warfare'. Buffalo Bill lights the fuse that destroys the southernmost of the two remaining pavilions. Here too the scene must have been coordinated with the wrecking crews. Two different cameras filmed the pavilion coming down, and footage from both was edited into the final cut so that the viewer sees the structure fall twice. The first time occurs immediately after a shot of a cannon firing; the film cuts then to a shot of the pavilion (which appears to be on a green screen) framed by the cannon and an officer's back. Presumably filmed on different stock, this sequence is grainier and slightly jumpy as it shows the pavilion fall in slow motion. This slow-motion fall presents a cliché of the film itself, which depicts the drawn-out and painful destruction of Les Halles. The camera cuts back to the reaction of the spectators before the structure hits the ground. One only hears the crash of glass and metal. But then the camera returns to the pavilion, which is somehow still half-upright. Buffalo Bill fires again (we see him light the fuse this time) and, on the same stock as the rest of the film, it crashes down in a giant cloud of dust.

On the set of Touche pas à la femme blanche/Don't Touch the White Woman! (Marco Ferreri, 1974): Buffalo Bill (Michel Piccoli) preparing to destroy one of the Baltard pavilions.

This second scene encapsulates the film's critical message: that the wanton destruction of cultures and peoples around the world too easily becomes someone else's spectacular entertainment. Ferreri himself had explained during the filming that he aimed to criticise much more than 19th-century American politicians or the demolition of Les Halles: '"On street corners in every city, we are still confronting the 7th cavalry regiment [...] The environment has changed, but the fight of oppressors against the oppressed continues."'³¹ He wanted to make a film about 'real Indians. But they might as well be Algerians, Portuguese ...' – precisely the two groups of immigrant workers then employed at Les Halles.³² *Libération*'s reviewer even commented that the blue uniforms of Custer's mounted troops were just a shade lighter than those of the CRS, the riot control unit of the French national police.³³ But the destructive forces at work in this scene are not just soldiers. Jean-Louis Bory declared it the most effective of *Touche pas à la femme blanche*:

> To show Custer bombarding Les Halles, is, with a violent ellipsis out of which springs forth simultaneously the comic and the vigorously politically engaged [*la vigueur pamphlétaire*], to show us an ancient civilisation disappear under the blows of its new conquerors. Swarming about like vermin on the ruins that they have created, we can no longer count our Custers and our Buffalo Bills.³⁴

The scene weds the destruction of the American West – its people, animals and land – to the careless waste of the 19th-century past within Paris itself and to the intertwined forces of imperialism, capitalism and entertainment. But Bory gets one important thing wrong here. Custer, the army man, did not bomb Les Halles. Buffalo Bill, the entertainer, did.

Through Buffalo Bill's presence and his key role in lighting the fuse, Ferreri criticises not just those who perpetuate such crimes, but also those who consume them as news and entertainment. Buffalo Bill was the stage name of William Cody, a former Army scout turned entertainer whose show 'Buffalo Bill's Wild West' toured the USA and Europe between 1883 and 1908. As played by Michel Piccoli, Cody draws crowds to a basement bar where he rides a stuffed bull and projects images of bloody battles.[35] Cody had, of course, actually played to Parisians for the first time during the 1889 World's Fair.[36] But here, Cody stands in for the significance of the experience of the destruction of Les Halles as produced and consumed in images. The grainy quality of the slowed-down sequence of the pavilion falling references the fact that most of France (and the world) would only witness the destruction of Les Halles as a media spectacle via grainy pictures on the television and in newspapers and magazines. It also refers to the television coverage of the Vietnam War that brought the conflict to living rooms around the world.[37] After all, portraits of Richard Nixon – not Ulysses S. Grant who was president in 1876 – preside over scenes through the film. The Native Americans are also constantly watched and arranged for display in *Touche pas à la femme blanche*. The soldiers track them with binoculars, from open windows, from the viewing platform of the Société d'Economie Mixte d'Aménagement des Halles (SEMAH) and from a hot-air balloon. The bodies of five Native Americans hanged for insurrection are cut down, stuffed with newspaper and exhibited at a local Native American school, a potential reference both to the display of people and their traditions at Paris's world's fairs and the public displays of the Paris morgue in the 19th century.[38]

Buffalo Bill might even stand in for Ferreri himself, as a clever criticism of the director's own desire to transform the destruction of Paris into, albeit politically engaged, entertainment. The film thus proposes a critical lens that one might apply to other films shot in and around Paris's construction sites in the 1970s and since. Pierre Tchernia, for example, shot the comedy *Les Gaspards/The Down-in-the-Hole Gang* (1974) that same summer in and around the vacant lots, and destruction and construction sites of the 5th, 6th, 13th and 14th *arrondissements*. When deployed in Roman Polanski's *Le Locataire/The Tenant* (1975), which takes place almost entirely in suffocating interior scenes, the construction site at Les Halles seems to foreshadow the pending psychological entrapment and destruction of the main character (played by Polanski). The most recent construction site at Les Halles, on the other hand, appears in Michel Gondry's 2013 *L'Ecume des jours/Blue Indigo* as a mere spectacular backdrop for the central couple's ride in a cloud-bubble. They marvel at its reappearance in the city and gape at an animated model of the old pit complete with clear plastic RER tunnels. But the scene functions to construct the characters' growing love, not to engage with what the most recent reconstruction of Les Halles might mean for the city and its people. Ferreri seemed aware of the possibility that images of the destruction and reconstruction of Paris might become vehicles for building consensus around the inevitability of urban change. He resisted this use by staging a tale of violent domination from the past in order to bring ongoing struggles and oppression into stark relief.

By engaging with *le trou des Halles* as a spectacular site in which to play with a present deeply rooted in the history of Paris, Ferreri's film seems to have avoided the peril of becoming just another Buffalo Bill. Reviewers at the time, for the most part, agreed. They praised the film, as Jean-Louis Bory did, for being both funny and politically engaged. For a few, however, the film had just too many critical targets. Michel Flacon, writing in *Le Point*, explained that 'the ponderous allegory, populated with puppets, leaves us cold'.[39] Louis Chauvet, writing in *Le Figaro*, claimed not only that the political critique of *Touche pas à la femme blanche* missed its mark but that it was not even funny.[40] Only critics on the right, however, failed to praise Ferreri's message, which suggests that *Touche pas à la femme blanche*'s criticism did actually hit home. For Ferreri does not play fast and loose with history here. Restaging Custer's last stand in the pit of Les Halles may seem fantastical, but the film's opening shots prove that this particular story has long roots in the site. They feature the frescoes commissioned for the 1889 opening of the Bourse de Commerce, which sits on the western edge of the site of Les Halles. As a bugle plays the reveille, long still shots of the portion painted by Évariste-Vital Luminais that celebrate North American commerce fill the screen with the stars and stripes, a steam engine, a group of nearly naked Native Americans and a man in a white safari suit. These shots become a montage of ominous music and visual details – drawn bows, a topless woman and children – that foreshadow the violence to come. All of the elements of the film's mythology are here, inscribed in the very site of Les Halles and the French popular imagination nearly a century earlier. In this sense, the film's opening therefore insists that the oppression of peoples is deeply rooted in the structures of international capitalism and 19th-century notions of progress.

The last paragraph of Chauvet's review of *Touche pas à la femme blanche* does concede that the film may have some value – not as a critique of any of the structures of contemporary society, but rather as 'a documentary about the old Halles de Paris and about their destruction'.[41] This, at least, he got right, for the film testifies to the role that cinema played in these events. The demolition that came to signify Paris's brutal rupture with its 19th-century past was in part shaped by the needs of the film shot within its bounds in the summer of 1973. Returning Marco Ferreri and the entire team of *Touche pas à la femme blanche*'s role in this process to the history of Les Halles recasts the history of the reconstruction of Paris in the 1960s and 1970s as not just the story of the deconstruction or the permanent alteration of the city's social fabric, but also the creation of the space and possibility for the production of culture itself.

Notes

1. Thank you to Max Page, Nicole Rudolph, Brian Jacobson, Vanessa Schwartz and Julie Elsky, as well as audiences at the 2015 meeting of the Society for French Historical Studies and the 2010 meeting of the Urban History Association who provided valuable feedback on this work.
2. 'Les Mauvais coups d'août', *l'Express*, 15 August 1971.
3. Noiret mentions this in an interview in Mario Canale's film *Marco Ferreri, il regista che venne dal futuro/Marco Ferreri: The Director Who Came from the Future* (2007). Deneuve, however, would look back on the filming of *Touche pas à la femme blanche* with distaste: Catherine Deneuve, 'Entretien avec Pascal Bonitzer', in *A l'ombre de moi-même* (Paris: Stock, 2004), pp. 201–3.

4. For more about these trends that shaped films such as *La Grande bouffe*, *Les Valseuses/Going Places* (Bertrand Blier, 1974), *Les Aventures du Rabbi Jacob/The Mad Adventures of Rabbi Jacob* (Gérard Oury, 1973), *L'An 01/The Year 01* (Jacques Doillon, Alain Resnais and Jean Rouch, 1973) and *Themroc* (Claude Faraldo, 1973), see Alison Smith, *French Cinema in the 1970s: The Echoes of May* (Manchester: Manchester University Press, 2005); Rémi Fournier Lanzoni, *French Comedy on Screen: A Cinematic History* (New York: Palgrave Macmillan, 2014); Guy Austin, *Contemporary French Cinema: An Introduction*, 2nd edn (Manchester: Manchester University Press, 2008).
5. For more about these changes, see Norma Evenson, *Paris: A Century of Change, 1878–1978* (New Haven, CT: Yale University Press, 1979).
6. Jean-Louis Saux, 'Embarras dans la ville', *Le Monde*, 22 August 1973.
7. Jean Gabin's character in *Voici le temps des assassins/Deadlier Than the Male* (Julien Duvivier, 1956) owns a restaurant in the neighbourhood. In *Charade* (Stanley Donen, 1963), the markets provide the setting for a middle-of-the-night rendezvous between Audrey Hepburn's character and a CIA agent, played by Walter Matthau. Crews at the Samuel Goldwyn Studios in Los Angeles also built a version of Les Halles for Billy Wilder's *Irma la Douce* (1963), in which Jack Lemmon's lovestruck ex-police officer works nights as a porter at the markets in order to pay for his prostitute/girlfriend Irma, played by Shirley Maclaine.
8. For more about the challenges and criticisms of the site, see Meredith TenHoor, 'Architecture and Biopolitics at Les Halles', *French Politics, Culture and Society*, vol. 25, no. 2 (Summer 2007), pp. 73–92.
9. See, for example, Louis Chevalier, *The Assassination of Paris*, trans. David P. Jordan (Chicago, IL: University of Chicago Press, 1994); André Fermigier, *La Bataille de Paris: des Halles à la Pyramide, chroniques d'urbanisme* (Paris: Gallimard, 1991); Norma Evenson, 'The Assassination of Les Halles', *The Journal of the Society of Architectural Historians*, vol. 32, no. 4 (December 1973), pp. 308–15; Rosemary Wakeman, 'Fascinating Les Halles', *French Politics, Culture and Society*, vol. 25, no. 2 (Summer 2007), pp. 46–72.
10. The historian Max Page has argued that the constant destruction and construction of New York City in the first half of the 20th century constituted a process of 'creative destruction'. I am building on his argument here to suggest that visual culture is part of what is created during the dynamic process of urban reconstruction. Max Page, *The Creative Destruction of Manhattan, 1900–1940* (Chicago, IL: University of Chicago Press, 1999).
11. Ornella Volta, 'Entretien avec Marco Ferreri', *Positif*, February 1974, p. 37. The artist Gordon Matta-Clark would be similarly inspired by the dynamics of this site. See Pamela M. Lee, *Object to Be Destroyed: The Work of Gordon Matta-Clark* (Cambridge, MA: MIT Press, 2000); Bruce Jenkins, *Gordon Matta-Clark: Conical Intersect* (London: Afterall, 2011).
12. Canale, *Marco Ferreri*.
13. '1973 à la Gare de Lyon', *Feuille d'avis des Halles*, 1 July 1973.
14. This documentation is part of a tradition, first forged in the 19th century, of documenting urban change in Paris through photographs. For more about the evolution of this tradition throughout the 20th century, see Catherine E. Clark, '"C'était Paris en 1970": histoire visuelle, photographie amateur et urbanisme', trans. Jean-François Allain, *Etudes photographiques*, no. 31 (Spring 2014), pp. 86–113.

15. The association, however, between working-class Parisians and the American West was not new. In Jean Renoir's Popular Front allegory *Le Crime de Monsieur Lange/The Crime of Monsieur Lange* (1936), for instance, a collectivised publishing house finds success with the serial tales of 'Arizona Jim', a cowboy hero who fights 'fascists' in the American West.
16. F. M., 'Custer à Paris', *L'Humanité*, 28 January 1974.
17. '1973 à la Gare de Lyon'.
18. M. D., 'Touche pas la femme blanche', *Le Canard enchaîné*, 30 January 1974.
19. Elvire Valois, 'A l'ombre de Saint-Eustache', *Le Monde*, 7 July 1973.
20. Urban historian Rosemary Wakeman offers an alternative interpretation of the film as satirical criticism of the planning ineptitude of city bureaucrats, while Peter Bondanella has read it as a condemnation of the American war in Vietnam. Wakeman, 'Fascinating les Halles', p. 61; Peter E. Bondanella, *Italian Cinema: From Neorealism to the Present*, 3rd edn (New York: Continuum, 2001), p. 270.
21. Volta, 'Entretien avec Marco Ferreri', p. 37.
22. Authors and journalists first likened the Parisian underclasses to North American 'savages' in the first half of the 19th century. The specific designation of *Apaches* for young, law-breaking Parisians emerged in 1900. It would remain current throughout the 1930s. See Dominique Kalifa, 'Archéologie de l'Apachisme: les représentations des Peaux-Rouges dans la France du XIXe siècle', *Revue d'histoire de l'enfance irrégulière*, no. 4 (2002), pp. 19–37.
23. Jean-Louis Bory, 'Cinéma: le grand canyon des Halles', *Le Nouvel Observateur*, 10 February 1974.
24. Valois, 'A l'ombre de Saint-Eustache'.
25. Les Halles, after all, is only steps from the Marais, from which just three decades earlier the city's Jewish population had also been deported. Given this engagement, it would be appropriate to count *Touche pas à la femme blanche* as part of the *mode rétro*, a wave of films about French experiences during World War Two made in the 1970s. For more about the *mode rétro*, see Austin, *Contemporary French Cinema*, pp. 29–33; Henry Rousso, *The Vichy Syndrome: History and Memory in France since 1944*, trans. Arthur Goldhammer (Cambridge, MA: Harvard University Press, 1991), pp. 127–31; Lynn A. Higgins, 'Old Waves, New Waves: French Cinema in 1974', *Contemporary French and Francophone Studies*, vol. 14, no. 5 (December 2010), pp. 469–76.
26. Jean de Baroncelli, '"Touche pas la femme blanche" de Marco Ferreri', *Le Monde*, 23 January 1974.
27. Michel Delain, 'Le Paris de Ferreri', *L'Express*, 9 July 1973.
28. Jean-René Huleu, '"Touche pas à la femme blanche" de Marco Ferreri', *Libération*, 24 January 1974.
29. Volta, 'Entretien avec Marco Ferreri', p. 37.
30. 'Il est vendredi matin, le 8 juin', *Feuille d'avis des Halles*, 15 June 1973.
31. C. F., '"Il y a un 7e de cavalerie dans toutes les villes"', *Le Monde*, 24 January 1974.
32. Volta, 'Entretien avec Marco Ferreri', p. 37.
33. Huleu, '"Touche pas à la femme blanche" de Marco Ferreri'.
34. Bory, 'Cinéma: le grand canyon des Halles'.
35. At one point, Buffalo Bill points the projector at Catherine Deneuve, splashing her white dress with blood in a reference to the *couleur du temps* (the colour of both weather and time) dress

in Jacques Demy's *Peau d'âne/Donkey Skin* (1970), created by directing footage of clouds and blue sky onto a dress made out of a projection screen.

36. For more about Buffalo Bill in France, see Susanne Berthier-Foglar, 'The 1889 World Exhibition in Paris: The French, the Age of Machines, and the Wild West', *Nineteenth-Century Contexts*, vol. 31, no. 2 (June 2009): pp. 129–42; Jill Jonnes, *Eiffel's Tower: The Thrilling Story behind Paris's Beloved Monument and the Extraordinary World's Fair That Introduced It* (New York: Penguin Books, 2010).
37. Michael J. Arlen, *Living Room War* (New York: Viking, 1969).
38. Vanessa R. Schwartz, *Spectacular Realities: Early Mass Culture in Fin-de-Siècle Paris* (Berkeley and Los Angeles: University of California Press, 1998); Shanny Peer, *France on Display: Peasants, Provincials, and Folklore in the 1937 Paris World's Fair* (Albany: SUNY Press, 1998).
39. Michel Flacon, 'Touche pas au western', *Le Point*, 21 January 1974.
40. Louis Chauvet, 'Touche pas la femme blanche', *Le Figaro*, 26 January 1974.
41. Ibid.

The Parisian *Banlieue* on Screen: So Close, Yet So Far

Ginette Vincendeau

'Paris in the cinema', as this volume itself confirms, virtually always refers to representations of inner Paris, the 20 *arrondissements* hemmed in[1] by the *périphérique* ring road which replaced the former belt of fortifications, and very rarely to the larger metropolis. Similarly, 'Parisians' evoke the inhabitants of the *intra-muros* city, whether positively (elegant, cultured) or negatively (arrogant, rude).[2] The rigid split between Paris and its suburbs is unique among major capital cities. As sociologist Annie Fourcaut explains, this is due on the one hand to 'the accumulation across centuries of images of a capital city whose symbolic importance has no equivalent elsewhere', and, on the other hand, of the 'peculiarities of urbanism during the *Trente Glorieuses* era'.[3] So stark is the division, geographically and culturally, that a whole mythology has developed around the populations living 'beyond' the ring road, as in the title of Bertrand Tavernier's 1997 documentary *De l'autre côté du périph'*/*On the Other Side of the Tracks*, or the comic thriller of the same title directed by David Charhon in 2012 – the very choice of words betraying the distancing, however sympathetic, point of view on the inhabitants of these nether regions. Even the word *banlieusard* is unflattering, as the 'ard' suffix is in itself derogatory.[4] Those who live in the Parisian suburbs are conceived as aliens, sometimes even 'savages', as observed by François Maspero, who conducted an anthropological study[5] of the populations living along the trans-regional RER B line, which joins Charles de Gaulle airport in Roissy-en-France (95[6]) to the north-east of Paris to Saint Rémy-lès-Chevreuse (78) in the south-west, slicing the inner city north to south on the way.

The marginalisation of the *banlieue* and its inhabitants has been in no small measure exacerbated by audiovisual representations. Films and television programmes have either ignored its vast and diverse territory or focused on one type of setting: the deprived high-rise *cités* (estates) built to house the displaced populations of the 'rural exodus' of the 1950s and the immigrant workers from the 1960s onwards. In the process, 10 million *banlieusards* have somehow been reduced to a narrow band of violent, alienated young men, epitomised by the heroes of *La Haine*/*Hate* (Mathieu Kassovitz, 1995),[7] while other suburban dwellers – that is, the vast majority – have received little attention. In this chapter I propose to shift our gaze towards a wider spectrum of suburban representations in post-war French cinema, focusing particularly on the last 20 years. After considering how the 'mytheme'[8] of the 'difficult' suburb has become entrenched, I explore the ways it has been challenged along gender lines, but also how alternative representations increasingly appear on screen that are paradoxically both widespread and 'invisible'.

From Invisibility to Stereotype

Until the massive post-war urban expansion, accompanied by an explosion in the population (from 6.5 million in 1946 to 11.8 million in 2012, out of which Paris itself includes about 2 million[9]) the Parisian *banlieue* appeared only sporadically in film, as a quasi-rural, often idyllic, setting. Marcel Carné's documentary *Nogent, Eldorado du dimanche* (1929) and Julien Duvivier's *La Belle équipe/They Were Five* (1936) summed up these pre-war bucolic delights with working-class Parisian families relaxing on Sundays on the banks of the Seine or the Marne.

After the war, a class and generational shift took place, and the – still relatively rare – films set in the Parisian suburbs were prone to show middle-aged, petit-bourgeois characters tending the gardens surrounding their modest detached houses known as *pavillons*. While the *zones pavillonnaires* grew exponentially (indeed are still growing) throughout the region, their absence of landmarks and quiet ordinariness rendered them almost invisible in film. They began to feature more prominently in the 1960s as a nostalgic foil to the new high-rise developments, with an emphasis on their liminal, semi-rural identity. In *Mélodie en sous-sol/Any Number Can Win* (Henri Verneuil, 1963) and *Le Chat* (Pierre Granier-Deferre, 1970), the small *pavillon* located in, respectively, Sarcelles (95) and Courbevoie (92), where the male protagonist (in both cases played by Jean Gabin) lives is seen as the last 'human' bastion against the encroaching concrete architecture, as is the hero – Gabin again – of *Le Jardinier d'Argenteuil/The Gardener of Argenteuil* (Jean-Paul Le Chanois, 1966).[10] A similar division animates Agnès Varda's *Le Bonheur/Happiness* (1965), in which the fragile 'happiness' of the central *ménage à trois* is mapped out against the difference in habitat (old *pavillon* vs new block of flats) in the south-west suburb of Fontenay-aux-Roses. In a more polemical mode, *La Ville-Bidon* (Jacques Baratier, 1971–76[11]) sets up a similar division between old, pre-urban, makeshift *banlieue* habitat and the 'brutal' new dwellings. The film, shot on location in Créteil (94), celebrates a community of marginal young men (and one woman played by Bernadette Lafont) who live between a rubbish tip and a shanty town. Despite bordering on delinquency, they are depicted as a warm community, against the corrupt politicians and 'inhuman' lifestyle promised by the new town in the process of being built.

When they do not view the traditional suburbs nostalgically, films pinpoint their 'dullness'. It is indicative in this respect that Jean-Luc Godard asked composer Michel Legrand to write a score that would echo 'the banality of the *banlieue*' for his film *Bande à part/Band of Outsiders* (1964).[12] Equally, Marguerite Duras's *Nathalie Granger* (1973) and *Le Camion/The Lorry* (1977) present the outskirts of Paris as forlorn and synonymous with ennui. After making documentaries on urban planning for French television, Eric Rohmer directed fiction films focused in more positive terms on the suburbs – in particular, *Les Nuits de la pleine lune/Full Moon in Paris* (1984) and *L'Ami de mon amie/Boyfriends and Girlfriends* (1988) – yet in each case the characters feel obliged to justify their choice of living there as opposed to central Paris. Indeed, in *Les Nuits de la pleine lune*, Octave (Fabrice Luchini) extolls in a long speech the 'magic' cultural aura of the capital.

The most significant turn in the representation of the *banlieue* came in the 1960s with the spread of the high-rise estates. The new habitat from the start was presented as soulless and alienating, and a hotbed of social problems. Jean-Luc Godard's *Deux ou trois choses que je sais d'elle/Two or Three Things I Know about Her* (1967), set in La Courneuve (93), shows housewives having recourse to prostitution. In comic mode, *Elle court, elle court, la banlieue/The Suburbs Are Everywhere* (Gérard Pirès, 1973), shot in Aubergenville (78), pinpoints noisy flats and stressful commuting. *Dernière sortie avant Roissy/Last Exit before Roissy* (Bernard Paul, 1977) uses the vast development at Sarcelles as background to couple breakdown, theft and rape. On the whole, these films portray white inhabitants. The emergence of the predominantly *banlieue*-based *cinéma beur* (made by and about second-generation immigrants, mostly from North Africa)[13] in the 1980s, notably *Le Thé au harem d'Archimède/Tea in the Harem* (Mehdi Charef, 1985) and *Hexagone* (Malik Chibane, 1994), added a new, racial dimension by focusing on multi-ethnic communities. In their wake, films by white directors, such as Mathieu Kassovitz's *La Haine* and Jean-François Richet's *Etat des lieux/Inner City* (1995) and *Ma 6-T va crack-er* (1997[14]), followed suit, largely defined by their location in the *banlieue*, now routinely qualified by adjectives such as 'difficult', 'critical' (*sensible*) or 'in difficulty'. The label *film de banlieue* thus gathered momentum, and through this process of naming,[15] a 'genre' was created.

Beyond their substantial differences, the *films de banlieue* endowed the *topos* of the difficult suburb with a consistent architectural and spatial iconography: high-rise estates dominated by towers (*tours*) and long blocks (*barres*), run-down staircases, graffiti, broken lifts, grim cellars and a cultural void signified by semi-derelict open spaces. Narratives privilege violence – riots, gunfights between gangs, clashes with the police and multiple social problems: unemployment, poverty, drugs and racism. The term *banlieusard* is now fully equated with young men from multi-ethnic backgrounds, archetypally the 'black-blanc-*beur*' trio of *La Haine*; in the process, women, children and old people are relegated to the margins or absent. Equally codified are their clothing (sportswear, leather jackets, hoods), aggressive gestures and language: accent, vocabulary and slang (especially *verlan*) immediately signal '*banlieue*-speak'. These spatial, narrative and thematic motifs are not confined to the films mentioned above. David-Alexandre Wagner's study of a vast corpus of *films de banlieue* confirms, among other things, that the prevailing protagonists are young men between 18 and 25.[16] The recurrence of such *mythemes*, which duplicate dominant media representations,[17] produced a deeply entrenched view of the *banlieue* that has become the default position when discussing the location and its social environment, up to the present day – even as the genre diversified, through action films – *District 13* (Pierre Morel, 2004) and *District 13: Ultimatum* (Patrick Alessandrin, 2009) – and especially comedy. Among the latter are *Mohamed Dubois* (Ernesto Oña, 2012), *Les Kaïras/Porn in the Hood* (Franck Gastambide, 2012), *Beur sur la ville* (Djamel Bensalah, 2011), *Halal police d'état* (Rachid Dhibou, 2011) and *De l'autre côté du périph'* (2012).

Auteur cinema too continued to mine the territory, including Jean-Claude Brisseau's *De bruit et de fureur/Sound and Fury* (1988), Abdellatif Kechiche's *L'Esquive/Games of Love and Chance* (2004)[18] and Jacques Audiard's *Dheepan* (2015). Yet, despite the resilience of such clichéd views of the *banlieue*, changes have been taking place, in two directions. On the one hand, there have been attempts at correcting the films' masculine bias; on the other hand, a more quiet *banlieue* has arisen in a wide range of film and television representations.

Feminising the *Banlieue*

The overwhelming masculine bias of the *film de banlieue* has a long and complex genealogy. The stereotype of the young male, semi-delinquent *banlieusard* finds its origins in 19th century art and literature set in the capital: the adolescent Revolutionary rebel immortalised by Victor Hugo as Gavroche in *Les Misérables* is a key figure, modified and modernised in turn through the *Apache* of the Belle Epoque and the *blousons noirs* of the post-World War Two era. As Sébastien Le Pajolec and Jean-Jacques Yvorel argue, 'The "*jeunes des cités*" constitute the ultimate version of the stereotype of dangerous youth in the Parisian imaginary [...] the meeting point of a spatial representation and social inscription specific to young men from the popular classes'.[19] Just as in this historical lineage, women appear rarely, except as allegorical figures, *beur* and *banlieue* films traditionally cast women in marginal roles, as mothers, sisters or girlfriends. In part thanks to the rise of women filmmakers, a few films have attempted to redress this gender imbalance by focusing on female protagonists – for instance, *Les Histoires d'amour finissent mal ... en general/Love Affairs Usually End Badly* (Anne Fontaine, 1993), *Souviens-toi de moi/Remember Me* (Zaida Ghorab-Volta, 1996), *La Squale* (Fabrice Genestal, 1999), *Samia* (Philippe Faucon, 1999), *Jeunesse dorée* (Ghorab-Volta, 2001) and *L'Année suivante* (Isabelle Czajka, 2006). While these films elicited critical interest,[20] they remained relatively marginal. By contrast, the three works discussed below have had a wider impact, critically and/or at the box office.

Tout ce qui brille/All That Glitters (co-directed by Hervé Mimran and Géraldine Nakache) was one of the surprise hits of 2010, with 1.3 million tickets sold. A cross between the teen movie, the romcom and the social film, it centres on the friendship between two young lower-middle-class women, the Jewish Ely (Nakache) and the Arab Lila (Leila Bekhti). They both live in Puteaux (92, next to the business area of La Défense) and are in pursuit of 'all that glitters', which for them means partying and designer clothes, and above all inner Paris. All of this they find, temporarily, through friendship with two wealthy young Parisian women, Agathe (Virginie Ledoyen) and Joan (Linh Dan Pham). The film, which constructs a strong feminine point of view, thanks to Nakache's double role as co-director and lead actress, nevertheless rereads the *film de banlieue* with explicit reference to *La Haine*. The trajectory of the two protagonists is littered with recurrent motifs from Kassovitz's film, such as being barred from a Parisian nightclub and a bemused encounter with avant-garde art. *Tout ce qui brille* similarly locates its heroines in a precise habitat, shot on location. One of the first shots shows them seated on a bench, surrounded by looming high-rise blocks. It also reiterates the key paradoxical relationship between the *banlieue* and the inner city: topographical proximity vs symbolic distance. While Chanteloup-les-Vignes where *La Haine* was shot is located on the far reaches of the region (78) a long train ride away, Puteaux is close to the city, underlined by the repeated

'So close yet so far': the Arc de Triomphe in the distance between Ely (Géraldine Nakache), left, and Lila (Leila Bekhti), right, in *Tout ce qui brille/All That Glitters* (Hervé Mimran and Géraldine Nakache, 2010).

mantra that 'it is [only] 10 minutes from Paris'. Yet the phrase is mostly used ironically as camerawork repeatedly constructs a sense of distance from it with the Arc de Triomphe shimmering in the sun, and the Eiffel Tower in the distance, reflected in windows or stuck between two buildings. Meanwhile, the contrast between the unprepossessing concrete blocks and the elegant Haussmann-style buildings in Paris constructs an obvious aesthetic hierarchy duplicated in the use of interiors. Nakache observed that

> in the cheap (HLM) suburban flats, at Lila's and at Ely's, we could not indulge in expansive camera movements, it was too narrow. As a result, [camera movements] mirror the life they lead there: they are constricted. On the other hand, in the Parisian interiors we could be more mobile.[21]

In many other ways, *Tout ce qui brille* is the antithesis of *La Haine*, starting with the decision to concentrate on a suburb that is 'rather an attractive place to live [...] no drugs, no gang rapes, no burning cars. In the end, a suburb that is representative of the majority of suburbs [and] that is of least interest to television news'.[22] But gender has the most decisive impact in renegotiating the gap between city and suburbs. The film pinpoints cultural differences between the suburban women and their Parisian friends, in language, food and wine. Yet, Agathe and Joan 'never judge Ely and Lila on their social condition. [...] they don't care about it',[23] contrasting with *La Haine*, where Parisians dismiss the *banlieusards* in an art gallery. Most significantly, where *La Haine* and its avatars approach class and cultural difference through violence, *Tout ce qui brille* acknowledges social domination but, like most other female-identified *banlieue* films, is characterised by a lack of crime and violence.[24] We can see in this the historical genealogy of the *banlieusard* (young women do not have access to the Revolutionary ancestry of their male counterparts). However, the film also acknowledges greater social mobility for women, through education on the one hand and consumerism on the other. Ely and Lila penetrate the nightclub and the wealthier crowd on the strength of their attractive looks and clothes that depart from familiar tropes. As Nakache put it, they 'were not going to be the cliché of the *banlieusarde* in jogging suit. They dress at Zara and H&M.'[25] Eventually, class reasserts itself: after the wealthy Max (Simon Buret) has abandoned her, Lila ends up as a salesgirl in a designer shop, where she sells a pair of shoes worth 500 euros to his new girlfriend. Nevertheless, Lila has a job and Ely moves to the city to study.

More caricatural in its vision of a feminised *banlieue* is the popular comedy *Paulette* (Jérôme Enrico, 2012). The eponymous central character played by Bernadette Lafont in her penultimate screen role is a grandmother who embarks on drug dealing for local gangs in her estate in order to supplement her meagre pension and provide for her mixed-race grandson. The film, part shot in Noisy-le-Sec (93), features the classic *banlieue* high-rise environment and mixed-race, male, hoodlums. Its classic comic device is the inversion of stereotypes: old woman vs young men, cake making vs drug dealing, educated language vs *banlieue* slang. Paulette adapts to, and at some point takes over, the male-dominated environment in order to survive. Her appearance as a 'typical' granny acts as a decoy (wearing dowdy clothes, carrying drugs in her shopping bag under bunches of leeks) and ensures her success. However, while it places a woman firmly at the centre, the film in other ways does not alter the representational paradigm of the difficult *banlieue*. Lafont's charismatic performance constructs an affecting character but she remains an exceptional – and improbable – figure in a familiar landscape of run-down estate, social and cultural deprivation and lawlessness, albeit presented comically. By contrast *Bande de filles/Girlhood* (Céline Sciamma, 2014) radically shifts to a young, black female-dominated world.

Set and part shot in the Cité de la Noue in Bagnolet (93), *Bande de filles* narrates the coming of age of Marieme/Vic (Karidja Touré) through her joining a tough 'band of girls', who give her the confidence to reject school, a job as a cleaner, her domineering older brother and a dangerous drug baron – although the open ending gives no clue as to what her future might be. From the *banlieue* film *Bande de filles* borrows many visual and oral tropes: concrete buildings, walkways and esplanades frame characters whose clothes and language label them as *banlieue* youth. As in the other films, Marieme and her friends' identity is partly defined by their encounters with Parisian space and characters: a ride on the RER, the shopping mall of Les Halles and the girls' noisy dance in the Métro. As in *Tout ce qui brille*, the hazy presence of the Eiffel Tower in the background further marks the distance from inner Paris.

Against the *banlieue* films' traditional confinement of women to the home, *Tout ce qui brille*, *Paulette* and *Bande de filles* show them conquering public space, sometimes with difficulty, as when Marieme and her friends run the gauntlet of men through their estate after playing football in the opening sequence. Yet despite *Bande de filles*'s more overtly realistic aesthetics – as opposed to the comic generic devices of the other two films – the social identity of its protagonists remains unexplored, including – paradoxically – their racial identity. The fact that Marieme, her friends and virtually everyone around them are black constructs an unrealistic space where racial difference (the rule in the real-life *banlieue*) has vanished. *Bande de filles*'s contradictory approach to the protagonists – ostensibly steeped in a social environment, yet detached from it – is reflected in the different ways of shooting exterior and interior spaces. Real locations are used for spectacular and/or aggressive displays outside (the violent fight between girl gangs; the girls dancing at La Défense), but the interior of Marieme's home was recreated in a studio, giving the director freedom to expand the volume and colour scheme of the flat, beyond what a real-life apartment in the estate would have permitted, contrary to *Tout ce qui brille*.[26] It is no accident in this respect that the high point of the film takes place in the neutral space of a bland hotel room, where the four girls dance ecstatically to Rhianna's 'Diamonds' number. Paradoxically then, the popular comedy *Tout ce qui brille* offers a more socially embedded view of the *banlieue* than *Bande de filles*, which is more concerned with a visualisation of the young women's mental space, in line with Sciamma's auteurist and feminist project. A similar point may be made about *Divines* (Houda Benyamina, 2016), in which familiar *banlieue* tropes – young women of immigrant origins rejecting school and attempting to escape social deprivation through violence and drugs – intersect uneasily with the director's auteurist stance.

While *Tout ce qui brille*, *Paulette*, *Bande de filles* and *Divines* to different degrees engage with, and nuance *banlieue* representation through gender difference, they continue to equate the location with the high-rise estates. By contrast, another type of representation of the Parisian suburbs has seen a marked development recently, and yet attracted little comment, by which I mean the quiet *banlieue* dominated by the *zones pavillonnaires* that is as ubiquitous as it is invisible.

The Quiet *Banlieue*

Over the past two decades, a large number of films (and television series) have featured *zones pavillonnaires* but in markedly different ways from the films of the 1950s and 1960s discussed earlier. Instead of using the small, detached houses in a nostalgic opposition to the brutal concrete blocks, they feature them as the new 'normality'. These are pleasant, bland, functional houses that include both the old *pavillons* from before World War Two and modern versions of them. In the only comprehensive scholarly study of popular French television fiction to date, Noël Burch and Geneviève Sellier note the recurrence of a 'pleasant' kind of suburb, made up of 'comfortable *pavillons* as well as numerous opulent villas, with only occasionally the odd high-rise block on the horizon'.[27] But such habitat also features in a rising number of film genres. In order to pinpoint the features of this 'invisible', quiet *banlieue*, I will examine examples from three types of audiovisual fiction across the spectrum: auteur film, television series and mainstream genre cinema.

The main character of *Après mai/There's Something in the Air* (2012), Olivier Assayas's recreation of the early 1970s, Gilles (Clément Métayer) lives in a suburb south-west of Paris. The location is signalled with the indication 'not far from Paris' superimposed on the opening images. Although the film features scenes in inner Paris and abroad (notably Italy), the suburban setting is present throughout. We see a quiet, leafy suburb. We are close to a park, and at one point chicken run in front of Gilles's moped as he leaves home. Paris is not far, but nor is nature. Gilles makes several journeys to and from Paris on the suburban train, and the railway station features on several occasions, as does the local college where Gilles and his friends clash with the authorities because of their left-wing political activities. Yet commentators on *Après mai* certainly did not call it a *film de banlieue*, focusing instead on its depiction of a generation's relation to May 1968. The characters' identity is anchored in their (bourgeois) class, age group and politics, not their habitat, which as a result becomes transparent.

Julie Lescaut was one of the most successful, long-running, French crime series, with 101 episodes spread over 22 years (1992–2014), initially broadcast on the privatised mainstream channel TF1. More than two-thirds of the episodes take place in the quiet suburb of 'Les Clairières' (shot in Vanves [92] [28]). At one point, the eponymous police inspector heroine, played by Véronique Genest, moves to Paris. On arrival her boss, high above the city in the Tour Montparnasse, warns her that things are about to get tougher for her: 'you know, here business is a bit more complicated than simple house break-ins gone wrong.' The message is clear: even crime is less exciting in the suburbs. Julie Lescaut however remains associated with 'Les Clairières' ('the clearings', evocative of nature); the homes we go into, following her and her team, correspond to Burch and Sellier's description. This includes Lescaut's own – an airy, light and comfortable *pavillon* – where she lives, as a middle-aged divorced woman, with her two teenage daughters, and soon a new partner, Pierre and his son (and later Pavel, a boy they adopt). The success of *Julie Lescaut* was due in part to the popular feminism of the series, clearly aimed at female spectators: as a working mother running in parallel job and 'recomposed' family, Lescaut is efficient, dynamic, respected. But it is her 'normality' as a suburban *pavillon* dweller that also defines her appeal. The *banlieue* and the *banlieusards* of *Julie Lescaut* are undoubtedly idealised: there appears to be no sexism or racism (her devoted team comprises two white men, a black man and a woman of Maghrebi origins), and very little poverty. A similar observation can be made about the more recent and also highly successful France 2 television comic series *Fais pas ci, fais pas ça* (2007–16, shot in Sèvres [92]), which follows two 'ordinary' middle-class families in an uneventful suburb. Yet at the same time, such series mirror the otherwise under-represented *classes moyennes* who inhabit such quiet suburbs and constitute large swathes of film and television audiences.

In popular genre cinema too, the quiet suburbs, unmarked by social problems or violence, seem to belong to female-oriented genres. Although central Paris has traditionally been associated with romantic comedy, especially for international audiences,[29] romcoms with domestic appeal tell a different story, as shown by two hit films starring Sophie Marceau. *De l'autre côté du lit/On the Other Side of the Bed* (Pascale Pouzadoux, 2009) features a young middle-class couple, Ariane (Marceau) and Hugo (Dany Boon), with two children, who decide to swap roles in order to save their marriage – she takes his place as a building company executive, he becomes a 'housewife' who sells jewellery on the side. As in *Après mai*, the opening signals the suburban location. A wide aerial shot shows Paris far on the horizon; the camera then swoops down to fly

The 'quiet' suburb's zone pavillonnaire: De l'autre côté du lit/On the Other Side of the Bed (Pascale Pouzadoux, 2009).

over a leafy suburb, on the edge of the countryside, dotted with identical, neat houses with gardens. Inside the couple's house, a relentless pastel colour scheme creates a comically unreal world, just as it does outside (for example, Ariane's pink car). While the couple is clearly well off, the plot makes them confront 'ordinary' problems: taking children to school or the dentist, shopping, dealing with a builder, etc. against the resolutely unremarkable suburban background. *Un bonheur n'arrive jamais seul/Happiness Never Comes Alone* (James Huth, 2012) is about single mother-of-three Charlotte (Marceau) and confirmed bachelor Sacha (Gad Elmaleh) who meet and fall in love, despite his initial horror of children. Thanks to her rich first husband, Charlotte lives in an opulent Parisian apartment, while, as befits an artist (he is a musician), Sacha lives in a Montmartre garret. After being temporarily estranged, Charlotte, her children and Sacha are blissfully reunited in an ending that takes place in the suburbs. Significantly, as Sacha tries to trace Charlotte, the concierge at her former Paris building says that she lives in Romainville, 'the back of beyond', a Parisian-centric joke, as Romainville (93) is actually close to Paris.[30] Charlotte's new home turns out to be a large old-fashioned *pavillon* with a garden, in a nice quiet street.

Beyond the practicalities of this type of housing for a family, as dictated by the plot of *Un bonheur n'arrive jamais seul* or *De l'autre côté du lit*, what can we make of the trend in featuring quiet suburbs and their 'ordinary' inhabitants in French cinema and television today? Three types of reasons can be invoked, which relate to the French film industry and cultural policy, French film genres and Parisian urban sociology.

Location, Location, Location

Since the days of the New Wave, when the excitement of shooting on location contributed significantly to putting Paris on the cinematic map,[31] conditions for filming in Paris and its region have changed beyond recognition. Moving about the city is vastly more difficult due to traffic, safety regulations are more stringent and production costs have increased exponentially. Yet the desire to promote the location has not abated. On the contrary, the whole region has developed marketing strategies to attract and manage film shoots on its territory, as a means to acquiring cultural prestige, tourism and revenue. A range of companies and initiatives, both public and private, has sprung up since the 1990s, working towards an increased professionalisation[32] of location scouting, as illustrated by official documentation put out by the Mairie de Paris and the Ile-de-France region,[33] the coining of the new profession of *repéreur* (scouter) and the existence of an annual Salon du Tournage.[34] While inner Paris definitely has the edge, with 110 films shot in the city in 2013 for instance,[35] suburban municipalities have been successful in attracting a range of contemporary French and international productions, from *Dheepan* to *The Hunger Games: Mockingjay Part 2* (Francis Lawrence, 2015).[36] The mayor of Noisy-le-Sec, where *Paulette* was shot, expressed his pride at the fact that his commune had featured in half a dozen films over one year and explained that

> Municipalities can receive revenue [from the shoots]. But many, including Noisy-le-Sec, opt for tax exemption against having the name of the city on the credits. It's a good way to contribute to cultural activities, promote our heritage and give a positive image of the commune.[37]

Thus, municipal action, cultural policy and the professionalisation of the film industry work hand in hand to exploit the city and its suburbs in a way that has begun to extend both the territorial meaning of 'Paris' and the range of previous narrow *banlieue* representations.

Equally significant is the increasing transnationalism of French cinema. While the *film de banlieue* claims realism as its major aesthetic trope, what François Jost calls its *effet d'actualité*,[38] its existence also derives from American urban dramas about 'housing projects', such as Spike Lee's *Clockers* (1995). Similarly, the growing prominence of the quiet suburbs in film and television finds part of its inspiration across the Atlantic but evidently in different genres. Charlotte and Hugo's habitat and lifestyle in *De l'autre côté du lit* are reminiscent of the bourgeois utopia of American suburbs as seen in numerous post-war films, and pastiched in series such as *Desperate Housewives* (written by Marc Cherry, 2004–12); François Ozon went as far as shooting his 2014 film *Une nouvelle amie/The New Girlfriend*, ostensibly set in a French suburb, in Canada in order to reproduce faithfully this type of quiet and leafy suburban habitat. So, as the romcom has emerged as a successful genre in France over the last two decades, new suburban visions have followed.

The rise of the quiet suburbs on French screens finally corresponds to a change in urban demographics and the housing market, with the growing gentrification of the city and, in turn, of parts of the *banlieue*. As young middle-class couples are pushed out of inner Paris by property prices, they begin to 'colonise' the ring of *communes* immediately surrounding the city. While the western suburbs of Neuilly and Boulogne-sur-Seine (92) have always functioned like extensions of well-off Paris, gentrification is now reaching places such as Levallois-Perret, Montrouge and Vanves (also in 92), Les Lilas (93) and Saint-Mandé (94).[39] Here, the inhabitants are no longer presented as alien *banlieusards* and, as in *Un Bonheur n'arrive jamais seul*, the move from inner Paris to suburb is smoother than in the *films de banlieue* that always insist on the unbridgeable gap between the two. Nevertheless, as we have seen, the films still feel the need to signal that there is a difference – through aerial shots, text inserts or dialogue. As Fourcaut points out, 'the suburbs can only be conceived in their relationship to Paris, the seat of political, economic and cultural power'.[40] Even the 'Grand Paris',[41] a long-term project launched in 2008 that will encompass the whole region and develop transport super-links and new administrative and regional structures, does not so far look set to challenge significantly the enduring division, and de facto relegation of the *banlieues* to the margins, not only of Paris, but of its representations on screen.

Notes

1. Eric Hazan, 'Paris va encore craquer', *Télérama*, no. 3272, 26 September 2012, p. 37.
2. A survey of (French) opinions of Parisians conducted in 2010 summed them up as 'cultivated' but also 'arrogant, aggressive […], snobbish'. *Marianne*, 26 February 2010. Available previously at: www.marianne.net/Les-Francais-et-leurs-Parisiens-l-autre-french-paradox_a189571.html (accessed September 2015).
3. Annie Fourcaut, 'Pour en finir avec la banlieue', *Géocarrefour*, vol. 75, no. 2 (2000), p. 103.
4. The more neutral *Francilien* tends to refer to the suburban railway network rather than the inhabitants of the Ile-de-France
5. François Maspero, *Roissy-Express: A Journey through the Paris Suburbs*. With photographs by Anaïs Frantz (London: Verso, 1994 [first published in French 1990]).
6. The Ile-de-France region surrounding Paris was divided by a 1964 law (implemented in January 1968) into seven *départements*, each with its own postal code: in addition to Paris itself (75), they are, immediately surrounding the city: Hauts-de-Seine (92) to the west, *Seine-Saint-Denis* (93) to the north-east and Val-de-Marne (94) to the south-east; further out are Val-d'Oise (95) to the north, Yvelines (78) to the west and Essone (91) to the south.
7. See Ginette Vincendeau, *La Haine* (London: I. B. Tauris, 2005).
8. 'Mytheme' is a concept developed by Claude Lévi-Straus; it refers to an irreducible, basic unit of myth around which various permutations are possible. See Claude Lévi-Strauss, *Structural Anthropology* (New York: Doubleday, 1967), p. 208.
9. Source: INSEE (Institut National de la Statistique et des Etudes Economiques) website. Available at: www.insee.fr/fr/themes/theme.asp?theme=2 (accessed November 2015).
10. See also Annie Fourcaut, 'Entre Gabin et Marina Vlady, les banlieusards au cinéma pendant les Trente Glorieuses', in *Etre Parisien, Paris et Ile de France Mémoires*, vol. 5 (Paris: Fédération des Sociétés Historiques et Archéologiques de Paris et de l'Ile de France, 2004), pp. 587–96.
11. The film was made in 1971 but suffered from censorship and was finally released in France in 1976. The title is a pun on *bidon* (phoney) and *bidonville* (shanty town).
12. Roland-François Lack, commentary for the film *Bande à part*, BFI Editions, B00008WQ56, 2003.
13. On *cinéma beur*, see Carrie Tarr, *Reframing Difference, Beur and Banlieue Filmmaking in France* (Manchester: Manchester University Press, 2005); see also Sylvie Durmelat and Vinay Swamy (eds), *Les Ecrans de l'intégration* (Saint-Denis: Presses Universitaires de Vincennes, 2015).
14. The title, which literally means 'my city is about to crack', is also a pun on 'crack' for drugs.

15. Raphaëlle Moine, *Cinema Genre* (Oxford: Blackwell, 2008), p. 198.
16. David-Alexandre Wagner, *De la banlieue stigmatisée à la cité démystifiée: la représentation de la banlieue des grands ensembles dans le cinéma français de 1981 à 2005* (Bern: Peter Lang, 2011), p. 81.
17. Marie-Claude Taranger, 'Télévision et "western urbain", enjeux et nuances de l'information sur les banlieues', *Les Cahiers de la cinémathèque*, no. 59/60 (February 1994), pp. 59–71.
18. See Ginette Vincendeau, 'Minority Report', *Sight and Sound*, vol. 25, no. 6 (June 2015), pp. 22–4.
19. Sébastien Le Pajolec and Jean-Jacques Yvorel, 'Du "gamin de Paris" aux "jeunes de banlieue": évolutions d'un stéréotype', in Myriam Tsikounas (ed.), *Imaginaires urbains du Paris romantique à nos jours* (Paris: Editions Le Manuscrit, 2011), p. 239.
20. See Wagner, *De la banlieue stigmatisée à la cité démystifiée*, pp. 81–4; Tarr, *Reframing Difference*; and Will Higbee, *Post-Beur Cinema: Maghrebi-French and North African Emigré Filmmaking in France since 2000* (Edinburgh: Edinburgh University Press, 2013).
21. Hervé Mimran, 'Entretien avec Géraldine Nakache et Hervé Mimran', in *Tout ce qui brille, scénario de Géraldine Nakache, Hervé Mimran* (La Madeleine: LettMotif, 2011), p. 138.
22. Géraldine Nakache, 'Entretien avec Géraldine Nakache et Hervé Mimran', p. 130.
23. Ibid., p. 133.
24. Michael R. Gott, '"Bouger pour voir les immeubles": *Jeunesse dorée* (2001), *L'année suivante* (2006) and the Creative Mobility of Women's *Banlieue* Cinema', *Modern & Contemporary France*, vol. 21, no. 4 (2013), p. 460.
25. Nakache, 'Entretien avec Géraldine Nakache et Hervé Mimran', p. 138.
26. Céline Sciamma, commentary for her film *Bande de filles*, Editions Pyramide Video, B00R1UV86C, 2015.
27. Noël Burch and Geneviève Sellier, *Ignorée de tous … sauf du public, quinze ans de fiction télévisée française* 1995–2010 (Paris: Editions INA, 2013), p. 15.
28. Philippe Le Guern, 'Les Professionnels de la profession: une enquête sur le tournage de la série *Julie Lescaut*', in Pierre Beylot and Geneviève Sellier (eds), *Les Séries policières* (Paris: L'Harmattan, 2004), p. 42.
29. Editors' note: see Mary Harrod's chapter in this volume.
30. The credits indicate the scene was shot in Asnières (north-west of Paris), even closer to the city.
31. Editors' note: as several authors discuss in this book; see chapters by Michel Marie, Roland-François Lack, Jennifer Wallace, and Hilary Radner & Alistair Fox.
32. Gwenaëlle Rot, 'Tournages et territoires. L'Ile-de-France, quel(s) territoire(s) de tournage, pour quels enjeux?', Université de Paris Ouest Nanterre La Défense, Laboratoire IDHE UMR 85 33 CNRS, Report (March 2011). Available at: www.urbanisme-puca.gouv.fr/IMG/pdf/rapport-idf-territoires-tournages-enjeux.pdf (accessed February 2016).
33. Mairie de Paris, Mission Cinéma, Paris Film, Guide des tournages à Paris (December 2013). Available at: www.parisfilm.fr/ (accessed April 2016).
34. The 2016 Salon des Lieux de Tournage took place at the Carreau du Temple (3rd *arrondissement*) on 2–3 February 2016.
35. See Mission Cinéma, Paris Film, op. cit.

36. The scenes of the run-down estate in *Dheepan* were shot at Les Coudraies in Poissy (78); major international productions, such as *Brazil* (Terry Gilliam, 1985) and *The Hunger Games: Mockingjay Part 2* chose the spectacular Palazzo d'Abraxas in Noisy-le-Grand (93).
37. Cited in Muriel Nicolau-Bergeret, 'Noisy-le-Sec, nouvelle terre d'accueil du cinéma', *You*, 31 January 2012. Available at: http://you.leparisien.fr/actu/2012/01/31/noisy-le-sec-nouvelle-terre-d-accueil-du-cinema-13024.html (accessed January 2016).
38. François Jost, 'Séries policières et stratégies de programmation', in Beylot and Sellier, *Les Séries policières*, p. 64.
39. On the gentrification of Paris and parts of the immediate *banlieue*, see Anne Clerval, *Paris sans le peuple* (Paris: La Découverte, 2013).
40. Fourcaut, 'Entre Gabin et Marina Vlady', p. 587.
41. See: www.societedugrandparis.fr/ (accessed April 2016).

Part II
CHARACTERS

Maigret from across the Channel

Charlotte Brunsdon

Paris as a cinematic city is inextricably bound up with theorisations of modernity, the early 20th century and, as the title of this book suggests, the *flâneur*. In this essay, I want to take a little distance from these debates – perhaps the width of the Channel – and explore Parisian modernity as it was imagined, produced and viewed in a British context. This I will do through one of the best-known Parisian characters, Georges Simenon's Commissaire Jules Maigret, and I want to consider Maigret's Paris not as a cinematic production, but as British television. While the television Maigrets of Jean Richard (1967–90) and Bruno Cremer (1991–2005) may be more familiar in France, in Britain the actor Rupert Davies brought Paris into the nation's living rooms, week after week, in the 51 adaptations made by the BBC in the early 1960s.[1]

There are three reasons for this exploration. The main one is that Maigret is a significant Parisian resident, whose investigations create and document a Paris resonant across audiovisual media in the 20th century.[2] The 1960s BBC adaptations of Maigret, which were very popular at home and exported worldwide, contributed to and recycled images of Paris which reached very substantial international audiences. Extremely unusually for television drama of the time, these programmes included specially shot location Paris footage. The second is that any serious considerations of cinematic Paris 'beyond the *flâneur*' needs to engage with that other audiovisual medium, television, which is in its own way a symbol of modernity in the mid-20th century. And finally, detailed attention to the production of a British Paris will illuminate both the international qualities and meanings of the city and something of how place is made in the audiovisual media.

The Television City

In the 1960s, television was dominated by national broadcasting, with very limited channel choice, and was watched domestically. As television production favours regular, predictable formats such as news, magazine and discussion programmes, as well as, in fiction, seriality, the city found on this television was created mainly through repetition. As the title of this book proposes, discussion of the cinematic city, and of Paris in particular, has been dominated by the figure of the *flâneur*. When we consider the television city, our focus must shift.[3] If the paradigms of the cinematic city are dominated by the figure of the solitary wanderer, those of the televisual city must attend to the armchair viewer. In this context, the television city, in the second half of the 20th century, when television is a terrestrial, nationally broadcast affair, has certain medium-specific characteristics. It is a city to which one returns repeatedly; it is domestic, it is mundane,

The opening title sequence of *Maigret*.

familiar and small (a little screen in the living room). In Britain, the structuring presence of the BBC shaped 20th-century British television, while the role, attitude to and development of television in France has been rather different, where cinematic, as opposed to televisual, culture is much stronger. However, in both countries, television, along with the fridge and the car, is one of the emblems of mid-20th-century domestic modernity. The domesticity of television forbids the metaphorical exchange which has been so significant in the theorisation of the cinematic city, and in which Paris has been so important: cinema-modernity-city. Watching television, we are not anonymous in a crowd of strangers, and if the cinema has been theorised as the medium of urban modernity, television has been conceived of as a suburban medium, identified not with a city crowd, but with the consuming nuclear family.

However, this overwhelming framing of familiarity and habit should not lead to neglect of the significance of television's role in bringing the strange, wonderful and unfamiliar into the home. It is the paradoxical bringing together of inside and outside, well known to scholars of the medium, which makes television so important to an understanding of the city. It is the outside inside, the city in the home. The wailing of the emergency siren is a significant aural signifier of a city location in television drama or news; the paradox of the city in the home which is the television city is that the sound can come from the box in the corner, or the streets outside. The television city brings viewers both the mundane – for example, local news and weather – and the exotic, and can render the strange and foreign familiar and recognisable – and to this I will return at the end.

British Paris

The 1960s British television *Maigret* has an opening title sequence that continues to resonate. The initial titles ('Georges Simenon's *Maigret*') are set against a dark, rough-textured wall on which a match is struck. The flare from the match illuminates the face of a man as he lights his pipe, and 'starring Rupert Davies' appears as the accordion-based theme tune invokes Paris. Ron Grainer's theme and the title sequence were so evocative that when I have told British people of a certain age that I am writing about this Maigret, many of them hum the notes to me, and describe the match striking in the dark. Ginette Vincendeau has commented on the irresistible simplicity of the iconography of the detective Jules Maigret ('the heavy silhouette of a mature man with big shoulders, hat and overcoat, pipe to his lips'), and this sequence renders this simplicity with great economy.[4] In the same passage, she also notes the exportability of the iconography of the French capital, and it is evident that the BBC was attentive to this too as it commissioned a Paris-set detective series which might, if successful, rival some of the shows crossing the Atlantic. For one of the most interesting aspects of the 1960s BBC *Maigret* series was that it was, from inception, a big prestige production for which the BBC planned overseas sales. This can be seen in the exceptional decision to record the episodes in 35mm, 16mm and videotape as it was not known which formats international purchasers would want.[5] Thus although the image of the BBC in this period is very much a national public-service broadcaster, in fact productions such as this were inaugurated with clear commercial ambitions.

The 'Notes for Directors' prepared by the series producer, Andrew Osborn, are explicit about the formal implications of this, insisting that episodes 'must be capable of having six commercials and at the same time be shown on our screens without these breaks being obtrusive'.[6] The double address that Osborn identifies here, in which each episode would have both a commercial and a public-service version, indicates that when the Paris of these programmes is considered, it is not just a British Paris. It is a British Paris imagined within a world market. The internationally recognised attractions of Paris, in combination with a reassuring detective, and a large number of stories, provided a package in which the BBC was eager to invest, to the extent of sending cast and crew to Paris on a regular basis to film the 5 to 10 minutes of exterior footage in each 50-minute episode.

The BBC archive production files, preserved in the magnificent paper detail of the 20th-century archive, indicate that this unusual commitment to regular overseas filming for a drama production was tricky to organise. Most of the British cast and crew spoke no French, and if they had experience of overseas travel, it was likely to be as members of the armed forces. For each minute of location-shot screen time, there were many hours of arrangements and memos, with the complex hierarchies of status reflected in different hotels and meals for different production employees.[7] In terms of the representation of Paris, though, the exceptional opportunity to provide location footage in each episode put contradictory pressures on the producers. On the one hand, they needed to demonstrate, every week, that they really had shot this in France – it really was Paris. For this, there must be landmarks, and scripts and shooting scripts often specify the use of a particular landmark early in the episode. On the other hand, they wanted to use their exceptional opportunities for location shooting to move away from tourist cliché and to consider a more banal Paris, an ordinary Paris ('the odd cul-de-sac to get a good montage'), which may not always be – particularly to a non-native – immediately identifiable as Paris.[8] And this is a problem for the production, because why spend all this money to go to France if the British viewer cannot tell that you have been there?

These dilemmas of the production raise the more general question of how place is signified in audiovisual fiction. Accent, music, props, writing, costume – each of these can tell an audience where a scene is set, and often these methods are more important in confirming location than where something was actually filmed. Accordion music and the uniform of a gendarme are clichés, but precisely because of this, they may identify a Paris location less ambiguously than a location-shot street, and clarity of setting was all important in constructing this Paris for domestic British and international domestic consumption. A character perceived as typically Parisian, such as a concierge (as Raphaëlle Moine notes elsewhere in this book) or a gendarme can simultaneously identify setting and create atmosphere. The internationally recognisable iconography of Paris – landmarks, characters and quotidian settings such as cafés and *tabacs* – can be invoked without expensively taking cast and crew over the Channel. This studio-created iconography is used extensively in these programmes, partly and paradoxically, *because* location shooting was also undertaken, and it was important that the ambiguities of the 'real' should not confuse the viewer about where it was set.

Great effort was expended in trying to dress the British studio sets with French objects and décor. As this was the BBC, permission had to be sought if this involved alcohol: 'Please may we have permission to use nine bottles of real continental beer in the studio?'[9] In this endeavour, the heroines of authenticity are two secretaries, Vanessa Virgo in Britain (secretary to Andrew Osborn) and Maud Vidal in Paris, the BBC's 'Television Secretary'. Vanessa must repeatedly contact Maud about details of arrangements, but also to ask urgently, in June 1960, for a map of Paris to be rushed over, 'as we cannot get one in this country with the writing in French'.[10] More trying is the question of sourcing French cigarettes. The production is using empty Gitanes packets for set-dressing, but the cleaners keep throwing them away and Vanessa must ask Maud to approach 'the company Gitanes Gauloises' to ensure a regular supply.[11] Another important prop was Perrier water because bottled water was unknown in Britain in this period. Perrier water, like cigarette packets, was also usefully portable, and could be introduced into domestic interiors to render them French, as well as featuring in the many different versions of café sets.[12]

This concern for authenticity was particularly challenging in relation to the handling of French names. Language is a significant element in the evocation of place, and it was decided, early in the production, to retain French pronunciation of names and to use some French phrases and modes of address.[13] Thus, Maigret himself is addressed as 'Patron', his colleague as 'Monsieur le juge' and other characters as 'Monsieur', 'Madame' and 'Mademoiselle'. Characters, particularly the Maigrets, bid each other 'Au revoir', and there is a consistent effort to use French stress patterns in the use of names. This decision had its travails, particularly for the British actors. As Andrew Osborn observed during the shooting of the first series, 'We are also in a bit of difficulty from time to time over the pronunciation of French words by people who can't speak French.'[14] This production decision to emphasise the Frenchness of the setting through the French pronunciation of words was, at the same time, judged likely to be confusing for a British audience, and there was some concern at 'the difficulty of understanding some of the rather unusual names – both of characters and of places – that we are continually coming up against in these plays'.[15] This translated directly into a contradictory instruction to the actors, which clearly elevates the comprehension of the English audience over the 'Frenchness' of the pronunciation: 'would you please have a word with Rupert and Ewen ... and ask them to take particular care that these difficult names are spoken slowly and clearly'.[16]

This paradoxical demand on the actors, that they both perform 'Frenchness' and speak 'these difficult [i.e. foreign] names' 'slowly and clearly', epitomises the challenges of the production.

Sexual Attractions and the Everyday

So Paris was both an attraction and a trouble for the BBC producers of *Maigret*. The question for the BBC was how to manage the presentation of the city both to demonstrate that licence-fee money has been well spent, but also to render the city easily recognisable to the notoriously insular British public. I have suggested this entailed the combination of three types of material: location-shot landmark imagery, location-shot 'ordinary Paris' and studio sets which use familiar icons of Paris and France in their production design and dressing. However, the most important – and for the BBC troubling – strategy was the invocation of Paris as the city of sexual attractions. If 'the Continent' has always meant sex and naughtiness to the British, then the invocation of the Moulin Rouge version of Paris plays a particularly important role in identifying the setting of the television series.

The film critic Barry Norman characterises this idea of Paris in his [1969] review, in 1969, of a one-off return of the Rupert Davies Maigret:

> ['Maigret at Bay'] ... was a pleasant reminder of how very good the series used to be, particularly in the way it reflected Simenon's knack of conjuring up the exciting Paris – a place where something delicious and probably naughty is about to happen any minute. Actually, Paris isn't really like that at all ... Still, Simenon makes you feel that the mythical Paris does exist if only you knew where to look, and the *Maigret* series recreated that impression quite vividly.[17]

As Norman points out, it is Georges Simenon's own interest in late-night Paris, and his repeated use of low-life milieux which necessitates this engagement with a Paris of cabaret dancers and professional criminals. Jules Maigret is radically democratic in his concern with the humanity of all social classes affected by criminal acts, and the stories feature tramps and petty thieves, heroin addicts, countesses and bar staff. But these settings of the Simenon stories coincide with the way in which 'the Continent' has always meant sex and naughtiness to the British, so it is an indicatively British judgement that this is 'exciting Paris' 'where something delicious and probably naughty is about to happen'. This impression of Maigret's Paris is confirmed by the decision to start the first series with a nightclub-set story. 'Murder in Montmartre' (*Maigret au Picratt's*) has the double focus of a murdered nightclub dancer and the later murder of an old lady about which the dancer had warned the police. The internal BBC synopsis declares, 'From out of the neon-lit jungle of Montmartre comes a frightened strip-tease dancer named Arlette',[18] and the episode has an explicit thematic concern with the question of how seriously the testimony of such a young woman should be taken, and thus introduces the inspector's attentiveness to characters often ignored by their social superiors.

The opening provides straightforward 'sexy Paris' promises which are so familiar that it was evidently decided that there was no need to waste expensive location shooting on the set-up. Ealing Studios provided a flashing sign and, thriftily, the production reused footage of street signs originally shot for the pilot episode (now lost), 'Maigret and the Lost Life'.[19] The episode opens with a night-time sequence of the flashing neon-lit exterior of the 'Folies Pigalle', accordion music providing a soundtrack to an image dominated by the glistening rain on the pavements reflecting the neon promises of 'Theatre Cabaret – Folies Pigalle – Naturistes – Nues – Striptease'.[20] This first story, with its *mise-en-scène* of bars and clubs and workers who trade in late-night pleasures, identifies one of the recurrent milieux for the series. However, with a junior policeman in love with a murdered striptease artiste, and Maigret's own pragmatic acceptance of this world, it also indicates how the series will deal with the demi-monde. The neon outline of a sensual woman's body which lights up the club exterior conforms to the promise of Paris as the city of attractions. But the particular manner in which Maigret interacts with the denizens of this world, the seriousness with which he takes them as people, inflects this location differently. This alluring city is made recognisable by the use of familiar imagery, but within that recognition, the world is treated as mundane and unremarkable, inhabited by working people like any other.

The location shooting in this first episode is reserved for daylight exteriors which are also very familiar – Montmartre and the place Pigalle. The instructions to the camera operators are precise – the shooting in Montmartre must 'show Sacre Coeur' [*sic*], while the funicular must also be captured.[21] The night tourism of the strip show will be accompanied by daytime images of a more respectable sightseeing. So as a whole, the opening episode makes promises to its audience that the series will both confirm and augment existing ideas and images of Paris, while also offering the familiar generic pleasures of the police story in which the main character is a bit French – he has French accoutrements, and uses familiar French words – but not too French.

The series promises a certain continental sophistication to its British viewers, a certain explicitness about the sexuality and the night-time professions which was otherwise absent from British screens. Because of the Simenon source, in which so much of Maigret's crime solving is achieved through his deep embeddedness in the everyday (and everynight) life of his locality, there is a noticeable lack of condemnation characterising Maigret's encounter with these characters. Identifying the location as Paris through studio-shot scenes of cabarets and bars carries with it certain lures and promises about what is just over the Channel, but also about attitudes to sexuality which might be less repressed and more modern – in some ways – than is characteristic of British culture.

There was however, still, anxiety about how acceptable this Paris would be, and just before transmission, a long memo from the General Manager, Television Promotions, Ronald Waldman, refers to the first episode's 'over-insistence and over-explicitness on sex'.[22] Audience reaction, though, vindicated the producers: 'Congratulations to everyone concerned on the splendid and fully earned press reaction to the first *Maigret* last night. This was a triumphant start.'[23]

The Modernity of Paris in Britain

Because the aim of the producers, in undertaking the expensive trips to Paris, was to shoot footage that would demonstrate that this was really set in the actual city, they had to aim for images that evoked recognition: 'Oh look, that's Paris'/'Oh look, it's really shot in Paris.' So for scholars of Paris, there are not, at first glance, many new images, or images which, in Pierre Sorlin's terms, incite reflection on the mode of representation.[24] However, because they were in Paris to shoot film, and because the nature of detective fiction means that often we see detectives observing sites in which crimes are about to happen, there is also, throughout these programmes, an inadvertent and partial documentation of early 1960s Paris, just as there is, as Ginette Vincendeau has observed, in the later 1960s Jean Richard version.[25] Long shots of empty, insignificant streets recur throughout the series, as do anonymous houses and apartment blocks. Juxtaposed with the extensive use of studio work to identify the setting unambiguously, these programmes present a fragmentary archive of a now vanished Paris articulated through commonplace and stereotypical British – and internationally resonant – ideas about Paris and French culture. The meals Mme Maigret prepares for her husband, which include a table laid with salad, bread and wine, and which he eats (unknown in British police series of the same period such as *Z Cars*, where any eating is done on the job or in the canteen), alone serve as an expression of iconic cultural difference.

What I want to argue in conclusion was that the 1960s British series, although it did not present particularly fresh images of Paris, did signify modernity in the British context. This is a modernity which comes precisely from the repetitions of the televisual city, the comfort and security of watching, from a British living room, a Paris in which ordinary people commit banal crimes, and are investigated and understood by Inspector Maigret. *Maigret* on British television in the early 1960s represented a new post-war world, a world in which many new experiences became possible for ordinary British citizens: going to Europe on foreign holidays, drinking wine, understanding a bit of French, considering the European Economic Community – and acknowledging the pleasures of sex.[26]

In histories of post-war Britain, the poet Philip Larkin's much-cited declaration that 'Sexual intercourse began in 1963 … between the end of the Chatterley ban and the Beatles' first LP' forms an emblematic inauguration of the 'swinging sixties'.[27] Recent historians of the period, such as Dominic Sandbrook, have argued that the swinging of the sixties has been much exaggerated, and for most people, life continued with hardly a ripple of the concerns of the metropolitan elite.[28] However, perhaps the BBC *Maigret* was one such ripple, broadcast between 1960 and 1963, a precursor to the sexual intercourse that began in 1963, and the radical liberalisation of the 1964 and 1966 Labour governments. The French setting taken for granted, Paris was watched in British living rooms by large audiences every week. Maigret's attention to the pleasures of the table coincided with the slow introduction of more Mediterranean cuisine to Britain, and the attention to France, Italy and Spain as desirable destinations with enviable lifestyles. While the British upper classes have always enjoyed Paris and 'The Riviera', to set detective genre fiction in France was quite a step for the British Broadcasting Corporation. It suggested a confidence in a popular engagement with 'the foreign'. After a very long 19th century, Britain was beginning to get modern.

The end credits of *Maigret*.

The awkwardness of the manner in which Rupert Davies inhabited his Frenchness can be seen to symbolise the awkwardness of these changes for Britain. Nevertheless, the composite French milieu of *Maigret* and Maigret's Paris meant modernity in this context, the beginning of the swinging sixties in London, and a period of extraordinary innovation in British television. And to support my point, let me draw attention to the end credits of the series. These elegant monochrome graphics are quite different to the opening titles, and draw on the pop sensibility which also created *The Avengers* and, precisely, the art-school chic of British popular music. The screen is all white, with a grey strip across the top of the bottom half. Across this grey strip are laid the credits, while isolated characters, one or two at a time, move and gesture in the abstraction of the white screen. The simplicity and cool of these 1960s credits demonstrate not just the modernity of Paris, but the modernity of *Maigret* in Britain.

All quotations from the BBC's Written Archives Centre, Caversham, are reproduced with kind permission. Copyright remains with the BBC.

Notes

1. The BBC, with producer Andrew Osborn, made four series of *Maigret* between 1960 and 1963, after a successful pilot in 1959 (with Basil Sydney as Maigret). There was a later 1969 reprise, also with Rupert Davies, as a 90-minute Play of the Month, *Maigret at Bay* (tx. 9 February 1969).

2. The large number of film and television versions of Maigret stories have been surveyed by Peter Haining, *The Complete Maigret* (London: Boxtree, 1994); Paul Willemen, 'Maigret', in Phil Hardy (ed.), *The BFI Companion to Crime* (London: Cassell, 1997), pp. 216–17; Anne-Marie Kosmicki, 'Les Maigret, de Jean Richard à Bruno Cremer', *CinémAction,* Littérature et télévision, no. 79 (1996), pp. 96–105; Ginette Vincendeau, 'Maigret pour toujours?', in Raphaëlle Moine, Brigitte Rollet and Geneviève Sellier (eds), *Policiers et criminals: un genre populaire européen sur grand et petit écrans* (Paris: L'Harmattan, 2009), pp. 89–100.
3. The very abbreviated outline of an argument I make here is presented in more detail in my forthcoming book, *Television Cities* (Duke University Press).
4. Vincendeau, 'Maigret pour toujours?', p. 90. The titles were shot using a wall of Shoreditch Public Library.
5. Senior Planning Assistant (II) (Dennis Souse), 'Maigret Recording Requirements', 20 April 1960, BBC Written Archives Centre (henceforth, WAC) T5/2, 166/5; General Manager, Television Promotions (Ronald Waldman), 'Maigret Recording Requirements', 26 April 1960, T5/2, 166/5; Andrew Osborn, 'Maigret Recordings', 20 October 1960, WAC, T5/2, 166/1.
6. Andrew Osborn, 'Maigret, Notes for Directors', WAC, T5/2, 166/1.
7. Maud Vidal, memo to Vanessa Virgo, 4 May 1960, WAC, T5/2,164/1.
8. Continuity notes, 'The Trap', WAC, T5/2, 204/1.
9. Ron Travers (A.F.M.), memo to Terry Williams (Property Master), 13 September 1962, WAC, T5/2, 204/1.
10. Vanessa Virgo, letter to Maud Vidal, 13 June 1960, WAC, T5/2, 166/1.
11. Vanessa Virgo, letter to Maud Vidal, 20 June 1960, WAC, T5/2,166/1. See note 20.
12. For example, in 'Peter the Lett' (tx. 17 December 1963).
13. The survival and detail of a document from 'The Winning Ticket', which gives a list of 58 words and phrases (mainly place, product and people's names) with phonetic pronunciation guides, suggests that equivalent documents were drawn up for all episodes, '"Maigret" No. 15 Pronunciations', n.d., WAC, T5/2, 185/1.
14. Andrew Osborn, memo to Eric Tayler and Gerry Glaister, 23 December 1960, WAC, T5/2,166/1.
15. Ibid.
16. Ibid.
17. Barry Norman, 'Review: *Maigret at Bay* (Play of the Month)', *Daily Mail,* 10 February 1969 (WAC, n.p.).
18. Synopsis, 'Murder in Montmartre', 23 November 1961, WAC, T5/2, 167/1.
19. WAC, T5/2, 167/1. This footage is thriftily used again in the first episode of the second series, 'The Winning Ticket' (tx. 13 November 1961).
20. Ginette Vincendeau has pointed out during the editing process that the normal French usage would be 'Nus', even though the 'nus' in question are women. The grammatical correctness of the sign in the titles, as opposed to its conformity to common usage, can be seen as an instance of the awkwardness of some of the engagements with French culture in this production, also exemplified by the formulation 'Gauloises-Gitanes', as opposed to the name of the state tobacco company, SEITA, and the general absence of accents in the BBC files (although it should be remembered that French accents were near impossible to include with British typewriter keyboards in the 1960s).

21. Film Schedule, WAC, T5/2, 167/1.
22. Ronald Waldman, memo to H. D. Tel, 13 September 1960, WAC, T5/2,166/1.
23. Controller of Programmes TV, memo, 1 November 1960, WAC, T5/2, 167/1.
24. Pierre Sorlin, *European Cinema, European Societies 1939–90* (London: Routledge, 1991), p. 12.
25. Vincendeau, 'Maigret pour toujours?', p. 99.
26. Elizabeth David had published her influential books on Mediterranean food throughout the previous decade (*A Book of Mediterranean Food* was first published in 1950, *French Country Cooking* in 1951 and *French Provincial Cooking* in 1960). Habitat, an interiors shop that imported goods such as earthenware dishes and pasta jars from the Continent, first opened in 1964.
27. The opening lines in full are: 'Sexual intercourse began/In nineteen sixty-three/(Which was rather late for me)/Between the end of the Chatterley ban/And the Beatles' first LP', but popular memory elides the line about the lateness. Philip Larkin, 'Annus Mirabilus' (first published in *High Windows*, 1967), *Collected Poems* (London: Marvell Press/Faber & Faber, 1988), p. 167.
28. Dominic Sandbrook, *Never Had It So Good: A History of Britain from Suez to the Beatles* (London: Abacus, 2005); Dominic Sandbrook, *White Heat: A History of Britain in the Swinging Sixties* (London: Abacus, 2006); see also Richard Davenport-Hines, *An English Affair: Sex, Class and Power in the Age of Profumo* (London: William Collins, 2013); Frank Mort, *Capital Affairs: London and the Making of the Permissive Society* (New Haven, CT, and London: Yale University Press, 2010); Christopher Bray, *1965: The Year Modern Britain Was Born* (London: Simon & Schuster, 2014).

Parisian Cinephiles and the Mac-Mahon

Leila Wimmer

Paris stands at the centre of the phenomenal passion for film that France has maintained since the first screening of the Cinématographe at the Salon Indien of the Grand Café on the boulevard des Capucines on 28 December 1895. From the silent era to the coming of sound, Paris, the capital of modern art, witnessed an explosion of interest in film typified by the specifically French intellectual fascination for the 'low art' of cinema, especially Hollywood and the work of D. W. Griffith, Thomas H. Ince, Cecil B. DeMille, Charlie Chaplin, Mack Sennett and others. A by-product of modernism, this fascination was from the outset the creation of a cultural elite,[1] a masculine culture of distinction[2] firmly embedded in the urban fabric of the city with the unprecedented rise of a cinephilic sociability through a network of critics, film journals, *ciné-clubs*, specialised theatres and film societies, special film lectures and exhibitions, not to mention the binding role of the Cinémathèque Française created in 1936 by Henri Langlois and Georges Franju. Reignited in the post-war period by New Wave critics and directors, this particular strand of cinephilia has acquired the status of a myth, evoking a specific 'site of memory'[3] – Paris in the 1950s.[4] In his authoritative history of cinephilia, Antoine de Baecque defines this type of cinephilia as essentially Parisian. The invention of a gaze and a culture, 'a way of watching films, speaking about them and then diffusing the discourse', Parisian cinephilia 'has the particularity of being located in the original birthplace, the world centre of the cultural legitimation of cinema as an art'.[5]

The story of the Cinémathèque is already well rehearsed[6] and here I want to focus on another iconic site of Parisian cinephilia, the Mac-Mahon, a still functioning cinema that bears the name of the avenue it is situated on in Paris, as well as those who frequented it, the 'Mac-Mahoniens', a particularly extreme and controversial version of the cinephile. Although the Mac-Mahon is rather small, its standing as a *cinéma d'art et essai* is legendary. It represents a high point in the history of 1950s and 1960s cinephilia conceived as a modernist and formalist masculine devotion to Hollywood. The epicentre and last surviving site of an intense cinematic culture, the Mac-Mahon has had a tremendous subterranean influence, even if it is often overlooked, or brushed aside, in histories of the period. The Mac-Mahon offers some suggestive insights into two sets of issues. Firstly, the primordial relationship between cinephile culture and the particular context of Paris, and, secondly, the means by which the high modernist cult of the autonomous artwork that dominated this strand of cinephilia, and which continues to play an important role to this day, took the politics of style to its logical extreme.

Cinephilia first emerged in Paris during the post-World War One silent era when Hollywood asserted its hegemony over French screens and for a whole generation of intellectuals, the cult of cinema, especially American cinema, offered an alternative to mainstream 'official' culture. For Louis Delluc, Ricciotto Canudo, Léon Moussinac et al., this almost religious devotion to film was structured around the provocative elevation of the disreputable medium of film into a good object of legitimate culture, the 'Seventh Art', and they set themselves against those *cinéphobes* who denounced film as a vulgar fairground attraction, in order to promote a radically modern French cinema.[7] To elevate the cultural status of cinema, this devotion produced a discourse revolving around the theorisation of cinema's specificity, and its aesthetic essence that was crystallised in the abstract and elusive term, *photogénie*.[8] This went hand in hand with the first conception of the *politique des auteurs*.[9] It should be mentioned at this stage that despite the involvement of women in early French film criticism, this strand of cinephilia remained exclusively related to the masculine domain of elite culture.[10]

This specific mode of reception and the cult of American cinema continued in Paris after World War Two when the influx of Hollywood films banned during the German Occupation ignited a new wave of discourse on film aesthetics. In an echo of the debates of the silent era about medium specificity, the *politique des auteurs*, and the issue of what exactly constituted *mise-en-scène*, once again dominated discussion. *Cahiers du cinéma* became the leading journal of this cinephilic tendency, polemically championing Hollywood directors such as Alfred Hitchcock and Howard Hawks and arguing that cinematic specificity resided in *mise-en-scène* alone. Providing the basis for a purely aesthetic approach to film, *mise-en-scène* criticism reached its apogee when the critics Michel Mourlet, Michel Fabre, Jacques Serguine, Jacques Lourcelles and Pierre Rissient gathered around the Mac-Mahon cinema and the now mythical film journal, *Présence du cinéma* (1959–67).[11]

In post-war Paris, cinemas that were central to cinephilia entered their golden age and cinema attendance remained at its peak until the late 1950s when the arrival of television in French households signalled the beginning of a decline in audiences. Cinephile culture was tied to the social ritual of filmgoing and the space of the cinema auditorium, a communal social experience bound to the projection of celluloid in the dark on the big screen. Therein 'lies the very fascination of the film', noted Roland Barthes, who described leaving the cinema as 'coming out of hypnosis'.[12] Hence also, perhaps, the idea of cinema as a medium of revelation.[13] Moussinac had argued in the silent period that one could only become a true cinephile by the assiduous frequentation of cinemas: 'One must frequent cinemas patiently and often. Faith doesn't come all of a sudden.'[14] The sociability of filmgoing was at the core of cinephile culture, since films often became the sites of symbolic battles between different cinephile groups revolving around a specific cinema and a film journal. Cinephilia was thus often defined as a highly localised activity closely connected to particular spaces of consumption. Cinephilic activities generally took place in the centre of the Parisian capital, with geographic clusters developing over the years.[15] Christophe Gauthier has observed that in the post-war period cinephiles gradually annexed Parisian locations, such as the 5th and 6th *arrondissements* on the Left Bank, already a hot spot of cinephile activity in the 1920s with the opening of the Vieux-Colombier (1924), Studio des Ursulines (1926), the Ciné-Latin (1927) and the Cluny-Cinéma (1929), among many others. After the Liberation, the number of cinemas exploded in the capital and Paris had around 350 first-run, second-run, art and experimental cinemas spread throughout the city. While the movie palaces were situated on the Champs-Elysées and along the Grands Boulevards (boulevard des Capucines and boulevard des Italiens in particular), working-class areas from the place de Clichy to the Barbès-Rochechouart Métro station (near Montmartre) were also packed with cinemas; there were 31 in the 18th *arrondissement*, 18 in the 19th and 26 in the 20th.[16] The Cinémathèque Française returned to full activity and the thriving *ciné-club* movement contributed to the strengthening of the place of cinema in the French intellectual and cultural sphere, especially in the capital. In November 1944 just one *ciné-club* was known to have existed, by June 1948 there were some 185, with a membership of over 100,000 by June 1947.[17] As Christian-Marc Bosséno has observed, film theatres once more became the temples of a new religion and the life of the cinephile a frantic race across Paris from cinema to cinema.[18]

The core audience was now made up of young, urban filmgoers; in a study of French audiences between the years 1957 and 1964, it was argued that 'The young, well-educated, "enlightened fanatic" is replacing the average spectator.'[19] The Mac-Mahon, the Studio Parnasse on the Left Bank and the Midi-Minuit on the Grands Boulevards, each hosted its own clan, cinephile tribe or 'chapel' with its own specific denomination: the 'Hitchcocko-Hawksians' and the *politique des auteurs*, the 'Midi-Minuistes' (from the journal *Midi-Minuit fantastique*) championing horror and the fantastic, especially the British horror films of Terence Fisher, the 'Mac-Mahoniens' promoting an ultra-formalist agenda through the absolute primacy of *mise-en-scène*.

The Mac-Mahon

The fabled Mac-Mahon cinema became the headquarters in the early 1950s of one of the most formalist strands of post-war Parisian cinephilia which, in pushing the definition of cinema in terms of its formal qualities to its extreme, gave rise to the critically controversial term 'Mac-Mahonisme'. Situated on 5 avenue Mac-Mahon near the Arc de Triomphe and the place de L'Etoile on the Right Bank in the 17th *arrondissement*, and close to the offices of *Cahiers du cinéma* at 146 avenue des Champs-Elysées, the Mac-Mahon was a small one-screen cinema that had originally been built in 1938. Requisitioned by German soldiers during the Occupation, it was regularly attended by US troops after the war. The programming of the cinema was highly significant. Its owner, Emile Villion, had decided to show American wartime films in their original English-language version. In the context of intense excitement about Hollywood cinema, the Mac-Mahon thus started to attract Parisian cinephiles shuttling between the Cinémathèque situated on avenue de Messine in the 8th *arrondissement*,[20] the Studio Parnasse on the Left Bank and the first-run film theatres of the Champs-Elysées. In the mid-1950s, a small group of cinephiles from the nearby Lycée Carnot, Pierre Rissient, Michel Fabre and Michel Mourlet, eventually convinced Villion that they be put in charge of programming. Initially concentrating on a handful of Hollywood directors such as Fritz Lang and Joseph Losey, this group of critics began to spread its influence wider in 1960 when the Mac-Mahon was turned into a first-run theatre. At the end of same year, the Cercle du Mac-Mahon *ciné-club* was founded under the chairmanship of director Joseph Losey. Four large black-and-white photographic portraits of Joseph Losey,

Fritz Lang, Otto Preminger and Raoul Walsh featured in the lobby of the basement projection hall: 'Losey, Lang, Preminger, Walsh, the four aces of the Mac Mahon'.[21] In the meantime, the 'Mac-Mahon school' was allowed a platform in *Cahiers du cinéma*. They set themselves apart from other *Cahiers* critics through their preference for Walsh and Preminger rather than Hitchcock and Hawks and by their ultra-formalist attachment to *mise-en-scène*. The absolute primacy of form was theorised with a manifesto published in 1959 in the journal. Signed by Michel Mourlet, it was framed by a statement in italics by the editor, Eric Rohmer, making it clear that although the views expressed were not entirely shared by the journal, he wished to offer it to readers 'without further comment'. This manifesto can now be regarded as the precise moment at which the formalist, modernist and masculine strands of cinephilia reached their peak:

> The curtain opens. The house goes dark. A rectangle of light presently vibrates before our eyes. Soon it is invaded by gestures and sound. Here we are absorbed by that unreal space and time. More or less absorbed. The mysterious energy that sustains with varying felicities the swirl of shadow and light and its foam of sound is called *mise-en-scène*. It is through *mise-en-scène* that our attention is set, organising a universe, covering the screen – *mise-en-scène* and nothing else [...] The arrangement of actors and objects, their placement within the frame, this must express everything, as we can see in the supreme perfection of Fritz Lang's two latest films, *The Bengal Tiger and The Indian Tomb*.[22]

The Mac-Mahoniens' theory of cinema that exalted *mise-en-scène* was founded on the valorisation of a taste for film as the art of fascination, an aesthetic posture through which this elite group of cinephiles affirmed its distinction and its difference. This radical formalism was linked to Catholicism through the figure of André Bazin and to the counter-culture of the literary Right made up of the group of writers dubbed the 'Hussards'.[23] This group that included Roger Nimier, Jacques Laurent, Antoine Blondin and Michel Déon differentiated themselves from the dominant Left by rejecting the idea of social and political commitment and by professing a sense of disengagement and art for art's sake. In the post-war intellectual context, this was tantamount 'to a declaration of right-wing affiliation'.[24]

This retreat into the confining realm of the aesthetic must also be understood in the context of the cultural changes brought about by rapid technocratic modernisation, the gender politics inaugurated by Simone de Beauvoir with the publication of *The Second Sex* in 1949 and the Right–Left split with the onset of the Cold War and decolonisation. In cinephile culture, these splits were played out on the terrain of form versus content, the aesthetic versus the political. The ideological debate over Hollywood was particularly intense. Beyond this radical posturing, the fetishisation of *mise-en-scène* can also be regarded as a defensive reaction against the hegemony of committed approaches to film, particularly those of Marxist film critics such as Georges Sadoul in the prestigious weekly *Les Lettres françaises*, the neo-surrealists at *Positif*, and the film journals *La Méthode*, *Miroir du cinéma*, *Cinéma* and *Image et son* united by their anti-colonialist articles on the worsening situation in Algeria.[25]

The critical strategy adopted by the proponents of *mise-en-scène* introduced a radical formalism built upon a highly exclusive counter-canon that exalted the genius of a select group of directors. It conceptualised cinema in terms of its interest in beautiful and violent bodies and dismissed as irrelevant films that didn't 'aim for this sublime' and which were 'content with posing sordid problems'.[26] In the name of these principles, Michel Mourlet's manifesto paved the way to a reversal of accepted hierarchies of taste as well as a radical overthrow of the *Cahiers du cinéma* pantheon. Cecil B. DeMille was superior to Alfred Hitchcock, while Orson Welles, one of André Bazin's favourite directors, was deemed another bête noire whose 'aggressive modernism and gratuitous originality conceals an expressionism that is a quarter of a century old'.[27]

At the heart of Mourlet's theory of film was the notion of the spectator being linked to the world of the film in a form of exalted fascination elicited by a classical continuity editing style unhindered by unusual or showy camera angles, framing or montage. Since cinema was the art of physical relationships between actors and setting, it was

> a gaze which is substituted for our own in order to give us a world that corresponds to our desires, it settles on faces, on radiant or bruised but always beautiful bodies, on this glory or this devastation which testifies to the same primordial nobility, on this chosen race that we recognise as our own, the ultimate projection of life towards God.[28]

While the *politique des auteurs* for *Cahiers* was tied to a certain moral vision (for instance, the idea of the transference of guilt in Alfred Hitchcock) and a conception of cinema as a religious narrative of the real,[29] it was linked for the Mac-Mahon school to a cinematic aesthetic consisting of the director 'stripping the spectator of any conscious distance to precipitate him in a state of hypnosis sustained by an incantation of gestures, looks, tiny movements of the face and the body and vocal inflexions'.[30] Hence the idea that *mise-en-scène* should be invisible. While this followed Bazin's analysis of cinema as the art of recording reality to the letter, Mourlet's axiomatic argument that *mise-en-scène* is the very building block of film was also predicated on a extreme experience of the cinema where 'the absorption of consciousness within the spectacle is called fascination: the impossibility to detach oneself from images'.[31]

In September 1960, the entire issue of *Cahiers du cinéma* was devoted to Mac-Mahon fetish auteur Joseph Losey, a moment which marked the peak and the end point of the controversial influence of the Mac-Mahon school. According to Antoine de Baecque and Noël Herpe, this episode led to a crisis at *Cahiers du cinéma* and the replacement of Eric Rohmer, who was blamed for the ideological slip-up of having sympathy for the reactionary dogmatic tenets of the Mac-Mahoniens.[32] The writers of the Mac-Mahon group thus moved elsewhere. In 1961, Michel Mourlet became editor with Jacques Lourcelles of *Présence du cinéma*. The Mac-Mahon pantheon was furthered enshrined with special issues dedicated to the 'Four Aces' noted above and a select – albeit eclectic – group of directors representing the 'purity of *mise-en-scène*': Vittorio Cottafavi, Don Weiss, Blake Edwards, Riccardo Freda, Raoul Walsh, Joseph L. Mankiewicz, Samuel Fuller, John Ford, Allan Dwan, Jacques Tourneur and Cecil B. DeMille. The journal folded in 1967.

Behind this disparate list of directors was an oppositional programme: *Présence du cinéma* stood against both Italian neo-realism, which had been lionised by left-wing critics and André Bazin, and modern European art cinema. It denigrated 'those intellectuals without taste, without judgement and genius that populate coffee shops, film journals and certain *ciné-clubs*, drunk on culture and politics' and complained that 'after Fellini, after Bergman, now it is Antonioni and Resnais that we have to suffer'.[33] *Présence du cinéma* championed the spectacular neo-mythological B-movies[34] of Ricardo Freda and Vittorio Cottafavi that had been discovered in local fleapits between 'Belleville and la Porte Saint-Martin'.[35] Cottafavi offered a radical aesthetic of libidinal fascination where the spectator's attention was fixed 'on the passage between the calm and the storm'. Comparing the *mise-en-scène* of these films to the *mise-en-scène* of the 17th-century French dramatist Racine, Mourlet argued that classical tragedy informed the way they were organised 'around love, secret passion-ripping, [and] certain female faces in a world of princes'.[36] Riccardo Freda, on the other hand, was 'a man alone' amid Italian cinema's neo-realist moment, a director lauded for a *mise-en-scène* where 'once decor is seen to logically include the actions that take place within it, everything will be said and known and the rest, themes, psychology, moral judgement, become pointless'.[37] French cinema and especially the New Wave were violently rejected, offering a catalyst for more politically motivated formalist arguments.[38] Despite such extreme views that went against the critical consensus of the time, the Mac-Mahoniens exerted an enormous influence beyond film fanatics. Joseph Losey, for instance, has frequently acknowledged how the Parisian release of *Time without Pity* in June 1960 by the group affiliated with the Mac-Mahon 'was a turning point' in a career he owed 'to the Mac-Mahon'.[39]

Jean-Luc Godard's *A bout de souffle/Breathless* (1960) remains a homage to the aesthetics of the Mac-Mahon. There is the physical presence of the Mac-Mahon itself when Patricia (Jean Seberg) ducks into the cinema to escape the police and we then hear dialogue from Otto Preminger's *Whirlpool* (1949). There is, too, the participation of Pierre Rissient as co-director (he was also assistant director to Claude Chabrol on *Les Cousins* [1959]) and there are numerous uncredited appearances by famed Mac-Mahoniens: Michel Mourlet as the studio photographer, Michel Fabre, who plays one of the two detectives pursuing Michel Poiccard (Jean-Paul Belmondo); Jacques Serguine, who is one of the spectators at the Mac-Mahon; and the owner of the Mac-Mahon himself, Emile Villion, who appears outside the cinema with the cashier. Godard's closeness to Mourlet and the Mac-Mahoniens is illustrated further by *Le Mépris/Contempt* (1963). In a piece written in 2011, 'L'Affaire Godard-Bazin', Mourlet specifically points out that Godard's famous spoken epigraph which begins the film –'"cinema", said André Bazin, "substitutes for our gaze a world more in harmony with our desires"' – was, as already seen, actually taken from his 1959 article 'Sur un art ignoré' published in *Cahiers du cinéma*.[40] The looming presence of Fritz Lang in this film also points to the Mac-Mahon cult of Lang against Hitchcock and specifically to *Moonfleet* (1955), released exclusively at the Mac-Mahon in March 1960, when MGM refused to distribute it in Paris.[41] *Moonfleet* was a core film of this strand of cinephilia, most crucially for Serge Daney, who joined *Cahiers du cinéma* in the mid-1960s.[42] Finally, the continuing influence of

The cover of Michel Mourlet's 2008 Ramsay edition of *Sur un art ignoré*, featuring the 'four aces' of the Mac-Mahon: (clockwise from top left) Fritz Lang, Otto Preminger, Joseph Losey, Raoul Walsh.

this key moment in the history of cinephilia figures in the revisionist portrayal of its political background in *Liberty Belle*, directed in 1983 by the former *Cahiers du cinéma* critic Pascal Kané. Set in early 1960s Paris during the intensification of the Franco-Algerian war, the conflict between proponents of Algerian independence and those against is played out on the terrain of cinephilia and the symbolic critical split between the 'Hitchcocko-Hawksiens' and the 'Mac-Mahoniens'. Julien (Jérôme Zucca) and Gilles (Philippe Caroit) are two young students from the Lycée Chaptal, on the boulevard des Batignolles, whose friendship is challenged by their divergent cinematic tastes and political inclinations. Julien is a *Cahiers du cinéma* reader who admires Fellini, Bergman and Antonioni; Gilles reads *Présence du cinéma* and 'would give up all of Antonioni for a single shot in Walsh'. While Gilles is actively involved with the right-wing OAS (Organisation Armée Secrète, the paramilitary organisation against Algerian independence), Julien will end up as a courier for the FLN (Algerian Liberation Front).

Today, cinephilia has shifted with the normalisation of the internet and now the passionate love of film takes many different forms, tastes and practices.[43] Yet, Paris is still famous as the capital city offering the widest range of different films to watch in the world. When Emile Villion died in 1968, the Mac-Mahon was eventually taken over by Alex Brucker, who, 'content to "lose money with Lubitsch" initially followed a programming philosophy that would be "*le pur et dur*, almost flagellatory"', though he would 'gradually shift his principles by linking treasures from the classical era with more recent fare'.[44] Since ownership transferred to Vincent Bolloré's holding group in 2000, this eclectic range of programming has increased, combining retrospectives of Hollywood classics with contemporary releases and special previews, film festivals and renting the venue for private screenings, debates and receptions.[45] In 2000, the Mac-Mahon was entirely renovated, thus preserving its 'Broadway style' art deco façade, as well as its small lobby and original 1940s ticket booth. As Danny Fairfaix points out, 'the aura of a bygone epoch continues when the spectator enters the cinema's single *salle*, with its 150 red velvet seats, gilded fittings and starry blue cupola overhead'.[46] In a time of multiplex cinemas, this antiquated interior design framed by two Roman statues helps to foster a close proximity between both spectators and the screen, and projects one back to a cinephile past. As I recently took my seat for the screening of a 35 mm print of *Notorious* (Alfred Hitchcock, 1946) in the intimate surroundings of the Mac-Mahon's darkened auditorium and the credits started to roll, I was immediately immersed in the images projected before me; no advertising, no fancy trailer; 'cinema, alone'[47] as the film unfolded. In this sense, the Mac-Mahon still stands as a space of cultural remembrance, a site charged with a past. It will be forever linked to the ritual of filmgoing and the experience of a certain kind of filmmaking as well as the home of the cinephile spectator, if no longer that of a coterie of film critics. In other words, the Mac-Mahon remains both a symbolic and physical embodiment of the enduring presence of cinema in the historical memory of the city and a monument to the unique and enduring relationship between Paris and cinephilia.

I would like to thank the head of programming, Bruno Vincent, for both his warm welcome during my visit and for kindly providing the photograph of the cinema that illustrates this chapter.

A 2015 screening of *Moonfleet* (Fritz Lang, 1955) at the Mac-Mahon.

Notes

1. Noël Burch, 'Cinéphilie et masculinité (I)', *Iris*, no. 26 (Autumn 1998), pp. 191–6 and Geneviève Sellier, 'Cinéphilie et masculinité (II)', *Iris*, no. 26 (Autumn 1998), pp. 197–206.
2. Pierre Bourdieu, *Distinction: A Social Critique of the Judgment of Taste* (London: Routledge & Kegan Paul, 1984).
3. Pierre Nora, *Realms of Memory: The Construction of the French Past*, three volumes (New York: Columbia University Press, 1996–98).
4. Laura Mulvey, 'Some Reflections on the Cinephilia Question', *Framework. The Journal of Cinema and Media*, vol. 50, nos. 1 and 2 (Spring and Autumn 2009), p. 190.
5. Antoine de Baecque, *La Cinéphilie. Invention d'un regard, histoire d'une culture, 1944–1968* (Paris: Fayard, 2003), p. 23.
6. See, for instance, Richard Roud, *A Passion for Film: Henri Langlois and the Cinémathèque Française* (London: Secker & Warburg, 1983); Pierre Barbin, *La Cinémathèque française: inventaire et légendes, 1936–1986* (Paris: Vuibert, 2005).
7. See Christophe Gauthier, *La Passion du cinéma. Cinéphiles, ciné-clubs et salles spécialisées à Paris de 1920 à 1929* (Paris: AFRHC/Ecole de Chartres, 1999).
8. According to Louis Delluc, the camera and the screen transformed the 'real', revealing something beyond appearances: 'the miracle of the cinema is that it stylizes without altering the plain truth', while for Jean Epstein, this ineffable quality of the moving image, *photogénie*, was impossible to pin down: 'one runs into a brick wall trying to define it'. See Richard Abel, *French Film Theory and Criticism, 1907–1939, Volume I: 1907–1929* (Princeton, NJ: Princeton University Press, 1988), pp. 110, 243.
9. Ibid., p. 103.
10. Paula Amad, '"Objects Become Witnesses": Eve Francis and the Emergence of French Cinephilia and Criticism', *Framework. The Journal of Cinema and Media*, vol. 46, no. 1 (Spring 2005), pp. 56–73.
11. Founded by Jean Curtelin and Michel Parsy in 1959.
12. Roland Barthes, 'Leaving the Movie Theatre', in *The Rustle of Language*, trans. Richard Howard (New York: Hill and Wang, 1986), pp. 345–6.
13. Paul Willemen, *Looks and Frictions: Essays in Cultural Studies and Film Theory* (Bloomington: Indiana University Press, 1994), p. 236.
14. Gauthier, *La Passion du cinéma*, p. 249.
15. Ibid., p. 263.
16. Rosemary Wakeman, *The Heroic City: Paris 1945–1958* (Chicago, IL, and London: University of Chicago Press, 2009), p. 204; Virginie Champion, Bertrand Lemoine and Claude Terraux, *Les Cinémas de Paris, 1945–1995* (Paris: Délégation à l'action artistique de la ville de Paris, 1995), p. 29.
17. Jeander, 'Les Ciné-clubs', in Denis Marion (ed.), *Le Cinéma par ceux qui le font* (Paris: Fayard, 1949), p. 392.
18. Christian-Marc Bosséno, *La Prochaine Séance. Les français et leurs cinés* (Paris: Gallimard, 1996), pp. 19–20.
19. In Richard Neupert, *A History of French New Wave Cinema* (Madison: University of Wisconsin Press, 2002), p. 11.

20. The Cinémathèque has travelled widely across Paris. It was located at 7 avenue de Messine (8th *arrondissement*) from 1948 to 1955, when it moved to 29 rue d'Ulm in the 5th *arrondissement*. It moved again in 1963 to the Palais de Chaillot, place du Trocadéro (16th *arrondissement*), and finally in 1998 to 51 rue de Bercy in the 12th *arrondissement*.
21. Jacques Serguine, 'Education du spectateur ou l'école du Mac Mahon', *Cahiers du cinéma*, no. 111 (September 1960), p. 44.
22. Michel Mourlet, 'Sur un art ignoré', *Cahiers du cinéma*, no. 98 (August 1959), p. 27.
23. The name of this group, originating from Roger Nimier's novel *Le Hussard bleu/ The Blue Hussar* was coined by the literary critic Bernard Frank in an article published in 1952 in *Les Temps modernes*.
24. Antoine de Baecque, *Camera Historica. The Century in Cinema*, trans. Ninon Vinsonneau and Jonathan Magidoff (New York: Columbia University Press, 2012), p. 112.
25. On the Algerian War in French film journals, see Sébastien Denis, 'Les Revues françaises de cinéma face à la guerre d'Algérie', *1895*, no. 42 (2004), pp. 35–56.
26. Mourlet, 'Sur un art ignoré', p. 30.
27. Ibid., p. 33.
28. Ibid., p. 34.
29. de Baecque, *La Cinéphilie*, p. 118.
30. Mourlet, 'Sur un art ignoré', p. 30.
31. Ibid., p. 31.
32. Antoine de Baecque and Noël Herpe, *Eric Rohmer* (Paris: Stock, 2014), p. 148.
33. Michel Mourlet, 'Du côté de Racine', *Présence du cinéma*, no. 9 (December 1961), p. 29.
34. Richard Dyer argues that the heroic masculinity of the peplum invokes colonial and fascist subtexts and a reactionary patriarchal status quo. See Richard Dyer, 'The White Man's Muscles', in *White* (London and New York: Routledge, 1997), pp. 145–83.
35. Michel Mourlet, 'Prélude à Cottafavi', *Cahiers du cinéma*, no. 99 (September 1959), p. 62. The first occurrence of the term 'peplum', according to Claude Aziza, was in the cinephile circle of Bertrand Tavernier's Nickel Odéon *ciné-club* who looked for B-movies in the Grands Boulevards cinemas. See Claude Aziza, 'Le Mot et la chose', *CinémAction*, no. 89 (1998), p. 10.
36. Mourlet, 'Du côté de Racine', pp. 29–32.
37. Jacques Lourcelles, 'Un homme seul', *Présence du cinéma*, no. 17 (November 1963), p.6.
38. Jean Curtelin, 'Sergent Croft, petit frère', *Présence du cinéma*, no. 13 (May 1962), p. 17.
39. Joseph Losey in Michel Ciment, *Le Livre de Losey* (Paris: Editions Stock, 1979), pp. 179–80.
40. 'L'Affaire Godard-Bazin', in Michel Mourlet, *L'Ecran éblouissant. Voyages en Cinéphilie 1958–2010* (Paris: Presses Universitaires de France, 2011), pp. 201–5.
41. Jacques Lourcelles, *Dictionnaire du cinéma. Les films* (Paris: Editions Robert Laffont, 1992), p. 986.
42. The title of Daney's *L'Exercise a été profitable, Monsieur* (Paris: P.O.L, 1993) is taken from a line of dialogue in the film. See *Persévérance* (Paris: P.O.L, 1994), p. 61.
43. See Laurent Jullier and Jean-Marc Leveratto, 'Cinephila in the Digital Age', in Ian Christie (ed.), *Audiences: Defining and Researching Screen Entertainment Reception* (Amsterdam: Amsterdam University Press, 2012), pp. 143–54.

44. Daniel Fairfax, 'Le Mac Mahon', in Jean-Michel Frodon and Dina Iordanova (eds), *Cinemas of Paris* (St Andrews: St Andrews Film Studies, 2016), pp. 330–1.
45. www.cinemamacmahon.com (accessed 8 April 2016).
46. Fairfax, 'Le Mac Mahon', p. 331.
47. 'In relation to the "cinema, alone", it is therefore at the very time when its uniqueness began to disappear that the consciousness and love of cinema were first forged', Raymond Bellour, '"Cinema, Alone"/Multiple "Cinemas"', trans. Jill Murphy in *Alphaville: Journal of Film and Screen Media*, no. 5 (2013). Available online: www.alphavillejournal.com/Issue5/HTML/ArticleBellour.html (accessed 3 September 2015).

Beyond the *Flâneuse*: The Uniqueness of *Cléo de 5 à 7*

Jennifer Wallace

Agnès Varda's New Wave film *Cléo de 5 à 7/Cleo from 5 to 7* (1962) tells the story of 90 minutes in the life of a Parisian pop singer, Cléo (Corinne Marchand), who is anxiously awaiting the results of a medical test on the longest day of the year. In the process, she moves through various parts of the city, using different forms of transportation. Contemporary critics praised Varda for deftly intertwining a fictional narrative within a documentary-style depiction of a recognisable Paris,[1] but it is only more recently that the film's status has risen, with two English-language monographs on the subject, and it has become a popular choice for analysis in areas such as feminist film studies, *auteur* cinema and cinema and the city. One of the most prevalent references in writings on the film is the figure of the *flâneuse*. Sandy Flitterman-Lewis, Janice Mouton, Valerie Orpen, Steven Ungar and Mark Betz have all discussed Cléo as the embodiment of a New Wave *flâneuse*, with each writer attributing various components of *flânerie* to her character according to their own interpretations. My aim in this chapter is to challenge the default labelling of Cléo as *flâneuse*. I believe that the film demonstrates such a rich and varied range of travelling around the city that to continuously refer to the term *flânerie* is to misrepresent the complexity of Cléo's journey and her transformation as a character. I also wish to establish the uniqueness of *Cléo de 5 à 7* in its treatment of the central female character in comparison to other contemporary examples. As I will illustrate, the film highlights a positive transformation for a woman in the city – something that is rarely seen in both New Wave and popular cinema of the early 1960s.

In her seminal work on Varda, Flitterman-Lewis compares Cléo to a 'Baudelairean *flâneur*' as she 'glides' through the Dôme café, overhearing snatches of conversation related to art and politics from other patrons around her.[2] Mouton argues that Cléo manages to break the cycle of objectification in becoming a *flâneuse* who does not fall into the same trap of objectification as a *flâneur*. She is not trying to possess the city or its people, she is responding to it as an observer for the first time.[3] Orpen is the author who most successfully problematises Cléo as a *flâneuse* in her monograph on the film; however, she remains persuaded that Cléo moves towards *flânerie* in the latter half of the film because she believes that Varda is consistently aware of 'Paris as the locus of modernity'[4] and because Cléo's outfit change into a black dress and sunglasses is reminiscent of the *flâneur* blending in.[5] Ungar sees *Cléo de 5 à 7* as the first treatment of the urban female walker,[6] and finally Betz applies a racial reading to the film in arguing that the image of the *flâneuse* in New Wave cinema is linked to 1960s colonial discourse.[7]

What many of these writers are engaging with is the historicised, 19th-century imagining of the *flâneur* and its more recent feminist revision, the *flâneuse*. In terms of the latter, the work of Elizabeth Wilson,[8] Anne Friedberg[9] and Giuliana Bruno[10] has been vital. They have taken the masculine attributes of the *flâneur* figure and explored spaces for his feminine counterpart that includes the figure of the prostitute, the shopper, the fairground visitor and even the cinemagoer. Whilst their arguments have been important and persuasive, they are grounded in the culture of the 19th century, and the term always entails some form of consumerism: the *flâneuse* as either a buyer or a seller of a specific commodity. There is also the continual threat of sexualisation by the male gaze: from the explicit dangers of prostitutes walking streets alone at night, to the prevailing social norm that a department store was one of the only places women of a certain class could be publicly seen without tarnishing their reputation. As Wilson has argued, a woman on the street in the 19th century carried with her a set of deeply embedded social codes relating to her class and gender:[11] it was not easy to be a *flâneuse*.

As I aim to prove, Cléo, being a woman of 1962, only briefly a shopper and not a prostitute, must be seen outside the restrictive parameters of the *flâneuse*. I will focus on Cléo's movement around the city in the second half of the film, demonstrating that it is not simply a synonym for *flânerie*, and examining how it authenticates Cléo's character as an urban woman who is developing a new subjectivity intertwined with a growing interest in the city. By also contextualising the film within other contemporary examples, I especially hope to reveal a hitherto unexplored uniqueness in Varda's representation of an urban woman that requires a form of analysis that departs significantly from the concept of *flânerie*.

On Foot

Cléo's first action upon leaving her apartment is to walk. Michel de Certeau writes of footsteps that: 'Their intertwined paths give their shape to spaces. They weave places together. In that respect, pedestrian movements form one of these "real systems whose existence in fact makes up the city."'[12] This quote suggests the possibility of Cléo's reciprocal interaction with Paris, and that her walk can 'make up the city'. Her first walk takes her from her home on rue Huyghens in the 14th *arrondissement* to the nearby Dôme café on the corner of boulevard Montparnasse. The journey lasts 1 minute and 45 seconds and includes a 30-second sequence of a street performer, swallowing frogs. The close-ups on the man's face are reminiscent of Varda's style of filming the residents of rue Mouffetard in the 5th *arrondissement* in *L'Opéra-Mouffe/Diary of a Pregnant Woman* (1958), and their inclusion is relevant to both a physical representation of Cléo's worry and disgust over her hidden illness, and also to Varda's taste for filming eccentric and unusual performances around the city.

Whilst in the Dôme café, Cléo overhears her friend Dorothée's name mentioned and she walks to the Académie de Sculpture, close by, across boulevard Edgar Quinet where Dorothée (Dorothée Blanck) works as an artists' model. This sequence is almost identical in length to the earlier walk and it features another grotesque spectacle of a man piercing his arm, and yet it differs in its formal qualities. In the first walking sequence, the camera depicted Cléo in the centre of the cityscape, and with smooth pans we followed her gaze onto people and signs. In this sequence, we see Cléo's subjective point of view mixed with both over-the-shoulder and frontal shots. It also contains flashbacks to encounters with other characters during the first 45 minutes of the film, but in poses that have not been seen before.

The effect is described by Mouton as a 'mental movie theatre':[13] visual representations of thought patterns (linked both thematically and formally), which constitute a mixture of Cléo's past and present self. It functions as the next step in this reciprocal interaction between character and location. Flitterman-Lewis describes it as a 'pivotal' moment for a 'meditation on vision, femininity and culture'.[14] The emotional weight of the sequence is still related to anguish and stress (with rapid cuts heightening the tension), but looking at others in the city has forced her to reflect upon the negative influence those close to her have upon her life. As she walks, men and women turn to look at her (and presumably the camera), but crucially they pose no threat, and she continues unimpeded, with the exception of a long funeral procession in her path (the boulevard leading to the Montparnasse cemetery). Her anguish is caused by internal conflict, not by the external city: the threatening gazes that confronted the historical figure of the *flâneuse* are not present in this sequence.

By Car

After Cléo meets Dorothée, whom we see posing naked at the Académie de Sculpture, the two women travel by car from the boulevard Edgar Quinet to a cinema on rue Delambre, only round the corner but with a brief stop outside Montparnasse station. The sequence is 5 minutes long and begins in a small side street. The image is a high-angle long shot as Dorothée's car begins to move down the rue du Départ (mentioned by name in the dialogue). It becomes clear that filming takes places on a parallel street which then joins the main road, along which the camera tracks the car journey for 53 seconds. To film this sequence, Varda must have been in another vehicle moving alongside the two women, as exemplified in Fig. 1, where we see Dorothée and Cléo turning onto the busy boulevard Edgar Quinet, laughing together whilst signalling with their arms. As has been widely documented, New Wave films deliberately avoided rear projection for vehicle sequences and found innovative ways to film in, on and around the car.[15] In total there are four different methods of filming the car throughout the sequence, which combine images of the women within the urban location, and glimpses of their own perspectives on the city too. Throughout the car sequence, Varda remains topographically exact.

After Dorothée has parked the car in front of Montparnasse station and Cléo is left alone, there is a montage of ten 'documentary' shots that show people arriving and leaving the station. The subjects filmed by Varda include nuns, sailors, babies and elderly men and women – and some notice the camera, whilst others remain unaware. This is again reminiscent of *L'Opéra-Mouffe*, and her later film *Daguerréotypes* (1975), which explores shopkeepers on the rue Daguerre, who first arrived in Paris via Montparnasse station. The sequence demonstrates that Cléo is learning to look, and it is also distinctly 'of its time'. The shots of sailors arriving and departing at the station remind the viewer of Montparnasse's link to the Breton coast, and seeing them (and nuns) around the

Cléo (Corinne Marchand, left) and Dorothée (Dorothée Blanck) signal to turn right onto the boulevard Edgar Quinet in *Cléo de 5 à 7/Cleo from 5 to 7* (Agnès Varda, 1962).

station would be a rare sight today. The specificity of these people anchors the film in the early 1960s, and the sequence serves as a precious archive, as the old station was bulldozed and the area entirely reconstructed later in the decade around the Montparnasse tower.

The conversation between the two women is an important aspect that makes this sequence unique. Whilst together in the car, they discuss their friendship over the years, Cléo's illness, her relationship with her lover, and it is Dorothée who encourages Cléo to look around her ('count the sailors' pom-poms!'). *Flânerie* is nearly always evoked as a solitary endeavour, and relationships between women are not examined in the literature on the *flâneuse*. So the very fact that these two women are travelling together shifts the analysis of Cléo's movements away from *flânerie* and into a shared experience that will be crucial for her transformation. This scene is comparable to a sequence in the first half of the film involving Cléo, her assistant Angèle (Dominique Davray) and a female taxi driver. There too, the narrative privileged female camaraderie, but Cléo had yet to undergo her transformation from spoiled pop star to awakened woman, and the conversation was not as intimate as it is here. The sequence also highlights a moment of female intimacy and places it within the area around Montparnasse station, and on a wider scale, Paris. Yvette Bíró and Catherine Portuges describe the effect of Cléo's personal journey continually being portrayed as part of a whole: 'Varda manages to suggest the infinite, the inconceivable richness of simultaneous events, the dizzying heterogeneity of things'.[16] This is not a conversation that is occurring in a vacuum – Cléo and Dorothée drive around a specific part of the city and thus become inhabitants of the landscape just like the other commuters in cars, buses and on foot around them. Furthermore, Varda is interested in more than just the stories of her protagonists. The dialogue we hear may give precedence to their important conversation (amplified in post-production), but it is heard alongside a soundtrack of growling engines and honking horns. An area such as Montparnasse station would have been congested and noisy, even in the early 1960s, and therefore this unpolished aesthetic that we now view as inherently New Wave is used to 'authenticate' the intertwined relationship of the narrative and the location. Jean Douchet describes this tendency (using *Cléo de 5 à 7* as an example) as 'extraordinary stories in ordinary locations'.[17]

By Taxi

After watching a short film at the cinema (*Les Fiancés du pont MacDonald* – a comedic homage to New Wave cinephilia), Cléo and Dorothée take a taxi from outside the Dôme café. The start of their journey in the car was marked by a high-angle long shot, and the beginning of this new journey is similar, although the angle of filming is straight on, and it contains the added detail of the precise month in which Varda is filming (June 1961) on a poster on the left-hand side of the frame.

This 3-minute taxi sequence continues to build upon the relationship of intimacy between the two women whilst privileging Cléo's gaze with more and more frequency. The camera frames Dorothée and Cléo in a medium close-up for much of their initial discussion, and we see both women's points of view when there are cuts to shots looking out of the taxi windows. It is also here that Cléo offers her fur hat to Dorothée, a symbolic moment of selflessness that shows Cléo leaving her 'caprices' behind, and cements the friendship between the two women. Just before Dorothée departs, the taxi circles around the place Denfert-Rochereau. The Lion of Belfort statue is glimpsed from the back seat (presumably from Cléo's perspective), and anchors the film once more in an identifiable and specific location. In 2003, this statue will be the star of Varda's short film *Le Lion volatil*.

Cléo is left alone in the taxi once Dorothée leaves. After 35 seconds, the taxi enters the parc Montsouris (still in the 14th *arrondissement*, but on the southern edge of the city), and the first image we see is of benches, trees and an observatory that was destroyed by a fire in 1991. In the bright summer sunshine, the park inspires connotations of nature and tranquillity. This sequence acts as a counterpoint to that of the taxi ride in the first half of the film from the rue de Rivoli to Cléo's home. That previous journey had been heavy with symbolic references to her anguish (African masks, rioting students, news about Algeria on the radio), whereas despite her continuing fear of her illness, the images she sees now are more soothing, although she is once more travelling alone. Cléo is apparently unfamiliar with the park, and yet she is willing to explore it. Each journey sequence so far has taken her somewhere important for her personal growth, and now she arrives at the park, where she will meet Antoine (Antoine Bourseiller), an erudite character who accompanies her on her final journey by bus to the hospital.

By Bus

As Sandy Flitterman-Lewis deftly analyses, Varda grants Cléo autonomy and subjectivity in the latter half of the film through both the narrative and the filmic form.[18] However, despite Cléo's growing agency and mobility in the city, Varda acknowledges that a woman alone in the park will almost inevitably be subjected to an approach by a *dragueur* (flirt): an aspect that does echo the more sexualised character traits of the *flâneuse*. When Antoine, a soldier on leave from Algeria, approaches Cléo in a pleasant, but nevertheless rather presumptuous way, he soon asks her if she is married, to which she replies, 'Why, do I look like a woman on the prowl?' However, he is not portrayed as a misogynistic seducer such as the likes of Jacques Charrier in *Les Dragueurs/The Chasers* (Jean-Pierre Mocky, 1959), and despite Cleo's initial hesitation to engage in conversation with a stranger, he soon wins her over with his gregarious and intelligent chatter. Antoine therefore is not shown to be a threatening or oppressive presence in Cléo's journey around the park, and he offers to escort her to the hospital for her results, via public transport, when he realises the depth of her anxiety.

The bus sequence is 6 minutes long, and the journey covers a distance of 2.7 kilometres from the rue Liard next to the parc Montsouris to the St Marcel Métro station outside the Pitié-Salpêtrière hospital. They take bus number 67, a line that still runs today from Stade Charlety in the south of the city to Pigalle in the north. Interestingly, despite the emphasis on Cléo's transformation in the final sequences of the film, her point of view is not privileged from within the bus. Many shots look out of the window onto the street, but the camera always returns via a pan to a central framing of the couple. One such instance is a 13-second shot of a premature baby in a glass incubator, which moves out of sight as the camera pans from right to left to return to Cléo and Antoine on the bus, with their backs to the camera. Although from the direction they are facing it appears they had been looking at the scene, it was in fact shot from neither Cléo nor Antoine's point of view; instead, the camera is deliberately observing them as they look out onto the city. The dialogue overheard as the camera pans is that of two unseen female passengers, who discuss their own premature children. There is no record of this sequence being staged. The baby is real (it moves inside the incubator) and it appears to be a chance occurrence that Varda captured. The layering of the dialogue over the image succeeds in relating the 'happy accident' to that of Cléo's own troubled thoughts of mortality: birth, death and motherhood are interconnected in the city, just as they were in *L'Opéra-Mouffe*. The city is reflecting Cléo's subjectivity, and she is now even more regularly framed by the camera as looking out onto its streets.

Throughout the entire bus journey there are consistent reminders of Parisian geography. François Penz praises this film's topographical precision as 'the yardstick against which all other films must be measured'.[19] The combination of recognisable landmarks throughout the journey across a section of the 13th *arrondissement* (the Rungis roundabout, the Butte aux Cailles swimming pool and place d'Italie) and the ticket inspector calling out place names locate the shooting precisely in this *quartier*. The fact that the most consistent shots in the sequence are of Cléo and Antoine framed together as the landscape passes by outside the window reiterates the anchoring of the fiction within the documentary and represents the visual establishment of the couple within a precise landscape. In Fig. 2, the sign for the *piscine* outside the bus window is clearly visible, with Cléo and Antoine in the foreground, facing one another in the frame.

Just as the display of intimacy between Dorothée and Cléo takes place on the move, so this is repeated in her friendly encounter with Antoine. Even when they were in the

The Butte aux Cailles swimming pool is visible in the background through the bus window, with Cléo (Corinne Marchand) and Antoine (Antoine Bourseiller) in the foreground in *Cléo de 5 à 7/Cleo from 5 to 7* (Agnès Varda, 1962).

park, they only paused briefly on a bench: they travel quite a distance in the city. Public transport marks a significant change from Cléo's usual taxi rides. It is once more a space for overlapping narratives, an efficient and safe manner for Cléo to move across the city and a place for intimacy to grow between her and Antoine. As Cléo looks out of the window and sees Parisian architecture, place names and people on the roadside, she absorbs and contemplates them. Finally, on the bus, Cléo declares: 'today everything amazes me'.

The Uniqueness of Cléo

As I hope to have demonstrated, *Cléo de 5 à 7* succeeds in representing female movement in an urban location with complexity and positivity, and this makes it strikingly unique compared to other films from the early 1960s (with one exception). The following examples exhibit many of the same traits that I explained were inherent in the discussion of female *flânerie*: they contain female characters sexualised by men and threatened by the urban location – the opposite of Cléo's experiences in the city by the end of her journey.

Paris nous appartient/Paris Belongs to Us (Jacques Rivette, 1961) offers a particularly labyrinthine view of the city. The female protagonist Anne (Betty Schneider) travels alone around the city on foot and in taxis, but it is in the pursuit of uncovering a complicated web of conspiracies, and she is consistently alienated within the urban location. On the other hand, nocturnal Paris is more glamorous for Florence (Jeanne Moreau) in *Ascenseur pour l'échafaud/Lift to the Scaffold* (Louis Malle, 1958), but her wanderings are symptomatic of her despair and (again) alienation, and her reason for walking is to pursue her missing lover. Orpen remarks how 'upbeat and therapeutic' Cléo's walk is compared to that of Florence.[20] In *Les Bonnes femmes/The Good Time Girls* (Claude Chabrol, 1960), the car is another space of seduction for men to prey on the female characters, and even when Jane (Bernadette Lafont) and Ginette (Stéphane Audran) are alone on the Métro, they do not speak to one another. The Métro is the everyday means for getting to work, a predictable step in their humdrum existence as 'working women'. Men and women die in and around cars in much of Godard's work from the 1960s, and particularly relevant for a comparison to Cléo is Nana (Anna Karina) in *Vivre sa vie/My Life to Live* (1962): a prostitute who wanders Parisian pavements and cafés looking to attract clients, and who collapses and dies next to a car after being shot.

Jean Rouch's *La Punition/The Punishment* (1962) makes for a compelling comparison to *Cléo de 5 à 7* as it also features a young woman walking around the Left Bank of Paris. Filmed in 1960, this 60-minute film follows Nadine (Nadine Ballot) as she is sent out of her *lycée* for a minor misdemeanour, and spends the day walking instead. The film oscillates between documentary and fiction (although leans more towards the former), yet despite the similar premise, *La Punition* differs in a number of ways. Firstly, Nadine is rarely alone for more than a few minutes before a male character approaches her, a trope that was deliberately repeated in her role in Rouch's episode 'Gare du Nord' for the omnibus film *Paris vu par ...*/*Six in Paris* (1965).[21] Secondly, the conversations with the first man (Jean-Claude) and the third (Jean-Marc) are heavy with innuendo. Like Antoine in *Cléo de 5 à 7*, the men are educated, but their manner of talking down to Nadine is filled with condescension, as they discuss literature, art and politics. Paul Henley argues that the film is criticising the patronising and bourgeois attitudes the male characters demonstrate towards Nadine.[22] However, I beg to differ, and argue that the superior cultural attitude adopted in the film is even more pointed than that of *Cléo de 5 à 7*, and, more importantly, Nadine's subjectivity is not privileged in the film's formal qualities. She is most frequently framed by the camera in a manner of observation, which does fit into the Cinéma Vérité style, but equally inscribes a male gaze over nearly all of the film.

In an emotional sequence in Jean Rouch and Edgar Morin's *Chronique d'un été/Chronicle of a Summer* (1961), Marceline Loridan-Ivens walks across place de la Concorde whilst revealing her past as a survivor of a concentration camp. Her story is narrated by both her own voice-over, and in real time, as she walks aimlessly across the enormous square. It is a distressing moment in the film and she is visibly shaken when talking about the death of her father in the Holocaust. As her story continues in the voice-over, the camera rapidly tracks away from her, leaving her isolated in Les Halles marketplace. Thus, in both *La Punition* and *Chronique d'un été*, despite the inclusion of walking sequences, Paris does not offer these women the same freeing possibilities as it does for Cléo. There are glimpses of female subjectivity in the films, but they come under the guise of rebuffing seduction and recalling trauma. Certainly, there is no evidence of positive transformation for the female subject in the city.

In popular cinema, there is also a tendency for either negative representations of women in the city, or highly sexualised ones. Mic (Pascale Petit), the female protagonist of *Les Tricheurs/Youthful Sinners* (Marcel Carné, 1958), dies in her car in what looks like suicide. The car is a space for solitude, and she is most frequently depicted alone at the wheel. Although there are examples of her subjectivity in the speeding sequence, she is most often in the centre of the frame, with what is clearly a rear projection behind her. Another example of rear projection occurs in *La Vérité/The Truth* (Henri-Georges Clouzot, 1960), after Dominique (Brigitte Bardot) accepts a lift home from her boss. His libidinous intentions in inviting her into his car are clear, even though she does not succumb to his seductions. However, just seeing her in the car with her boss is enough to convince her boyfriend Gilbert that she is unfaithful. Thus, the car contributes to the end of their relationship, indirectly his death and her subsequent self-destructive behaviour.

Nicoleta Bazgan remarks upon the 'photogenic quality'[23] of both star and city in her analysis of Brigitte Bardot and Paris in Michel Boisrond's *Une Parisienne* (1957). Bazgan rightly points out Brigitte Laurier's (Bardot) ability to move freely around the urban environment as a 'modern' woman, exemplified in the opening sequence of her driving alone down the Champs-Elysées, but this freedom is tied to a highly sexualised image in which Bardot's curvaceous figure is literally mapped onto the city, as illustrated by the poster and certain DVD covers.[24] Vanessa Schwartz argues that the formal qualities of this sequence predate that of New Wave cinema, as filming is taking place on the streets and in a car, not in a studio.[25] Despite Bazgan's argument for spectator and star alignment in the narrative,[26] there is little evidence of Brigitte's subjectivity, and her character is highly sexualised by nearly all the male characters. However, Bardot's star persona complicates this analysis and means that, whilst the distinction with Cléo remains, she cannot be equated with the other female characters I have mentioned above either.

Les Petits matins/Hitch-Hike (1962) directed by Jacqueline Audry, the only other major French female director of the era, offers the only challenge to the patterns just evoked. The film follows Agathe (Agathe Aems), a young woman who hitchhikes across France. In a sequence filmed in Paris, an older man (François Périer) takes her to the famous luxury restaurant Maxim's in a smart convertible. Interestingly, much of the sequence in which they drive from Maxim's to avenue Victor Hugo (in the 16th *arrondissement*) is filmed in real time with a rear-mounted camera, and there are also location shots of the car going around the Arc de Triomphe filmed from the pavement. The main use of the car space throughout the entire film is ostensibly that of seduction. However, whilst the location shooting shows adoption of New Wave techniques, Agathe successfully rebuffs even the most persistent of male characters, with her subjectivity consistently privileged in the narrative.

The moment Cléo leaves her apartment and begins to travel around the city, spaces shared with others (the car, the taxi and the bus) become spaces for intimacy and connection that explore both female and male friendship, and the growth of Cléo's subjectivity. Varda's frequent depiction of these vehicles as located within the cityscape anchors the fictional narrative in the documentary-style shooting of the city, and locates the film very much in a specific time and place. The final journey on the bus is also the pinnacle of Cléo's transformation-by-movement, as she repeatedly looks out at the city and its people. Finally, whether Cléo is on foot or in a vehicle, the city is not represented as a threatening presence: she consistently travels unimpeded and unchallenged by others. This is precisely why the film is unique. Vehicles are not stolen, women are not seduced in them, and nobody is shot or seen careening to their death. In a more general sense, the female characters I touched upon in Paris (with the notable exception of the heroine of Les Petits matins, and, to some extent, Bardot in Une Parisienne) found the city threatening, alienating, uninviting: a strong undercurrent running through all the films, alongside their lack of female subjectivity. And if they are not alienated by the city, then they are sexualised within it, either by characterisation or by other male characters. By contrast, Paris is a landscape for positive transformation in Cléo de 5 à 7, and travelling around the Left Bank alone and with others, Cléo defies the sexualised, commoditised and restrictive vision of the flâneuse, moving into spaces that encourage her transformation towards autonomy, agency and subjectivity.

Notes

1. Richard Roud, 'Cléo de 5 à 7', Sight and Sound, vol. 31, no. 3 (Summer 1962), p. 145.
2. Sandy Flitterman-Lewis, To Desire Differently: Feminism and the French Cinema (New York: Columbia University Press, 1996), p. 274.
3. Janice Mouton, 'From Feminine Masquerade to Flâneuse: Agnès Varda's Cléo in the City', Cinema Journal, vol. 40, no. 2 (Winter 2001), p. 9.
4. Valerie Orpen, Cléo de 5 à 7: (Agnès Varda, 1961) (Urbana: University of Illinois Press, 2007), p. 57.
5. Ibid., p. 75.
6. Steven Ungar, Cléo de 5 à 7 (Basingstoke and New York: Palgrave/BFI, 2008), p. 45.
7. Mark Betz, Beyond the Subtitle: Remapping European Art Cinema (Minneapolis: University of Minnesota Press, 2009), p. 139.
8. Elizabeth Wilson, 'The Invisible Flâneur', New Left Review, vol. 1, no. 191 (February 1992), pp. 90–3.
9. Anne Friedberg, Window Shopping: Cinema and the Postmodern (Berkeley: University of California Press, 1993).
10. Giuliana Bruno, Atlas of Emotion: Journeys in Art, Architecture, and Film (New York: Verso, 2002).
11. Wilson, 'The Invisible Flâneur', pp. 90–3.
12. Michel de Certeau and Steven Rendall, The Practice of Everyday Life (Berkeley: University of California Press, 1984), p. 97.
13. Mouton, 'From Feminine Masquerade to Flâneuse, p. 11.
14. Flitterman-Lewis, To Desire Differently, p. 275.
15. Michel Marie and Richard Neupert, The French New Wave: An Artistic School (Malden, MA: Blackwell Publishers, 2003), pp. 81–92. And Richard Neupert, A History of the French New Wave Cinema (Madison: University of Wisconsin Press, 2009), pp. 39–40.
16. Yvette Bíró and Catherine Portuges, 'Caryatids of Time: Temporality in the Cinema of Agnès Varda', p.16. Performing Arts Journal, vol. 19, no. 3 (1997), p. 2.
17. Jean Douchet and Cédric Anger, Nouvelle Vague (Paris: Cinémathèque française/ Hazan, 1998), p. 125.
18. Flitterman-Lewis, To Desire Differently, pp. 268–84.

19. François Penz, 'From Topographical Coherence to Creative Geography: Rohmer's *The Aviator's Wife* and Rivette's *Pont du Nord*', in Andrew Webber and Emma Wilson (eds), *Cities in Transition: The Moving Image and the Modern Metropolis* (London: Wallflower Press, 2008), p. 126.
20. Orpen, *Cléo de 5 à 7*, p. 60.
21. Robert Daudelin and Michel Patenaude, 'Michel Brault et Claude Jutra racontent Jean Rouch. Entretien', *Nouvelles Vues*, vol. 14 (Winter 2012–13). Available at: www.nouvellesvues.ulaval.ca/no-14-hiver-2012-13-nouvelle-vague-et-cinema-direct-rencontres-france-quebec-en-construction/documents/michel-brault-et-claude-jutra-racontent-jean-rouch/ (accessed 30 April 2015).
22. Paul Henley, *The Adventure of the Real: Jean Rouch and the Craft of Ethnographic Cinema* (Chicago, IL: University of Chicago Press, 2010), p. 187.
23. Nicoleta Bazgan, 'Female Bodies in Paris: Iconic Femininity and Parisian Journeys', *Studies in French Cinema*, vol. 10, no. 2 (2010), p. 99.
24. Ibid.
25. Vanessa Schwartz, 'Who Killed Brigitte Bardot? Perspectives on the New Wave at Fifty', *Cinema Journal*, vol. 49, no. 4 (Summer 2010), p. 150.
26. Bazgan, 'Female Bodies in Paris', p. 100.

Amateur Filmmakers' Paris: Home Movies at the Forum des Images

Roger Odin

Amateur filmmaking is often looked down on – this is the case with family home movies, even though most people make them – or else dismissed condescendingly as 'amateurish'. Yet such films have gradually come to be recognised as having documentary value, particularly as regards local history.[1] This process has resulted in the setting up of many specialised archives, some of them regional (in Brittany, Normandy, Savoie and Corsica, for example), and others municipal (in Nancy, Saint-Etienne and Strasbourg, among others). In Paris, that recognition came with the creation, in 1986, of the Paris Vidéothèque, which in 1998 became the Forum des Images.[2]

It is worth pausing for a moment to examine the origins of that institution. The idea for it was launched in 1980 by the poet Pierre Emmanuel, who felt it should serve two aims:

> The first will be to set up a live memory which, through the use of animated images, will show how Paris and its population have changed. It will do this not only by going back into the past, but by filming cultural, social and political events and changes in the city's structure as they take place.

The second aim was to make it possible

> to know the city as it is at a given moment in time, in its duration and as it changes, and therefore to enter into the life of its various districts and of its human groups, both associative and professional, by drawing on a wide range of documentary output as well as possible contributions by those groups as they become able to use audio-visual media as a means of informing and becoming informed.

The overall aim is in line with the democratic ideals held by Emmanuel, a left-wing Christian:

> Thus the city, captured on a daily basis by its citizens, will cease to be what it most often tends to be – a milieu that standardises and isolates – and will instead give them the impression that they are having a hand in its rich life and on-going creation. (Paris, 14 March 1983)[3]

We can see how ambitious as well as innovative the project originally was. Many of the recommendations in those guidelines have in fact been followed. One of them proposed, from the outset, that the Vidéothèque should concern itself with amateur filmmakers, on the one hand to archive the part of their output devoted to Paris, and on the other to encourage further productions through competitions and collaboration with associations. Indeed, the Vidéothèque co-produced, with the television channel La Sept, what was to be the first series of programmes (in France at least) wholly devoted to home movies: *Objectif amateur* ('The Amateur Lens', Chantal Desanges, Alain Esmery and Philippe Venault, 1990, transmitted first Thursday of each month, 8 p.m.). This was a series hosted by the popular TV presenter Pierre Tchernia, who was known as 'Television's Mr Cinema', making it hard to find a more striking token of recognition. The series consisted of 12 26-minute programmes illustrating the wealth and diversity of home movies (family films, dramas, documentaries, genre films, and so on).

Lastly, it is worth noting that the Vidéothèque has always striven to make such output available to the general public, first by installing a particularly sophisticated robot capable of delivering videocassettes for viewing on request, later by making two rooms available for consultation on computer, one of them for individual viewing, the other designed to accommodate a group or a class. Alain Esmery, who managed the home movie collection for many years, was fully aware of the fact that if such films were to mean anything to the general public, they needed to be contextualised. So each film was accompanied by very detailed notes indicating not only its technical and factual specifications (format, original medium, year of production), and information about the context of its production (by an individual or a family, in a club or association, or as part of a competition), but also information about the person or persons who made the film (who the family was, what the filmmaker did in life, what his or her social class was, what the intentions were behind the filming, and so on), as well as a list of the places in Paris shown in one way or another in the film. Today, all those details can be accessed via the Internet on the Forum's database.

I would now like to look more closely at the films in that home movie collection in an attempt to understand the relationship between amateur filmmakers and city, as well as to establish what they tell us about Paris.

Family Home Movies

The Forum contains several collections of family home movies.

The first thing that strikes one is that a large proportion of the films in the collections have nothing to do with Paris. Since most Parisians are not Paris-born, they do not film the city much: they get out their cine cameras during the holidays, when they visit the house where they were born or their family home in the provincial town or village they come from, or when they travel elsewhere. The Pigeaire collection, for example, features a day's skiing on the Mont Dore in the Auvergne and a holiday, including doing school homework, at Cournonterral (Hérault, in the south of France). The Meunier collection comprises a trip to Milly-la-Forêt (Essonne, south of Paris), holidays in the Dordogne and the Lot, as well as trips to New Caledonia and the French West Indies (Guadeloupe and Martinique).

Paris itself can be seen on the occasion of family events. Interiors are often filmed, as well as outings to try out a new bicycle, walks in the park with baby in a pram, visits to the zoo, and so on. In such cases, the filmmaker's aim is clearly not to document Paris, but to set up a family memory – as Alain Esmery remarks, even 'Marie Curie, one of France's most celebrated figures, is depicted solely as a grandmother looking after her grandchildren'.[4] From a technical point of view, the quality often leaves much to be desired (many of the images are wobbly, out of focus or incorrectly exposed).

An effort therefore needs to be made to 'wrench these images from the gangue in which they remain stuck [...] so they can produce a meaning and in the end say something about what is and about what we are,' as Georges Perec put it so beautifully when referring to *les choses communes* (everyday life).[5] Less poetically, I would say the images need to be interpreted in 'documentarising mode'.[6] They then yield a host of factual details about everyday life in Paris (about the way people dressed and ate their meals, about the decoration of their apartments, about shops and cars, and about what was going on in the streets). All that information is invaluable for sociologists, ethnologists and historians.

There are however two points that need to be kept in mind. First, the images provide us with an incomplete picture of Paris society insofar as they are filmed by wealthy people. Making home movies used to be expensive and could be afforded only by members of a certain social class: M. Malvaison was a dental surgeon, P. Meunier a civil aviation engineer, and P. Boggio head of personnel in a bank. What is more, these images show nothing but happy events. Now it is inconceivable that the families portrayed never endured tragedies – 'tragedies that take place within walls, shuttered windows and bruised hearts', as the filmmaker Olivier Smolders puts it in *Mort à Vignole/ Death in Vignole* (1998), a film that draws on his family's home movies[7] – or the natural moments of unhappiness that every family experiences (illness, death). Equally, it is somewhat surprising that the 'family = happiness' equation lingers on into the 1970s and 1980s, at a time when the image of the family and its true situation (a decrease in the number of marriages, a higher divorce rate and a rise in the number of reconstituted families) had seriously deteriorated.[8] No trace of those changes can be detected in the films.

The fact remains that by depicting 'what happens every day and recurs every day, the banal, the everyday, the obvious, the commonplace, the ordinary, the infra-ordinary, the background noise, the habitual' (to quote Perec again[9]), such images illustrate something that professional filmmakers do not normally film.

Filmmakers in Love with Paris and the Work of Memory

Alongside home movie makers, certain amateur filmmakers (sometimes one and the same person simply playing a different role) who are in love with Paris devote some or much of their time to filming the city.

That is true of L. Estevez, an architect and diplomat who between 1923 and 1965 used a silent 9.5 mm cine camera to film famous Paris landmarks, neon signs at night (in colour), particularly on the Champs-Elysées, and a parade of automobiles, as well as some of his friends (one sequence shows Marcel Pagnol being admitted into the French Academy) and film actors, whom he filmed on set (Viviane Romance, Louis Jouvet, Jean-Louis Barrault, Arletty, Raimu and Marguerite Moreno, among others).

Other filmmakers set themselves up as reporters and shot what might be termed 'newsreels': L. Roubanovitch, for instance, filmed between 1948 and 1950 an event in honour of Jewish war veterans, a student march at the Buffalo stadium, a meeting with General Charles de Gaulle and a Labour Day parade. Others covered major events (*L'Exposition coloniale de 1937* [the Colonial Exhibition of 1937], L. Tellier), chronicled life in various districts of Paris (rue des Rosiers in the Marais, the embankments of the Seine, Belleville, and so on) or focused on a specific area of activity: Les Halles market at Christmas time (collective, 1989), public baths in the 19th *arrondissement* (E. Sebillet, Y. Shaller, L. Maisant, 1993) and life in the barracks (M. Com, 1958).

The amateur filmmaker as reporter: L. Roubanovitch films a Labour Day parade.

In their capacity as inhabitants of Paris, amateur filmmakers depicted public works in progress (the 'hole' caused by the reconstruction of Les Halles, the building of the Georges Pompidou Centre), demolitions (M. Aubert's Super 8 *Peine de mort pour une prison/Death Penalty for a Prison* [1974] is a final testimony to the Petite Roquette prison, a women's jail in the 11th *arrondissement*) and, more generally, major changes in the Paris landscape. Some filmmakers employ a systematic approach. In the commentary to one of his films, for example, L. Roth goes so far as to claim, rather presumptuously, that he 'scoured Paris in order to do what [Albert] Kahn did in the 1920s with the archives of the planet'. In his own view, his visual approach is 'very plastic, very symmetrical': 'I possess the eye of Lumière's cameramen; I frame with an expertise typical of the cinema's very beginnings'; 'the aim: a skyline two-thirds of the way up'. Roth comments on his film as it proceeds; often he does no more than utter a hesitant 'er' or two. His commentary is of course tinged with nostalgia: 'That cop in white is what my grandmother used to call a *sergent de ville* ([city sergeant]); look how he owns his street, his territory – he is on his home ground ... all that's a thing of the past.' In another example, when we see a Baltard newspaper kiosk, he comments: 'Those were the real ones.' Some of his remarks hint at an interpretation in terms of a family movie: 'My mother can be seen on the left; she generally accompanied me as she shared my enthusiasm.' Roth even reveals his deeper motivation: 'I was looking for my father's lost 16 mm reel, featuring his brothers and sisters, who were deported during the war; my father had left the reel in the projector he sold; from a fantasmatic point of view, that had a considerable impact on my documentary approach.'

Amateur Filmmakers Bear Witness to Their Age

Anyone can at some point or another be caught up in a historical event and become a witness. The collections demonstrate how home movie makers can suddenly decide to bear witness:[10] to do that, they have to feel directly involved. It may be a case of reacting as a user (J. P. Causse, for instance, depicts the chaos caused by the public transport strike of 1947); reacting as an activist (for example, the many films describing strikes and demonstrations, or those covering funerals such as the burial of Maurice Thorez[11]); reacting as an inhabitant of a city (P. Staub filmed a long sequence showing the façades of buildings gutted by bombs, even taking a number of risks in order to film: an inter-title mentions the fact that 'this film was shot despite a ban on doing so, a few days after Germans troops came through in June 1940'); or else reacting as a citizen.

The best-known images in this respect are those of the Liberation of Paris. The Forum des Images possesses several films on that topic, which have often been used in documentaries. The most remarkable of these is probably the film shot by 30 or so members of the Amateur Club of French Filmmakers between 15 and 25 August 1944. In an accompanying note, the historian Michèle Lagny remarks:

> These images are neither more nor less 'true' in their ability to show and explain what the Liberation of Paris really consisted of in August 1944. But they are more specific, more moving, more gripping, and surprisingly animated, carnal and joyful. [...] Among the most fascinating images are shots of young women clambering on to French or American tanks, in a whirl of bright summer dresses, short skirts revealing slender legs, and hair more or less held in place over their foreheads and somewhat ruffled at the back; a flurry of kisses and puffs of smoke, soldiers' helmets, resistants' berets, fag-ends sticking out of mouths and weapons slung over shoulders. There is also, naturally, an ironic touch: two street urchins sitting on a pavement (apparently uninterested in what is going on) and a cutaway to the bare thighs of women leaning over a parapet! Some of the funniest shots are of an unperturbed rabbit, the mascot of General Leclerc's tanks, which appears in several shots, and the linguistic efforts of an American soldier: 'the people of Paris are beautiful and pretty ...'

Community Films

A number of home movies can be described as 'community films': they are part and parcel of life in the community and aim to help cement it (they have a performative function).

This is true of *Nos oeuvres en 1931/Our Good Works in 1931*, an anonymous silent film devoted to Catholic missions). The enunciative formulation of the title (*Our* good works) and the inter-titles clearly announce its community-related objectives: the accent on personal pronouns combined with a referential system based on proper names (the proper name, when not left blank, is understood only by those who belong to the community and who are therefore already familiar with the reference), recourse to turns of phrase that give a positive image of the community, and a reliance on affects liable to give a dynamic impulse to the group:

'To keep up to date, all *our children* visited the Colonial Exhibition.'

'The outing. Watched by Father Danion and Hergé, the author of the Tintin & Snowy stories who had flown in specially from Brussels, Pierre Rougement brings back *his* Saint Pierre de Montrouge children.' [My italics]

'On Thursday April 30, 5,000 Brave Hearts filled the huge Trocadéro auditorium with their youthful and vibrant enthusiasm.'

The same is true of the film *Fête de l'Humanité 1970* (organised by the eponymous Communist newspaper), which centres on the activity of a stand representing the town of Nogent-le-Rotrou. It was shot by an activist, A. Durand, who supplies a commentary accompanied by the strains of the Internationale: activists are introduced by name and we are told what they happen to be doing ('You have just seen comrade Guyot, who is preparing his game of darts'; 'comrade Guerin, who is making coffee'; 'comrade Cousin, who is going to the kitchen'). Knowing glances are exchanged between the filmmaker and those filmed. Banners displaying the community's common values are emphasised ('Printing works in the service of the working class').

Such films are valuable documents for an ethnographical approach within certain specific milieux.

Home Movies by Filmmakers from the Provinces or Abroad

Paris is visited by very large numbers of tourists from the provinces or from other countries, who naturally film what everyone else is filming. Here again, it would be a mistake to underestimate such films, for they tell us a lot about foreigners' imaginary relationship with Paris (the 'legendary' Paris): we are shown the best-known landmarks (the Eiffel Tower, the Trocadéro, the Arc de Triomphe) and the aspects that left the greatest impression on them – luxury, cabarets, cafés with terraces, champagne and, of course, Parisian women (it should be remembered that until Super 8 and, above all, camcorders became available – Kodak's advertising campaign aimed at feminising Super 8 flopped completely[12] – the vast majority of amateur filmmakers were men). In some cases, the observation can be more precise: a woman in *Le Paris des années 30 filmé par des cinéastes amateurs belges/Paris of the 1930s Filmed by Belgian Amateur Filmmakers* explains that the first thing she needed to learn in Paris was how to alight from a moving bus like a Parisian woman: 'It's a knack: you have to throw your body and your foot pointing backwards while remaining upright; it's very tricky'. (These films have been collected by A. Huet for his programme screened on RTBF in 1989.)

Here again, it sometimes happens that the historical context can make a film particularly valuable: *France, la vie des soldats allemands/France, the Life of German Soldiers* (1941), filmed by an officer, H. Lorenz, who was in charge of finding entertainment for soldiers occupying Paris, depicts their summer pursuits: chess tournaments, sporting competitions, outings on steamers, and so on.

Films Made with the Encouragement of the Forum des Images

Pierre Emmanuel emphasised the need to pursue a proactive policy aimed at encouraging film productions featuring Paris and at mobilising universities, schools and various other bodies. The Forum des Images was all too happy to follow that advice by organising competitions and initiating or assisting productions made by associations (Young Reporters and the House of Gesture and Image, for example).

The film *Empreinte/The Mark* (1993) was the result of a school class mobilising to protest against a development that threatened to affect the rue Watt in the 13th *arrondissement*, a street dedicated to the memory of a young resistant shot by the Milice as he was painting an anti-Pétainist slogan on a wall. Several films offer a consistently picturesque and sometimes moving portrait gallery: pizza delivery men (*Spizza 30*, collective [1991]), a landlady (*La Logeuse*, N. Siouofi [1991]), Father Christmas (*Les Habits rouges/Red Outfits*, collective [1989]), tramps (*clochards*) in *Un soleil à Paris/A Sun in Paris* (A. Charlet, F. Breniaux and F. Suard, 1993) and *Le Mandarin et le marabout/ The Mandarin and the Witch Doctor* (M. Boussat and B. Branque, 1982). There is even one film devoted to another denizen of Paris: the rat. It is well known that below ground Paris teems with rats, which occasionally emerge, to the alarm of Parisians (*Ratopolis*, D. Camus [1993]).

Several films portray artistic figures: M. Manouchian, an Armenian poet and Resistance hero who was shot by the Germans in 1944, and whose photo was displayed on Vichy's notorious propaganda poster, the Affiche Rouge (*Le Sang d'un poète/The Poet's Blood*, M. Ionascu [1989]); S. Kessler, pianist, visited at his home by the filmmakers K. Bah, D. Bressy and Charles Neuville (*162 Avenue d'Italie* [1991]); and a collective of marginal painters occupying a squat in the rue Juliette-Dodu in the 19th *arrondissement* (*Vaches maigres chez Juliette Dodu/Lean Times at Juliette Dodu's*,[13] S. Backes [1991]), and so on. Lastly, other films take us on Paris walks in the footsteps of this or that celebrity: *Sur les pas d'Henry Miller; Paris 1930–1939/In the Footsteps of Henry Miller; Paris 1930–1939* (Ph. Boig and D. Jouventin, 1991) and *François Truffaut* (L. Chartin and Th. Deshayes, with a commentary spoken by André Dussollier, 1991).

In other words, such works by amateur filmmakers treat a whole series of minor subjects that professionals would perhaps not bother to film.

Filming as a Professional

Lastly, a very limited number of examples clearly show, from their scripting, photography, editing and soundtracks, that the director was determined to make a film that had all the qualities of a professional production.

In the silent era, such films were usually made by experienced amateur filmmakers belonging to a film club; in the context of amateur film competitions, those films fell into the category known as 'genre films', where the director's main concern was formal experimentation. *La Parisienne* (P. Boyer, 1937) is a remarkable example of this approach: it is structured around a series of inter-titles referring to the Parisian woman ('Essentially multifaceted/diverse and fickle/sometimes too well known/often little known/disapproved of by some, lusted after by others/ always captivating/ the *Parisienne* is ...'), and relies on sumptuous black-and-white photography to outline the various facets of the legend of the Parisienne (the seductress, the whore, the gold-digger, the consumer, the mother always rushing to perform her many tasks). The director skilfully resorts to elaborate lighting effects, multiple superimpositions and unusual framings (a couple getting out of a car are reflected on the front wing of the vehicle).

The amateur filmmaker and formal experimentation: P. Boyer's *La Parisienne* (1937).

Since the advent of video, what we mainly find is films by young directors using the facilities of associations. There are feature films: *Le Génie de Paris/The Spirit of Paris* (collective, 1993) chronicles the tribulations of two Parisian men, one of them very self-assured, Mr Floche, and the other clumsy, Mr Plock, in an entertaining series of six tableaux orchestrated by a conjuror. There are filmed essays: the epigraph of one film – 'Paris: coming back, leaving and going round in circles' – is illustrated by cross-cutting between lions in a cage, filmed at the Jardin des Plantes zoo, and the faces of Parisians shot at the Gare du Nord and the Gare de l'Est (*Parisiens*, V. Guadissart, N. Roméro and P. Dubosc [1991]). An even more experimental approach is used in *L'Echo des carreaux/The Echo of Windows* (Ch. Morin, 1994): a series of shots of the windows of Paris apartment buildings is accompanied on the soundtrack by snatches of conversation. In such films, while Paris is always the setting, and sometimes even the source of inspiration, the real mainspring of the direction is a determination to produce a creative work through the cinematic medium. It is all about a desire to make films rather than a desire for Paris.

As we have seen, the relationship between amateur filmmakers and the city of Paris as revealed by an analysis of the Forum des Images collection is extremely diverse in terms of the production set-up (family, school, association, club, individual or collective), the type of film (family home movie, document, testimony, documentary, drama, film essay) and the motivation behind it (family memory, collective memory, desire to document or to bear witness, artistic approach). Major roles can be identified: the involuntary endotic ethnographer (the home movie maker), the passionate lover of his or her city, the reporter, the witness, the member of a community, the visitor, the documentary maker, the filmmaker.

By way of conclusion, I would like to shift my perspective from filmmakers to users of the Forum in order to stress what seems to me to be the major difference between the Forum des Images and other archives devoted to home movies. The Forum, like other archives, is a place where researchers and other interested persons can consult documents, while at the same time acting as an educational tool for students. But people do not go there filled with a fervent desire to join together in a recollection of the past and an almost sacred celebration of the community of the kind I was able to observe at the Saint-Etienne Cinémathèque[14] and other regional archives. The reason for this could be that, as we saw with home movies, Paris remains a city of provincials whose hearts are elsewhere.[15] Or perhaps, above a certain threshold in terms of size, the inhabitants' relationship with their city changes; in Paris, it is at the level of the district or even the building that emotional relations come into play. The same is true of the relationship between the amateur filmmaker and the other inhabitants of the city (in the provinces people go to watch films made by filmmakers they know; screenings fall into the category of extended home movie events). In other words, it could be said that the Forum des Images is more of an archive than a 'site of memory' as understood by Pierre Nora,[16] though it unquestionably forms part of the memory of Paris.

I would like to thank Jean-Yves de Lépinay and Mathilde Oskeritzian of the Forum des Images for their help.

Translated from the French by Peter Graham.

Notes

1. Roger Odin, 'Reflections on the Family Home Movie as Document: A Semio-Pragmatic Approach', in Karen L. Ishizuka and Patricia R. Zimmermann (eds), *Mining the Home Movie: Excavations in Histories and Memories* (Berkeley, Los Angeles and London: University of California Press, 2008), pp. 255–71.
2. Editors' note: see Jean-Yves de Lépinay's chapter 'The Mirror of a City: The "Parisian Collection" of the Forum des Images' in this volume for further discussion of this institution.
3. I would like to thank Alain Esmery for having made available to me some of Pierre Emmanuel's unpublished documents.
4. Alain Esmery, 'C'est le cinéma du bonheur', *Le Figaro*, 18 May 2013 (interview with Claire Bommelaer). Marie Curie, together with her husband Pierre and Antoine Henri Becquerel, won the Nobel Prize in Physics in 1903 for their work on radiation; Marie Curie also won, singly, the Nobel Prize in Chemistry in 1911 for her work on radium.
5. Georges Perec, 'Approche de quoi', in *Le Pourrissement des sociétés* (Paris: 10/18, Cause commune, 1975), pp. 251–5.
6. Roger Odin, *Les Espaces de communication. Introduction à la sémio-pragmatique* (Grenoble: PUG, 2011), pp. 53–8.
7. Olivier Smolders, *La Part de l'ombre* (Paris and Brussels: Les Impressions nouvelles, 2005), p. 33.
8. Philippe Ariès and Georges Duby (eds), *Histoire de la vie privée, de la première guerre mondiale à nos jours*, vol. 5 (Paris: Seuil, 1987), p. 286ff.
9. Perec, 'Approche de quoi', pp. 251–5.

10. Renaud Dulong, *Les Conditions sociales de l'attestation personnelle. Le Témoin oculaire* (Paris: EHSS, 1998).
11. Editors' note: Maurice Thorez was the leader of the French Communist Party from 1930 to his death in 1964.
12. On this topic, see Bernard Germain, 'Madame Kodak contre l'amateur, ou les conquêtes du Super-8', in Roger Odin (ed.), *Communication*, no. 68: 'Le Cinéma en amateur' (Paris: Seuil, 1999), pp. 171–92.
13. Editors' note: the title is a pun on the street name 'Juliette Dodu', after a (controversial) heroine of the Franco-Prussian War of 1870, as 'dodu' also means plump, contrasted to 'lean times'.
14. Roger Odin, 'Which Role for the Cinema in a Working-class City ? The Case of Saint-Etienne', in François Penz and Andong Lu (eds), *Urban Cinematics. Understanding Urban Phenomena through the Moving Image* (Bristol and Chicago, IL: Intellect, 2011), pp. 93–105.
15. Guy Pourcher argues that most people moved to Paris for financial reasons – promotion and the prospect of a higher income ('Le Peuplement de Paris. Origine régionale. Composition sociale. Attitudes et motivations'. Presentation of research by INED and the Préfecture of the Seine, in *Population*, 18th year, no. 3 [1963], pp. 545–64) – and that, while on the whole people integrate well, the fact remains that they like to keep their family ties in the provinces, and sometimes even a house to which they return as often as possible to 'recharge their batteries'; indeed, many Parisians move back to the provinces when they reach retirement age, happy to be able to return to their roots.
16. Pierre Nora, 'Between Memory and History: Les Lieux de mémoire', *Representations*, no. 26, Special Issue: *Memory and Counter-memory* (Spring 1989), pp. 7–24.

The Concierge in Contemporary French Cinema

Raphaëlle Moine

Historically, the emergence of the figure of the concierge is tied to the development of a modern type of urban housing, the apartment block. In the second half of the 19th century, the concierge even came to epitomise the Parisian environment, as an ongoing series of depictions shows: the Pipelet couple in Eugène Sue's *Les Mystères des Paris* (1842–43), Honoré Daumier's caricatures, Bébert's aunt in Louis-Ferdinand Céline's *Voyage au bout de la nuit/Journey to the End of the Night* (1932), Robert Doisneau's photographs, the description of Madame Nochère's *loge*[1] in Georges Perec's *La Vie mode d'emploi* (*Life: A User's Manual*, 1978) and, more recently, Madeleine Wallace in Jean-Pierre Jeunet's *Le Fabuleux destin d'Amélie Poulain/Amélie* (2001). Likewise, a chapter of André Maurois's 1954 book *Femmes de Paris*, lavishly illustrated by the Dutch photographer Nico Jesse, is dedicated to concierges, giving them a position of choice in the gallery of 'typical' post-war Parisian women, next to 'students, artists and models', 'ballerinas', 'grocers' and 'women of Saint-Germain-des-Prés':

> The concierge is an essentially Parisian type. […] From her *loge*, she watches who comes in and who goes out, then makes knowing inferences about the intimate history of tenants; the master of the bell-pull at night, she lets people in or out upon identification; she distributes the mail, cleans the staircase, helps the bachelor on the ground floor. This kind of woman may only be found in Paris and delights foreigners: she is often their first contact with working-class France and elicits a wonderful feeling of strangeness in them.[2]

Insofar as concierges also exist in other countries and cities where the apartment block has become the main type of urban housing, from the Spanish *portero* to the British caretaker, the almost mythological dimension of the Parisian concierge may surprise. Indeed, it exceeds by far the necessities of realistic representation. This mythology is due to the origins of the profession in Paris between 1820 and 1840 with *maisons à allées* (two- or three-storey residential buildings, usually situated one behind the other with a small courtyard or a ventilation shaft separating them).[3] It also has to do with the more political dimensions of some of the concierge's duties: taking care of the building, providing information to visitors, delivering mail, but also keeping an eye on comings and goings and, where necessary, collecting the rent. Throughout the 19th century, these last two functions contributed to turning concierges into constant targets for satire and caricature. On the one hand, they were feared for their contacts with the police and their 'power' over the building and its occupants; on the other hand, their status as servants earned them much contempt.[4] Two archetypal figures, occasionally bound up in caricature, thus developed: the comical, laughable concierge, a variant on the vaudeville servant; the inflexible doorkeeper who collaborated with 'Monsieur Vautour' ('Mister Vulture', a nickname for greedy landlords) and the police in bringing rollicking residential bohemian writers and artists under control.[5] A third, more likeable figure appeared in the first half of the 20th century with the first 'HBM',[6] or controlled-rent buildings, and the hygienist principles that accompanied their development:[7] the concierge preoccupied with the well-being of tenants, who brought a touch of humanity to modern urban space, as André Maurois's description attests. Finally, the strong connection between the concierge and the French capital was reinforced by the growth of various art movements that revolved around a quest for realism as well as the representation of the city and its ordinary inhabitants: the naturalist and realist novels in the 19th century, Poetic Realism in the 1930s and the 'humanist photography' of the post-war period (Edouard Boubat, Robert Doisneau, Willy Ronis) all contributed to cementing the place of concierges and their living quarters in the gallery of picturesque Parisian places and popular social archetypes.

Over the course of the 20th century, French cinema itself recycled and altered this typical and typified Parisian figure. While few films featured a concierge in a lead role, as did *L'Impossible Monsieur Pipelet* (André Hunebelle, 1955) and *Le Concierge* (Jean Girault, 1973), many included a concierge in their setting, more often than not a woman, for a few shots or a sequence at the entrance of a building or in a staircase. In French cinema, the concierge is thus part of the Parisian landscape, and more specifically part of its most iconic popular locations. As Elizabeth Main noted in a survey of the 130 films produced between 1895 and 2000 featuring a concierge in a more substantial role, only one is situated outside Paris, while Montmartre and the 18th *arrondissement* are over-represented.[8] Nonetheless, against this background, the concierge still does not truly constitute a character in the narratological and dramatic senses of the term.

Having said this, at a time when concierges are becoming rarer in real Paris, several contemporary French films are breaking with the long tradition of concierges-as-cameos to turn them into fully fledged, sometimes leading characters: this is the case in *J'ai faim!!!* (Florence Quentin, 2001), *Le Bison (et sa voisine Dorine)* (Isabelle Nanty, 2003), *Le Hérisson/The Hedgehog* (Mona Achache, 2009), *La Cage dorée* (Ruben Alves, 2013). This article will examine the recent status of the concierge on film and compare it to the typical Parisian concierge in earlier French cinema. In so doing, it will explore the persistence and renewal of this colourful type. Now that the proverbial notice '*La concierge est dans l'escalier*' ('The concierge is on the staircase') that once hung on the door of their *loge* to indicate that they were busy cleaning the building's communal parts has disappeared, what function do concierges serve?

A Typified Character

The countless number of often brief on-screen appearances make it impossible to synthesise the figure of the Parisian concierge into a single type. In French films, even when considered by genre, no ideal-type of concierge may be identified across successive variations. Instead, a set of stereotypes emerges from the three prevailing configurations found in 19th- and early 20th-century discourse and representation: the doorkeeper, the comic concierge and the compassionate (female) concierge. According to Elizabeth Main, while early French cinema privileged the comic kind, with their naivety and the tricks played on them by tenants, as in *Le Locataire diabolique/The Devilish Tenant* (Georges Méliès, 1910), or by nosy characters, as in *Par le trou de la serrure/ What Happened: The Inquisitive Janitor* (Ferdinand Zecca, 1901), films soon emphasised other dimensions: concierges maintaining order and standards of morality, as in *Quatorze juillet/July 14* (René Clair, 1933) and *La Vérité/The Truth* (Henri-Georges Clouzot, 1960); gossiping, prying and inquisitive concierges, as in *Pas sur la bouche* (Nicolas Rimsky and Nicolas Evreinoff, 1931) and *L'Ecole des cocottes* (Pierre Colombier, 1935) and *Porte des Lilas/The Gates of Paris* (René Clair, 1957); naive concierges, as in *La Vengeance du serpent à plumes* (Gérard Oury, 1984); or holier-than-thou concierges, as in *La Grande lessive(!)* (Jean-Pierre Mocky, 1968) and *Ma petite entreprise* (Pierre Jolivet, 1998); not to mention helpful and understanding concierges. As for this last type, Elizabeth Main notes a recurring trope: the relationship between a concierge and 'her' bachelor, whom she takes care of and protects, pampers and spoils. *L'Arpète* (Donatien, 1928), *Pas sur la bouche, L'Ecole des cocottes, Bob le flambeur* (Jean-Pierre Melville, 1955), *Mon oncle* (Jacques Tati, 1958) and *Les Cousins* (Claude Chabrol, 1959) provide some examples.[9]

The concierge is overwhelmingly a female character on screen, in keeping with the sociology of the profession. Visually, she can be immediately identified by her body language (standing straight at the entrance of the building, hands on the hips or arms crossed) as well as by her iconic attributes (the broom and, later on, the vacuum cleaner) and her clothes. Working-class women from the countryside wearing a long apron and a shawl, hair arranged in a bun or hidden under a bonnet, dominated representations until World War Two, an instance being Madame Charles in *Le Jour se lève* (Marcel Carné, 1939). Since then, and to this day, however, the concierge has mostly been dressed in a cardigan, short apron, slippers or worn-out old shoes and somewhat shapeless layers that betray a professional identity and lifestyle as well as a degree of carelessness.[10] Like the relationship between the concierge and her bachelor, which invariably alternates between mothering and ridicule, the careless look of the concierge on screen functions as both a negative social marker (a working-class woman without elegance) and a gendered marker (a woman excluded from the circuit of desire).

A final characteristic of the concierge is her liminal position. Films tend to place her between the street and the building, either at the entrance of her *loge*, on the staircase or in the hallway. In fact, films favour the functions of mediation and communication and thus often limit her role to one part of her duties and to a brief sequence: providing or declining to provide information, conveying a message, reporting, betraying, spying, protecting, and so on. What makes the concierge immediately recognisable, more than a complex set of signs and cultural markers, is her position in the space of the building, between the private homes of residents (and the main protagonists of the plot) and the public space of the city. And what gives these characters visibility and saliency, at least in classical cinema, is their frequent embodiment by a supporting cast referred to as 'the eccentrics of French cinema' by Raymond Chirat and Olivier Barrot.[11] Indeed, a pleasure anticipated by audiences would be a performance, no matter how brief, by one of these actors. Even though not all concierges look like Pauline Carton, the actress is a case in point here. She played the part more than ten times from the 1920s to the 1960s and her successive appearances as a concierge gave the character a prominence and visibility that far surpassed its function in the plot. Pauline Carton's unattractive face, her tiny, button-like dark eyes, her unaffected appearance, the high pitch of her voice and her hair arranged in a little bun defined the figure to such an extent that Hergé modelled Tintin's as well as Captain Haddock's concierges after the actress.

Sans laisser d'adresse (Jean-Paul Le Chanois, 1951) features three concierges in brief appearances and thus rather well encapsulates their functions and their mode of representation. The plot recounts the trials of a taxi driver (Bernard Blier) and one of his passengers (Danièle Delorme), a young unmarried mother, whom he takes on at Gare de Lyon. She is trying to find the father of her child, a search that brings the two characters to three buildings located in Montmartre, the Marais and the 15th *arrondissement*, respectively. Each time, they ask a concierge for information. The first concierge, in Montmartre, shown only in two shots and only as she interacts with Delorme or Blier, is constructed on the old model of the country woman who has emigrated to the city. We see her sitting on the doorstep as she would have done in her village, wearing a black skirt and a long apron, and she informs the visitors while sorting beans. The second concierge, played by Georgette Anys, one of the 'eccentrics' of classical French cinema previously mentioned, is depicted at more at length. She is shown in her *loge*, grinding coffee, then pictured on the doorstep onto the courtyard of the building where, in her own words, 'we enjoy bourgeois comfort'. Hands on her hips, she is quite abrupt as she provides the visitors with information. The arrival of her husband, a policeman, in the course of the conversation, reinforces the traditional association between concierge and order. Unlike the previous two, the third concierge proves difficult to find. Blier initially mistakes the front of the modern complex for a military barracks and wonders where the concierge is, until a resident points out that the *loge* of the night concierge, who we see smoking his pipe on the doorstep, is located in the middle of the square. The three concierges in the film thus clearly represent three eras of collective urban housing: past, present and 1950s modernity.

The Concierge in Contemporary French Cinema: Recurrence and Pastiche

What happens to the mythological and familiar type on screen when the concierge disappears from the actual Parisian urban landscape? While the concierge has been in long-term decline (85,000 concierges in 1939, 60,000 in 1965, 24,000 in 1990[12]), the phenomenon now regularly draws press attention in the early 21st century. In 2010, for instance, *Le Monde*'s weekend supplement devoted a long article to the suppression of *loges* in private real estate. The piece noted that 20 per cent of *loges* had disappeared between the professional censuses of 1990 and 2006, and that the figure was now below the 20,000 mark. The article explained that the concierge was the only part of the budget on which the co-owners of the building could save money, by outsourcing services such as the cleaning and the putting out of bins, or by renting or selling the *loge* whenever it was not turned into a room for pushchairs or bikes.[13] It should also be noted that, since 2001, the decrease in the number of concierges has been tempered by the obligation for controlled-rent or private residential properties of more than 100 housing units to hire *gardiens*, or caretakers.¹⁴ This has maintained or brought back the kind of concierges in Parisian buildings that appear rarely in contemporary French cinema, *Agathe Cléry* (Etienne Chatiliez, 2008) being one recent exception.

It would be problematic to assert that the number of concierges, as they are typically featured in the cinema, has declined in proportion to what has happened in the social sphere, and in fact impossible without a systematic review of all the films in question. Still, after looking into contemporary production trends, I would claim that this familiar figure is generally less present today than it used to be. A degree of faithfulness to reality is thus operating. Significantly, in the romantic comedy *Mon pire cauchemar/My Worst Nightmare* (Anne Fontaine, 2011), the very bourgeois Agathe (Isabelle Huppert) lives in a 200 square metre apartment in the 5th *arrondissement* of Paris, while social misfit Patrick (Benoît Poelvoorde) squats in the now unused *loge* of a Portuguese concierge in the same neighbourhood, near the Pantheon.

However, a first, striking aspect in the contemporary persistence of typical concierges is that they appear in films whose action is situated in the most bourgeois neighbourhoods of the French capital – primarily west of the city, and in the 5th and 6th *arrondissements* – which is sociologically accurate. The predilection of *auteur* cinema for characters belonging to the intellectual Parisian bourgeoisie partly explains the permanence of figures such as the Hungarian concierge in Jeanne Labrune's 2002 fantasy *C'est le bouquet!* or the concierge and her husband in Michael Haneke's *Amour* (2012). Another strong trend is that concierges are becoming a more discrete presence in the contemporary French crime film, a genre in which they traditionally were a staple as the police's first contacts in an investigation. Adaptations of Simenon's stories come to mind, particularly those involving Maigret, with their many scenes in which the Inspector gathers information from a concierge. While realism and the location of a number of detective films outside Paris may explain this evolution, I would argue that it is also inherent in the genre's own shift, away from the investigative model to a new emphasis on the thriller and 'old-style film noir'.¹⁵ In both of these, the character of the concierge becomes irrelevant.

Another new development is the second-degree treatment of the concierge as a type: by exaggerating and producing a pastiche of the character, films lose the familiar transparency of the figure and signal its obsolescence, but in the process they also give the concierge a three-dimensionality absent in the earlier representations. *Le Fabuleux destin d'Amélie Poulain* presents a mannerist version of this in the shape of Madeleine Wallace (Yolande Moreau), a sentimental and teary-eyed concierge who wears ankle socks and an apron and lives with her stuffed dog in a *loge* overflowing with knick-knacks and religious trinkets. The vector of a nostalgic myth of a picturesque working-class Paris (like Amélie Poulain's world as a whole), Madeleine Wallace is also over-typified by her name, formed through a figure of antonomasia. Indeed, the concierge, who cries all the time, evokes through her name both the expression '*pleurer comme une madeleine*' and '*pleurer comme une fontaine*'; both mean to cry one's heart out and, as it happens, Paris's most famous fountains are the Fontaines Wallace. While

Madeleine Wallace (Yolande Moreau), the sentimental *concierge* of *Le Fabuleux destin d'Amélie Poulain/Amélie* (Jean-Pierre Jeunet, 2001).

the choice of Darry Cowl to play madame Veuve Foin in *Pas sur la bouche/Not on the Lips* (Alain Resnais, 2003) contributes to the distanced tone and kitsch aesthetic of the film, the transvestite concierge is also a nod by Resnais to one of the conventions in early 20th-century vaudeville and operetta, in which the parts of female concierges were played by either women or men.[16] Finally, the concierge in *Les Femmes du 6e étage/The Women on the 6th Floor* (Philippe Le Guay, 2011), Madame Triboulet (Annie Mercier), who bears the ridiculous name of François I's court jester, is an irascible, racist and accusatory caricature who seems to issue directly from the dark mythology of concierges during the Occupation.[17] This historical-social comedy (the action takes place in the 1960s) uses the concierge as a counterpoint to the kind Spanish maids living on the sixth floor – stereotypical yet much more structured as characters. Madame Triboulet embodies the commitment to a social order disturbed by the romance between a rich landlord and one of the Spanish maids: in her view, everyone should know his/her place in the hierarchy of the building, which also translates spatially (the concierge in the courtyard, the maids in attic rooms, the residents on the other floors).

The Concierge as Character: A Woman Like Any Other?

Two years after *Les Femmes du 6e étage*, *La Cage dorée* tapped into a similar vein of 'comedies of ethnic integration'[18] with a Portuguese family as its central characters. The Ribeiros live in a *loge* in an upscale Parisian neighbourhood. Maria, the mother (Rita Blanco), keeps the place neat with unwavering care and selflessness. While the film consciously and deliberately repeats a series of clichés about Portuguese immigrants to France (the husband is a mason, everyone loves work, Catholicism is very present, children are perfectly integrated in French society and successful), it gives Portuguese concierges an unprecedented visibility. Even as they represent between a third and a half of Parisian concierges (sources differ on the exact proportion),[19] French cinema disregards the current diversity of origin in the profession, almost exclusively representing French concierges.[20] *La Cage dorée* satirises the selfish domination of some well-off French characters (the bourgeois residents of the building, employers) who take advantage of the devotion of the Portuguese couple. Still, the depiction of a community is more central to the film than social critique, due in part to its narrative backbone: the Portuguese family, who settled down in France long ago, face a dilemma when they receive an unexpected inheritance. Should they return to Portugal or stay in France in their 'gilded cage'? The subject of the film is thus not so much life in a Parisian *loge* (referred to as 'more than a *loge*: heaven' on the poster) but, rather, an empathetic depiction of the Portuguese community in the context of a difficult decision involving emigration and integration.

Similarly, the three other films promoting the concierge to the status of fully fledged character displace her identity beyond what defines her professionally and socially. *J'ai faim!!!* tells of the sentimental disappointments of a young woman, Lily (Catherine Jacob). To win her boyfriend back, she sets out on a drastic diet and decides to ruin the life of the person she wrongly believes to be her rival. Three other women clearly presented as a group of friends second her in these efforts. It is only by the end of the film that the audience finds out that one of them, Yolande (Garance Clavel), is in fact both the caretaker of the building and a sociology student. Approaching the concierge primarily as a friend, the film turns her into a woman like any other.

A comparable levelling of the social differences and domestic service once central to the identity of the concierge is also at work in *Le Bison (et sa voisine Dorine)*, starting with the title, since Dorine (Isabelle Nanty) is not referred to as a concierge, which she is. Her first name 'Dorine' reinforces the ambivalence of the character, since it equally elicits positive connotations through the allusion to Molière's eponymous servant in *Tartuffe*. The film initially recycles the typified figure of the concierge, contrasting an unattractive, sour and slovenly Dorine, her husband and four children with Le Bison (Edouard Baer), a young, idle dandy, a reveller and seducer. The two cross paths as Dorine puts the bins out and Bison returns from a party. The early morning encounter does not so much function to situate the characters in opposing social worlds as to launch the conventional formula of the romantic comedy. As the DVD's promotional description puts it, 'in short, this caretaker and her bohemian neighbour have nothing in common. Still, an unexpected event (Dorine's husband walking out on her and the family) leaves them with no choice but to help each other.' The film then alternates, rather unimaginatively, sequences of confrontation and cooperation between the two characters and concludes with a happy ending that has Dorine, her children and Le Bison run away from the building – and from a returning husband and a girlfriend, respectively – and drive together to the sea, like a reconstituted family. Here, the concierge is an unusual romantic-comedy heroine and the sentimental relationship, subsuming all social differences, is far removed from the cliché of the concierge and her bachelor. The horizontal proximity of the *loge* with Le Bison's flat, also located on the ground floor, contributes to establishing the characters as ordinary neighbours.

The idea for *Le Hérisson* (as well as for the bestselling novel from which it was adapted[21]) is that of a two-faced concierge, Renée (Josiane Balasko). On the one hand, she is a stereotypical concierge shown performing her duties as she takes care of the building; on the other hand, she is an art and literature lover who hides a library at the rear of her *loge* and has chosen to live her life behind the façade afforded by her profession. The film explicitly posits the figure of the concierge as a construction and as a cliché against which Renée, as a character, comes to constitute a 'counter-stereotype'. In a sequence in which she is interviewed by Paloma, the gifted, neurotic rich little girl who films her relatives, Renée declares that she 'fits to perfection the archetype of the building caretaker: an ugly, sour, old woman endlessly watching television while her fat cat dozes off on cushions with crocheted covers, the smell of cassoulet hanging in her *loge*'. *Le Hérisson* focuses on the friendship between Paloma and Renée, whose accidental death restores the girl's appetite for life, but most of all on the developing relationship between Renée and a new flat owner, Monsieur Ozu, who senses the genuine nature of the concierge, her sensibility and culture, hidden beneath her prickly exterior. Like *Le Bison (et sa voisine Dorine)*, the film follows the path of the romantic comedy, insisting on the budding romance between the two characters. While the novel let Renée's encyclopaedic culture show through long literary, linguistic or philosophical first-person developments, her culture in the film is limited to *Anna Karenina* (a subtext to the love affair and the tragic ending when Renée is run over by a van) and an Ozu film she watches with the character who bears the same name.

Contemporary French cinema thus adds new strata of representations to the mythology of the Parisian concierge. While concierges are now less frequently seen as a utilitarian and contextual element, thus echoing their actual decline in Parisian social space, their presence is also manifested by a change in status: they are no longer a 'natural' part of the setting. Some films overplay the typicality of a now-fossilised role more than that of a character, with the result that the concierge has become the vehicle of a nostalgic myth, that of a picturesque working-class Paris and/or a form of bygone popular spectacle. Other films, on the contrary, extract the concierge from

Renée (Josiane Balasko), the bookish *concierge* in *Le Hérisson/The Hedgehog* (Mona Achache, 2009).

her typicality, running counter to clichés for instance. But as the concierge becomes a – full – character, she also becomes a woman like any other, whose clothing or social and professional condition have to be shed. What can then be embodied is an 'ordinary' femininity whose diversity appears in the four films analysed at the end of this chapter, a development confirmed by the recent *Le Grand partage* (Alexandra Leclère, 2015). This comic film deploys a range of blatant stereotypes to depict the inhabitants of a bourgeois block of flats forced by the government to take in people with housing needs. But even the racist concierge (Josiane Balasko, again), whose only love is her stuffed one-eyed cat called Jean-Marie, in honour of Jean-Marie Le Pen, the founder and former president of the National Front party, softens up, like everyone else. She ends up sharing and caring for others and falls in love with a black man, remaining with him at the end of the film when the requisition order has been withdrawn. Either way, whether films deploy clichés in the second degree or deconstruct them to allow a character to emerge, the idea of the transparency and the innocence of the concierge is now outdated. In that sense, on screen, as everywhere else, the concierge is no longer on the staircase.

Translated from the French by Franck Le Gac.

Notes

1. Editors' note: in most 19th- and 20th-century Parisian buildings, the concierge traditionally had a small apartment (called a *loge*) on the ground floor near the entrance.
2. André Maurois, *Femmes de Paris* (Paris: Plon, 1954), p. 29.
3. Jean-Louis Deaucourt, *Premières loges. Paris et ses concierges au XIXe siècle* (Paris: Aubier, 1992), p. 21.
4. Hervé Marchal, *Le Petit Monde des gardiens-concierges* (Paris: L'Harmattan/Collection Logiques sociales, 2006), pp. 28–9.
5. Jean-Marc Stébé, Hervé Marchal, Roselyne de Villanova, Eliane Nicolino, 'Le Métier en France: de la domesticité à la profession', in Roselyne de Villanova and Philippe Bonnin (eds), *Loges & gardiens* (Paris: Editions Créaphis, 2006), p. 35.
6. Editors' note: the HBM, *Habitations à bon marché* (literally cheap housing), were the ancestors of the HLM, *Habitations à loyer modéré*, the social housing of the post-war period.
7. Marchal, *Le Petit Monde des gardiens-concierges*, pp. 32–5.
8. Elizabeth Main, *Quand les concierges balaient l'écran (1895–2000). Figures de concierge dans le cinéma français. Essai d'analyse de la représentation à partir d'un corpus de films de fiction de long métrage*, doctoral dissertation in Contemporary, Social and Cultural History (Université Paris 1, 2007), pp. 52–3.
9. Ibid., pp. 101–4.
10. Ibid., p. 92.
11. Raymond Chirat and Olivier Barrot, *Les Excentriques du cinéma français (1929–1958)* (Paris: Henry Veyrier, 1983).
12. Stébé *et al.*, 'Le Métier en France', p. 35.
13. Rafaële Rivais, 'Les Concierges s'effacent au profit des gardiens', *Le Monde*, 13 January 2010, p. 22.

14. Decree no. 2001-1361, 28 December 2001, *JORF* no. 303, 30 December 2001, p. 21475, text no. 67. Available at: www.legifrance.gouv.fr/affichTexte.do?cidTexte=JORFTEXT000000226267&categorieLien=id (accessed 9 September 2017).
15. Thomas Pillard, 'Between Tradition and Innovation: French Crime Films during the 2000s', in Alistair Fox, Michel Marie, Hilary Radner and Raphaëlle Moine (eds), *A Companion to Contemporary French Cinema* (Chichester: John Wiley & Sons, 2015), pp. 256–74.
16. Elizabeth Main, 'La Concierge dans l'imaginaire parisien 1830–2004', in Myriam Tsikounas (ed.), *Imaginaires urbains. Du Paris romantique à nos jours* (Paris: Le Manuscrit, 2011), p. 284.
17. Historians agree that the disproportionate number of concierges put on trial after the Liberation has to do with the characteristic duties of their work, not with a supposed inclination to report people rather than to resist during the Occupation. See Marc Bergère, 'Délations ordinaires dans la France occupée', in Laurent Joly (ed.), *La Délation dans la France des années noires* (Paris: Perrin, 2012), pp. 181–94.
18. Ginette Vincendeau, 'From the Margins to the Center: French Stardom and Ethnicity', in Fox et al. (eds), *A Companion to Contemporary French Cinema*, pp. 547–68.
19. Eliane Nicolino and Roselyne Villanova, 'Concierges et gardiens en chiffres', in Villanova and Bonnin (eds), *Loges & gardiens*, p. 44.
20. Main, *Quand les concierges balaient l'écran*, p. 40.
21. Muriel Barbery, *L'Elégance du hérisson* (Paris: Gallimard, 2006). *The Elegance of the Hedgehog* (London: Gallic Books, 2008).

Parisian Lovers in the Contemporary Romcom

Mary Harrod

Paris has long held a formative place in geo-spatial imaginaries of love. The Gallic tendency to embrace carnal desire more for its own sake than do many other cultures, including Anglo-American, has lent Frenchness sex appeal. In this context, as Celestino Deleyto has noted, the appearance of the capital in Hollywood romantic comedies always acts as 'shorthand [...] for an Americanised version of European attitudes to love and sexuality'.[1] Since around the late 1990s, Paris has also featured recurrently in another cycle of romcoms: indigenous French ones, which have proliferated over the last two decades and which are themselves necessarily in dialogue with their Hollywood predecessors, including in their deployment of the capital as the setting for romantic plotlines.[2] This chapter seeks to identify trends in the representation of Paris via the heavily determined generic space of recent romcoms originating in both cultures. It thus considers the city's representation in a handful of Hollywood romcoms of the current post-1990 cycle, in particular *French Kiss* (Lawrence Kasdan, 1995) and *Le Divorce* (James Ivory, 2003), before discussing its manifestation in a range of French films of the genre, such as the transnationally conceived (in both thematic and marketing terms) *Amour et turbulences/Love Is in the Air* (Alexandra Castagnetti, 2013), as well as the more locally positioned *Clara et moi* (Arnaud Viard, 2004) and *Je vais te manquer* (Amanda Sthers, 2009). From this analysis, I will argue that several recent romcoms across the board construct a version of the French capital that is closer to Deborah Jermyn's description of New York in the genre as a 'romantic playground' than to her designation of Paris's traditional value as the City of Love, and that this co-opting of a generic space that is marked as foreign typifies the genre's integrationist impulses with regards to French and US popular film culture.[3] Finally, I will show how this reinvention of Paris along neo-globalised lines dovetails perfectly with the reconciliatory work of romantic comedy itself.

A precept of this study is the impossibility of 'authentic' spatial representation in cinema. Texts prompt the assignment of meanings, including generic ones; moreover, the creation of what Deleyto calls a 'magical space of transformation and fantasy' is one of the defining elements of romantic comedy. While Shakespearean comedy typically removed events to a pastoral idyll or 'green space', the imbrication of early cinema and modernity saw the medium's close ties to the city extend to resituating romcom's magic space within the metropolis, notably with the classical screwball comedies. Deleyto argues that romantic fantasies are all the more powerful when declined within a space less removed from the everyday lived reality of the majority of cinemagoers.[4]

This may be true, and certainly all romcoms blend elements of recognisable everyday reality with tropes that mark events as 'special' in various ways. However, the staging of romantic comedy within the western metropolis tends to imply a balance between these referential spheres that is skewed away from romantic wonderment – particularly in more recent decades. According to Jermyn, New York is the pre-eminent setting for US romcoms;[5] and the director who cemented this trend and whose films epitomise it is Woody Allen. Both David R. Shumway and Frank Krutnik have shown how Allen's urban romcoms depart substantially from more traditionally romantic discourses to usher in a relatively new view of relationships, characterised by emotional cynicism, intellectualism, the granting of relative freedom to women and above all restlessness.[6] The flipside of the city's 'sense of infinite promise'[7] is that all relationships are conceived as provisional. This aspect speaks in turns to the metropolitan space's links with realism, dovetailing with Allen's European art cinema influences. And if the post-classical urban romcom has transnational roots, Julia Hallam and Margaret Marshment have shown conversely how its cousin social realism has become a global cinematic brand that includes the success of the 1995 Paris-set (in the broadest sense) *La Haine/Hate* (Mathieu Kassovitz).[8]

If traditional romance emphasises a timeless narrative and one that privileges the individual over the social, social realism conceives the individual as fundamentally subject to social forces and change.[9] The links between French culture and the genre of realism, as well as between post-1970s city romcoms and a pragmatic and contingent view of love, give the lie to any preconceptions of Paris's status as the City of Love – a phrase whose capitalisation emphasises immutability – in a number of recent examples of the genre. Indeed, where classical Hollywood films such as *Ninotchka* (Ernst Lubitsch, 1939) or *Funny Face* (Stanley Donen, 1957) tended to gloss over the social contradictions implied by the French cultural fetishisation of relatively untrammelled desire, to construct Paris as a tourist space of 'enchanted' (monogamous, heterosexual) love, the tensions inherent in bringing 'European attitudes towards desire and sexuality' to bear on romance prove more worrisomely visible in a group of more recent Paris-set romcoms from both sides of the Atlantic.

Deconstructing the Eiffel Tower

The most traditional of the contemporary crop of Parisian Hollywood romcoms under discussion is the 1995 *French Kiss*. The film mobilises caricatural views of both US and French culture and stars romcom queen Meg Ryan opposite Kevin Kline, who 'passes' as French; rather than attempting to debunk stereotypes, it endorses them as endearing, in pairing Ryan's unadventurous Kate with Kline's loveable rogue Luc. Despite a poster emblazoned with the couple framed against the quintessential Parisian romantic symbol, the Eiffel Tower, however, the film's deployment of Parisian iconography does not conform to expectations.

Kate's opening lines presage the film's gently subversive intervention into urban signification in romantic comedy: '[singing] I love Paris in the Springtime [... grumpy speaking voice] I don't love Paris, I don't like the French [...]' These are pronounced in the space of what appears to be an aeroplane – until her verbal reversal is echoed by a physical one when it is revealed that she is in fact inside a flight simulator, attempting in vain to overcome a fear of flying to accompany her 'wrong partner' fiancé to the French capital. When her failure to do so propels him into the arms of another, Kate grasps the nettle and follows him to Paris to save their relationship, only to fall for the petty criminal she meets on the plane, via a series of plot machinations involving his smuggled goods and her handbag. The Paris of *French Kiss* is thus populated pre-eminently by criminals: not only Luc but the mealy-mouthed confidence trickster Bob (François Cluzet), who provides a foil to the protagonist's lesser vices. The locations captured by the film span the red-light district of Pigalle in the 18th *arrondissement*, an area more commonly associated with 'neo-noir' cinema, and the upscale Champs-Elysées with its luxury shops, as well as the baroque interiors of the nearby Hôtel George V.[10] These latter spaces, however, connote exclusion: the implacable receptionist at the hotel treats Kate's request for her fiancé's room number, and subsequent attempt to bribe him, with disdain; by the time she has reached the unwelcoming reflective glass of the shop windows, she has been robbed of her possessions and reduced to sleeping on the street. The disjuncture between Kate's notionally desirable physical locations and her state of extreme deterritorialisation (her status as an American domiciled in Canada also means she can access no help from either embassy) reaches its apotheosis as she sobs, 'I will triumph!', with heavy irony, before the Arc de Triomphe. And this is not the only monument whose grandeur and symbolic status are undercut by the film. A running joke sees Kate's one touristic desire in Paris, to see the Eiffel Tower,[11] thwarted again and again, as the building ghosts her unhappy itinerary: once, she turns around just as the tower's lights are extinguished to render it invisible against the night sky; on another occasion, she captures a tantalising glimpse of its reflection in a window. The only Eiffel Tower Kate does manage to bring into her orbit is a souvenir figurine which crumples in on itself at the press of a button, and which comes to stand in for the hinted notion that Luc is suffering from erectile dysfunction, as Kate explicitly taunts him on the subject. This metaphor highlights the simultaneous failure of not only old-fashioned ideas of love but specifically of the ideal partner, especially male, to live up to contemporary realities: instead of offering eternal love, Luc tells Kate that 'when someone tells me they're happy, my ass begins to twitch'. It is here that *French Kiss* is at its most contemporary. However, the film's ending jettisons its interrogative mode on the compatibility of romantic desire and commitment, metaphorically healing Luc's sexual problems alongside his social ones by coupling the protagonists, far from the city's perils, in a vineyard in the sun-drenched rural *midi* where a phallic-looking vine Luc has smuggled from the US can be blended with a French variety to produce a harmonious and intoxicating union.

Given that the contemporary cycle of Hollywood 'new romances' is typified by an ambivalent attitude towards the signs of old-fashioned romance, which are cited in a post-modern, self-conscious way that allows them to be embraced only once their clichéd nature has first been acknowledged, it is no wonder that *French Kiss* seeks to disavow the romance of Paris – even if this is the site in which Kate does, after all, begin to fall in love. The narrative sets the trend for a spate of films that take an increasingly distanced stance towards the romanticism of France's capital city. In *Le Divorce*

Kate's (Meg Ryan) one touristic desire in Paris thwarted again and again in *French Kiss* (Lawrence Kasdan, 1995).

Isabel's (Kate Hudson) romantic Parisian affair with a much older, married man Edgar (Thierry Lhermitte) is not only short-lived, but it is shadowed by a melodramatic thread that has her sister Roxeanne (Naomi Watts), abandoned for another woman by her husband Charles-Henri (Melvil Poupaud) while pregnant, attempt suicide. Moreover, the film's secondary plotline weaves in a discourse about the precarious relationship between seductive appearances and value that bleeds into its portrayal of love. Thus, one aspect of Roxeanne's ugly divorce concerns her husband's desire to get his hands on a potentially valuable painting owned by her family, a campaign that is abandoned when the Louvre mistakenly fail to identify the piece as a Delacroix. At the end of the film, the American heroines may seem both wealthier and happier than their French counterparts, as Isabel shakes off her feelings for the supposedly unsuitable Edgar and Roxeanne marries again, but the relationship between appearances and reality has been destabilised. And this destabilisation of the sign-referent bond applies equally to Paris, as underlined by sequences that bookend the film. The opening sequence's picture-postcard view of the city's rooftops at sunset is accompanied by Roxeanne's overeager stipulation that the beams in her exorbitantly priced shabby-chic apartment are nothing like 'the fake ones' in their East Coast home, but rather represent 'the real load-bearing ones'. The film's climactic sequence, in turn, reinvents the Eiffel Tower not as a site of romance but one where the tragic consequences of failed love are played out. Thus, the husband of Charles-Henri's lover, having murdered his French rival, pursues Roxeanne for some sort of cathartic note-comparing, still armed, causing the tower to be closed and cordoned off by police, as unglamorous crowds of kagoul-clad Japanese tourists cower until he is led away.

Given the generic lineage of Paris-set US romcoms detailed above, it is unsurprising that, by 2011, for Paris to return as a less problematically romantic space in a film by city romcom *auteur* par excellence Woody Allen, *Midnight in Paris*, it must be for the most part recast explicitly as a distant fantasy projected into the historical past. Nor is this heavily attenuated view of the romanticism of Paris limited to US filmmakers. In the case of French director Julie Delpy's 2007 English-language *2 Days in Paris*, notably,

The picture-postcard view of the city's rooftops at sunset in Le Divorce (James Ivory, 2003).

Neil Archer has shown how 'the dissemination of cinematic self-imagery' is in question, in a narrative that has its anti-heroic tourist male protagonist driven to re-enact iconic scenes from the romantic history of Paris on film – for instance, Marlon Brando's scream on the Bir-Hakeim bridge that opened Last Tango in Paris (Bernardo Bertolucci, 1972). Here, the sojourn in the 'City of Love' is the death knell for the central couple's relationship, with the breakup filmed in front of the canal St Martin, so mythologised in Poetic Realist films and then re-aestheticised in Le Fabuleux destin d'Amélie Poulain/Amélie (Jean-Pierre Jeunet, 2001).[12] The less successful but nonetheless transnationally positioned Amour et turbulences – shot partly in New York as well as Paris, starring Ludivine Sagnier, who has enjoyed some international recognition since appearing in several films by François Ozon, and released in the USA – is even more overtly self-reflexive about the cinematic overdeterminacy of Paris when it comes to romance specifically. The film returns again to a reflection on the Eiffel Tower as emblematic of romance. Here, the couple's initial encounter, when they share a taxi home from a party, evolves into an impromptu date up the tower after hours. Producing a bottle of champagne as if by magic, playboy Antoine (Nicolas Bedos) has no qualms in admitting to Sagnier's Julie that this is his party trick for seducing women (he knows a security guard there), adding: 'But who cares? It's great.' By constructing Julie's reaction as more amused than lovestruck, the film taps into a contemporary intimate discourse that validates 'authentic' communication, such that romance proves '*the obstacle* which the desirable love relationship must overcome' ;[13] indeed, Antoine himself dimly acknowledges the obsolescence of his approach when he laments the choice of champagne as too 1980s. However, the redundancy of romance is problematised by a subsequent scene where Julie tells her mother that Antoine's failure to kiss her was in fact disappointing: as so often, romantic clichés are both disowned and endorsed as powerfully seductive. As regards the Eiffel Tower itself, though, the film ultimately echoes French Kiss's more cynical impulse to equate the tower, and by extension Paris, not with ethereal love but with phallic desire, as Julie's mother remarks that the only thing Antoine wants to get her on top of is his cock.

The Girl in the Next-Door Seat

Amour et turbulences simultaneously contributes to a contemporary trend I have elsewhere identified as originating in early 2000s Parisian French romcoms, which reflect post-modern mobility by having a couple meet in what Marc Augé has dubbed 'non-places', or places of transience too insignificant to be regarded as places.[14] These arguably include such prominent French romcoms as *Le Fabuleux destin d'Amélie Poulain*, which – despite being generally traditional-cum-nostalgic in its view of Paris – uses a Métro station (on which more later), and *Décalage horaire/Jet Lag* (Danièle Thompson, 2002), set mostly in an airport. *Amour et turbulences* in fact takes place principally on a plane itself, as the couple are seated next to one another some time after an acrimonious breakup and spend the flight reminiscing about their relationship via flashbacks before being reconciled. Thus, the romanticism of the Eiffel Tower is in fact doubly displaced, by being ironised but also by being situated in the diegetic past, while the couple's current courtship is played out in a context Augé equates with 'supermodernity' (that is, the period associated with the post-modern sensibility). This tendency is not exclusive to the French romcom. Indeed, *French Kiss*'s couple also meet on a plane – and the identical internal body of the flight simulator underlines such spaces' placelessness – just as British romcoms such as *Love, Actually* (2003) have made substantial use of airports. This can in both cases be linked to the films' transatlantic settings, and in the second works to underline an affinity with the US genre too – a drive that also frequently applies to French examples. However, uniting couples in places of transience is strikingly common in French romcoms, as part and parcel of their greater penchant for realism. For instance, various romcoms featuring this trope are multi-protagonist films portraying the intersection of Parisian trajectories. Beyond their possibilities for linking different spaces of regional belonging, such pairings represent a post-modern twist on the emblem of traditional community coupling, the girl next door, who becomes either figuratively or literally the girl in the next-door seat.

Just as for Augé (citing Michel de Certeau), to frequent busy public spaces is 'to be other, and go over to the other, in a place', staging encounters in liminal spaces endows them with a sense of heightened possibility for extraordinary intersubjective fusion (even if this is in romcom typically limited to the white, heterosexual middle classes).[15] The non-place in Augé's description facilitates a regression to the experience of infancy – the very fusional return psychoanalytic theory identifies as driving human desire for the other. This is reflected in romcoms' stress on the childish wonder of fantasy narratives: their construction of a 'romantic playground' of multifarious urban delights, where love may be fickle, but it is marvellous. Such a view of Paris overlaps rather than contrasts with the city's previous representations, since the *flâneur*'s own restlessness is bound up with the city's status as 'a site of almost infinite pleasures'.[16] *Le Fabuleux destin d'Amélie Poulain* has more than once been discussed in terms which chime with Janice Radway's argument that romances rework the female Oedipal drama. However, 'the reestablishment of that original, blissful symbiotic union between mother and child' need not be limited to female experience and, along with *Décalage horaire*, the romcoms *Je vais te manquer* and *Clara et moi* address this aspect of romance also from a male perspective.[17] In the broadly realistically framed ensemble piece *Je vais te manquer*, terminally ill Julia (Carole Bouquet), on her way to commit suicide in Canada, meets embittered, misanthropic writer Marcel (Pierre Arditi) in a bookshop at Charles de Gaulle airport. They strike up an unlikely rapport when she recognises him as one of her favourite authors, which leads to a long talk over coffee, then culminates in one romantic kiss before she sets off and, crucially, in Marcel giving her his intimate journal. Although the couple, in their fifties, are far from children, his act is revealing of the extent to which Marcel's interaction with Julia constitutes a pleasurable opening up and unburdening, as he lets down his habitually cast-iron defences, returning him to a childlike, un-symbolised (in the Lacanian sense) state. In this case, the dynamic is commutative, as Julia too unburdens herself to Marcel about her illness and intentions, which she has been (unsuccessfully) hiding from her daughters, perhaps suggesting the human urge for a primal return to origins in the face of death. In any case, the regressive possibilities fostered by frequenting non-places are once more celebrated by *Je vais te manquer* as propitious for intersubjective communion, seen as an antidote to a human solitude magnified in the face of death.

In *Clara et moi*, the couple meet when Antoine (Julien Boissellier), seeing beautiful stranger Clara (Julie Gayet) opposite him on a Métro train, writes a note requesting a date. Not only does this contrivance avoid the generic problem of how to express the inexpressible through hackneyed language, it also points up a change in the configuration and problematic of the romantic encounter. Where for Jane Austen's heroines the difficulty was how to rethink the familiar as alluringly other, today the challenge is to bridge the divide between beings for whom anonymous otherness has become standardised. Writing offers here a less threatening means than the spoken word to approach the stranger Antoine is attracted to but has no excuse to address. This moment of emotional warmth stands out within a *mise-en-scène* whose chilly, grey-toned palette and naturalistic lighting, captured at times digitally through a hand-held camera, reinforces the social realist codification of a Paris presented as frequently drab and fairly anonymously urban. It is worth noting here that Augé in fact designated the Parisian underground system not a post-modern space but rather one where private memory meets a collective history channelled through older passengers' experiences and the historicity of station names. The Métro featured in *Le Fabuleux destin d'Amélie Poulain* retains something of this modernity, with photography of the station name Abbesses rooting events in an anachronistically reimagined Montmartre – even if Augé himself notes that supermodernity is born merely of an acceleration of 'the determining constituents of modernity'.[18] The anonymity of the crowded Métro carriage in *Clara et moi*, whose geographical moorings are not given, shifts its narrative further into supermodernity – as do scenes showing Clara working as a TGV hostess.[19] The anchorage of events in a recognisable contemporary setting makes it still more surprising when, during their first date against the romantic backdrop of the Seine by night, Antoine and Clara burst into a romantic song complete with dancing.[20]

From Nation to Non-place

Identifying the non-place as central to Parisian romcoms is striking in view of Paris's status in Augé's writing as quintessentially 'a place, or rather an agglomeration of places'.[21] However, such an observation serves as a reminder of the distance between physical settings and the imaginary spaces of highly contrived genres such as romcom. Indeed, Jermyn argues that one explanation for New York's centrality to the iconography of romcom concerns precisely its history as a fulcrum for immigration, which fuels the mythos that 'anything can happen here, *for anyone*' [sic].[22] *Dépaysement*, or a pleasurable sense of unfamiliarity, is one of the intrinsic qualities of romance, which highlights the logic of blending intersubjective encounters with intercultural ones.[23] In Paris-set romcoms, this may be a question of pairing different cultural identities (notably US and French). More often, though, *dépaysement* is evoked by staging romcoms in un-Parisian Parisian locations, either denaturalised versions of the city's traditionally romantic spaces or else places whose Frenchness is reimagined along neo-globalised lines – much, as I have noted, like the Hollywood-indebted indigenous genre as a whole. Old Paris itself is no longer sufficiently exotic to fulfil the generic requirements of romcom, even in films made in the USA: it has become a tired symbol of what Umberto Eco has called 'the already said'.[24] Indeed, Augé has argued that national monuments – like the Eiffel Tower – themselves become non-places when fixed with the distant tourist gaze.[25]

However, if the non-place can be a function of the gaze, a loving gaze can also invest anonymous spaces with meaning. Deterritorialising the Parisian romcom by annexing non-places as sites of intimate romance can thus be read as an act of control over the overwhelming aspects of post-modernity. Interpolating these spaces as loci for human contact makes of them a kind of silver lining to the onward march of 'anonymising' globalisation, as intermittently decried by Augé in the Parisian context.[26] A comparison can thus be made here that addresses one of the central concerns of this collection: Paris's contemporary relation to the city of the Baudelairian modernist *flâneur*. While Augé associated the figure of the traveller with *flânerie*'s deliberate, prolonged and pleasurable meanderings through culturally specific places, for him the passenger – a mere interloper frequenting non-places – was in contrast defined not by the journey but only by the destination stamped on his or her ticket. Genre cinema in general and the romcom in particular appear to me to mobilise elements of both these experiences: the pleasure in watching such films is rooted in the combination of knowing roughly where we will end up, but being along for the joy of the ride. Fascinatingly, Thomas Elsaesser has argued that some of the most important technologies of the 20th century were focused on transport and mobility and that the moving image has participated in the investment of these with subjectivity and fantasy. For Elsaesser, indeed, transport (rather than the ocular qualities associated with modernist *flânerie*) provides a compelling metaphor for the experience of post-modern cinema itself.[27] To comment on the similarities between the experiences of physical motion and sexual desire, or 'falling' in love, is banal: Kline's character Luc makes this very comparison, with a bawdy chortle, during take-off in *French Kiss*. In romcom, however, I would add that the potential for subjective transport on the part of audiences is somewhat circular, in the sense of shoring up our understanding of the world – with incremental modifications – by meeting expectations to a considerable degree. Just as romance may be a means to reinforce the imaginary wholeness and coherence of the subject, paradoxically by interaction with the other, so romcoms are as much concerned with homecoming and destination as they are with the journey.[28] Seen from this angle, the deterritorialised Parisian spaces of contemporary French romcoms suggest not a rejection of national culture but rather the latter's hybridised recalibration for the contemporary world.

Notes

1. Celestino Deleyto, 'Tales of the Millennium (Park): The Happy Ending and the Magic Cityscape of Contemporary Romantic Comedy', in Armelle Parry, Isabelle Roblin and Dominique Spière (eds), *Happy Endings and Films* (Paris: Michel Houdiard, 2010), p. 107.
2. For a full discussion of the phenomenon, see Mary Harrod, *From France with Love: Gender and Identity in French Romantic Comedy* (London: I. B. Tauris, 2015).
3. Deborah Jermyn, 'I ♥ NY: Rom-Com's Love Affair with New York City', in Deborah Jermyn and Stacey Abbott (eds), *Falling in Love Again: Romantic Comedy in Contemporary Culture* (London: I. B. Tauris, 2009), pp. 9–24.
4. Deleyto, 'Millennium (Park)', pp. 103–7.
5. Jermyn, 'I ♥ NY', p. 10.
6. David R. Shumway, *Modern Love: Romance, Intimacy and the Marriage Crisis* (New York and London: New York University Press, 2003), pp. 157–87; Frank Krutnik, 'The Faint Aroma of Performing Seals: The "Nervous" Romance and the Comedy of the Sexes', *The Velvet Light Trap*, no. 26 (Autumn 1990), pp. 57–72.
7. Deleyto, 'Millennium (Park)', p. 107, discussing New York.
8. Julia Hallam and Margaret Marshment, *Realism and Popular Cinema* (Manchester: Manchester University Press, 2000), p. 195.
9. Kathleen Rowe, *The Unruly Woman: Gender and the Genres of Laughter* (Austin: University of Texas Press, 1995), p. 111.
10. See Ginette Vincendeau, 'The New Lower Depths: Paris in French Neo-Noir Cinema', in Mark Bould, Kathrina Glitre and Greg Tuck (eds), *Neo-Noir* (London and New York: Wallflower Press, 2009), p. 111, on the associations between the 18th *arrondissement* and criminality in French cinema of the past and today.
11. Editors' note: see Nicoleta Bazgan's chapter in this volume for a more detailed discussion of the Eiffel Tower in cinema.
12. Neil Archer, 'The City Presented to Itself: Perspective, Performance and the Anxiety of Authenticity in Recent Parisian Films', *Studies in European Cinema*, vol. 8, no. 1 (2011), p. 38.
13. Lynne Pearce and Jackie Stacey, 'The Heart of the Matter: Feminists Revisit Romance', in Lynne Pearce and Jackie Stacey (eds), *Romance Revisited* (London: Lawrence and Wishart, 1995), p. 37.
14. Marc Augé, *Non-places: Introduction to an Anthology of Supermodernity*, trans. John Howe (London and New York: Verso, 1995); Harrod, *From France with Love*, pp. 35–40.
15. Augé, *Non-places*, p. 83.
16. Laura Rascaroli and Ewa Mazierska, *Crossing New Europe: Postmodern Travel and the European Road Movie* (London: Wallflower Press, 2006), p. 44.
17. Janice Radway, *Reading the Romance: Women, Patriarchy and Popular Literature* (Chapel Hill and London: University of North Carolina Press, 1991), p. 156, citing the work of psychoanalyst Nancy Chodorow.

18. Marc Augé, 'Paris and the Ethnography of the Contemporary World', in Michael Sheringham (ed.), Parisian Fields (Critical Views) (London: Reaktion Books, 1996), p. 177; see also Augé, Un ethnologue dans le métro (Paris: Hachette, 1986).
19. The hyper-mobile Clara is also associated with both sexual permissiveness (she later contracts HIV) and with a watered-down form of prostitution, through a second job as a sex phone-line employee. This recalls the de facto identity of the woman streetwalker as prostitute in Walter Benjamin's contribution to the conceptualisation of *flânerie* in *Illuminations* (1950), giving rise to Giuliana Bruno's formative remarks on the 'impossibility' of female *flânerie* in 'Streetwalking around Plato's Cave', *October*, vol. 60 (Spring 1992), p. 126.
20. For a fuller discussion of the interaction of romance and realism in these scenes from *Clara et moi*, see Harrod, *From France with Love*, pp. 37–8.
21. Augé, 'Paris', pp. 175–9.
22. Jermyn, 'I ♥ NY', p. 17.
23. See Diana Holmes, *Romance and Readership in Twentieth-Century France: Love Stories* (Oxford: Oxford University Press, 2006), p. 123.
24. Cited in Frank Krutnik, 'Conforming Passions?: Contemporary Romantic Comedy', in Steve Neale (ed.), *Contemporary Hollywood* (London: BFI, 2002), p. 139.
25. Augé, 'Paris', p. 179.
26. The romcom's drive to tame the metropolis is also much in evidence in the recent Hollywood blockbuster *Friends with Benefits* (Will Gluck, 2011). Here, New York is conscripted in the service of a fantasy of control in a climactic sequence in which the female protagonist exerts her local influence to harness the organic life of the city, street-dancers, into a choreographed sequence in Times Square that is designed as a backdrop to the couple's union.
27. Thomas Elsaesser, 'City of Light, Gardens of Delight: *Metropolis vs Kuhle Wampe*', in Andrew Webber and Emma Wilson (eds), *Cities in Transition* (London: Wallflower Press, 2008), p. 98.
28. See Will Brooker's research on the pertinence of the notion of pilgrimage to the experience of audiovisual consumers, where he cites Victor Witter Turner's work on the way in which pilgrimage is conceived as homecoming in Christian doctrine and imagery. Brooker, 'A Sort of Homecoming: Fan Viewing and Symbolic Pilgrimage', in Jonathan Gray, Cornell Sandvoss and C. Lee Harrington (eds), *Fandom: Identities and Communities in a Mediated World* (New York: New York University Press, 2007), p. 164.

The Enduring Glamour of the Parisienne

Stephen Gundle

Writing in 1910, the bibliophile and cultural critic Octave Uzanne declared that the Parisienne was 'an aristocrat among the world's women',[1] because 'at all levels of the social scale, woman is a hundred times more woman in Paris than in any other city in the universe'.[2] This was so because its particular atmosphere of charm modelled 'pretty women', by 'slimming, polishing, refining, beautifying and staging' them. A bewitching seductiveness, a delightful coquettishness, unleashed at the highest power, was apparent in the gestures, the gait, the smile, the expression and the bearing of the women, which together were 'of a marvellous harmony, science and justice'.[3] They were the expression of a 'perfect art' that remained constant over time. No matter how much the city might change, woman 'conserved her excellence ... and her indisputable supremacy'.[4] The hallmarks of the Parisienne, he argued, were beauty, gaiety and goodness. Together they fuelled a mood of joy and pleasure that typified the city and made its streets 'artistic and lovely, a fairytale Eden of subtle desires, of sudden admirations, of strange adventures'.[5]

Uzanne was not offering an original analysis or labelling a hitherto unidentified phenomenon. He was merely elaborating and celebrating notions which became widespread in the Belle Epoque and which, in some ways, would forever be associated with that period through popular song and literature, painting, touristic literature and fashion advertising.[6] Singing the praises of Paris and enumerating its delights was commonplace among male journalists, commentators and novelists, who invariably included the city's uniquely seductive women among these. The Parisienne or, more accurately, the male fantasy of the Parisian woman, acutely analysed by Elizabeth Wilson,[7] was accorded unique symbolic importance during the Universal Exposition of 1900, when a statue of a proud, beautiful and indisputably modern woman, fashionably attired in flowing robes, had been placed over the monumental gateway in the place de la Concorde. Critics, who saw in the statue traits of the courtesan, had condemned it as a hymn to prostitution, but this was no impediment to writers for whom the *demi-monde* in any case constituted one of the city's great attractions.

The aim of this chapter is to explore the legacy of the fantasy of the Parisienne in post-war cinema. In the 1950s and 1960s, France underwent a far-reaching process of industrialisation which uprooted traditions and extended mass consumption to the country as a whole. In the course of this, established symbols of Frenchness and of French modernity were thrown into question. In the discussion that follows, it will be shown that tensions existed between continuities and nostalgic evocations on the one hand, and ruptures and reconfigurations on the other. After several of the purposes served by the myth have been outlined, the chapter will explore some of the ways in which the pre-World War One era was revisited in film and will consider the subsequent emergence and affirmation of Catherine Deneuve as the quintessential Parisienne.

The Parisienne Fantasy

For Charles Rearick, the fantasy figure of the Parisienne actually consisted of two emblematic figures: 'the sexy fun-loving young Parisienne' and 'the elegant high-fashion woman'.[8] For convenience, these were often rolled into one in rhapsodic descriptions of the personification of the soul of Paris. The fantasy was fuelled by drawings and cartoons in magazines like *La Vie Parisienne*, the vibrant posters of Jules Chéret, as well as a range of actresses, dancers, singers, society beauties and *demimondaines* whose portraits were painted by such artists as Giovanni Boldini, Carolus Duran and Henri Béraud.[9] Two key aspects of the myth were institutionalised in the economic and cultural life of the city. First, there was the fashion industry. The first couture houses in the mid-19th century built on the reputation Paris had acquired in the pre-Revolutionary era. They prospered under the Second Empire as the court of Napoleon III absorbed the newly wealthy of the world. Houses like Worth and Doucet were joined in later years by Paquin and Patou. Second, there was the entertainment world. The theatre, music hall and operetta provided platforms for narratives, songs and performers who would give shape and voice to the atmospheres of the city. Paris acquired a special reputation for daring, eroticised entertainment that was confirmed when several courtesans took to the stage in the late 19th century. Unlike predecessors including Alphonsine Duplessis, the inspiration for Alexandre Dumas fils' *La Dame aux camélias*, La Belle Otero, Liane De Pougy and others were performers who veiled their sexual commerce with art. Their adventures and antics, amply reported in the press, constituted the stuff of the lore of Paris as a centre of luxury and erotic refinement.

This legend of Paris as a city imbued with a special vocation for female entertainment and for love took special shape in the aftermath of the Franco-Prussian War, reaching full bloom between the end of the 19th century and the early years of the 20th. Under the Third Republic, notions of joy, charm and seductiveness, ostensibly deriving from the *ancien régime*, were resuscitated as a form of national pride, as 'a civilised trait to which the Prussians could never aspire'.[10] Noémi Hepp has argued that 'all the forms of old-time aristocratic *galanterie* were re-proposed in various *nouveau riche*, *petit-bourgeois* and popular settings'. In the novels of Emile Zola and Guy de Maupassant, these qualities were to be found not only in interpersonal relations but in the press and the department store.[11]

This particular cultural disposition declined in the aftermath of World War One, when greater numbers of women entered the labour market, societal norms changed and the idea of 'the woman enveloped in leisure, dreams and mystery' lost relevance.[12] However, as Hepp argues, it never completely disappeared.[13] Indeed, notions of lighthearted eroticism formed part of the rosy collective memory of the Belle Epoque as a vanished golden age which flourished in the 1920s and 1930s.[14]

The Historical Parisiennes of Post-war Cinema

Ideas of the Belle Epoque also brought consolation following World War Two in the aftermath of defeat and German occupation. At this time, memories served as what Rearick calls an 'emotional touchstone' for thinking on Paris's present and future. In contrast to the last decades of the 19th century, cinema more than the press and literature provided the vehicle for this use of the past. The Belle Epoque films flourished as a subgenre of the historical film, which, according to Rearick, provided 'a pleasant daydream and entertainment, offering the nation distractions from painful memories of war, strife, insecurity and misery'.[15] They provided an important way in which national identity was asserted and a shared idea of the national past affirmed. Films like *Casque d'or* (Jacques Becker, 1952) and *French Cancan* (Jean Renoir, 1954) evoked strong notions of Frenchness and thus pleased domestic and foreign audiences. The Belle Epoque was especially popular as a setting for these films on account of its spectacular possibilities, its association with capitalist growth and the period's famed light-hearted gaiety.[16] Many of the dozens of films belonging to this subgenre were set in Paris and over half of them were centred on a female protagonist. However, they were not purely nostalgic, Geneviève Sellier argues, for they allowed directors to explore women's points of view in a period remote from the present.[17] The genre, Sellier continues, 'became the privileged site for [...] a strong representation of women', a role that differentiated them from contemporary-set films, which continued to be imbued with traditional and patriarchal views about the life possibilities of women. Parisiennes of the past were given fresh, contemporary faces in films, which contributed to a revival of the city's associations with modernity and femininity. As Susan Hayward has shown, costume films were an excellent vehicle for fashion and thus confirmed 'the lengthy heritage of France's fashion supremacy, and thus its legitimacy as a nation of taste'.[18] In some cases, narratives were woven around prominent archetypal figures like the stage artiste or the great courtesan. La Belle Otero was revived in the eponymous film (1954), with Maria Felix in the title role, while one of the most popular stars of the time, Martine Carol, played Zola's anti-heroine Nana in the film of the same title by Christian-Jacque (1955), as well as Lola Montès in Ophuls's biopic of an earlier courtesan (1955).

Women of the past were reinvented and proposed to new audiences in ways that strongly evoked Paris as a city of opportunity with a special capacity for celebrating and moulding female beauty. The sense of possibility was exemplified, for example, by the story of Nini, the laundry girl who becomes a theatrical star, which constitutes a key narrative thread of *French Cancan*. Nini's tale is not one without shadows and regrets, but the film dramatises opportunities, choices and pleasures. The role brought Françoise Arnoul unprecedented recognition. Her character starts as a lively, unpretentious but pretty girl who plans to marry her working-class boyfriend.[19] Over the course of the film, she is transformed into a figure of desire who, while still in a relationship with the boyfriend, begins an affair with the theatrical impresario Danglard (Jean Gabin) and is wooed by a prince. Her appearance, while not being her sole appeal, contributes to her success. Writers of the late 19th century, like the distinguished Italian anthropologist Alfredo Niceforo, had been quite specific about the physical type of the Parisienne.[20]

She was slim, dynamic and sinuous; she possessed 'a barely noticeable bust, a tiny waist, small white hands, slender feet, a delicate face and abundant well-cared-for locks'.[21] Some of these characteristics carried over easily into the post-war period, while others diminished in importance. Arnoul, however, possessed them all.

The association of entertainment with the urban scene had contributed in the 19th century to an idea of Paris as what Vanessa Schwartz has called 'the metropolis par excellence'.[22] Commercialism and a diffuse entertainment culture entailed a marked emphasis on the artificial and on the manipulation of beauty. *French Cancan*'s Danglard is presented as a master of beauty in the mould of Florenz Ziegfeld, a Svengali who creates female stars for public enjoyment and profit. Renoir's film, his first after returning from the USA, asserts Paris's role in the origins of glamour, a special allure that Hollywood had virtually branded as its own. If, as I have argued elsewhere, glamour can be defined as an enticing image that invites consumption, a manufactured illusion of wealth, beauty and desirability aimed at the masses,[23] then Danglard's dream of an entertainment palace offering the illusion of the high life for modest purses is fully compatible with it. Indeed, the realisation of his dream in the Moulin Rouge is the film's assertion of a French and specifically Parisian patent over glamour.[24] It is significant that Renoir should have done this at a time when American power was at its zenith and glamour and Hollywood were virtually synonymous for film audiences. Recovering France's pre-eminent place as the centre of allure bolstered national pride and complemented the relaunch of Parisian style and taste. The way the three colours of the French flag were woven into the film's *mise-en-scène* helped turn it into an explicit expression of French cultural influence.[25]

Martine Carol's career was intimately bound up with costume drama. A Parisian by birth, she first emerged in *Caroline chérie/Dear Caroline* (Richard Pottier, 1951), a historical romance set in the Revolutionary era, in which she played a young aristocrat who falls for a soldier. Over the next five years, she consolidated her position as 'the number one French sex symbol', offering the public a series of performances of a highly constructed type. For Alastair Phillips, 'from the start, there was nothing natural in the persona of Martine Carol'; her physique, acting style and costuming distinguished her from everyday reality.[26] She was invariably 'a hyper-sexualised object of male desire' whose physical attributes, notably her bosom and legs, were amply displayed. Embedded in her screen image were obsessions with appearances and consumption. Thus, her costumes are often sumptuous and eye-catching, with an haute couture feel to them. Her star persona also incorporated this element. Her association with post-war fashion was first established when *Elle* magazine dressed her in Dior for a cover feature in 1947,[27] and in the contemporary-set romantic comedy *Adorables créatures* (Christian-Jacque, 1952), she visits a Parisian fashion boutique.

Carol was in her thirties at the height of her success and thus, for Phillips, she 'cannot be associated with the values of youth, liberty and modernity'.[28] She corresponded more to Rearick's 'elegant high-fashion woman' than to the youthful version of the Parisienne. In *Nana*, she quickly exchanges the gauche mannerisms of the working-class upstart for those of the professional coquette. As Hayward has shown, Carol's Nana was much 'toned-down' from Zola's original and 'softened-up' in terms of the sensual appeal that replaces the original's unbridled sexuality.[29] In the film's glamorised euphemism, little remains of the novelist's condemnation of the society that placed the likes of Nana on a pedestal, and the protagonist herself is spared degradation and the physical disfigurement of smallpox. Instead, the screen Nana meets an untimely end when her enraged former lover, Count Muffat (Charles Boyer), strangles her. The film's Second Empire setting is adjusted to incorporate both the star persona of the actress and the *galanterie* of the Belle Epoque, which the boulevard newspaper *Gil Blas* had defined as 'a light heart, a carefree character, a joyful attitude, pronounced taste for change and the unexpected, a horror of regularity, uniformity, routine and convention, a degree of leisure, a certain amount of philosophy and almost total personal independence'.[30] The film made a spectacle of Caro's physical appeals and showed her deriving enjoyment from teasing and tormenting her suitors and lovers. The film's ultimate message, however, was conventional. For Hayward, it offered 'a safe portrayal of loose morality that is suitably punished, and which stands as a warning to women who transgress'.[31]

Changes to Carol's appearance were much discussed and on occasion staged for the illustrated press. Her magnificently artificial blonde hair marked her out as glamorous. It was subject to constant restyling, with curls and waves adding to her allure according to the roles she played.[32] In her historical films, it is especially long and abundant and functions as a sign of her physical desirability. Like Marilyn Monroe, to whom she was compared, she was the very embodiment of the idea of the star. But there was nothing of the 'dumb blonde' cliché about her.[33] Even if her characters are frequently inserted in narratives which result in their comeuppance, they display a knowingness and resilience that comes from experience and which is culturally validated by the long association of Paris with the arts of love.

Catherine Deneuve as Parisienne

The historical genre flourished at the start of a phase of great social and economic modernisation during which France would exchange a rural, imperialist identity for an urban, consumerist one. The Paris cityscape itself was subject to significant reshaping and rebuilding at this time, with the result that the visual symbols of the modern city of 1900, where they survived, came to be seen as quaint reminders of what Rearick terms 'dear old Paris'.[34] Representations of the city in film increasingly took in busy real-life streets and motor vehicles, the cultural significance of which has been explored by Kristin Ross.[35] As these changes came to be widely felt, the historical genre lost appeal,[36] while new stars emerged, first among them Brigitte Bardot.

Although she was born and raised in Paris, Bardot was not in any meaningful way a cinematic Parisienne. As a film star, she was the cultural symbol of an entire country that was breaking with tradition and embracing mass culture.[37] Nevertheless, on occasion a linkage with the established female imagery of the capital was embraced. The film Bardot made immediately after the scandalous *Et Dieu ... créa la femme/And God Created Woman* (1956), which would associate her in the public mind with the Côte d'Azur, was *Une Parisienne* (1957), a light romantic comedy which included both conventional tropes and new themes. Bardot's character, also named Brigitte, is the daughter of the prime minister. A headstrong young woman, she manipulates situations to her advantage and, in order to gain revenge over her straying spouse, plays a game of love with a visiting prince (played by the charming master of old-style *galanterie*, Charles Boyer) that would have won applause from a Belle Epoque courtesan, were it not for the 'fundamental innocence' of the character and indeed of the young actress, despite the potency of her erotic display, as Ginette Vincendeau argues. Despite this, Brigitte is as fashionable and urbane as any Parisienne. When she poses as a maid to serve her husband's mistress, the latter is perplexed to find a domestic employee dressed in Balmain. When the prince whisks her down to the Côte d'Azur in his plane, a local restaurateur remarks that he can tell at a glance that she is from Paris on account of her look and style.

The alignment of Bardot with Paris fashion was unusual as she was very far removed from Rearick's ideal of 'the elegant high-fashion woman'. Indeed, she contributed decisively to the demise of the old-school elegance that was associated with the Paris fashion world by rejecting traditional couture and embracing the creations of 'a new breed of trendy young couturiers such as Jacques Estérel and Louis Féraud'.[38] By popularising their simple dresses, she helped promote prêt-à-porter. Among the new couturiers who reconnected Paris fashion with novelty was Yves Saint Laurent. Hired to replace Christian Dior after his untimely death, Saint Laurent brought street style dramatically to the catwalk in his 1960 'Beat' collection. Under his own name, he would appropriate youth themes and shift the focus of fashion towards youth culture, opening his first Rive Gauche boutique in 1966.[39] He would also establish a long-running creative partnership with Catherine Deneuve, whose costumes he designed in *Belle de jour* (1967) and many other films.

More than any other film actress, Deneuve would come to represent over time the different faces of the Parisienne, giving them a contemporary and predominantly bourgeois edge. The way she came to be associated so closely with Paris has to do with her personal biography (she was born in the capital to actor parents), an artistic career which saw her work with the best directors and actors, a fashion persona forged through her associations with Saint Laurent and to a lesser extent Chanel (whose perfumes she advertised), her unconventional private life and, finally, the creative flair with which she shaped her own image over the decades.

Her first role, at the age of 18, saw her take the part of the *lycéenne* Sophie in an episode of the 1962 film *Les Parisiennes/Tales of Paris*, directed by Marc Allégret. Her famed poise and self-containment are already in evidence in a character who acquires a sexual allure when her friends erroneously suspect that she has a lover. In order not to disappoint them, she fakes a night-time rendezvous at her friend's apartment, only to encounter, as she flees across the rooftops and stumbles into a bed-sitting room, the man who will truly become her lover. This is none other than Johnny Hallyday, who plays an aspiring rock musician. Soon afterwards, the pair find themselves in Sophie's parents' very bourgeois apartment and there they begin a musical interlude which will see the action temporarily cut to a stage where Hallyday is playing with backing musicians. Deneuve joins him on stage for a memorable twist before the action switches back to the apartment.

Rock star Johnny Halliday serenades Sophie (Catherine Deneuve) in *Les Parisiennes/Tales of Paris* (episode 'Sophie', Marc Allégret, 1962).

In this film, Deneuve is a relatively ordinary Parisian girl. She and Hallyday walk arm in arm in the street like any contemporary couple, but even at this stage in her career the actress had little in common with the working-class girls of Parisian mythology. It was thanks to her enigmatic beauty that Deneuve would establish herself as one of the most famous faces of French cinema. In 1968, *Look* magazine labelled her 'the most beautiful woman in the world'. Over time, she would become a quintessential symbol of Paris. As Agnès Rocamora writes:

> With films such as Buñuel's 1967 *Belle de Jour*, Truffaut's 1980 *Le Dernier Métro* or Nicole Garcia's 1998 *Place Vendôme*, Deneuve's face has superimposed itself onto that of the anonymous *Parisienne*, in the process cementing the actress's position at the junction of both the imagined and the lived. For Catherine Deneuve, by virtue of living in Paris, is a *Parisienne*, whilst at the same time her identity cannot be disassociated from the glamorous fictional images – the imagined Parisian women that have made her famous the world over.[40]

The interplay of the real and the fictional, as well as of past and present, is crucial to the Deneuve persona. As an actress, she belonged to the entertainment industry, while as a star she always cultivated links to fashion, which is the other quintessentially Parisian industry. In her roles, she is often positioned between the traditional and the contemporary. Her Janus-faced character in *Belle de jour* lives in an apartment which is decorated with a curious mixture of Louis XV furniture and contemporary art. While many of her films are contemporary in setting, others project her back into the past. In *Le Dernier Métro/The Last Metro* (1980), set during the German occupation of Paris, she is a theatre manager who becomes embroiled in a *ménage à trois* with her husband,

Positioned between the traditional and the contemporary: Séverine (Catherine Deneuve) in *Belle de jour* (Luis Buñuel, 1967).

who is hiding in the bowels of the theatre, and a young actor who woos her. Her character's elegant exterior, and perhaps also her frosty hauteur (both inseparable from the Deneuve image), are explained by the fact that Deneuve worked for Chanel before taking up acting.

The transgressive aspects of Deneuve's star persona, which were often configured as the flip side of her legendary self-containment, did not prevent her from winning official approval. By the 1980s, she was firmly established as the internationally recognised face of 'French chic'. For Sue Harris, the mature actress embodied 'physical elegance, bourgeois sophistication, intellectual strength and the suggestion of sexual desire held in check by social and historical circumstances'.[41] She was widely seen as 'an icon of compassionate French identity, accessed through her established cinematic femininity'.[42] This role meant that she was an obvious candidate in 1985 to be the new face of Marianne, the symbolic embodiment of the French Republic. Her association with an 'enduring narrative of national maternal authority intensified the aura and appeal of her screen incarnations'.[43]

For Deneuve, fashion was a realm in which she was to some extent trapped by an image, like Agnès Varda's Cléo in *Cléo de 5 à 7/Cleo from 5 to 7* (1962). Rocamora shows that Paris *Vogue* used her repeatedly as an example of the chic Parisienne, her celebrity serving as a way to connect her with discourses about the city, femininity and fashion which the magazine controlled.[44] But it was also a sphere in which she creatively developed both an off-screen and an on-screen identity. The actress displayed a propensity for reinvention, playing against her established image, demonstrating a 'rare capacity for visible self-deconstruction'.[45] The fantasy Parisienne had always been a figure interested in fashion and creative in her relations with it. Deneuve enjoyed a commercial relationship with fashion companies but disguised this by cloaking it with the aura of art. Saint Laurent was not, for her, a business associate but a kindred spirit.

Deneuve's Paris was not obviously a city of lively streets. It is difficult to imagine her mature persona strolling along the boulevards like some of the female characters of the New Wave. Rather, her Paris is more institutional and rarefied; it is the bourgeois city of capitalism and consumption, which is populated by the couture houses, the salons, the large hotels and public buildings. In any event, the city streets which had offered observers so many delightful pleasures in the Belle Epoque, and which still afforded opportunities for sights and encounters in the early 1960s, had by the 1970s given way to the traffic. The modernisation that many had resisted or criticised up to that point as un-French had become a fact of life.

Deneuve, finally, represents a reconciliation of old and new images of the Parisian woman. She has incorporated long-standing fantasies and the changes of the postwar decades, changes which have brought prosperity to the city as well as a certain class levelling (Morin wrote in the early 1960s of the gentrification heralded by mass culture[46]). She has synthesised both into an image which has become both fixed and ever-changing. It is appropriate therefore that the actress has often commented on the changing city, offering views which blend nostalgia with a certain openness to novelty.

> I used to live in the 16th *arrondissement*, between the Porte d'Auteuil and the Boulevard Exelmans, and when I walk near there I see the viaduct which no longer exists, the Molitor swimming pool which has also gone, my high school ... But I am not wedded to the past. I think there have been some fantastic innovations in Paris. The Great Arch of La Défense, the Othoniel Métro station,[47] Bernard Benet's sculptures in the Tuileries gardens ... I am very open to this evolving Paris.[48]

'The more I travel, the more I love Paris,' she added. 'There are visions of it that never leave me. Every day offers some pleasure for the eyes. It really has to rain a lot for me not to notice something I adore about Paris.'

Notes

1. Octave Uzanne, *Parisiennes de ce temps en leurs divers milieux, états et conditions* (Paris: Mercure de France, 1910), p. 20.
2. Ibid., p. 18.
3. Ibid., p. 19.
4. Ibid.
5. Ibid., p. 23.
6. On the genesis of the myth of the Parisienne, see Patrice Higonnet, *Paris: Capital of the World* (Cambridge, MA: Harvard University Press, 2002), pp. 95–120.
7. Elizabeth Wilson, *The Sphinx in the City: Urban Life, the Control of Disorder, and Women* (London: Virago, 1991), Chapter 4.
8. Charles Rearick, *Paris Dreams, Paris Memories: The City and Its Mystique* (Stanford, CA: Stanford University Press, 2011), p. 34.
9. Ibid., p. 35.

10. Noémi Hepp, 'La Galanterie', in Pierre Nora (ed.), *Les Lieux de mémoire*, vol. 3 (Paris: Gallimard, 1997), p. 3702.
11. Guy de Maupassant's *Bel-Ami* (1885) and Emile Zola's *Au bonheur des dames* (1883), respectively set in the worlds of the press and the department store, both show how eroticism was harnessed by modern commercial organisations.
12. Hepp, 'La Galanterie', p. 3702.
13. Ibid.
14. Rearick, *Paris Dreams*, p. 69.
15. Ibid., p. 89.
16. The majority of the historical films of the post-war years were set in the 19th century and the most popular period was that of the Belle Epoque, which is generally taken to cover the years 1889–1914. See Susan Hayward, *French Costume Drama of the 1950s* (Bristol: Intellect Press, 2010), pp. 31–2.
17. Geneviève Sellier, 'The Belle Epoque Genre in Postwar French Cinema: A Woman's Film *à la francaise*?' *Studies in French Cinema*, vol. 3, no. 1 (2003), pp. 47–53.
18. Hayward, *French Costume Drama*, p. 19.
19. In other words, she corresponds to Rearick's fun-loving young Parisienne, a figure similar to the working-class *grisette*. See Valerie Steele, *Paris Fashion: A Cultural History* (New York: Oxford University Press, 1988), pp. 70–5.
20. Alfredo Niceforo, *Parigi: una città rinnovata* (Turin: Bocca, 1911), pp. 188–9.
21. Ibid., p. 189.
22. Vanessa Schwartz, *Spectacular Realities: Early Mass Culture in Fin-de-Siècle Paris* (Berkeley: University of California Press, 1998), p. 13.
23. Stephen Gundle, *Glamour: A History* (Oxford: Oxford University Press, 2008).
24. On Paris's historical contribution to glamour, see Stephen Gundle, 'Mapping the Origins of Glamour: Giovanni Boldini, Paris and the Belle Epoque', *Journal of European Studies*, vol. 29, no. 3 (1999), pp. 269–95.
25. Janet Bergstrom, 'Jean Renoir's Return to France', *Poetics Today*, vol. 17, no. 3 (1996), pp. 453–89.
26. Alastair Phillips, '"La Séductrice française no.1": le cas de "Martine chérie"', *Iris*, no. 26 (1998), p. 103.
27. 26 August 1947.
28. Phillips, '"La Séductrice française no.1"', p. 105.
29. Hayward, *French Costume Drama*, p. 292.
30. Anon., 'Journal d'un fantasiste: sur la galanterie', *Gil Blas*, 3 July 1895, p. 1.
31. Hayward, *French Costume Drama*, p. 292.
32. Phillips, '"La Séductrice française no.1"', p. 104.
33. Ibid.
34. Rearick, *Paris Dreams*, p. 44.
35. Kristin Ross, *Fast Cars, Clean Bodies: Decolonization and the Reordering of French Culture* (Cambridge, MA: MIT Press, 1996).
36. Hayward suggests that the golden age of the costume drama came to an end in 1959. See *French Costume Drama*, p. 18.

37. Edgar Morin described this process as '*le grand cracking*' in his *L'Esprit du temps* (Paris: Grasset, 1962), pp. 59–74.
38. Ginette Vincendeau, 'Hot Couture: Brigitte Bardot's Fashion Revolution', in Rachel Moseley (ed.), *Fashioning Film Stars: Dress, Culture, Identity* (London: BFI, 2005), p. 142. Féraud in fact designed some of her costumes for *Une Parisienne*.
39. Steele, *Paris Fashion*, pp. 276–81.
40. Agnès Rocamora, *Fashioning the City: Paris, Fashion and the Media* (London: I. B. Tauris, 2009), p. 94.
41. Sue Harris, '"Madame La France": Deneuve as Heritage Icon', in Lisa Downing and Sue Harris (eds), *From Perversion to Purity: The Stardom of Catherine Deneuve* (Manchester: Manchester University Press, 2007), p. 96.
42. Ibid., p. 97.
43. Ibid., p. 107.
44. Rocamora, *Fashioning the City*, p. 98.
45. Lisa Downing and Sue Harris, 'Introduction', in Downing and Harris (eds), *From Perversion to Purity*, p. 5.
46. Morin, *L'Esprit du temps,* pp. 37–45.
47. Editors' note: Jean-Michel Othoniel designed the Palais-Royal Métro station.
48. This and the quotations that follow are all taken from 'Le Paris de Catherine Deneuve'. Available at: http://toutsurdeneuve.free.fr/Francais/Pages/Interviews_Presse0009/ANousParis04.htm (accessed 8 January 2016).

Part III
HISTORY

Charles Dickens's Two Cities

Colin Jones

In 1853, while holidaying in France, the usually clean-shaven Charles Dickens grew a moustache. It was, he informed a writer friend, 'the pride of Albion and the admiration of Gaul'.¹ This light-hearted remark highlights the fact that a writer who is often seen as quintessentially English had a strong identification with France as well as his native England. In particular, Dickens adored Paris. If London was his principal place of residence and the location of many of the plots of his novels, Paris was where he had fun. From the 1840s, he was a frequent visitor to the city, which he judged 'the most extraordinary place in all the world', and where he indulged in endless theatre-going, tourist visiting and general *flânerie*.² Yet when he incorporated the city into his historical novel, *A Tale of Two Cities* (1859), he transformed this site of private hedonism into an abyss of social emiseration and political tyranny.

The Paris of *A Tale of Two Cities* was not the 19th-century city of Dickens's jaunts and *flânerie*, but rather the Revolutionary stronghold of the late 18th century. The plot unfolds through the last decades of the century in both London and Paris, and its famous denouement takes place in the French capital at the height of the Terror of 1793–94. In essence a love story, the novel encompasses an account of the French Revolution that has been highly influential in British culture, and indeed, as I shall argue, in the culture of Britishness.³ Dickens was delighted by the 'extraordinary success' that what he regarded as 'the best story I ever wrote' enjoyed among the British public.⁴ In contrast, the novel was little known in France – and where it was known it was viewed in a hostile fashion. The aim of the present chapter is to explore how this tale of two receptions provides an instructive context for analysing the two best-known cinematic adaptations of the novel – namely, the 1935 MGM Hollywood version, produced by David O. Selznick, directed by Jack Conway and starring Ronald Coleman, and the Rank Organisation's British version, directed by Ralph Thomas and produced by Betty Box, starring Dirk Bogarde, which was released in 1958.⁵

Franco-British Reception of the Novel

An infallible sign of *A Tale of Two Cities*'s popularity and the privileged place it enjoys in British culture is that the wording of the opening and closing passages has passed into common English parlance. 'It was the best of times, it was the worst of times' introduces an overview of 1774, but in fact refers to the whole period that the novel covers, up to 1793–94. In the last scene, the hero (or rather, anti-hero) Sydney Carton mounts the steps to the guillotine – stoically sacrificing himself for a woman he adored, after substituting himself in prison for his rival in love (Charles Darnay) – and utters the words, 'It is a far, far better thing that I do than I have ever done'. This has become a *locus classicus* of the arch-British notion of a stiff upper lip.

By the late 19th century, *A Tale of Two Cities* had become one of the works of Dickens that was most read in British schools. This seems also to have been the case in the USA. David O. Selznick, for example, read it when a boy; it was, he later maintained, 'revered by tens of millions of individuals'.[6] Its growing place in Anglophone culture was endorsed by stage adaptations, long before filmmakers got hold of it. Towards the end of the century, a play closely based on the novel, entitled *The Only Way*, opened at the Lyceum Theatre and continued the work of diffusion.[7] With actor-director John Martin-Harvey as Sydney Carton, the play achieved notoriety by being performed in 1899 by besieged English troops, under the Ur-Boy Scout, Robert Baden-Powell, at the siege of Mafeking during the Boer War. The guillotine scene's 'Far, far better thing …' had the effect of boosting troop morale – as was widely and enthusiastically reported when Mafeking was relieved, to much chauvinistic rejoicing on British streets. The final scene's nationalistic popularity was confirmed in World War One. Martin-Harvey toured the battlefields, and Carton's guillotine scene and 'Far, far better thing …' became the preferred entertainment of Tommies in the trenches, beating into second place Henry V's similarly upper-lip stiffening exhortation, 'Once more unto the breach'.

One might never suspect from these examples that Britain fought both World Wars against the Germans, with the French as their allies! The Francophobic element in English culture testifies to the much earlier role that the French had played in the 18th and early 19th centuries as Britain's most redoubtable enemy. It was at this moment, Linda Colley has argued, that emergent British national identity was crystallised around a French 'other'.[8] In 1940, George Orwell noted that the 'average Englishman' still regarded the French Revolution as nothing but 'a pyramid of guillotined heads'.[9] This highlighted an enduring tendency to contrast 'evolutionary' Anglo-American politics against a revolutionary tradition in France that was viewed almost entirely negatively.[10]

It is worth noting that this British view of *A Tale of Two Cities* as a quintessentially anti-French, anti-revolutionary text has been widely shared in France too. Dickens's novels have always been popular across the Channel, and he himself was something of a celebrity in Paris. Yet *A Tale of Two Cities* has always been almost invisible in France. Symptomatically, French publishers have had difficulty in even agreeing a title for the work. Only in the late 20th century did the straightforward *Un conte de deux villes* prevail.[11] This neglect owes something too to the overtly counter-revolutionary politics of the most authoritative specialist on English literature in the late 19th century, Hyppolite Taine. Although he never commented at length on *A Tale of Two Cities*, Taine was the most loquacious French commentator on Dickens. His hyper-reactionary politics seems to have cast a shadow over the novel, so that, by a process of a kind of guilt by association in the years leading to World War One, Dickens was placed in the same camp in most French minds as the Baroness d'Orczy, author of the very overtly reactionary Scarlet Pimpernel novels.[12]

Charles Dickens, Paris and London

Despite the role of the novel in feeding national stereotypes in both countries, there is good reason to believe that Dickens himself had a quite different appreciation of his story. Dickens received encouragement and stimulation from the wild and largely reactionary history of the French Revolution by his friend Thomas Carlyle.[13] But Dickens was far from sharing Carlyle's – any more than Taine's – political views. His own politics were liberal rather than conservative. In fact, they bordered on populist radicalism, especially as regards the seriousness with which he took the social question in British industrial cities. He was highly critical of politically motivated crowds – but he was even more hostile towards social elites that showed sadistic indifference to the sufferings of the poor. The real villain of *A Tale of Two Cities* was not the legendarily malignant *tricoteuse*, Madame Defarge, vengeful emanation of the sinister faubourg Saint-Antoine, but rather the etiolated and cruelly insouciant aristocrat, the Marquis d'Evrémonde. By the same token, Dickens was severe in regard to the conduct of the English elites of his own time. His attacks on French Revolutionary crowds were targeted less at the French and more at revolutionary crowds per se.[14] He held that the people were invariably driven to excess by the unfeeling conduct of their social superiors. Although it has been little remarked on, the most ferocious mobs to be found in Dickens's oeuvre are not in *A Tale of Two Cities* at all, but in his other historical novel, the lesser-known *Barnaby Rudge* (1841), in which he paints a chilling picture of the anti-Catholic mobs that wrecked much of central London in the Gordon Riots of 1780.[15]

Dickens was thus not the reactionary Francophobe he is often painted. On the contrary, as we have suggested, he was Francophilic and 'Parisomaniac'. The Paris he admired was not the city of the 1790s, however, but that of the 1840s and 1850s. In these years, Paris was transformed by Napoleon III and the Paris Prefect, Baron Georges Haussmann, from '*le vieux Paris*' into the fabled 'City of Light': 'Haussmannisation' involved the erasure of dirt and disease from central Paris and their replacement by wide, tree-lined boulevards, outdoor cafés, excellent public services, and manicured parks and squares – a perfect setting in fact for Dickens's *flânerie*.[16]

From this perspective, *A Tales of Two Cities* may be viewed less as a Francophobic or counter-revolutionary parable, than as a wake-up call to British elites to take social and urban problems more seriously – or face potentially revolutionary consequences. The underlying causes of Parisian street radicalism, Dickens states, were 'cold, dirt, sickness, ignorance and want' – and in the era in which he lived, these were more to be found, he held, in London than in Haussmannising Paris.[17] Symptomatically, the scenes of Parisian poverty within the faubourg Saint-Antoine in the novel (contrasting with a hyper-prosperous Soho that features strongly in the films) are based more on Dickens's experience of London's East End than on Paris: for close analysis of his movements within the city in his frequent visits shows that he most of all haunted the touristy boulevard neighbourhoods in the north-west of the city, and never once set foot in the faubourg Saint-Antoine.[18]

Film Versions: Confirming Stereotypes

When we view the film versions of *A Tale of Two Cities*, it is very apparent that they take their inspiration much more from the nationalistic stereotypes that grew up around the novel after Dickens's death than the author's own estimation of his cherished novel. Those stereotypes highlighted antagonism between French and British values, with the latter always regarded as superior. The cultural resonance of this vision has proved sufficiently strong to preclude a film version of the novel being made in France.[19]

The first film adaptation of the novel appears to have been in 1908 in the USA, but the first still accessible is the 45-minute Vitagraph film, directed by William Humphrey, which came out in the USA in 1911. A further version, directed by Frank Lloyd, appeared in 1917 and this was followed in 1935 by the lavish David O. Selznick MGM production.[20] In it, Sydney Carton was played by the British actor Ronald Coleman, who had already achieved celebrity in the USA by perfectly incarnating what Americans imagined a true gentleman from 'Old England' was like: handsome, debonair, seductive, imperturbable, slightly ironic (with a penchant for mild self-mockery) and proud possessor of an iconically stiff upper lip. In 1958, it would be the turn of another matinee idol and leading man to take the role, namely Dirk Bogarde, who was then at the height of his fame. Wisely perhaps, he emulated the ultra-English stiff-upper-lip demeanour that Coleman had displayed.

Other casting confirmed this stereotypically nationalistic version of the leading man. In the films, sympathetic characters are always located on the English side. The transformation of Charles Darnay from French physician and aristocrat to English gentleman is warmly approved. The Miss Pross character – Edna May Oliver in 1935 and the cherishable Athene Seyler in 1958 – also plays to a classic English stereotype: the strict but fiercely loyal and ultimately loveable middle-class spinster-servant, who glories in the name of 'Briton' in her battle with Madame Defarge, as recorded in the novel and in both films.

On the French side, sympathy is altogether scarcer. Up to 1789, the impoverished Parisians are viewed pityingly, and our antagonism is drawn more towards the heartless and insouciant aristocracy. But by the time of the Terror, the plebeian radical population of the faubourg Saint-Antoine are exhibiting swarthy, greasy and feral physiognomies. The two films vie in their disapproval of the drunken, loutish and sadistic behaviour on view. Then again, Madame Defarge is revealed to owe her deep-dyed class hatred of the Saint-Evrémonde family to the rape of her sister and murder of her father and brother by the Marquis in her childhood. But she is presented – by both Blanche Yurka in 1935 and Rosalie Crutchley in 1958 – as a daemonic maenad rather than a long-suffering, sadly traumatised victim.

In an odd paradox, the two great cities in which the action of *A Tale of Two Cities* takes place are remarkable in the film versions only by their absence. There are pragmatic reasons for this: the 1935 version was filmed in the studio – making it a Film of Three Countries in fact! – and although the 1958 version had some outdoor scenes, resources did not stretch to filming in Paris. It was becoming a film cliché to evoke a great city by a passing shot of a mythic public building – producing that 'It's so *French!*' reaction which has been analysed by Vanessa Schwartz.[21] For Paris, it is invariably the

Eiffel Tower or the Sacré-Coeur basilica in Montmartre which have come to perform this role; for London, it is Trafalgar Square or Big Ben. The directors of *A Tale of Two Cities* were constrained, however, by the fact that none of these buildings existed in 1794.[22] Even the Bastille prison, whose storming marked the Revolution's outbreak, giving both films the opportunity for big crowd scenes, was demolished in 1789, so could not form part of the cityscape of the Terror of 1793–94. The prison-fortress's profile was, however, insufficiently etched on English and US minds for it to require exact replication: the 1935 film has a rather impressive studio recreation, the 1958 version much less so, and its unconvincing street scenes were evidently shot in a middling French provincial town.

The novel unobtrusively references the cathedrals of Notre-Dame in Paris and St Paul's in London as broodingly benign presences floating above the streets of the city. The rendezvous for the escape scene in the final part of the novel is indeed located outside 'the great cathedral door between the two towers'.[23] Yet these cues are studiously ignored in both film versions. Although the religious theme of redemption in the novel features very prominently in the 1935 film – whose musical score recurrently melds 'O Come All You Faithful' with the Marseillaise – there are no religious monuments in view.[24] The cityscape for Carton's guillotining references the place de la Concorde (with some degree of accuracy in fact), but the skyline only shows with any degree of prominence the dome of Les Invalides, not Notre-Dame.

Given that no public monument from the Revolutionary period could provide that 'It's so *French!*' moment of recognition,[25] the Paris and London of the films are characterised by streets and largely generic buildings of a timeless 'Olde England' and '*le vieux Paris*' sort. In the novel, the built environment of the two cities are very much of a muchness – a fact that highlighted the extent to which Dickens was as revolted by the dirt and decay of his own city as by what he found in Paris. But in the films, Paris comes off far worse at all levels. The Revolutionary Tribunal at the height of the Terror is dominated by darkly threatening revolutionary hordes in a Kafka-esque setting. Yet in both films, the scenes at London's Old Bailey seem light and even comic in contrast, with lashings of benign local colour. Then again, Parisian streets are anonymous, dirty, unkempt and, once Revolution comes, full of impoverished rebellious crowds, marshalled by Monsieur and Madame Defarge. Class violence on the street precedes the Revolution too: the coach of the villainous and utterly remorseless Marquis de Saint-Evrémonde runs over and kills a street urchin (he will pay for it by his murder). London streets seem very tranquil in contrast, and although the passengers on the Dover coach in the films' opening scenes are fearful of highwaymen, nothing untoward occurs. The main outdoor scene in London in the 1935 version takes place at Christmas, when the streets present a pristine white, snowflake (studio-based) vision, with Christmas carols and quasi-Pickwickian seasonal good cheer as sonic accompaniment.

Both films thus tend to highlight undifferentiated private or semi-private spaces rather than specific monuments. And here again, a major divergence is evident. In both films, it is only in London that we see a true 'home', a comfortable, middle-class domestic interior – namely, the residence of Doctor Manette in Soho, where his daughter, the heroine of the piece, is brought up. The home is viewed as a refuge against the threatening violence that comes from outside and that is represented – in both the novel and the films – by a tempest and also by the rushing sound of footsteps in the streets. The idealised dwelling of Dr Manette serves as the moral centre of the plot and provides a moral compass for the narrative as a whole.

In France, in contrast, no such homely space is shown. The aristocratic Parisian salon that we see – characterised in the Selznick version by 'the mincing measures of the minuet' – is shown as a cold, insincere and heartless space. Saint-Evrémonde's huge country chateau is the setting for him to be viciously cruel, rapacious and violent towards his peasants. In Paris, we see the gloomy offices of a surveillance committee and the cells of the prisons of the Terror, in which lurk suspicion and treason. But the pivotal Parisian interior in both films in terms of the plot is the Defarge wine shop, presided over by the sinister and threatening figure of Madame Defarge at her knitting. Tiny, sparsely decorated and lacking amenity, the wine shop is the polar opposite of the refined and mildly luxurious décor of the Manette household. It bears no comparison either with the bustling and good-natured taverns and restaurants of London, staffed by politely jovial types and with roaring fires and prominent chinaware, or even with the salubrious business of Tellson's bank.

In sum, it is clear that the films of *A Tale of Two Cities* – in their casting, settings and plotting – maintain and endorse the stereotypical versions of the novel that had been increasingly evident in British culture from the late 19th century onwards. Perhaps Dickens's own much more even-handed approach was too subtle and too generous towards the French to provide the basis of a Hollywood spectacular or a Rank Organisation emulator. It probably also made commercial sense to accept and to work with stereotypes widely subscribed to in US as well as British culture.

In addition, the wider political setting evidently counted for something in this. As we have seen, the revolutionary French served as a whetstone on which British nationalism sharpened its axe – even when, in the two World Wars, the French were allies and the Germans enemies. Since the Russian Revolution, however, the French Revolution has often served as a proxy for its Soviet successor. Whereas the French stood in for the Germans in the late 19th and early 20th century, Russian Bolsheviks took this role after 1917.[26] The atavistic and pathologised crowds of the two films served as a heavy-handed reminder to audiences of what Bolshevism might mean for peaceful, overtly freedom-loving countries. If the Cold War top notes present in the 1958 film are less evident, linking text in the 1935 film obtrusively evokes 'the approaching footsteps of a bitter people', spreading 'messages of hate'. The nightmarish trial of Charles Darnay by the Revolutionary Tribunal in the 1935 film implicitly evokes Soviet justice, just as Stalin's show trials were about to start. In Anglo-American political culture, the French Revolution stands as an indication of How Not To Do It. Despite Dickens's much more qualified views, and as I have suggested, *malgré lui*, *A Tale of Two Cities* seems to be destined always to be viewed as an iconically nationalistic tale.

Notes

1. *The British Academy Pilgrim Edition of the Letters of Charles Dickens*, ed. Graham Storey *et al.*, 12 vols. (Oxford, 1965–2002), vii, p. 60.
2. Ibid., iv, pp. 166–7.

3. This essay draws especially on the essays in Colin Jones, Josephine McDonagh and Jon Mee (eds), *Charles Dickens, the French Revolution and* A Tale of Two Cities (London: Palgrave Macmillan, 2009). See too Colin Jones, 'French Crossings I: Tales of Two Cities', *Transactions of the Royal Historical Society*, no. 20 (2010), pp. 1–26. The most accessible scholarly edition of the novel is the Penguin Classics version, ed. Richard Maxwell (London: Penguin Random House, 2003).
4. *Letters of Charles Dickens*, ix, p. 132.
5. The best comparative study of the 1935 and 1958 films is Charles Barr, 'Two Cities, Two Films', in Jones et al., *Charles Dickens*, pp. 166–87. Much more attention has been given to the earlier film. See especially Jason W. Stevens, 'Insurrection and Depression-Era Politics in Selznick's *A Tale of Two Cities* (1935)', *Literature Film Quarterly*, vol. 34, no. 3 (2006), pp. 176–93; Brian Bialkowski, 'Facing up to the Question of Fidelity: The Example of "A Tale of Two Cities"', *Literature Film Quarterly*, vol. 29, no. 3 (2001), pp. 27–42; and Pascal Dupuy, 'La Diffusion des stéréotypes révolutionnaires dans la littérature et le cinéma anglo-saxons, 1789–1989', *Annales historiques de la Révolution française*, vol. 35, no. 1 (1966), pp. 511–28. For the earlier 1917 film, see Judith Buchanan and Alex Newhouse, 'Sanguine Mirages, Cinematic Dreams: Things Seen and Things Imagined in the 1917 Fox Feature Film *A Tale of Two Cities*', in Jones et al., *Charles Dickens*, pp. 146–65.
6. Memo, 3 October 1935, cited in 'Memos from David O. Selznick', in The Sheila Variations. Available at: www.sheilaomalley.com/?p=10060 (accessed 4 October 2015).
7. See Joss Marsh, 'Mimi and the Matinee Idol: Martin-Harvey, Sydney Carton and the Staging of *A Tale of Two Cities*', in Jones et al., *Charles Dickens*, pp. 126–45.
8. Linda Colley, *Britons: Forging the Nation, 1707–1837* (London: Yale University Press, 1992).
9. George Orwell, 'Charles Dickens', in *Inside the Whale and Other Essays* (London: Victor Gollancz, 1940), p. 25.
10. This simple narrative was complicated by the fact of the American Revolution itself.
11. See the discussion in Annie Sadrin, 'Traductions et adaptations de *A Tale of Two Cities*', in Sylvère Monod (ed.), *Charles Dickens et la France. Colloque international de Boulogne-sur-Mer, 3 juin 1978* (Lille: Presses Universitaires de Lille, 1979) and Jones et al., *Charles Dickens*, especially p. 7.
12. D'Orzcy's *Scarlet Pimpernel* appeared in 1903 and was followed by sequels. For a latter-day bracketing of d'Orczy and Dickens, in a highly scholarly source, see Jean-Noël Jeanneney, 'Quand Google défie l'Europe', *Le Monde*, 24 January 2005, p. 13.
13. Carlyle's *The French Revolution: A History* was published in 1837. For relations between the two men, see the Penguin edition, pp. 401–6.
14. Jones, 'Tales of Two Cities', especially pp. 22–3.
15. *Barnaby Rudge* came out in serial form in 1841. It is Dickens's only other historical novel. It is not widely known or appreciated and has rarely given rise to adaptations for other media.
16. *Letters*, v, p. 42; ibid., v, pp. 256–7; ibid., iv, pp. 166–7. See in general, for example, David P. Jordan, *Transforming Paris: The Life and Labors of Baron Haussmann* (New York: Free Press, 1995).
17. Penguin edition, p. 32.
18. See the map of Dickens's Parisian peregrinations in Jones, 'Tales of Two Cities', p. 14. Cf. Claire Hancock, *Paris et Londres au XIXe siècle: représentations dans les guides et récits de voyage* (Paris: Editions CNRS, 2003).

19. There was, however, a French TV version in 1989, directed by Philippe Monnier.
20. See the references above, at note 5.
21. Vanessa Schwartz, *It's So French! Hollywood, Paris and the Making of Cosmopolitan Film Culture* (Chicago, IL: Chicago University Press, 2007).
22. Big Ben was built in 1858, and Trafalgar Square was constructed in 1840. The Eiffel Tower dates from 1889 and the Sacré-Coeur basilica, started in 1875, was only completed in 1914.
23. Penguin edition, p. 349. Cf., for example, pp. 38, 107, 110, 326.
24. Stevens, 'Insurrection and Depression-Era Politics', pp. 180, 186–7.
25. Schwartz, *It's So French!*
26. See Barr, 'Two Cities, Two Films', p. 167, and the more general discussion of this point in Stevens, 'Insurrection and Depression-Era Politics', pp. 183–7.

From Meryon to Ulmer's *Bluebeard*: A Baudelairian Iconography

Jean-Loup Bourget

Edgar George Ulmer, the 'King of the Bs', made *Bluebeard* in 1944, about halfway through a long, prolific and extremely uneven career. Ostensibly a run-of-the mill, low-budget feature about a serial killer, the film shows a number of intriguing features which warrant close examination. It is set in Paris in the mid-19th century and its very economical visual rendition of this time and place is freely inspired by the 'Old Paris' etchings of Charles Meryon, a contemporary of Baudelaire who was much admired by the *flâneur* poet. This specific aspect of *Bluebeard* might be ascribed at least in part to its cinematographer, Eugen Schüfftan,[1] another European exile, although Ulmer, as was his wont, claimed most of the credit, telling Peter Bogdanovich: 'All my love for Paris came out in the picture. [...] I did the sets myself [...]. As an art director, from my earliest time on, I adored the Île-de-France, Montparnasse and Montmartre, and whatever I did I always wound up in that. I adore Paris.'[2] *Bluebeard*'s connection with Baudelaire and Meryon is strengthened by various thematic and narrative elements in the film that refer to Edgar Allan Poe (a favourite of both the poet and the artist), in particular to his story 'The Mystery of Marie Rogêt', ostensibly set in Paris. Perhaps the most fascinating feature of *Bluebeard*, however, is its use of a puppet show of Gounod's opera *Faust*, which, as we will see, presents the scholar with a bit of a puzzle.

Like the minimalist *Detour* (1945), a noir film which is widely regarded as Ulmer's masterpiece, and *Strange Illusion* (also 1945), one of Ulmer's better films, whose plot is a thinly veiled transposition of Shakespeare's *Hamlet* in modern, explicitly psycho-analytical terms, *Bluebeard* was produced by Leon Fromkess for his PRC (Producers Releasing Corporation) Pictures and shot, according to Ulmer, in six days. The title role is played with commendable and unusual understatement by John Carradine, a well-known character actor in several films directed by John Ford. The 30-year-old actress Jean Parker gets second billing, followed (in the typical practice of B-movies) by two veteran actors of European origin, the Swede Nils Asther in the role of the Paris police inspector Lefèvre, and the Austrian Ludwig Stossel as Lamarté, the gallery owner who exploits Gaston Morel/'Bluebeard'.

Also of interest is Eugen Schüfftan's credit as production designer. The German-born cinematographer, who had photographed Robert Siodmak and Ulmer's *Menschen am Sonntag*/*People on Sunday* (1930) – an outstanding quasi-documentary portrait of Berlin and of five young Berliners, played by non-professional actors, on a leisurely Sunday – moved to France in 1933. There he worked for several German exiles, among whom were G. W. Pabst, Max Ophuls and Siodmak, as well as for Marcel

Carné, acting as cinematographer for his *Le Quai des brumes/Port of Shadows* (1938). In 1940, he went on to the US, and worked again with German exiles in various fictitious capacities, since his application to the ASC (American Society of Cinematographers) having been turned down, he could not be credited for his work as a cinematographer. According to Ulmer, Schüfftan was actually responsible for *Bluebeard*'s cinematography (credited to the camera operator Jockey Arthur Feindel) but got billing for its production design, which in fact had been done by Ulmer himself.[3]

The film's script, by Pierre Gendron (a former silent cinema actor turned screenwriter for a handful of Poverty Row productions), is both unnecessarily convoluted and derivative. Unnecessarily convoluted because the identification of Gaston Morel (Carradine) as the 'Bluebeard' of the title is established quite early on, first implicitly (in a shot reminiscent of Fritz Lang's *M* [1931], which frames the supposedly innocent puppeteer in close proximity to a poster warning the women of Paris against the 'Bluebeard' monster), then explicitly. The Morel character combines three aspects: that of a painter who does idealised portraits of the women he loves; that of the serial killer 'Bluebeard' who, originally disappointed because his first model did not live up to his lofty expectations, strangled her and now feels compelled to strangle all the women whose portraits he paints, then throw their bodies into the Seine; that of a melancholy puppeteer who stages a show of Gounod's *Faust* for his new love, Lucille (Jean Parker).

The action takes place in Paris in the 19th century, the exact date being unspecified. The film refers once to the (probably Third) Republic but various elements, such as the date of Gounod's *Faust* (1859) and the gendarmes' two-cornered hats, point rather to the (immediately earlier) Second Empire of Napoleon III (1852–70).

The first striking thing about *Bluebeard* is its opening credits sequence, which shows a series of highly stylised black-and-white pictures of Parisian urban landscapes that do not 'quote' or reproduce, but are very much in the manner and spirit of, Charles Meryon's *Eaux-fortes sur Paris/Etchings on Paris* (1852). Meryon (1821–66), the son of an English physician and a French opera dancer, was a naval officer and an etcher of genius, greatly admired by Victor Hugo and by Baudelaire, who wrote at length about him and saw in Meryon's etchings of Old Paris – fast disappearing to make way for Haussmann's boulevards – a kind of visual equivalent of his own *Petits Poèmes en prose*, also known as *Le Spleen de Paris* (*Little Poems in Prose/Paris Spleen*, published posthumously in 1869). Baudelaire long hoped to collaborate with the artist and to write short pieces of either verse or prose, 'the philosophical musings of a Parisian *flâneur*', to accompany Meryon's etchings.[4] Largely because of Meryon's unstable moods, this did not materialise, which Walter Benjamin deemed 'a fantastic loss'.[5] Meryon's mastery of the severe black-and-white drama of etching, also commented on by Edward Hopper – himself an accomplished etcher – is paradoxically combined, in the later states of some engravings, with a hallucinatory drift which shows the skies of Paris invaded by balloons and flocks of ducks and seagulls (*Le Pont-au-change*) or by fantastic flying fish and charioteers (*Le Ministère de la marine/The Admiralty*). Meryon went mad and died in the Charenton mental asylum.[6]

Several of the Meryon-like cityscapes of *Bluebeard*'s opening titles reappear in the film proper, notably the massive twin towers of Notre-Dame cathedral, somewhat reminiscent of

Meryon's famous etching *Le Petit Pont*, and a bridge on the river Seine, with equally massive piers, framed diagonally as in Meryon's rendition of *Le Pont-Neuf*. Another set reprised from the opening credits is that of the Paris sewers, clearly 'drawn' on a flat surface rather than tri-dimensional, thus emphasising the architecture's strict geometry and bringing to mind Meryon's *Antechamber of the Palais de Justice*.

Notre-Dame cathedral in Edgar J. Ulmer's *Bluebeard* (1944).

Nowhere is Meryon explicitly referred to, either visually or by name, in *Bluebeard*, whereas, to take an opposite, almost contemporary, example, the opening credits of *Bedlam* (a Val Lewton production directed by Mark Robson [1946]) unfold on a background of engravings by Hogarth and of his painting *The Madhouse*, which provides loose inspiration for the film's plot and title.[7] An equivalent would have been a 'quote' or reproduction of what is probably Meryon's best-known engraving, *Le Stryge/The Vampire*, which shows Viollet-le-Duc's famous statue of a grotesque devilish figure 'looking out' from a tower of Notre-Dame, with the Tour St Jacques and an aerial view of Paris in the background. Often wrongly referred to as a 'gargoyle', the figure (designated in Meryon's caption as 'The Insatiable Vampire, Eternal Lust') was soon made popular both by Meryon's etching and by a photograph by Charles Nègre, probably dating from the same year (1853), and much reproduced by later illustrators. One may imagine that Ulmer himself had the Stryge in mind when in 1970 he told Bogdanovich: 'Every picture [Buñuel] makes is a morality play, only he goes and brings the gargoyles down from their niches up on Notre Dame.'[8]

Other circumstantial evidence, however, tends to confirm *Bluebeard*'s association with Meryon, and more generally with 19th-century Paris as described or evoked by Baudelaire and Poe, and also by Victor Hugo. To start with, the focus of the action is firmly placed on the area near Notre-Dame cathedral, which is also the heart of Paris as depicted by Meryon, who never strays far from the Ile de la Cité and the Latin Quarter. Notre-Dame cathedral had been, of course, the subject of an extremely popular historical novel by Victor Hugo, published in 1831–32, with numerous illustrated editions from 1844 on, and several adaptations to the screen, notably *The Hunchback of Notre Dame*, an RKO production directed by the German exile director William Dieterle in 1938.[9]

Mention should also be made of the essential part played in Ulmer's film by the Seine. The opening scene shows the discovery of a woman's corpse floating down the

Charles Meryon's etching *Le Petit Pont* (1858).

river, in the area of Notre-Dame cathedral and the Petit Pont, which was most familiar to Meryon, and in a series of shots whose atmosphere recalls that of Meryon's ominous etching of *Le Petit Pont*, with its strong contrast of light and darkness, its twin cathedral towers of fantastic height and the mysterious, supposedly not intentional, human shadow cast by a portion of the stonework on the side wall of the bridge, and representing the profile of the 'Sphinx' Napoleon III.[10] A similar scene occurs after Morel, having fallen in love with Lucille, strangles his jealous lover and partner Renée (Sonia Sorel); and in the film's final sequence, Morel, chased by the Paris police, who have at last identified him as 'Bluebeard', escapes to the rooftops but falls to his death into the river's dark waters.

The theme of drowning – a leitmotiv of Ulmer's films, it is also found in *Strange Illusion*, *The Strange Woman* (1946), *Ruthless* (1948) and *Sette contro la morte/The Cavern* (1965)[11] – can be related both to Poe's 'The Mystery of Marie Rogêt', in which Poe's amateur detective Dupin elucidates the murder of a young woman whose body has been found floating down the Seine,[12] and to another famous etching by Meryon, *La Morgue/The Mortuary* (1854). This impressive, essentially architectural rendition of the old mortuary (then located on the Ile de la Cité) depicts a 'miniature melodrama',[13] very similar to the opening scene of *Bluebeard*: a body which has just been pulled from the river is being taken to the mortuary under the direction of a gesturing gendarme wearing a two-cornered hat. A crowd of curious but indifferent onlookers watches from above, while a woman and a girl near the corpse show signs of grief and a second gendarme keeps another woman from approaching the scene.

From Baudelaire, who translated Poe's short stories, we hear of Meryon's idiosyncratic reading of the most famous of them, 'The Murders in the Rue Morgue'. Meryon questioned Poe's identity, convinced as he was that the Paris-set story actually referred to his etching of *The Mortuary*, that the orang-utan was none other than Meryon himself, who had 'often been compared to an ape' and had been accused of the 'moral assassination' of a woman and her daughter, the incident being transposed, in Poe's story, into the actual killing of the two victims by an orang-utan.[14]

Finally, the part played by the Paris sewer towards the conclusion of *Bluebeard* and its neat geometry, reminiscent of Meryon, bring to mind, from both a narrative and a formal point of view, the famous episode in the last book of Hugo's *Les Misérables*, in which the hero, the ex-convict Jean Valjean, escapes via the sewer system ('Leviathan's Intestine') after the fall of the Republican barricade in the June 1832 riot. Jean Valjean carries the wounded Marius on his back, thus saving him from arrest and summary execution. When he comes out of the sewer, he is met by Javert, the police inspector and spy who has long been chasing him mercilessly but is now 'derailed' because the ex-convict has just spared his life on the barricade instead of killing him as Javert expected. Eventually, Javert lets Jean Valjean go free but, incapable of condoning this breach of duty, he commits suicide and throws himself into the Seine, in the 'rapid' between the Pont Notre-Dame and the Pont-au-change – in other words, in the exact spot depicted by Meryon in his etching *An Arch of the Notre-Dame Bridge* (1853), with the arch framing the Pont-au-change in the distance.[15]

The use of quasi-'abstract' sets reminiscent of Meryon's etchings, far removed from the picturesque and/or gothic trappings of other horror films set in Paris (such as Robert Florey's *Murders in the Rue Morgue* [1932] or Karl Freund's *Mad Love* [1935]), gives *Bluebeard* its unique melancholy flavour, closer to Baudelaire's *spleen* than to conventional gothic horror. This feeling is reinforced by the use of music – not just the diegetic *Faust* music in the first part of the film, but also the subtle and effective 'pit music'[16] of the film as a whole, written by the frequent Ulmer collaborator, Hungarian-born Leo Erdody. In essence Erdody's score alternates a melancholy (rather than frightening) 'Bluebeard' leitmotiv associated with Morel and a lively 'Gay Paris' dance tune which enhances the impression of local/historical colour, with occasional quotes from Mussorgsky's *Pictures at an Exhibition*.

As already mentioned, the other striking feature about *Bluebeard* is the use, in the early part of the film, of a puppet show of Gounod's *Faust*. The device helps to turn the Bluebeard 'Monster' or serial killer into a figure of pathos and pity: Morel is both puppeteer and puppet, an apparent 'puller of strings' who is in fact more of a Faust than a Mephisto figure. On an almost literal, immediate level, Morel the puppeteer turns out to be a puppet in the hands of Lamarté the gallery owner; but when the puppet rebels and Morel finally gets rid of his nemesis, the feeling is very far from one of liberation. The outcome simply confirms that Morel was doomed to kill Lamarté, as he was doomed to kill the women he loved, and that he will not be granted the happy ending which favours Faust through the intercession of Marguerite's sublime love (a scene which is beautifully staged in the puppet show, with Nazarene angels descending from the flies).[17]

The puppet show, however, is puzzling. In a sense, there is nothing surprising in the appearance of the Faust legend in a story set in 19th-century Paris: the immense popularity of Goethe's drama in France is well attested to by Gérard de Nerval's translation (1828 and later), Eugène Delacroix's lithographs (1827–29), the operas by Hector Berlioz (*La Damnation de Faust*, 1846) and by Charles Gounod (*Faust*, 1859). What gives pause is that we are dealing with a filmmaker who was brought up in Vienna and who claimed to have worked closely with F. W. Murnau, whose own *Faust* of 1926 is explicitly based on the old German legend rather than on Goethe's version of the drama. The fact that Gounod's *Faust* is here performed by puppets is intriguing, and raises the question of whether this is a plausible bit of local (or historical) colour, or an Ulmer 'graft' onto the otherwise 'Parisian' material. Puppet shows of the Faust legend have long been popular in German-speaking countries, so it is tempting to assume that the unusual introduction of the legend *in this particular form* is a German (or Viennese) adjunct by Ulmer.[18] Historians of the performing arts in 19th-century France tell us that there were indeed puppet shows adapted from literary and operatic subjects for the literati, but that these tended to take place in salons or in private theatres in order to eschew the very strict censorship to which shows meant for the 'people' and for children (such as the one we witness in *Bluebeard*) were submitted.[19]

Ulmer's 'collapsing' of Gounod's 'grand opera' into a puppet show may well be due to budgetary reasons (which also account for the minimalist painted or drawn sets of *Bluebeard*), which does not lessen the singular inventiveness of the device. It brings to mind Marcel Proust's felicitous use, at the beginning of *Du côté de chez Swann/Swann's Way*, of the magic lantern to introduce the medieval story of the criminal Golo – a 'Bluebeard' figure – and of 'poor Geneviève de Brabant' before relating it to the more prestigious stained-glass windows of the church in Combray. Perhaps this is the reason why I like to think that the use of the puppet show may have been connected with some childhood memory on Ulmer's part.

Be that as it may, the obviously 'popular' appeal of the puppet show to *Bluebeard*'s diegetic audience also goes to prove that the conflict in Ulmer's work between High (European) culture, exemplified by (among others) classical music and opera, and Low (American) culture, exemplified by noir films, jazz music, and so on, is not as clear-cut as assumed by some recent commentators.[20] 'Bluebeard' is, after all, originally a fairy tale, and similarly *Faust*, even in the guise of Gounod's opera, retains some of the vernacular flavour of the 'German legend'. In Ulmer's *Bluebeard*, the Faust puppet show is *both* opera and popular culture, or rather it is opera reintegrated into popular culture, Paris under the Second Empire reintegrated into the twin visual culture of Meryon's etchings and of a Faust puppet tradition alive to this day in German-speaking countries. If the film as a whole is definitely written in the Hollywood idiom of 'Poverty Row', including Carradine's hammy but subdued impersonation of Morel's Monster or Stryge, it feeds on disparate elements which are not just French, but also German; not just examples of European 'high' culture, but also examples of European popular culture.

To conclude, I have to admit that my various intuitions about the sources and authorship of *Bluebeard* remain just that: intuitions and hypotheses, which have been neither confirmed nor denied in a definitive way. If the similarity between the sets of *Bluebeard* and Meryon's engravings seems to me to be beyond question, I have been unable to find definite proof that Meryon was a source of inspiration for the filmmakers. Meryon's single most famous subject, the *Stryge* or Vampire, is conspicuously absent from Ulmer's film, although it would not be far-fetched to argue that it is Morel himself (Carradine), the serial killer and puppeteer, who plays the symbolic and melancholy part of Meryon's 'gargoyle' or 'chimera', that of *The Monster*, to quote the mistaken but apt title that Baudelaire gave the etching.[21] My second intuition was that Schüfftan, who had lived in Paris for several years and was more familiar with the French capital than Ulmer, had a hand in the production design he gets credit for, as well as in the cinematography; yet on this specific point, the evidence seems to confirm Ulmer's claim to have been responsible for the film's art direction. We recall that in his interview with Bogdanovich, Ulmer talks effusively about his fondness for Paris; perhaps for once we are to take his statement at face value, despite the fact that it was made long after the event and that he seems to confuse the Ile de France region with the Ile de la Cité – essentially Meryon territory – at the heart of Paris. Finally, there remains the intriguing question of the Faust puppet show, which is the most inventive device of *Bluebeard*, and which – although the opera is French and was created during the Second Empire – I continue to associate with a German rather than a French tradition. In the final analysis, we can only wonder at the felicitous achievement of two German/Austrian exiles, a Hollywood B-movie which conveys to perfection the sharp vision and baleful spirit of Meryon's etchings and of Baudelaire's prose poems *Le Spleen de Paris*.

Notes

1. Credited as Schufftan in this film.
2. Interview with Peter Bogdanovich, February 1970, here quoted from the shorter version reprinted in Todd McCarthy and Charles Flynn (eds), *Kings of the Bs: Working within the Hollywood System. An Anthology of Film History and Criticism* (New York: E. P. Dutton & Co., 1975), p. 401.
3. Ibid.
4. Baudelaire's letter to his publisher Poulet-Malassis, 16 February 1860, in Charles Baudelaire, *Oeuvres complètes*, ed. Yves Florenne (Paris: Club français du livre, 1966), vol. 3, p. 844. Baudelaire's 'public' writings on Meryon can be found essentially in his 'Salon of 1859' and in his 'Painters and Etchers' of 1862.
5. Benjamin (1936) quoted by Elisabetta Villari, 'Walter Benjamin sur *Le Stryge* de Charles Meryon', in Ségolène Le Men (ed.), 'Ceci tuera cela?', *Livraisons d'histoire de l'architecture*, no. 20 (Paris: Association Livraisons d'histoire de l'architecture, 2010), p. 79.
6. On Meryon, see among others Charles Meryon, *Old Paris. Twenty Etchings by Charles Méryon* [sic] *with an Essay on the Etcher by Philip Gilbert Hamerton* (Liverpool: Henry Young & Sons, 1914); Gustave Geffroy, *Charles Meryon* (Paris: H. Floury, 1926); Robert L. Schneiderman, *The Catalogue Raisonné of the Prints of Charles Meryon* (London: Garton & Co., 1990).
7. A reproduction of The Madhouse serves as background to the title, which reads: 'Suggested by/The WILLIAM HOGARTH Painting/BEDLAM/Plate 8 "The Rake's Progress".' In fact, neither the painting (now in Sir John Soane's Museum, London) nor the engraving based on it (*Madness*) is called *Bedlam*, although their 'madhouse' has long been identified with the Royal Bethlehem Hospital or 'Bedlam'.
8. Ulmer's interview with Bogdanovich, *Kings of the Bs*, p. 408.
9. Ségolène Le Men traces the *Stryge's* ancestry to Hugo's novel in 'De *Notre-Dame de Paris* au *Stryge*: l'invention d'une image', in Le Men (ed.), 'Ceci tuera cela?', pp. 49–73.
10. Baudelaire's letter of 8 January 1860 to his publisher Poulet-Malassis, in Bernard Gheerbrant (ed.), *Baudelaire critique d'art* (Paris: Club des Libraires de France, 1956), pp. 171–2.
11. John Belton has remarked on Ulmer's frequent use of the image of a drowning man and of 'watery death'. Belton, *Howard Hawks, Frank Borzage, Edgar G. Ulmer. The Hollywood Professionals*, vol. 3 (London and New York: The Tantivy Press/A. S. Barnes & Co., 1974), pp. 152–3.
12. Poe described 'The Mystery of Marie Rogêt' as a sequel to his 'Murders in the Rue Morgue'. Whereas only its title relates Ulmer's earlier film *The Black Cat* (1934) to Poe's eponymous short story, in *Bluebeard*, on the other hand, there is a definite echo of Poe's 'The Oval Portrait' in the scene where Morel, who does not wish to be seen by Francine (Lucille's sister), paints her portrait not directly but from her reflection in an oval mirror.
13. Schneiderman, *The Catalogue Raisonné of the Prints of Charles Meryon*, p. 87.
14. In the already quoted letter of 8 January 1860 to Poulet-Malassis; Gheerbrant, *Baudelaire critique d'art*, p. 172.
15. See Part 5 ('Jean Valjean') of *Les Misérables*, especially Books 2 ('Leviathan's Intestine'), 3 ('The Mud, but the Soul') and 4 ('Javert Derailed'). That (final) part of the novel was completed in 1862. Other etchings by Meryon depicting locations close to that of Javert's suicide include the panoramic and visionary *Pont-au-change* already referred to and the *Pompe Notre-Dame*.

16. I am referring to Michel Chion's classic distinction between *pit music* (non-diegetic music) and *screen music* (diegetic music); see Michel Chion, *Audio-Vision: Sound on Screen* (New York: Columbia University Press, 1994), p. 80.
17. On the puppets' Faustian symbolism, see Belton, *Howard Hawks, Frank Borzage, Edgar G. Ulmer*, pp. 158–61.
18. At the outset of his 'Journey to the East', Nerval, stopping by in Augsburg (Bavaria), hesitated between going to the opera house, to see Weber's *Preciosa*, or to a puppet show of *Doctor Faustus*. Having decided for the grand opera, he soon came to regret 'the unfortunate idea of neglecting the opportunity to see the naive and childish drama which has inspired Goethe's eternal masterpiece'. Nerval's 'Travel Letters', *La Presse*, 26 March 1840, in Oeuvres complètes, vol. 2, pp. 1414–15.
19. Olga Krakovitch, who researched the censorship records of the French National Archives, did find the trace of an anonymous Faust parody, *Faust et Marguerite* (10 November 1858, last item in box F 18 1328), whose tone and coarse punning are far removed from the romantic fervour of Gounod and of the puppet show in *Bluebeard*. Personal e-mail communication from Olga Krakovitch, 27 December 2012. With warmest thanks to Ms Krakovitch and to Joël Huthwohl, who put me in touch with her.
20. Thus, Scott Loren writes about Ulmer '[m]erging American low-budget popular (or even sub-) culture with European "high" culture' in his 'Dead Fathers and Other Detours: Ulmer's *Noir*', in Gary D. Rhodes (ed.), *Edgar G. Ulmer: Detour on Poverty Row* (Plymouth: Lexington Books, 2008), p. 84; similarly, Bernd Herzogenrath states that 'it is in fact the inoculation of that high [European] culture into [Ulmer's] B-movies that turn these films into something else, staging strange dissonances between European high culture and American trash cinema'. 'Ulmer and Cult/ure', in Bernd Herzogenrath, *Edgar G. Ulmer: Essays on the King of the B's* (Jefferson, NC: McFarland & Company, 2009), p. 23.
21. Baudelaire's letter to his mother, 4 March 1860; in Baudelaire, *Oeuvres complètes*, vol. 3, p. 854.

Site of Infamy: The Vel' d'Hiv in French Cinema

Sandy Flitterman-Lewis

The 15th *arrondissement* of Paris is sometimes called the 'parks quarter' because of the tiny islands of greenery laid out in the 19th century.[1] In the early 20th century, this Left Bank quarter was a mixture of populous working-class lodgings to the north and a remote wasteland of factories and slaughterhouses to the south. Today, despite the radically anti-aesthetic rebuilding of the 1960s and 1970s, with the Montparnasse Tower and river-front development, guidebooks suggest pleasant walks along tree-lined streets of what has now become a peaceful residential neighbourhood.

However, the north-west corner of this tranquil *arrondissement* harbours a dark secret: it is the site of an infamous tragedy that took place in the middle of World War Two and changed the lives of France's Jewish population for ever. Long suppressed in the cultural memory of the nation, it took the French several decades to fully come to terms with the events. Known as 'La Grande Rafle du Vel' d'Hiv (or simply the Vel' d'Hiv), the raid is named after the glass-domed sports arena (the Vel' d'Hiv, short for Vélodrome d'Hiver, or Winter Cycling Stadium) where, after a massive roundup of Jews in Paris, the families were deposited and left to suffer miserably without food, water or proper sanitation for a week. From there they were sent in boxcars to French detention camps either in the suburb of Drancy, or Beaune-la-Rolande and Pithiviers in the Loiret 100 kilometres to the south, where the children were separated from their anguished mothers, before being sent in separate convoys to their deaths in Auschwitz. On 16 and 17 July 1942, a total of 13,152 people (including 5,919 women and 4,115 children) were arrested by French police and detained in the Vel' d'Hiv, exactly six months after Adolph Eichmann presented his Final Solution for the eradication of Europe's Jews at Wannsee. Fewer than a hundred returned and none of the children who arrived at Auschwitz survived. Several factors make the Vel' d'Hiv significant: the raid (called 'Operation Spring Wind' by its organisers) was entirely carried out by French police; the totals are staggering; women and children were arrested for the very first time; and, most important, the first trains from the west to the death camps of Auschwitz came from the Vel' d'Hiv, sealing its inaugural position in the Nazi machinery of destruction.[2]

For years, the site of the velodrome (destroyed in 1959) remained an obscure part of the urban landscape. A single photograph exists from the day of the raid, a shot of unoccupied buses lined up by the stadium entrance, in a vision of haunting emptiness. Post-war orders to destroy all records of the roundup enacted a policy of organised amnesia. Today at this site on the rue Nélaton, in full view of the Eiffel Tower, the Ministry of the Interior has its offices. Around the corner, a small plaque calls for remembrance. President François Mitterrand commissioned a more visible monument on the Quai de Grenelle, where a sculpture by Holocaust survivor Walter Spitzer depicts a group of deportees on the stadium floor. But Mitterrand fed the popular myth by blaming the Nazi invader and constructing an ideal, resisting French Republic. In 1995, at the square de la place du Martyr Juif, newly elected president Jacques Chirac asserted France's responsibility: 'France, home of the Enlightenment and of Human Rights, land of refuge and asylum ... upon that day committed an irreparable act.' 70 years after the roundup, President François Hollande fully acknowledged national complicity: 'The truth is that a crime was committed in France, by France.'[3] Five years later on 17 July 2017, on the 75th anniversary of the events, President Emmanuel Macron again denounced the role of the French state in the Vel' d'Hiv atroticities.

Site of infamy, the Vel' d' Hiv has become shorthand for the particularly brutal way that France participated in the Shoah. The cinematic memory of that dark chapter has been necessarily vexed; across seven decades only five feature films have treated the subject, and of them only two, the most recent, take us inside the stadium walls. The three films discussed here trace the representational history of the Vel' d'Hiv from the eyewitness account of a non-Jew – *Les Guichets du Louvre/Black Thursday* (Michel Mitrani, 1974) – to symbolic allegory of anti-Semitism, paranoia and identity – *Monsieur Klein/Mr. Klein* (Joseph Losey, 1976) – and finally to a detailed, historically accurate narrative culled from histories, documents and testimonies – *La Rafle/The Roundup* (Roselyne Bosch, 2010).[4]

The analyses both traverse occupied Paris and trace the cinematic figuration of the Vélodrome d'Hiver. First there is the Jewish Quarter in the Marais in *Les Guichets du Louvre*, where the roundup is woven into a *Bildungsroman* of young love. And, while the tragic hunt with its historical signifiers (the police, the buses, the Jews with their yellow stars and suitcases) is integral to the story, the stadium itself is neither seen nor mentioned. Next there are the luxurious hotels, cafés and auction houses of the 7th *arrondissement*, plus seedy Pigalle and its shadowy corners in *Monsieur Klein*, where the creation of a claustrophobic atmosphere of mysterious anxiety combines with the organised anti-Semitism of the raid, and we have glimpses of an unidentified stadium associated with the roundup. Finally, in *La Rafle*, we are inside the Vélodrome d'Hiver itself (and in the camp) where most of the action takes place, while the film begins with the popular working-class quarter of Montmartre and ends with the incongruously fashionable Hôtel Lutetia in the 6th *arrondissement* where shattered families try to regroup after the war.[5]

All three films emphasise the role of the French police and dramatise Jewish subjectivity; all seek to redress the official history. Each filmmaker evokes the horror in a way that awakens public consciousness, and each uses different representational strategies to portray not only the roundup, but also French complicity and the atmosphere of indifference that surrounded it. Each director's era frames what can be historically articulated, from the first evocation of the forbidden in *Les Guichets du Louvre*, through the burgeoning fascination with the Occupation years in *Monsieur Klein*,[6] to the present era of research, enlightenment and responsibility that grounds the specific historical project of *La Rafle*. These films share one disturbing aspect of the Vel' d'Hiv: while none of the Jews knew their terrible fate, all three filmmakers are painfully aware of the destination of death. Thus, each director finds a way to keep the shadow of Auschwitz always hovering at the interstices in their depictions of the Vel' d'Hiv.

Les Guichets du Louvre

In 1960, 18 years after the roundup, Roger Boussinot, a 20-year-old student at the time of the arrests, published his memoir of witnessing the raid and trying to save some Jews. Taking his title, Les Guichets du Louvre, from the portals of the museum through which he had hoped to lead them, Boussinot describes their unwillingness to follow him or to remove their yellow stars. He meets a young Jewish woman and something other than altruism begins to guide his efforts.[7] Both memoir and film end as she decides to turn away from imagined freedom towards the Jewish quarter where her mother and sister have disappeared. In 1974, the Bulgarian-French director Michel Mitrani transferred the subjective voice of the memoir into a narrative film, with Christian Rist as Paul and Christine Pascal as Jeanne, thus creating the first representation in film of the Vel' d'Hiv roundup. Where in the novel the narrating consciousness is the author himself, in the film it is the chaos of the roundup that speaks, giving full priority to the historic events.[8]

Boussinot begins: 'On July 16, at around four in the morning in a Paris still asleep, buses and vans with their bluish headlights left barracks, military camps, and depots and, despite the curfew, started toward the neighbourhoods of Belleville, Saint Paul, Popincourt, Poissonnière, and the Temple.'[9] Mitrani visually plunges us into Boussinot's scene, creating an air of disturbing tension even before the action starts: Paris, for its Jews, will be a city under siege. A delirious musical score in a minor key, a sort of *danse macabre*,[10] enhances this, as police vans race in darkness, gendarmes wordlessly pass around bread and fruit, and some glimpse Parisian sights while others stare blankly.

Paul begins his project in this tense atmosphere. Diverse encounters, vignettes of persecution, range across classes, denominations and generations of Jews; different configurations of arrested people articulate the tragedy of xenophobia. One common thread that links Jews who assert their Frenchness, those who obey religion and those

Alain Delon playing the eponymous ambiguous hero of *Monsieur Klein* (Joseph Losey, 1976) with 'glacial indifference'.

who simply feel that they have done nothing wrong is the belief that they will return to Paris.[11] The mystification is democratic – the French police believe this too. Jeanne's presence changes Paul from observer to participant; they are now both on the run. The organised sweep of this Jewish neighbourhood continues throughout the film, with mixed bystander reactions ranging from 'Good riddance' to 'Pour souls'. Most disturbing is the looting – everything from furniture to coveted sewing machines – by the good French citizens, who appreciate the 'cleansing' that the arrests bring. City buses filled with Jews cross the Marais, while posters of Marshall Pétain claim, 'Work, Family, Country', to be interpreted as reassuring or threatening, depending on identity.

The film's dramatic apex is the removal of Jeanne's yellow star, the badge of discrimination, to which she clings as if it were a talisman.[12] Without this identity, despised or not, Jeanne seems even more desperate and confused. Still, even without the star, Jeanne performs her Jewish identity when she sings a Yiddish lullaby to an abandoned baby. She refuses to tell Paul her name until the very end of the film, when, hesitating on the bridge, she decides to return to the place where the star is most prominent, the Marais, to find her mother and sister. Rather than a move towards victimisation, as some have claimed, this is a courageous assertion of Jewish identity in the midst of those who would deny it.[13] Mitrani's film conveys the fear and panic of that day from the dual perspective of a sympathetic Frenchman and a Jewish woman, while the spectre of the first destination, the Vélodrome d'Hiver, is an absent presence that haunts every action.

Monsieur Klein

In *Monsieur Klein*, Joseph Losey takes a very different approach, for as he famously said, 'I've always detested naturalism.'[14] While the film is a profound meditation on French anti-Semitism and government-ordered exclusion, Losey is careful to avoid literal representation, choosing the symbolic and conceptual over the historically specific. He explained, 'This film is not a precise reconstitution of the Grande Rafle. It's an attempt to grasp the essence of this period and the events that it produced, in the form of a documented moral fable, as a warning.'[15] While the Vel' d'Hiv took place in mid-July, the raid in the film occurs in midwinter; while the actual velodrome was enclosed and tragically disorganised, the film depicts an outdoor stadium with barbed wire and alphabetical sections; while the Vel' d'Hiv was in west-central Paris and requisitioned buses carried the prisoners to transit camps where they were then put on trains to Auschwitz, in the film the trains leading to Auschwitz are right next to the stadium and the stadium is at Vincennes on the eastern outskirts of Paris. Additionally, day turns to night rapidly, completely frustrating the logical sense of time spent in the stadium. Scripted by Franco Solinas, *Monsieur Klein* references the Vel' d'Hiv in order to examine the mechanisms of racial prejudice. An atmosphere of uneasy mystery is created by emblematic scenes of police preparations for the roundup, puzzling because they seem unrelated to the central plot. By the time we see the stadium and its captives at the very end of the film, these previously unrelated shots become imbued with narrative meaning.

Losey also stated that the central theme of the film is 'indifference ... the inhumanity of the French towards sections of their own people',[16] while its images have been described as palpably evoking 'the black machine of the Occupation, implacable and infernal'.[17] To reinforce this double move from history to moral fable, a title at the beginning of the film states: 'Mr Klein is a fictitious character, a composite of the experiences of many individuals. The facts are a matter of history. They took place in France in 1942.'[18] Specificity of dates, generality of experience: *Monsieur Klein* embodies 'the political numbness of a population that ... enabled intolerance and racism to turn into institutionalized murder'.[19] Nowhere is the indifference more evident than in the last moments of the film when the roundup is fully portrayed; people obliviously continue their shopping at the marketplace, a note thrown from a bus is ignored and the sight of terrified Jews on city buses garners no response.

In the film, the atmosphere of anxiety is constructed through a dual series of narrative images. The first is an enigmatic exploration of Jewish identity through the story of one Robert Klein (played with glacial indifference by Alain Delon),[20] an art dealer who lives in luxury while he profits from desperate Jews selling family heirlooms. He finds himself confused with another Robert Klein, Jewish and invisible, and becomes obsessed with meeting his mysterious doppelgänger, if only to prove the case of mistaken religion. When he finally and unexpectedly merges with him in the chaos of the roundup, he is unable to extricate himself from the crowd of Jews. In his search, he encounters the other Klein's seedy lodgings and his concierge, a strange tapestry representing indifference and remorse, an anti-Semitic cabaret performance, a mysterious chateau sheltering wealthy Jews who later escape to Mexico, and other unyielding locations. All the while he is intent on proving his 'French French' heritage (he is actually Alsatian of several generations) with the help of his lawyer friend Pierre (Michael Lonsdale). But as he gets closer to this proof, the further he gets from his original grand bourgeois identity, and the closer he gets to assuming the identity of the debased other. Alexandre Trauner's haunting art direction constructs places bathed in dusk or twilight; the claustrophobic interiors, the labyrinth of dark streets or alleyways, the shadows, mirrors and polished surfaces all indicate a world destabilised by uncertainty.[21]

The second strand of the narrative appears throughout the film in momentary, puzzling scenes interspersed with Klein's story. There is no apparent connection between these and Klein until the end, when the two strands finally meet in the panic of the roundup, and both he and the other Klein are herded into a boxcar. The two are finally taken for one – a Jew. This strand is made up of iconic scenes of preparations for the roundup – officials plan with a large map of Paris, gendarmes and secret police prepare the stadium, clerks assemble addresses of Jewish families on index cards, black cars drop off groups of officers in the Paris streets, they prepare staging areas. Often these are accompanied by eerie electronic chords of a threatening nature in an evocative score composed by Egisto Macchi.[22]

At the very end of the film when Klein is absorbed into the doomed crowd, the definition of Jewish identity seems to be primarily 'someone designated for death'. The yellow stars are visible everywhere. Robert Klein, having been divested of every material thing in his luxurious apartment at 136 rue du Bac (7th *arrondissement*), now definitively taken for a Jew by the police who arrest him, is compelled to follow the man who answers to his name into the stadium. With a futile 'I'll be back' to Pierre, who has the documents that could save him, Klein finds himself crammed in a boxcar with the

Annette Monod (Mélanie Laurent), the 'heroic Protestant nurse' in *La Rafle/The Roundup* (Roselyne Bosch, 2010).

desperate Jewish client we saw him swindle at the beginning of the film, now with a prominent Star of David on his coat. In an atmosphere described as 'more hallucinatory than historical',[23] the Jewish bodies destined for annihilation act as a response to the full corporeality of the stark, puzzling sequence that opens the film: a frightened middle-aged woman, naked before the cold eye of a bureaucrat, is examined like a horse or other beast, to determine if she is Jewish. Measurements taken, posture observed, teeth and nostrils examined, the result is 'inconclusive'. And the question that haunts the film – 'What is a Jew?' – continues to hover, unanswered, as it ends, while it solemnly dramatises 'the disappearance of the Jewish body from the European scene'.[24]

La Rafle

La Rafle takes a third approach to the tragic events of July 1942 with its focus on children and its comprehensive historical form. There were 4,115 Jewish children arrested in the Vel' d'Hiv; only a tiny number of them survived.[25] These arrests set a horrifying precedent by putting every Jewish child at risk. Some historians refer to this organised infanticide as the 'Massacre of the Innocents'.[26] Moved by the specific tragedy of the children, Roselyne Bosch made *La Rafle* out of a desire to tell the story from their point of view.[27] She also wanted to describe the Vel' d'Hiv from the inside, believing that fiction can reveal truths unavailable to the documentary form.[28] She created a fictional account of true events, and prefaced her film with a statement that historicises it. 'All of the events in this film, even the most extreme, truly occurred in the summer of 1942.'[29] She developed a sort of epic mosaic that represents both the historical and subjective realities of the Vel' d'Hiv through a multifaceted view of intersecting destinies: the increasingly difficult life of Jewish families; the commitment of some of the French to helping them; the crowded, anguished suffering in the hellish stadium; the bargaining Vichy and Nazi officials (even Hitler himself) responsible for the decision to deport the children; the horrific life in limbo at the detention camp; the terrifying barbarity of the separation of mothers from children; and the tragic return of the few survivors after the war.

Concerned with historical realism, Bosch consulted many sources, among them Blanche Finger and William Karel's influential *Opération 'Vent Printanier'*.[30] It provided two of her main characters: Joseph Weismann (Hugo Leverdez), who, as an 11-year-old, managed to escape from Beaune-La-Rolande and, while he lost his entire family, survived both the Vel' d'Hiv and the Loiret camp; and Annette Monod (Mélanie Laurent), a heroic Protestant nurse who showed tremendous compassion and courage by caring for the children at the Vel' d'Hiv, Beaune-La-Rolande and the Hôtel Lutetia.[31] A third main character, Dr David Sheinbaum (Jean Reno), is a composite, while most of the other characters and incidents have analogues in specific accounts; every single episode can be historically documented.

One can say that the film's main character is actually the Vel' d'Hiv, for most of the action takes place during the roundup and its aftermath. But before Jewish families are torn apart, the film places us in the vibrant immigrant community of Montmartre where both Yiddish and French are spoken, while Jewish life is increasingly restricted.[32] Jo, star marked 'Juif' on his sweater, goes to school, where the children sing allegiance to Marshall Pétain. Our first vision of Jo thus evokes the contradictory struggle of Jewish children who must revere the source of their exclusion. Sequences in Montmartre introduce other families, while some scenes convey moments of sublime tenderness (Shabbat, bedtime) that rewrite the iconic clichés of Jewish victimhood by substituting real human qualities for the familiar emaciated forms in prison garb. Soon after Montmartre goes to sleep to the soft music of Chopin and soundtrack composer Christian Henson,[33] all are abruptly awakened by the swarms of police who have come to arrest the families. The horror of the roundup, with its scenes of chaos and panic, is depicted from within the action: suicides, looting, brutality, hostile bystanders (and some who are sympathetic), tears, pleas, anger, resignation.

We are introduced to the infamous interior of the Vel' d'Hiv as nurse Annette Monod enters; her shock is ours. An overhead shot provides a startling view of the confusion and chaos, filth and degradation, as thousands of people are crammed into the stadium without food, water or sanitation. 'Eyewitness testimony to the horror of the Vel' d'Hiv abounds ... A Red Cross nurse later recalled: "The atmosphere was stuffy and nauseating: nervous breakdowns, shouting, weeping of children and even of adults who were at the end of their tether."'[34] Amid this squalor and despair, acts of heroism and conscience were in fact possible. Anna Traube brazenly leaves by having plumber Gaston Roques write a pass.[35] Her escape to freedom, past the Eiffel Tower, repeats Monod's original entry in reverse. Compassionate firemen turn on hoses to aid people literally dying of thirst. They post letters, scribbled in haste and hope.[36] The exhausted Annette and Dr Sheinbaum develop a friendship, and when finally the Jews are let out of the Vel' d'Hiv, only to be imprisoned in the transit camps, Annette decides, out of conscience and love for the children, that she will go with them.

Even though in the open, Beaune-La-Rolande is not much better, surrounded by barbed wire and watchtowers, its captives nearly starved. Still, there are moments of lightness as when Annette procures madeleines and a makeshift picnic takes place. However, this is a prelude to perhaps the worst horror of the Shoah in France: the separation of the mothers and children. Permission to deport the young children had not yet arrived from Berlin, so a decision to send parents and older children was made; the younger ones would follow later. The decision to leave the children behind in the camp produces the most dramatic event of the film. Beatings, hosings, machine guns, traumatic cries of agony abound as pure terror accompanies the separations, and once again this is depicted from within the action.[37] Finally, at the Hôtel Lutetia, Annette Monod is unexpectedly reunited with Jo, who has found kind adoptive parents, and with little Nono, who, traumatised and mute, is the image of the tragedy of the Vel' d'Hiv.[38]

Testament

What can be said of the cinematic legacy of the Vel' d'Hiv? There is certainly the obligation to remember, the continued desire to tell the truth of France's complicity in the Shoah. These three films, *Les Guichets du Louvre*, *Monsieur Klein* and *La Rafle*, have begun the task of representation, as the last of the eyewitnesses disappears. Each film's strategies contribute a perspective, from the symbolic, to the more abstract and thought-provoking, to a scrupulously detailed realism. Each film succeeds in tearing a bit of the blindfold away. And, unexpectedly, they have also provided us with a modicum of hope. Today, the Vel' d'Hiv remains an excruciating symbol of one of the most tragic moments in French history. Yet a proud antithesis to this icon of terror can be found in some images of women of indomitable strength depicted in these films. In *Les Guichets du Louvre*, Jeanne's return to the Marais is an act of defiance and an assertion of her Jewish identity. She bravely claims her part in the community of Jews in the face of an unknown fate. In *Monsieur Klein*, this strength comes unexpectedly in the form of the unnamed Jewish woman who maintains her composure during the brusque and humiliating physical examination. Of the many reactions one might have in this situation, this silent resignation is a kind of strength. And *La Rafle* gives us an array of admirable women, from Anna Traube and Annette Monod, whose bravery and commitment existed in reality, to Jo's anguished mother Sura, who at the moment of deepest sorrow, the separation, breaks from the tormented crowd to make sure Jo will escape and tell the world. Today, nothing remains of the Vélodrome d'Hiver in the 15th *arrondissement*. The Eiffel Tower, immutable, stands watch as the Seine flows languidly by, past the statue, plaque and monument that silently enjoin us to remember. They are easily ignored. But the increased visibility of this forgotten place, brought into focus by the gradual cinematic representation of the Vel' d'Hiv, echoes the growing recognition of its role in history. Finally, these films give voice to the impossible perceptions of vanished lives and in so doing begin the reciprocal work of memory and representation so necessary to the recovery of these traumatic Parisian sites.

Notes

1. *Nelles Paris Guide* (Munich: Nelles Verlag GmbH, 1996), p. 115.
2. Two of the most useful summaries of the Vel' d'Hiv roundup can be found in Robert Paxton and Michael Marrus, *Vichy France and the Jews* (Stanford, CA: Stanford University Press, 1995), and Susan Zuccotti, *The Holocaust, the French, and the Jews* (New York: Basic Books, 1993).

3. Hollande's recognition brings to light one of the paradoxes of the Vel' d'Hiv, for while finally acknowledging the crime, it alludes to the fact that about 12,000 of the 25,000 Jews demanded for the roundup avoided capture and 75 per cent of France's Jewish population survived the war. Various independent ways of protecting Jews were enacted.
4. The other two films are *Les Violons du bal* (Michel Drach, 1974), and *Elle s'appelait Sarah/Sarah's Key* (Gilles Paquet-Brenner, 2011), based on the bestselling novel by Tatiana de Rosnay.
5. The Hôtel Lutetia was used by the Red Cross as an assembly point where both prisoners and families went to find out what had happened to their loved ones.
6. This fascination is sometimes referred to as the '*mode rétro*'. '[F]ascinated with the aesthetic trappings of the period ... la mode retro was not simply nostalgia for a fascist past but a wholly more complex renegotiation of what the past represented.' Ferzina Banaji, *France, Film, and the Holocaust: From le génocide to la shoah* (New York: Palgrave Macmillan, 2012), pp. 71–2.
7. Roger Boussinot, *Les Guichets du Louvre* (Paris: Denoel, 1960). Reprinted in 1999 by Gaïa Editions with a new postscript by the author. The English title of the film, *Black Thursday*, is taken from '*le jeudi noir*', which is how many Jews referred to that day of 16 July.
8. Between novel and film, the 1967 book *Ce jour-là 16 juillet 1942: la grande rafle du Vel d'Hiv* by Claude Lévy and Paul Tillard was published. This first (and still best) documentary collection of testimonies and eyewitness accounts broke the silence and brought the trauma of the Vel' d'Hiv to a wide public. Claude Lévy and Paul Tillard, *Ce jour-là 16 juillet 1942: la grande rafle du Vel d'Hiv* (Paris: Robert Laffont, 1967). The book was then translated into English and published as *Betrayal at the Vel d'Hiv* in 1969. This is about the time that France was beginning to see many testimonies and histories, among them Eberhard Jaekel, *La France dans l'Europe de Hitler* (Paris: Fayard, 1968), Robert Paxton, *La France de Vichy, 1940–1944* (Paris: Editions de Seuil, 1973) and Georges Wellers, *L'Etoile jaune à l'heure de Vichy* (Paris: Fayard, 1973). Of course, the groundbreaking documentary film by Marcel Ophuls, *The Sorrow and the Pity* (1973), did much to awaken the knowledge of French complicity.
9. Boussinot, *Les Guichets du Louvre*, p. 9.
10. The score was composed by Mort Shuman of Industrial Music, who is best known for his pop anthems, such as 'Save the Last Dance for Me' and for songs he wrote for artists from Elvis to Johnny Hallyday. He wrote the off-Broadway musical *Jacques Brel Is Alive and Well in Paris*. He became a popular entertainer in France, and scored 15 films.
11. Several sources refer to a closing title of the film: 'Only thirty adults survived that "Great Roundup." Not a single child returned.' But this does not exist on the three DVDs that I viewed, and I assume it was on the English-language version, which is unavailable.
12. The German ordinance of 29 May 1942, enforced by French police, stated that every Jew, French or foreign, over the age of 6 was required to wear a six-pointed yellow Star of David with the word 'Juif' inscribed in black gothic letters, clearly visible and solidly sewn on the upper left side of their outerwear. This ignominious badge of difference caused consternation and remains a devastating memory in almost all survivor testimonies.
13. See Annette Insdorf, *Indelible Shadows: Film and the Holocaust* (Cambridge: Cambridge University Press, 1989), 2nd edn, p. 86. Among those critiques of Jeanne's timidity, see Banaji, *France, Film, and the Holocaust*, and Judith Doneson, 'The Jew as a Female Figure in Holocaust Film' cited by Insdorf, *Indelible Shadows*, p. 81.

14. Cited in David Caute, *Joseph Losey: A Revenge on Life* (New York: Oxford University Press, 1994), p. 281.
15. Joseph Losey, *Positif*, no. 186 (October 1976). Quoted by Anny Dayan Rosenman in her excellent essay 'La Rafle du Vel' d'Hiv entre apologue et histoire: *Monsieur Klein* de Joseph Losey', in Alain Kleinberger and Philippe Mesnard (eds), *La Shoah: théâtre et cinéma aux limites de la représentation* (Paris: Editions Kimé, 2013), p. 362.
16. Caute, *Joseph Losey*, p. 414.
17. Quoted in ibid., p. 411.
18. Claude Lévy, one of the authors of the history of the Vel' d'Hiv mentioned above, was a technical advisor on the film. However, since Losey was not interested in technical accuracy, I'm assuming his work had to do with the atmosphere the director wanted to create.
19. André Pierre Colombat, *The Holocaust in French Film* (Metuchen, NJ: Scarecrow Press, 1993), p. 297.
20. Delon also co-produced the film, and was troubled by its disappointing reception.
21. Art director Alexandre Trauner, who was himself a Jew in hiding during the war, is best known for his highly evocative work with Poetic Realists of the 1930s. He worked with Losey on several films and later with both well-known Hollywood and French directors.
22. Egisto Macchi is known for his work in avant-garde music. He worked with Ennio Morricone and Nino Rota, and composed scores for 20 films.
23. Insdorf, *Indelible Shadows*, p. 177.
24. Jacques Mandelbaum, 'Recovery', in Jean-Michel Frodon (ed.), *Cinema and the Shoah: An Art Confronts the Tragedy of the Twentieth Century* (Albany: SUNY Press, 2010), p. 38.
25. All of the deported children were killed; the only children who survived were those who managed to escape either the Vel d'Hiv or the Loiret camps.
26. Paxton and Marrus, *Vichy France and the Jews*, p. 263. Several years after *La Rafle* appeared, the Hôtel de Ville in Paris had an extensive exhibit about the children entitled, 'C'étaient des enfants: déportation et sauvetage des enfants juifs à Paris', in 2012.
27. There was also a personal investment. While Bosch is not Jewish herself, her husband's (producer Ilan Goldman) family who lived in Montmartre had avoided the roundup and gone into hiding. Bosch had always wanted to tell their story and spent three years on the scenario, creating 74 speaking parts and documenting everything with historical evidence.
28. Press book, p. 15. 'We tell the story from the inside. There is no other way.'
29. Serge Klarsfeld, whose legendary work on the Shoah in France is revered, served as technical advisor. Among Klarsfeld's numerous and important works is *French Children of the Holocaust: A Memorial* (New York University Press, 1996). The French edition preceded it in 1994. This monumental volume outlines the names, places and dates of birth, last addresses and convoys of every single one of the 11,403 Jewish children deported from France to the east.
30. Blanche Finger and William Karel, *Opération 'Vent Printanier'* (Paris: Editions La Découverte, 1992). Composed of survivor testimonies, it was published on the 50th anniversary of the roundup, and these testimonies were made into a documentary film.
31. Weismann escaped with another boy of his age, Joseph Kogan, who was reunited with his friend 50 years later. After the war, Annette Monod devoted her life to prisoners of all kinds and was always willing to share her memories of the Vel' d'Hiv. She died in 2003, so Bosch was unable to interview her for the film. On the other hand, it was through countless interviews

with the octogenarian Joseph Weismann that Bosch was able to write her scenario in the style she wished. Weismann was able to write his own memoir, *Après la rafle*, after the film's release.
32. A quarter of the children in the Vel' d'Hiv came from Montmartre. Press book, p. 17. The German ordinance of 8 July forbade Jews from going to public places such as parks, cinemas, theatres, libraries, museums, cafes or restaurants. Zuccotti, *The Holocaust, the French, and the Jews*, p. 93. The list was expanded to include concert halls, swimming pools, beaches, exhibitions, historic monuments, sporting events, racecourses, campgrounds and even phone booths.
33. This British composer has created music for 45 films and worked with Brian Eno and Steve Reich.
34. Zuccotti, *The Holocaust, the French, and the Jews*, p. 111. Also on that page is a description of Sarah Castel, then aged 5: 'Those cries of grief, of horror, of fear, in my spirit as a young child, the memory of those cries, that horrible odor, the tears of the children and that constant blue light day and night.'
35. Anna Traube's memoir, *Evadée du Vel' d'Hiv'*, was published in 2005 in the Collection Témoignages de la Shoah. In the film she is played by Adèle Exarchopoulos.
36. Some of these letters were recently found and published as *Je vous écris du Vél' d'Hiv*, introduced by Karen Taib (Paris: Robert Laffont, 2011).
37. 'They waged war against children because they were Jewish. Do you know of any civilization capable of such cruelty? It is inhuman to make children suffer so.' Joseph Weismann in Finger and Karel, *'Vent Printanier'*, p. 82.
38. 'My whole life was overwhelmed and shaped by that roundup of the Vel' d'Hiv, that has left so few traces in people's memory, about which they seldom speak.' Annette Monod, in Finger and Karel, *'Vent Printanier'*, p. 194. As for Nono, he is based on a little boy who became Annette's protégé. Annette Monod, quoted in Zuccotti, *The Holocaust, the French, and the Jews*, p. 114, and in Lévy and Tillard, *La Grande Rafle du Vel d'Hiv*, p. 159.

'Unremarkable Paris': Jacques Becker's Urban Everyday

Alastair Phillips

To move 'beyond the *flâneur*' in terms of understanding Paris as a cinematic city means, in one sense, to re-examine the conventional ways that the topography of the French capital may be configured as a site of narrative attention. If the Parisian *flâneur* existed as an individual mobile figure, perhaps uniquely engaged with the momentary sensations and distractions of modernity,[1] what happens in the kind of popular mainstream cinema that privileges instead the more understated, and thus more ordinary, realities of quotidian urban life? Where does the Parisian everyday specifically occur on film and how are its constituent sites and activities within the capital managed not just in terms of their geography, but also their unique temporality? In this chapter, I want to argue that two of Jacques Becker's films of the immediate post-war – *Antoine et Antoinette* (1947) and *Rendez-vous de juillet/Rendezvous in July* (1949) – may be fruitfully contextualised by some of the important critical and aesthetic questions emerging from the introduction of 'the everyday' as a key conceptual term within French culture. In so doing, I will suggest there is actually something quite distinctive about the way that Paris is configured in Becker's work, and that this might, in turn, mean adjusting some of the conventional vocabularies deployed in thinking about the relationship between the French capital and its historic cinematic representation.

In writing on the attractions of the cinematic city, Charlotte Brunsdon has suggested a recognisable kind of 'city discourse' that conveys what one might call a notion of melancholic city wandering: of unexpected encounters, fleeting glimpses of beauty, disregarded detail and material traces of past urban history.[2] Clearly, modern Paris in Becker's films offers few of these qualities except certain material aspects of the city's historical architecture. It largely requires a different notion of being at home in the capital. How then *does* Becker show Paris? I want to think about the ways in which *Antoine et Antoinette* and *Rendez-vous de juillet* do three things: assimilate the everyday, potentially reconvene the everyday and then convey an apprehension of what the future everyday might eventually entail. In both embodying the ordinary realities of Paris and raising questions about the relationship between the old and the new within the contemporary urban everyday, Becker's work thus also allows us to fruitfully reconsider the traditional nexus of film, modernity and the city. In short, it permits us to address some of the broader, hitherto unexplored, problems of conceptualising Paris as a major cinematic city that govern the inclusion of several other chapters in this book.

The cinema of Jacques Becker is intimately linked to the French capital and its most quotidian aspects. As befitting someone who closely collaborated with Jean Renoir in the 1930s – he was an assistant director, for example, on Renoir's *Boudu sauvé des eaux*/*Boudu Saved from Drowning* (1932)[3] – the majority of his post-war films such as *Falbalas* (1945), *Casque d'or* (1952), *Rue de l'Estrapade* (1953) and *Touchez pas au grisbi* (1954) are carefully delineated genre portraits of Parisians in their ordinary social milieux. In the words of René Gilson, 'Jacques Becker was the only filmmaker of his generation to be truly and authentically without any self-mythology, without any artifice, a discrete painter of Paris and certain aspects of *la vie parisienne*.'[4] Claude Naumann is typical of many French scholars of his generation who situate Becker somewhere between the achievements of French classical cinema of the 1930s and the observational aesthetics and bravura experimentation with cinematic temporality that marked the emergence of the New Wave. Placing the director as a bridge 'between classicism and modernity', Naumann argues that Becker's astute camera positioning and movement constantly allowed the director to 'situate the film's characters in the social or human reality with which they are linked'.[5] As if to reinforce this view, in a canonical interview with the critical progenitors of the New Wave, Jacques Rivette and François Truffaut, Becker himself declared: 'I don't feel I have any real interest ... in that which is exceptional.'[6]

Becker's interest in the unexceptional realities of French urban life overlaps with two contemporaneous discourses that underpin the wider significance of his work to the specificities of the French cinematic city. Firstly, there is the complex question of cinematic realism that is acutely underscored, for instance, in the fascinating critical debate between Becker and the scriptwriter Charles Spaak, published in *L'Ecran français* the year of *Antoine et Antoinette*'s release. Entitled 'To Paint Reality or to Turn One's Back on It?',[7] the piece appears to pre-empt François Truffaut's later and more famous polemical interventions about authorship and film style in *Cahiers du cinéma*[8] and *Arts*.[9] It essentially argues, through Becker's own words, for a modern French cinema that recognises the medium's differential capacity to dramatise human action in real time in a manner completely devoid of the necessary artifice of literary adaptation. The discussion was preceded by a related feature in the journal that investigated *Antoine et Antoinette*'s intended realism by interviewing various Parisians from the specific urban locations in the working-class districts of the 18th *arrondissement* where the film was actually shot.[10] In this sense, it is not surprising that, according to Jean Nery at the time, the original title of the film was to have been *Les Gens de Paris* ('the people of Paris').[11]

Part of the wider context for this concern lay, of course, in the vexed issue of to what extent French cinema should respond to the aesthetic imperatives of Italian neo-realism; something articulated, for example, by André Bazin in his now landmark piece, published in *Esprit* in January 1948, in which he observed that '[t]he Italian cinema retains something of the human quality of the Bell and Howell newsreel camera, a projection of hand and eye, almost a living part of the operator, instantly in tune with his awareness.'[12] At the very same time, too, French sociologists and anthropologists were beginning to theorise and explore what the notion of 'the everyday' might specifically entail. In 1938, the novelist and anthropologist Michel Leiris had given a formative lecture at the Collège de Sociologie, entitled 'The Sacred in Everyday Life', in which he argued for an ethnographic attention to the dialogue between the self and ordinary experience.

The first volume of Henri Lefebvre's *Critique of Everyday Life*, published in 1947, built on this by arguing from a Marxist perspective that it was only at the level of one's lived experience of everyday activity that the political consequences of social and cultural modernity could be scrutinised. Elsewhere, the formation of Section VI of the Ecole Practique des Hautes Etudes, devoted to the Economic and Social Sciences, coincided with a growing interest in mass society and urbanism. In his foreword to the first edition of his book (actually written in 1945), Lefebvre wrote, '[i]f we can consider the critique of everyday life as an aspect of a concrete sociology, we can envisage a vast enquiry which will look at professional life, family life and leisure activities in terms of their many-sided interactions.'[13] Becker was obviously working in a quite different political and aesthetic register, one more related to the popular dramatised fictional lives of French people and their homes and occupations, yet I want to argue that his attentive but undemonstrative cinema nonetheless proposed a significant form of enquiry into the same ethnographic realm of the French quotidian then beginning to be discussed by his intellectual contemporaries. As the director later put it simply to Rivette and Truffaut, 'I am French, my work is about the French, I look at the French, I am interested in the French.'[14]

The question of temporality underpinned much critical theorisation of the everyday. For Lefebvre, the everyday was 'situated at the intersection of two modes of repetition: the cyclical, which dominates in nature, and the linear, which dominates in processes known as "rational"'.[15] In his magisterial study of the topic, Michael Sheringham reframes this formulation by asking whether there are 'events or acts that are uniquely "everyday", or ... [whether] the *quotidian* [is] a way of thinking about events and acts in the "here and now" as opposed to the longer term'.[16] Certainly, Becker was not especially interested in extricating the everyday 'from the continuum in which it is embedded',[17] yet, at the same time, his work, particularly the many films set in Paris, and perhaps especially *Antoine et Antoinette*, pays scrupulous attention to the modulation of time as a means of evoking the texture of everyday lived experience. And, as we shall see, the film stresses both of Sheringham's modalities.

Antoine et Antoinette is the story of a young Parisian couple who share the ordinary rituals and routines of their neighbours and wider circle of friends, colleagues and workmates in the city. The narrative, such as it is, follows the course of a series of misadventures and misunderstandings based around the discovery, loss and recuperation of a winning lottery ticket – an item that has the potential to disrupt the circumscription of the couple's everyday lives and reshape their shared imagined dreams of a better future. The film begins with an exemplarily detailed and compassionate portrait of one ordinary working day in their lives: at the printer's, in the case of Antoine (Roger Pigaut), and at the department store, in the case of Antoinette (Claire Mafféi). Becker's scrupulously detailed *mise-en-scène* documents the routine interaction of the two characters with the machinery of their respective workplaces. We first see the serial routine of the mass production of popular novels, one of which, *The Ace of Clubs*, will play a pivotal role in the organisation of the narrative time of the film. Next, we see Antoinette interact with a customer at the store's 'Photomat', where she guides him in the process of having an identity photograph taken by the camera in the kiosk. On one level, Becker is showing us a series of moments that are clearly embedded in a sense of the structured repetition of time – this could be any day in any week in any month – but on another level, he is also setting up the means by which the film achieves an important sense of counterpoint to these two forms of media practice. Becker's film presents a different proposition to the viewer than that of pulp fiction and photography: that the world of its story is neither special nor fantastic (like the fictional world of the cheap novel) and neither fixable and still (like the regimented expectations of the official printed photograph). In this sense, his urban everyday is both contingent and in flux. His characters, in their different facets, are uniformly absorbed within its ongoing flow.

This notion is reinforced in multiple ways within the film's visual grammar. The lives of the main characters are shown as circumscribed by various domestic and work-related routines. Much of this involves an almost forensic attention to their coming and going from one city space to another, to their entering various ordinary Parisian homes, cafés, shops and buildings. It is no accident that Antoinette's closest female friend, Juliette (Annette Poivre), works as a ticket vendor on the Métro, for this permits a further circle of mobile encounters, conversations and ordinary interactions with apparently real-life Parisians. When we cut to distinctive high-angle long shots from an adjacent window of either Antoine cycling in the street below the couple's apartment or Antoinette exiting La Fourche Métro station, the camera is thus painting a way of seeing how the couple are specifically integrated within the ordinary everyday movement of Parisian life *as it is now*. Becker's sensitive attention to the human environment of the city and its multiple temporal textures produces a cinema in which, according to Claude Naumann, its characters actually 'take their time'.[18] But this is also a time which is resolutely supposed to be happening in front of our eyes.

A way of seeing that is specifically integrated within the ordinary everyday movement of Parisian life. Antoine (Roger Pigaut) leaves the apartment in *Antoine et Antoinette* (Jacques Becker, 1947).

Having said this, as Valérie Vignaux has discussed,[19] there are exceptions when the film imagines a different awareness of the progression of ordinary urban time. One element is, of course, the projected sense of a different future enabled by the anticipated prosperity of the lottery win. The point is underscored by the gaze directed at their neighbour's daughter by the childless couple who are babysitting while the parents pursue their routine Saturday evening entertainment at the cinema. Another is the film's ability to slow its registration of the external spaces of the city and enter the internalised thought processes of Antoine as he anxiously paces the streets worrying about the possible loss of the winning lottery ticket. Here, the film's visual style noticeably shifts key from both the documentary real of the weekend leisure sequences at the football match and boating lake and the fluid interaction of faces and gestures that marks the director's engaging portrayal of the local characters' domestic banter and conversation in the couple's *quartier*.

The majority of the critics of the time certainly saw *Antoine et Antoinette* as a film invested in an authentic representation of the urban everyday, with Georges Charensol being typical of many when he noted that Becker's attention to detail ensured the thoughts and actions of the film's many characters 'corresponded exactly to the way that the people of Paris behave'.[20] Becker's dual narrative ambition of assimilating the codes of ordinary Parisian representation and then reconvening them in terms of a briefly imagined alternative to routine was well received. These tensions, albeit through the prism of a different element of the Parisian class structure, similarly inform *Rendez-vous de juillet*. The street, the body and the subject of Frenchness matter to the picture of Paris we have in *Antoine et Antoinette*, but they become even more pressing in this vivacious and romantic story set amongst a group of young jazz musicians, filmmakers and actors on the Left Bank.

Even today, *Rendez-vous de juillet* remains a subtle and evocative exploration of place and the relationship between the group and the individual in a society on the cusp of a vital explosion in youth culture. At the centre of a number of oppositions that the film explores is an intense and ardent undergraduate documentary filmmaker, Lucien Bonnard (Daniel Gélin), who appears to exist in a world of theatricality, duplicity and bourgeois confinement. Lucien, based on the real-life ethnographer Francis Mazière,[21] spends the film occupied between his precarious romance with an aspiring actress, Christine (Nicole Courcel), and his efforts to raise the money to make a new form of anthropological documentary in Africa. The film ends with Lucien's departure en route to foreign parts after discovering Christine in a compromising position with the oily and smooth playwright François (Philippe Mareuil) in an effort to secure a promising stage role for herself.

The key negotiation made in the film's narrative rests in this acute tension between the conventions of theatrical artifice (a performance of Sacha Guitry's *Le Beau mariage*) and the fluidity of the documentary real. Becker's narrative moves, for instance, from Lucien's oppressive and formal Parisian bourgeois family home to the various social and domestic worlds of his young comrades. The parts of the film set in the theatre were filmed in the studio, whilst the journeying around the city to the clubs and bars involved filming on location at such places as rue des Carmes (in the 5th *arrondissement*), the

Trocadéro, the Jardin des Plantes and the Pont Neuf.[22] The film also includes, for the very first time in mainstream French cinema, a carefully delineated portrayal of the newly emergent and energetic Left Bank youth culture of beatniks and jazz aficionados who populated such venues as the Lorientais, a *cave* which is faithfully recreated within the film and which Gélin and Becker both knew intimately.[23] The film's principal character is an ethnographic filmmaker who studies anthropology at the Musée de l'Homme. This move within the diegesis from the representation of live performance towards the quest for a more scientifically verifiable lived-in authenticity marks an interesting set of questions about the nature of the urban world within the film and the film's own wider relationship to discourses around urban youth and modernity in French cinema and society of the time. As Michèle Lagny has argued convincingly, Becker's method in *Rendez-vous de juillet* is thus far more complex than mere descriptive realism. His film offers a sort of meditation on how the real may be construed and then reimagined within the terms of narrative representation.[24] It is fascinating to note, for example, that the various aspirational professions featured in the film are ethnographer, cameraman, actor, scriptwriter: the various creative roles featured in early critical discourse about the representation of the city in the French New Wave – a point I shall return to at the end of this chapter.

Despite the general rhetoric within much early scholarship on the cinema and the city that privileged 'the street' as an almost abstract space, Parisian streets are generally one of the major ways by which French cinema most ably distinguishes where one is specifically located within the capital. This is partly a question of architecture and the historical organisation of the city through a system of separate *arrondissements* with their individual geographical and cultural identities, and partly a question of the dialectic between typicality and the exceptional achieved through the notion of the urban landmark. In thinking about Paris as a cinematic city, one has to always attend to both the typical and the exceptional, but accept that in Becker's cinema, neither might be especially foregrounded. As we saw in the case of *Antoine et Antoinette*, Becker's protagonists are clearly immersed in the ordinariness of an urban daily reality, and what the director is suggesting is that what normally goes unnoticed might in fact be quite interesting to observe in its own right. This is especially true in the film's conception of location cinematography.

In *Rendez-vous de juillet*, for example, the street is largely conveyed through a sense of shared improvisation, rather than the anonymous direct gaze. The film is more or less devoid of touristic landmarks and instead conveys an underlying spirit of urban connectedness rather than solitary, masculine alienation. We largely just see the ordinary reality of people going about their daily business in the heart of the city. In the words of Becker, in an article he wrote about the film, revealingly titled 'Rendez-vous with Life':

> It's not a question here of a sentimental film, of a social film, of a drama or ordinary comedy, it's a question of a real journey that will transport the spectator in the midst of strangers ... troubled by the twin mirages of theatre and cinema.[25]

If prominent Parisian sites such as the Panthéon, the place de la Concorde or the towers of Notre-Dame thus feature at all, they occur only in the background to remind us of a general locale; they have no specific narrative function. The street is just a space to get from A to B, even in the famous sequence when the young friends move across the city and take to the Seine in an amphibious vehicle. Here, the river simply conveys an image of quotidian flow that is momentarily punctured by a specific act of human and mechanical improvisation.

It is difficult to think about French cinema's conception of Paris without also considering the relationship between the body and space and especially the idea of a communal or shared sense of being in the city. As Valérie Vignaux has argued, the expression of ordinary bodily freedom becomes a central facet of the ways in which Paris is signified in Becker's films.[26] This is especially true through the careful rendering of generational difference in *Rendez-vous de juillet*. Where then is the everyday in this sense? In one sense, it is in the urban home (a favourite space of Becker's) but in another, it is located in the new reality of public youth culture and its reinvention of this particular conception of 'being Parisian'. Interestingly, therefore, the cinematic everyday thus depends in part on the principle of counterpoint. We might think, for example, of the contrast between the tiresome bourgeois meal at the beginning of the film and the conviviality of the *gigot* and piano later on in the friends' bohemian garret as a typical instantiation of this broader narrative pattern.

Becker is thus still interested, like the *flâneur*, in the idea of the Parisian urban body within the Parisian here and now. He certainly presents an almost kinaesthetic sense of belonging in the modern world and an interest in presentation, ephemera and surface. But here, there is no perceptual shock; instead, there is a 'live' and improvised sense of everyday conviviality and community. This is emphasised in both films by their editor Marguerite Renoir's practice of cutting on movement that leads to an intensified scrutiny of the ordinary spatio-temporal rhythms of Parisians as they variously walk, rest, chatter and converse in the city.[27] Jacques Chastel, writing on *Rendez-vous de juillet* in *Combat*, was, like many contemporary critics of the film, especially sensitive to its structured melding of the dramatic and the quotidian in terms of Becker's portrayal of the city. The director 'proposes a geography of faces and makes us follow their perpetual modification', he wrote. 'From the first images onwards, the behaviour of these young people is rigorously implicated within ... a way of life, its timing and its geography, that [also] forms part of the narrative action.' For Chastel, 'the presence of whatever time it is, is profoundly felt. ... The Paris of *Rendez-Vous de juillet* is the first cinematic Paris that resembles that of Parisians.'[28]

Becker's *mise-en-scène* pays scrupulous attention to the material nature of transition within the urban everyday, hence a recurring attention to mobile objects, portals and machines such as telephones, doors and vehicles within much of his work. In the film's opening montage, for example, the relationship between the different characters and their specific milieux is managed through a series of intercut telephone conversations linking the spectator to the various bedrooms, living rooms and other ordinary domestic spaces of the main protagonists. As Claude Naumann observes, Becker's camera scrupulously observes the various pressures and attachments between the generations and across the classes, singling out the constraints of Lucien's excessively bourgeois home for special critique.[29] In both *Antoine et Antoinette* and *Rendez-vous de juillet*,

Becker's *mise-en-scène* pays scrupulous attention to the material nature of transition within the urban everyday. Lucien (Daniel Gélin, seen from the back) goes out into the street in *Rendez-vous de juillet* (Jacques Becker, 1949).

this level of attention is especially configured in terms of the intensity of unexceptional lived experience in largely indistinguishable parts of the city. When Lucien leaves a banal airline office in his bid to raise travel funds, for instance, Becker's camera pans right to track him exiting through the building's main door. Lucien rubs shoulders with an anonymous woman coming in the opposite direction and he then disappears screen right into the flow of an ordinary Parisian street. We are left watching life pass by for a moment before the film fades and a wipe then reintroduces Lucien walking in the Jardin des Plantes plotting what to do next with one of his friends. This is a form of cinema about the precise moment, but not one that proposes a temporality based on the sensation of impermanence à *la flâneur*. Instead, we largely have a sensation that one particular moment in one particular day might be special just because being in the ordinary continuum of the everyday might itself actually be too much to bear. Just as urban space can be divided ordinarily between the typical and the landmark, so urban time – in all cities, but especially Paris at this point – can thus be clearly divided in terms of the routine and the exceptional (when the everyday might be said to be resisted).

Becker's particular attention to city space in *Rendez-vous de juillet* is therefore based on a principle of assimilation rather than fragmentation; one that simultaneously proposes a model of urban integration and a mode of distraction. On the one hand, the friends move knowledgeably and seamlessly from one space to another with a striking degree of geographical familiarity. On the other hand, the city remains depicted as a kind of formative playground within which the characters rehearse a set of playful alternatives to the occupations of adult life. Thus, whilst aware of the lived present – what ordinary life in Paris might be like now for young people of a certain class background – the film is also beginning to ask questions about the material transformation of the postwar everyday. The film's characters are Parisians explicitly resisting a Fordist, and thus American, model of urban life based around the principles of punctuality, durability, reliability and consumption. In this sense, the representation of American popular culture activates a notion of Paris as both home and site of resistance or escape. It is no accident that jazz becomes a dominant issue in the film, because as a cultural form it relies on a finely tuned synthesis of internal structure and improvisation. The way jazz music simultaneously emphasises the radical spontaneity of the present moment along with the necessary complicity of group coordination in terms of performance relates precisely to the film's overall musical structure in terms of its presentation of Paris (and the presentation of the possibilities of filmmaking within the film), to the extent that it still feels profoundly authentic despite its ambivalent mobilisation of national identity.

To conclude, both *Antoine et Antoinette* and *Rendez-vous de juillet* are therefore films that pose a number of methodological problems when it comes to understanding Paris as a cinematic city in French cinema of the late classical period. There is no especial use of prominent scenic sites such as the *quais* and boulevards to orientate the spectator and evoke a sense of Paris as either 'landmark' or 'postcard' that could be targeted to an international audience. Both films lack any representation of conventional genre topoi such as the Pigalle nightclub, the urban courtyard or the city police office. There is no sense of anxiety or anomie as seen either in the vein of city/cinema writing focusing on real or imagined urban dystopia[30] or in the more literary influenced discourse of Paris as a site of danger or suffocating metropolitan sophistication.[31]

Jacques Becker's conception of Paris instead is of a city as a site of exemplary social and cinematic transition in which both the nature of the everyday and the means of its disavowal are in flux. One of the ways this is achieved is through a new configuration of the city as a mobile space that may be characterised by both a sense of routine and play. This is something that, as many have observed, explicitly predates the concerns of the French New Wave. The characters in these two, still undervalued, Paris films are all beginning to see and be in the city that place them already 'beyond the *flâneur*'. Some of the ways in which this may be especially true include an interest in the city that requires a specific kind of unobtrusive attention: a notion of the city as an anonymous backdrop that could nonetheless be seen as topographically familiar. In other words, what we might call 'unremarkable Paris'.

Notes

1. See, to give but one example, Anke Gleber, *The Art of Taking a Walk* (Princeton, NJ: Princeton University Press, 1999).
2. Charlotte Brunsdon, 'The Attractions of the Cinematic City', *Screen*, vol. 53, no. 3 (2012), p. 209.
3. According to Jean Castanier, the film's production designer, it was Becker who had the idea of the celebrated extensive lateral travelling shot following Boudu (Michel Simon) along the *quais* by a hidden camera. See Claude Naumann, *Jacques Becker* (Paris and Courbevoie: BiFi/Durante, 2001), pp. 17–18.
4. René Gilson, 'Becker', in *Anthologie du cinéma/2* (Paris: L'Avant-Scène Cinéma, 1967), p. 176.
5. Claude Naumann, 'Becker entre classicisme et modernité', in Claude Naumann and Freddy Buache (eds) *Jacques Becker* (Locarno: Editions du Festival International du Film de Locarno, 1991) p. 28.
6. Jacques Rivette and François Truffaut, 'Entretien avec Jacques Becker', *Cahiers du cinéma*, vol. 6, no. 32 (February 1954), p. 4.
7. *L'Ecran français*, no. 121 (21 October 1947), page number unknown.

8. François Truffaut, 'A Certain Tendency in French Cinema', in Peter Graham with Ginette Vincendeau (eds), *The French New Wave. Critical Landmarks* (London: BFI/Palgrave Macmillan, 2009), pp. 17–23 (originally published in *Cahiers du cinéma*, vol. 6, no. 31 [January 1954], pp. 15–29).
9. François Truffaut, 'Le Cinéma français crève sous les fausses légendes', *Arts*, no. 616 (15 May 1957), pp. 3–4.
10. *L'Ecran français*, no. 119 (7 October 1947), page number unknown. [Editors' note: see Thomas Pillard's chapter in this volume for further discussion of the representation of the 18th *arrondissement*.]
11. *Franc-Tireur*, 1 November 1947, page number unknown.
12. André Bazin, 'An Aesthetic of Reality. Cinematic Realism and the Italian School of the Liberation', in Hugh Gray (ed.), *What Is Cinema? Volume 2* (Berkeley: University of California Press, 1967) p. 33 (originally published in *Esprit*, no. 141 [January 1948]).
13. Henri Lefebvre, 'Foreword', in *Critique of Everyday Life* (London and New York: Verso, 1991), p. 42.
14. Becker in Rivette and Truffaut, 'Entretien avec Jacques Becker', p. 8.
15. Henri Lefebvre, "The Everyday and Everydayness', *Yale French Studies*, 'Everyday Life', no. 73 (1987), p. 10.
16. Michael Sheringham, *Everyday Life. Theories and Practices from Surrealism to the Present* (Oxford: Oxford University Press, 2006), pp. 14–15.
17. The act which Kristin Ross argues lay at the heart of the politics of Lefebvre's analytical project. See Kristin Ross, 'French Quotidien', in Lynn Gumpert (ed.), *The Art of the Everyday. The Quotidien in Postwar French Culture* (New York and London: New York University Press, 1997), pp. 19–20.
18. Claude Naumann, 'Becker ou le regard singulier sur les personnages', *Focales*, no. 2 (1993), p. 85.
19. Valérie Vignaux, *Jacques Becker ou l'exercice de la liberté* (Liège: Editions du Céfal, 2000), p. 91.
20. Georges Charensol, *Nouvelles littéraires*, 6 November 1947, page number unknown.
21. Francis Mazière (1924–94) actually appears in the film as Frédéric, a member of Lucien's proposed exhibition team. He also assisted the director in the set decoration. Mazière went on to achieve considerable success in the 1950s with a number of publications on Amazonian and Polynesian culture.
22. The 'Théâtre Saint-Jacques' in the film is actually the Théâtre Saint-Georges on 51 rue Saint-Georges in the 9th *arrondissement*.
23. Resident home, for example, of the jazz musician Claude Luter (1923–2006), who recorded as 'Claude Luter et Ses Lorientais' for the Swing record label. The Caveau des Lorientais was forced to close its doors in 1948 due to fire regulations. [Editors' note: for a further discussion of the *caves* of Saint-Germain-des Prés, see Sébastien Layerle's chapter in this volume.]
24. Michèle Lagny, 'Le Réalisme imaginaire du cinéma de la quatrième république', in Raymond Chirat (ed.), *Le Cinéma français de la Quatrième République. Conférences du Collège d'Histoire de l'Art Cinématographique*, no. 4 (Paris: Cinémathèque Française, 1993), pp. 1–14.
25. Jacques Becker, 'Rendez-vous avec la vie', *Ciné-Digest*, no. 3 (July 1949), page number unknown.

26. See, for example, Vignaux, *Jacques Becker ou l'exercice de la liberté*, pp. 103–8.
27. Alain Resnais notes that there are around 1,200 cuts in *Antoine et Antoinette*. See the aptly titled 'Le Bonheur au quotidien', in Naumann and Buache, *Jacques Becker*, p. 230.
28. Jacques Chastel, *Combat*, 20 August 1949.
29. Naumann, *Jacques Becker*, pp. 51–2.
30. See, for example, Giuliana Bruno, 'Ramble City: Postmodernism and *Blade Runner*', *October*, no. 41 (Summer 1987), pp. 61–74.
31. Such as Honoré de Balzac's *Illusions perdues* (1843).

Television and the Renewal of Paris: From Official Discourse to Social Criticism

Hélène Jannière

La Rénovation urbaine ('Urban Renewal') was the title of a French television documentary typical of the late 1960s and early 1970s that was broadcast on 26 April 1971. The expression 'urban renewal' encompassed the demolition of slums and, more generally, sparsely built or run-down areas deemed to be not worth preserving. The term is characteristic of this period of urban planning in Paris, which allowed very large-scale redevelopments that the historian Norma Evenson has likened to those that took place during France's Second Empire (1852–70). From the mid-1950s to the 1970s, changes in the urban landscape of Paris were the subject of many documentaries, reports and television news items. Up to the beginning of the 1960s, such coverage was an integral part of public information and even what might be termed propaganda put out by the Construction and Housing Ministry. In association with the Construction and Urban Planning Commission for the Paris Region, the ministry organised in 1961, for example, the exhibition Demain … Paris ('Tomorrow … Paris')[1] at the Grand Palais: Paris urban planning reflected government policy. Symptomatic of the blurring of boundaries between municipal and national areas of responsibility was the appointment of Pierre Sudreau – the main person responsible for implementing the capital's urban renewal policy (or 'reconquest of Paris'), who had been commissioner for Construction and Urban Planning in the Paris region since 1955 – as minister of Construction and Housing by Charles de Gaulle in 1958. In a series of five television programmes broadcast that same year, Sudreau explained the government's regional development policy to the French public, described the Paris Region's problems – which were very much in the news at the time – and outlined the first steps in the renewal of the capital.[2]

But the television reports broadcast between 1954 and 1977 also served as a vehicle for criticism of the redevelopment of Paris, which was extremely virulent in the mainstream, cultural and political media. This chapter describes how the approach of general news magazines and television documentaries changed between 1954 and 1977.[3] It examines how television, after being used by the Paris administration and the government in the late 1950s as a tool to explain their redevelopment plans, contributed to criticism of centralised urban planning in the 1960s and 1970s. Did the criticism of urban renewal that could be sensed in several reports, documentaries and magazines broadcast at the beginning of the 1970s act as a vehicle for more general social criticism?

Paris Urban Planning, French Television and Critical Discourse

The television reports I have viewed (dating from 1957 to 1974) were all shaped by three concurrent contexts – that of French television, that of Paris urban planning, and that of the social and political criticism of urban planning that gathered momentum at the end of the 1960s.

As regards the relationship between television and politics, it is worth remembering, because of the considerable impact it had on televisual content at the time, De Gaulle's return to power just after the beginning of the period under consideration. Although the number of households with television sets was then rather low,[4] the new regime regarded the medium as a tool that could influence public opinion. As the historian Evelyne Cohen has noted: 'From 1959 to 1968, television was a national medium capable of sending out a single message to the French. It saw itself as a "national language".'[5] De Gaulle's presidency, which ended in 1969, was a period marked by a very strict control of television by the Ministry of Information. This eased up under the influence of the May 1968 events and President Georges Pompidou's prime minister, Jacques Chaban-Delmas, and his project for a 'new society', debated (though never implemented) between 1969 and 1972. At that point, there was a fresh clampdown on information. Changes in television had also been triggered by the mounting importance of current affairs programmes during the 1960s, particularly at the beginning of the decade, when they were encouraged by the 'art documentaries' section of the French Radio and Television Office (ORTF)[6] and its research department. The department was founded in 1960 and run by the composer Pierre Schaeffer, a pioneer of *musique concrète*. In the 1960s, current affairs programmes were also aided by the arrival of lighter cine cameras.[7] The practice of getting 'ordinary' people to express their views was popularised on television by the now legendary magazine *Cinq colonnes à la une* ('Front-page Headlines'), which was launched in 1959 to compensate for the conventionality and scarcity of field reporting in the 1950s. In the eyes of the ORTF's management, it was also important to counterbalance television news programmes' reputation as a government mouthpiece. At the same time, programmes that directly toed the government line were replaced by current affairs magazines that touched upon social issues: the presence of a director alongside a journalist ensured that they enjoyed *auteur* status. Other ingredients were in-depth reports, uncompromising interviews and clashes with the powers that be.[8] Lastly, the period running from the end of the 1960s up until 1974 was marked by serious industrial unrest at the ORTF. This was also true of other French corporations and public services, but the many strikes affecting television were sparked above all by plans to break up the ORTF and oblige television channels to compete with each other – a process which in effect took place in 1974.

Urban transformation was effected over a period of several decades, from 1954 with the Lafay Plan (so called because it was initiated by Bernard Lafay, a member of parliament for the Seine *département* and president of the Paris City Council) up until the introduction of a new land-use scheme in 1977, which put an end to the earlier policy. While the first renewal operations were implemented by the City Council in 1953, it was only in 1955 that the authorities initiated the policy known as the 'reconquest of

Paris'.[9] A decade after the end of World War Two, the policy was intended to come up with solutions to the capital's urgent problems by getting rid of slums[10] and rationalising land use in outlying areas, as opposed to the central historical districts which the Lafay Plan, bedrock of the 'reconquest of Paris',[11] proposed to leave untouched under the appellation 'crystallised Paris'.[12]

But in the middle of the 1960s, these urban transformations were affected by changes in the institutional framework of planning, ranging from public renovation, as in the 'reconquest of Paris', to the private development which was the dominant – and controversial – system in the early 1970s. In 1964, the balance between public operations and private investment was reversed at the instigation of the government. That year, Prime Minister Georges Pompidou called on the Paris prefect, Raymond Haas-Picard, to 'encourage private initiative to take an active interest in the construction of Paris and, more particularly, the major work of renovating the capital'. In the early 1970s, the operations carried out by private investors that were the subject of scathing attacks in the left-wing and centrist press were also denounced in television reports.

Finally, mounting social and political criticism of urban redevelopment was palpable in television programmes and magazines. It was not always expressed as radically in television documentaries as in the print media. But it was nonetheless remarkably virulent, given that such programmes were produced and broadcast by state television.

Prominent Themes

Whether toeing the official line or coming from more anti-authoritarian quarters, coverage of the transformation of Paris consistently tackled several issues.

In the 1960s, congestion was treated in many brief items concerning road traffic. Take, for example, the report entitled 'Traffic Problems' (1962) in *Cinq colonnes à la une*, in which the Paris prefect of police, Maurice Papon,[13] discussed the action that needed to be taken. At about the same time, traffic congestion prompted the formulation of Utopian and technologically inspired projects. These included proposals made by the Study Group on Underground Urban Planning and by architects such as Yona Friedman and Paul Maymont, highlighted by the critic Michel Ragon,[14] who in 1961 and 1962 denounced the obsolete organisation of Paris in the weekly magazine *Arts*. On television, congestion was soon superseded by motor pollution.

A second recurring theme was the clash of old and new, also evident in the cinema.[15] Up until the mid-1960s, an old building was seen as something run-down, unhealthy and unfit for human habitation; a new building was synonymous with all modern conveniences. That antithesis was reinforced by visual rhetoric. Reversals in the composition of images can be observed between the end of the 1950s and the beginning of the 1970s, which reflected a new perception of modern buildings. Praised as examples of the government's campaign against slums at the beginning of that period, recent buildings were on the other hand perceived in the early 1970s as eyesores that came to symbolise the disappearance of local social life and of urban planning with a human face. For example, the 1974 documentary *Le Carrefour de la Butte-aux-Cailles* ('The Butte-aux-Cailles Intersection'),[16] produced by the ORTF for the magazine *Lieux communs* ('Commonplaces'[17]), described, without a single word of commentary, the events that take place during one day at that intersection from the time the shops open until nightfall, when they close. Numerous high-angle shots show the daily comings and goings of the residents of that – then – working-class area of the 13th *arrondissement*, which consisted of rather low-rise, traditional buildings typical of the inner *faubourgs*. The camera then pans away from the intersection to reveal recently built tower blocks on the horizon at the nearby place d'Italie, on a completely different scale. Visually, the film harps on this contrast of scale. A similar rhetoric of the image can be found in a great many documentaries of that period.

At this point (the beginning of the 1970s), a third theme comes to the fore: nostalgia for a fast-disappearing working-class Paris. It is not so much nostalgia for the picturesque – even though this increased during that decade, which saw the rise of heritage culture – as a hankering for the forms of sociability provided by local communities. Finally, from the very beginning of the 1970s,[18] one of the dominant themes of the current-affairs magazines is the contrast between public renovation, such as the construction of HLMs (low-rent social housing), in which local residents are rehoused in the same area, and private development. Such items contain not only criticism of centralised urban planning but, more generally, political criticism.

Urban destruction thus was a key preoccupation throughout the period under consideration. Reactions to it, however, ranged from enthusiasm for the grand undertaking of urban renewal policies to their condemnation, not only from an urban-planning angle, but from a political and social viewpoint.

Positive Images of Urban Destruction

The discourse of urban planners and architects generally tends to focus more readily and more often on construction than on destruction. And yet urban transformation cannot take place without destruction or, at the very least, planned demolition. Demolition nearly always makes its presence felt, like a kind of subtext or obverse of urban transformation – an aspect that the discourse of urban planners and architects tends to play down.[19] It is all the more interesting, then, to note that at the end of the 1950s a first wave of television programmes revealed the government's attitude towards the demolition of slums, which was regarded as a form of rehabilitation: this can be judged from the title of a news report produced by Les Actualités françaises (12 February 1958), namely 'L'Art d'abattre les vieux immeubles' ('The Art of Knocking Down Old Buildings'), which shows what a positive image the act of demolition enjoyed.

Filming destruction and demolition was a leitmotif of television programmes about urban development. Destruction and demolition – the nuance between the two terms is important, since destruction is truly violent and symbolic, while demolition is planned and scheduled[20] – featured more prominently on the screen than in other media. Absent at the time from architecture and urban-planning publications, the themes however were widely covered by the daily and weekly press later, in particular following the demolition of Victor Baltard's pavilions in Les Halles (which began in 1971).[21] In the 1970s, the filming of destruction was in some cases fuelled by strong disagreements with development policies and their social repercussions, and in others by a concern to preserve an architectural heritage.

At the end of the 1950s, filming of the destruction of buildings made it possible to illustrate government action. This was in the (temporary) absence of other concrete results of urban-planning policies, since construction of the new developments had yet to begin. Television reports and studio broadcasts alternated between scenes of slums being pulled down and close-ups of spanking-new urban planners' models, commented on by architects and politicians.

In a series of five television programmes shown during prime time in October and November 1958, the Construction and Housing Minister Pierre Sudreau addressed French viewers directly in order to explain the government's policy on regional development, aiming to convince them of the wisdom of demolishing slums and building large housing complexes. It is fair to say that such programmes formed part of De Gaulle's election campaign. As Evelyne Cohen points out, they were made 'at the request of the government and in a specific electoral context', between the referendum on the proposed constitution of the Fifth Republic and the general election.[22] They alternated between close-ups of Sudreau as he was interviewed by the celebrated television anchorman Pierre Sabbagh,[23] comments by experts (such as the Paris prefect, urban planners and City of Paris architects demonstrating their arguments with models) and clips from documentaries. In voice-over, Sudreau commented on those extracts, whose sources were not always indicated.

The articulation between housing policy, slums and destruction was developed in the second programme in the series, which illustrated the destruction of several substandard groups of buildings in the 13th *arrondissement* and Ménilmontant in the 20th *arrondissement*. In such programmes, which could be described as 'propaganda', the filming of slums being demolished was part and parcel of a *mise-en-scène* of destruction. With regard to the renovation of the 13th *arrondissement*, for example, the minister urged Parisians to go and admire the process of destruction, which he described as 'spectacular'. Whole buildings did indeed cave in on themselves. This controlled destruction was therefore tantamount to demolition; but the tools used were winches, pickaxes and traction. In the second half of the 20th century, the use of such tools, when employed to illustrate a policy of rationalised urban planning at a time when prefabrication had already been introduced, was strikingly artisanal, anachronistic and indeed violent. In the most striking part of the programme – an extract from a film on the Ménilmontant area and commented on by Sudreau – destruction no longer takes place in piecemeal fashion, but on the scale of a whole district, involving planned and organised destruction and deliberate fires: antiquated buildings are set alight by firemen and then carved up with fire hoses, thus replacing spontaneous, 'wild' fire with a controlled, almost surgical process. In his commentary, the minister points out that the reason for using fire to destroy most of Block 11 (Ménilmontant) is of course to provide Paris firefighters with an opportunity to carry out a 'life-size' exercise, but also to 'decontaminate'. In a sense, this form of destruction shields neighbouring buildings and protects their residents from disease. The rhetoric hinges on the twin forces of protection and destruction. As Sudreau puts it, 'Destruction first began in 1954 – it has been a grandiose undertaking.'

This example conflates two antithetical images, that of *controlled destruction* and that of fire. The scale of the fire, which engulfed a whole district of Paris, suggested an accidental and destructive disaster rather than a scheduled and patient process. The high-angle shots of the event are reminiscent of the aerial shots of bombed cities taken during World War Two, and conjure up the imagery of great fires which Paris has never had to endure – except, partially, during the Commune of 1871 – on the scale of London in 1666, Rennes in 1720 or Lisbon in 1755. In the case of several such cities, fires triggered radical changes in their appearance and structure – an allusion that had some relevance in a television programme aimed at explaining an urban policy that was going to cause major upheavals. By evoking the Paris Commune, these images appealed to the historical imaginary of the destruction of Paris during the 19th century.[24]

The themes of demolition and destruction recur throughout the 1960s. We are repeatedly shown the instruments of demolition, from pickaxes to mechanised equipment. In November 1965, a television report entitled *Le XXe arrondissement de Paris et le logement*[25] and devoted to the demolition of slums in Ménilmontant depicts men with pickaxes perched on a wall and silhouetted against the sky. The framing of the images, the low-angle shots and the backlighting result in an aestheticisation of destruction that is both violent and artisanal. Beyond this particular programme, it is worth noting that in the early 1960s most films on the subject of reconstruction, including the construction of housing complexes, display a striking discrepancy between the artisanal demolition methods employed and the triumphalist approach to the industrialisation of construction.

From Destruction to Nostalgia

At the beginning of the 1970s, there occurred a distinct reversal of this approach – and of the images serving its purpose. Together with the reversal of values concerning destruction, now perceived as negative, television programmes also displayed a change of attitude towards working-class Paris and began to highlight its positive qualities of sociability.

It is true that from the end of the 1950s, in counterpoint to the government's positive line on the changes taking place in Paris, several documentaries began to engage in a social analysis of the various districts of the capital and their future transformation. They pointed to the side effects of displacing inhabitants when urban renewal took place. In 1956, Jacques Krier made a television docudrama on the severe housing crisis, *Rue du Moulin de la Pointe*.[26] The two-part film is set in a 13th *arrondissement* courtyard. Krier, a member of the French Communist Party (PCF), had been one of the authors behind a series of social reports on sections of the working classes, *A la découverte des Français* ('Exploring the French').[27] In the case of *Rue du Moulin de la Pointe*, the filmmakers called on the help of sociologists from the Social Ethnology Group at the CNRS (National Centre for Scientific Research) and the anthropologist Paul-Henry Chombart de Lauwe, whose book *Paris et l'agglomération parisienne* (1952) correlated urban space with social representations of working-class life. As early as 1956, *Rue du Moulin de la Pointe* tackled the theme of a disappearing working-class Paris. While denouncing living conditions in slums, the commentary highlighted forms of sociability inherent in older Paris housing (the inner courtyard forming a community of inhabitants). The second part of the docudrama,

La Butte à la Reine, broadcast a week later, illustrated the problems of people being rehoused in some remote suburb, having to endure hours of commuting to work and a lack of neighbourhood stores – themes to be found at the end of the 1950s in criticism of large housing complexes. *La Butte à la Reine* extolled the positive aspect of working-class areas, despite their unsuitability for human habitation. Isabelle Coutant argues that the two-part film illustrates the ambivalent attitude of the PCF towards urban renewal:

> Between 1944 and 1964, the PCF was faced with a dilemma: it came to the defence of people living in substandard housing in their struggle against criminal landlords and irresponsible local authorities, yet urban renewal often resulted in their being banished to the suburbs. That being the case, any encouragement to demolish slums and replace them with new housing could result in the party's electorate shrinking.[28]

From the beginning of the 1970s, television news magazines and documentaries reinforced this positive image of life in the inner Paris *faubourgs*, their inhabitants and their community spirit. At university level, there was a proliferation of Marxist studies of urban renewal which denounced rehousing in the suburbs and the social transformation of certain Paris areas whose less affluent inhabitants had been forced to move out. One of these studies was Henri Coing's *Rénovation urbaine et changement social* (1966), which focused on the sweeping changes in the landscape of the 13th *arrondissement*. In addition to Marxist criticism levelled at both government urban planners and private developers, increased awareness of the national heritage gathered momentum in other quarters, particularly in the general-interest and cultural press. The theme of 'vandalism' resurfaced (typically in the magazine *Arts*) in the 1960s as a reaction against the widespread destruction of buildings as a result of property speculation, and the trend was boosted by the traumatic destruction of Les Halles. In television programmes, the theme of the *quartier*, formerly approached from a social point of view, was now seen in terms of heritage, with commentaries regretting the disappearance of atypical urban typologies and 'minor' architecture.

While regional development, urban planning and environmental issues were the subject of many television magazines, some of them prime time, government spokespersons also occasionally voiced fresh concern over development. For instance, from 1973 on, the first, then the second, state television channels broadcast a series entitled *La France défigurée* ('Disfigured France'). It had been preceded by another series, *Chefs-d'oeuvre en péril* ('Endangered Landmarks'), which focused on derelict ancient monuments and attacked the authorities' or private owners' failure to maintain them. *La France défigurée*, on the other hand, criticised public decision-making, but in a rather ambivalent way.

Broadcast on Sunday afternoons, *La France défigurée* regularly denounced pollution, pointed up the incongruities of landscaping and questioned new forms of visual environment. The programme was part of the communication plan to promote Prime Minister Jacques Chaban-Delmas's project for a 'new society'. In conjunction with the

Lamenting the disappearance of the old *quartier*: *Charonne, un village qui se meurt* ('Charonne, a Dying Village', 1973).

setting up in 1971 of an Environment Ministry, government policy then began to embrace environmental concerns. The programme was also intended to put across the notion of a change of policy and of the modernisation of France. In that respect it recognised, in veiled terms, the mistakes that had been made during the previous decade. One episode, 'Charonne, un village qui se meurt' ('Charonne, a Dying Village'), lamented the disappearance of that old *quartier* in the 11th *arrondissement*, thus highlighting heritage concerns and a love of the picturesque rather than social preoccupations.

Social and Political Criticism of Renewal

The 1970s saw the heyday of general-interest television magazines covering the disappearance of old *quartiers*.[29] However, the private interests that were by then dominating urban renewal also attracted criticism. That criticism came to a head from 1970 to 1973, a period when politically committed directors clashed with ORTF management.

Jacques Frémontier's *La Rénovation urbaine* ('Urban Renewal') (1974), a typical example of such criticism, targets private investment's stranglehold on policies of renewal. Its sweeping political and social broadside is barely veiled; the city is presented as an object of speculation and a proving ground for the domination of capital. The film's editing alternates between images of destruction and shots of local shopkeepers and artisans, who are interviewed about what it is like to live in their district (Belleville, Ménilmontant, Montparnasse) while it is being demolished. These contrasting images are echoed by the contrast between the muffled quiet of their threatened homes and the deafening clatter of destructive machinery – excavators, tractors and bulldozers. The film directly accuses private developers of emptying working-class areas of their residents and banishing them to housing complexes. *La Rénovation urbaine* did not go down well with ORTF management and underwent indirect censorship designed to reduce the number of viewers. While not actually banned from being broadcast, the documentary was shown one Sunday evening at a time when the only other channel scheduled the highly successful film *Zorba the Greek* (Michael Cacoyannis, 1964).

The personal and political trajectories of the directors of such programmes, which fuelled the social criticism to be found in their work, were partly responsible for these examples of censorship. From the 1950s to the beginning of the 1970s, many directors working for French television were Communists. Paradoxically, in the 1950s and early 1960s (years when television was inspired by 'republican humanism'[30]), there was a convergence between the social and cultural aims of television as accepted by the government and the aspirations of such directors. This 'consensus between Gaullist management

Criticizing private speculation: *La Rénovation urbaine* ('Urban Renewal', Jacques Frémontier, 1974).

and Communist directors'[31] was based on a joint desire to pass on the national cultural heritage. The already mentioned case of Jacques Krier, the Communist director of the series *A la découverte des Français*, was an illustration of that phenomenon. From 1964 on, following the introduction of new staff regulations and a new remit assigned to television, including the requirement to entertain, relations with the government became strained. At the beginning of the 1970s, despite the relative freedom of expression enjoyed by television journalists while Chaban-Delmas was prime minister, such unrest became more marked. Strikes were called in protest against the sacking of directors who had been the most critical of large corporations and government policies.

Frémontier, who made *La Rénovation urbaine*, was a trained sociologist and journalist, as well as a graduate of the Ecole Nationale d'Administration (ENA), and in that capacity destined for a high-flying political or administrative career. He became a television producer in 1967 (and worked as such until 1983). After being disconcerted by the lukewarm response of workers to the May 1968 student-initiated uprising, he decided to centre his investigations on the working classes, more specifically in the programme series *Vivre aujourd'hui* ('Life Today') from 1970 to 1974.[32] He joined the French Communist Party in 1971 and remained a member until 1978. In that series, Frémontier made several controversial films, such as *L'Usine* ('The Factory'), on the working conditions in the car-maker Renault's factories in Billancourt. It was scheduled to be shown on 16 April 1970, but ORTF management decided in the end not to broadcast the film on the grounds that Frémontier was too politically committed and even posed 'a threat to the Fifth [five-year] Plan's objectives'[33] because he openly criticised major French corporations. In 1970, he focused his disenchanted and accusing eye on urban planning in *Les Espaces verts* ('Green Spaces'). In 1973, he made *L'Enfer du décor* ('Stage-set from Hell'), a documentary about the Grande Borne housing complex in the Paris suburb of Grigny.[34] Like his earlier documentaries, it sparked intense controversy, which was compounded by tensions in the world of television production. For

Frémontier, housing and urban planning were domains where social domination was rife, as in the case of factories and the status of women.

Social criticism on television occasionally went hand in hand with the criticism of modern urban planning formulated by young architects at about the same time. The documentary *La Rue et la tour* ('The Street and the Tower') (1972),[35] for instance, highlighted the contrast between the two worlds. Its first part, 'La Rue', highlighted the Aligre district (12th *arrondissement*) and its street market. The film praises the street as a breeding ground for sociability in all its forms; in interviews, local residents see a parallel between their district and a village-like community. The architect Gérard Thurnauer, when questioned, argues that what is 'anti-urban' is not necessarily the new buildings themselves, but the forms of contemporary urban planning which grew out of modernist urban planning, and which need to be combated. The second part of the documentary, 'La Tour', centres on several families who had recently moved into the Tour Keller, one of the first tower blocks to be erected on the Front de Seine development (15th *arrondissement*), built on an elevated concrete plaza. The interviews focus mainly on the social life made possible by this novel form of housing and regret the disappearance of any relationship with the street as a result of the so-called 'plaza' form of urban planning.

The film encapsulates the criticism of modern urban planning formulated at about the same time in architectural circles. The message of *La Rue et la tour*, with its emphasis on reinventing the street and its campaign against plaza-orientated urban planning and tower blocks as an architectural model, could perhaps be regarded as the watchword of a new generation of architects who, after arriving on the scene in the 1960s and coming to prominence in the wake of the May 1968 events, found an outlet in criticism and teaching in the early 1970s. They advocated a 'return to the city' and strove to bring to a close, first symbolically, then concretely, the modernist urban-planning ethos that predominated during the so-called 'Trente Glorieuses'.[36]

Translated from the French by Peter Graham.

Notes

1. See Jacques Lucan (ed.), *Eau et gaz à tous les étages: Paris 100 ans de logement* (Paris: Editions du Pavillon de l'Arsenal/Picard, 1992), p. 142.
2. See Evelyne Cohen, 'Expliquer Paris à la télévision: Pierre Sudreau et les problèmes de la construction 1958', *Sociétés & représentations*, vol. 1, no. 17 (2004), pp. 117–27.
3. This corpus includes documentaries, reports and lifestyle magazines broadcast by French television between 1955 and 1977. I have not included in this exploratory corpus clips from television news programmes broadcast by the first and second channels of the ORTF (see note 6).
4. About 5 per cent, as opposed to 33 per cent in the UK and 82 per cent in the USA. That percentage had risen to 39.3 per cent by 1964 and 82.4 per cent by 1974. Source: Evelyne Cohen, *La Télévision sur la scène du politique: un service public pendant les Trente Glorieuses* (Paris: L'Harmattan, 2009), p. 7.
5. Ibid., p. 8.
6. Radio Télévision Française was set up in 1949 and became Office de Radio Télévision Française (ORTF) in 1964. That same year, the second channel was created.

7. During the 1960s, the bulky Tolona cameras, which needed to be powered by a generator, were superseded by Coutan cameras.
8. Hélène Bousser-Eck and Monique Sauvage, 'Le Règne de *Cinq colonnes*, 1959–1965', in Jean-Noël Jeanneney and Monique Sauvage (eds), *Télévision, nouvelle mémoire. Les magazines de grands reportage* (Paris: Seuil/INA, 1982), p. 44.
9. This was facilitated by legislation introduced in 1957 and 1958, which covered not only ZUP (Areas in Urgent Need of Urbanisation) but urban renewal in general.
10. See Simon Texier, *Paris contemporain* (Paris: Parigramme, 2005), p. 22.
11. Initiated as early as 1950 by André Thirion. The recommendations in his report (1951) included the preservation of historic districts, in particular the Marais, a reorganisation of the 11th and 20th *arrondissements*, in other words the north-eastern *faubourgs* of the capital, and the creation of a business quarter (within the triangle formed by the Gare Saint-Lazare, the Gare du Nord and République). See Philippe Nivet, 'Le Conseil municipal face aux rénovations, 1945–1977', in Lucan, *Eau et gaz à tous les étages*, pp. 118–35.
12. Bernard Lafay, with Raymond Lopez, 'Problèmes de Paris, contribution aux travaux du Conseil municipal: esquisse d'un plan directeur et d'un programme d'action', *Rapports et documents du Conseil municipal*, no. 11 (11 December 1954).
13. The French civil servant Maurice Papon (1910–2007) collaborated with the Vichy regime during World War Two, in his capacity as the official in charge of 'Jewish questions' in Bordeaux. As prefect of police for Paris under De Gaulle's government, he was implicated in the massacre of Algerians during a demonstration by the Algerian National Liberation Front in October 1961. He continued his ministerial career up until 1981.
14. See Hélène Jannière, 'L'Urbanisme contre la ville: Michel Ragon et la critique de la ville, années 1960 et 1970', in Richard Leeman and Hélène Jannière (eds), *Michel Ragon, critique d'art et d'architecture* (Rennes: Presses Universitaires de Rennes, 2013), pp. 181–201.
15. Camille Canteux, *Filmer les grands ensembles: villes rêvées, villes introuvables: une histoire des représentations audiovisuelles des grands ensembles, milieu des années 1930–début des années 1980* (Paris: Créaphis, 2014).
16. *Le Carrefour de la Butte-aux-Cailles* (1974), colour, 25', produced by Patrick Volson, written by Derri Berkani and directed by Jean-Claude Guidicelli. It was only broadcast 18 years later, on 23 June 1992.
17. In French, *lieu commun* means both a platitude and a communal space.
18. For example, the documentary *La Rénovation urbaine*, in the series *Vivre aujourd'hui* ('Life Today'), produced by Jacques Frémontier, written by Frémontier, directed by Philippe Laïk, reports by Frémontier and Victoria Llanso. ORTF, 16 mm, colour, 53'32", tx. 25 April 1971 on Channel 2.
19. See Daryl Lee, 'Peur sur la ville: Paris à l'image de Pompéi', in Myriam Tsikounas (ed.), *Imaginaires urbains du Paris romantique à nos jours* (Paris: Le Manuscrit, 2011), p. 62.
20. Bruno Vayssière and Olivier Quérouil, 'Démolition et destruction', *Traverses*, no. 9 (November 1977), pp. 47–51.
21. Editors' note: for discussions of the demolition of Les Halles' pavilions, see the chapters by Catherine E. Clark, Marie Gaimard & Marguerite Vappereau, and Jean-Yves de Lépinay in this volume.

22. The five programmes, entitled *Les Problèmes de la construction* ('The Problems of Construction'), were broadcast between 23 October and 20 November 1958. (*Logement notre honte*, tx. 23 October, 48'; *Destruction des taudis*, tx. 30 October, 48'; *Aménagement du territoire*, tx. 6 November, 30', *La Région parisienne*, tx. 13 November, 37', *La France de demain*, tx. 20 November, 32'.) See Cohen, 'Expliquer Paris à la télévision', p. 118.
23. The journalist, director and producer Pierre Sabbagh (1918–94) joined French television in 1946 and anchored the first French television news in 1949.
24. Lee, 'Peur sur la ville: Paris à l'image de Pompéi', p. 62.
25. *Le XXe arrondissement de Paris et le logement*, programme 'Bonsoir Paris' ('Good Evening Paris'), tx. 19 November 1965, an ORTF production directed by Jacques Rutman.
26. *Rue du Moulin de la Pointe*, 1957 (shot in 1956). In the series *A la découverte des Français*, directed by Jacques Krier and produced by Jean-Claude Bergeret; RTF, 16 mm, black and white, 27'27", tx. 5 April 1957.
27. Co-directed by Jean-Claude Bergeret.
28. Isabelle Coutant, 'Les Réalisateurs communistes à la télévision. L'engagement politique: ressource ou stigmate', *Sociétés & représentations*, special issue of *Artistes/Politiques*, ed. Benoît Lambert and Frédérique Matonti, no. 11 (February 2001), p. 357, note 53.
29. Between 1971 and 1975. The topic was also covered by television news reports, which have not been taken into account in this survey.
30. Marie-Françoise Lévy, 'Télévision, publics, citoyenneté', in Evelyne Cohen and Marie-Françoise Lévy, *La Télévision des Trente Glorieuses, culture et politique* (Paris: CNRS Editions, 2007), p. 97.
31. Coutant, 'Les Réalisateurs communistes à la télévision', p. 370.
32. See Jacques Frémontier, *Vive la télévision, messieurs!* (Paris: Editions du Rocher, 1975).
33. 'L'usine', *Télé liberté information*, no. 41 (August–September 1970), p. 14.
34. See Hélène Jannière, 'Stage-set from Hell. The Grands Ensembles between Social and Aesthetic Criticism: The Case of Grigny la Grande Borne, 1969–1974', *Candide. Journal for Architectural Knowledge* (Aachen University), no. 7 (Fall 2013), pp. 37–60.
35. Broadcast on ORTF's Channel 1 on 15 May 1972 (in the magazine programme *Arguments*, produced by Jean-Emile Jeannesson, 61'28").
36. Les Trente Glorieuses, literally the 'Thirty Glorious Years', refers to the 30 years of economic growth in France from the end of World War Two to the mid-1970s.

Parisian Building Sites (1945–75): From Modernity to Abstraction

Marie Gaimard and Marguerite Vappereau

> Yesterday I surveyed the enormous city from the Notre Dame tower. Who built the first house? When will the last one collapse and the ground of Paris look like the ground of Thebes and Babylon?[1]

Protean and transient, the construction site fascinates, impresses and excites the imagination. It figures, variably, as urban landscape, technical object, social microcosm or poetic space.[2] As a fluid object, the building site is characterised by its double temporality; its typically intense daytime activity dissolves into stillness and desertion at night. During the second half of the 20th century, a number of artists, such as the Frenchman Robert Filliou, the Italian Giuseppe Uncini and the American Robert Smithson, found in the building site a motif ripe for metaphor, a supply of unexplored material and fertile ground for experimentation. Filmmakers are no exception; in taking the building site as décor, subject or motif, they demonstrate, reinvent and contribute to a fantasy – a projection of the site as a battleground, a hostile territory, wasteland or space suitable for escape. Curiously, however, the 20th-century construction site has largely been ignored by historians of architecture.

The reasons for this historiographical peculiarity can be explained in part by the changing role of the architect in the early modern era. The medieval master builders, who first worked closely with masons, gradually distanced themselves from the manufacturing process (*fabrica*) in order to exercise a more intellectual and solitary art.[3] Today, as a rule,[4] architects do not conceptualise building sites and yet the latter have long figured as a motif in art and literature. Cinema is a source of documentation that must however be explored with caution. With this in mind, an interdisciplinary approach is advisable, as the combination of methodological tools from Film Studies and Architectural History can contribute to our understanding of what is at stake in the representation of the building site.

The image of Paris as an eternal city, at once monumental and picturesque, has been crystallised in the lyrical prose of Victor Hugo or Honoré de Balzac, but like any metropolis, it is a constantly changing organism. All it takes is a glance at the panorama from the steps of Montmartre or from atop the towers of Notre-Dame to see how cranes and scaffolding are integral to the Parisian skyline, as are half-filled gaps and pieces of waste ground. For centuries, French centralism has subjected the capital to continuous and inexorable growth,[5] making Paris the home of the most emblematic building sites. One could reconstruct a heroic history of the city based on representations of the great construction projects that shaped it. Perrault's[6] prints of the unlikely machines that built the Colonnade of the Louvre or, later, the photographs taken by Louis-Emile Durandelle of the Opéra Garnier's renovation and the construction of the Eiffel Tower helped fashion the mythic quality of these monuments. According to Walter Benjamin, the Haussmannian building works of the 1850s to 1870s played a major part in shaping the idea of modernity as Baudelaire understood it. As Le Corbusier put it admiringly: 'The city of Paris entered the twentieth century in the form that Haussmann gave it. He revolutionized the physiognomy of the city with the humblest means imaginable: spades, pickaxes, crowbars and the like.'[7] Conversely, photographs by Charles Marville of the clearing of slums to make way for the avenue de l'Opéra, or those taken by the indefatigable wanderer Eugène Atget of neighbourhoods full of ghostly empty lots or gutted buildings, capture a Paris in the process of disappearing. Finally, the 19th-century building site became an important location for social struggle; the artists Théophile Alexandre Steinlen and Maximilien Luce, for example, drew attention to the construction workers' plight through depictions of their long and arduous days.

After World War Two, the economic boom in France inaugurated a period known as Les Trente Glorieuses ('Thirty Glorious Years'): three decades during which an 'invisible revolution' reached all layers of society.[8] The major architectural projects of the time reveal the wholehearted embrace of modernism on the part of the authorities, with Paris at the forefront of this movement. However, the major urban developments that took place during this period – the medical school on the rue des Saint-Pères (6th *arrondissement*), the Montparnasse tower, the business district of La Défense, the *périphérique* ring road and the regional cross-rail system that became the Réseau Express Régional (RER) in 1977, together with the destruction of Les Halles – provoked violent controversy, exacerbated by the disruptions such large-scale projects generated. In order to find out how the cinema has addressed these profound changes, the collection of films about Paris at the Forum des Images acts as a veritable memory for the city and is an invaluable resource. Of the 400 fiction films released between 1945 and 1975 that are in the collection, about 30 depict the transformations the city has been subjected to.[9]

The first impression left by these works is predictable: oscillating between realist tragedy and fantasy, they frequently convey the prejudices of their era. The construction site's dangerous and shady character is emphasised, sometimes heavily. It is perceived as threatening or disastrous, and used metaphorically to express the character's inner self. The building site stands for a crisis zone, reflecting larger social and political themes from 19th-century political art. However, it also raises narrative and formal issues for the filmmakers. While it is closed to the public, the building site is not populated solely with construction workers; other social groups infuse it with life. The *badaud* (bystander), hitherto a passive observer of the movements of excavators, becomes an active agent. Named 'theatre' in the 19th century,[10] the Parisian building site becomes, through filmmakers' eyes, a new agora: at once proletarian place, public space, metaphor or literally battlefield. Thus sublimated, the building site works as a backdrop and generates a narrative, while also functioning as part of a composition within which realist cinematography drifts towards abstraction.

A Critique of Modernity

In the 17th century, Nicolas Boileau featured the building site in his poem *Les Embarras de Paris*:

> As pavers here block my way;
> I find a cross, a gruesome omen,[11]
> And from workers up on the roof of a house
> Slate and tiles profusely hail down[12]

Boileau thereby inaugurated a literary tradition, maintained by Parisians since harassed by the noise, confusion and nuisances that plague the city. We find the same satirical rendition in the cinema a century later, in the third episode of the portmanteau film *Tant qu'on a la santé/As Long as You've Got Health*, directed by Pierre Etaix in 1966.[13] The building site is a menace for old-fashioned trades, everyday tranquillity and even the health of Paris. Thus, the voices of the glazier and of the street singers are drowned by the terrifying noise of machines at work. The vibrations of invisible pneumatic drills disturb not only public but also private space: it is impossible to play the piano, or keep the family china safe within the frail glass-fronted cabinets that shatter from the tremors. Always off screen, the building site is pure, nerve-wracking sonic nuisance. This scene is not about urban embellishment but about a city that is sick, and in which the doctors are as ill as their patients. The deafening Parisian soundscape, dominated by the sound of traffic, jumps and starts in sync with the cement mixer's gyrations and the explosive din of the pneumatic drills. In the tradition of American burlesque, the construction site becomes a pretext for slapstick. For example, the racket caused by machines in Daniel Goldenberg's *Le Portrait de Marianne/Portrait of Marianne* (1971) allows for the introduction of mimed sequences in which the exasperated protagonists silently and emphatically gesticulate. In the same vein, in his 1965 short film 'Place de l'Etoile',[14] Eric Rohmer uses the building site to comic effect; the construction of the future RER around the Arc de Triomphe becomes an obstacle course that blocks the once-seamless route of an employee's path to work. His impeccable suit and composure are severely put to the test. Rohmer mocks the supposed functionality of the modern city.

Also in a satirical register, in *Les Gaspards/The Down-in-the-Hole Gang* (1974), Pierre Tchernia tells the story of a group of characters who for decades have lived under the city to escape the cacophony of construction work above. Former mines and catacombs are framed as places out of time. For the sake of caricature, Tchernia tweaks history and creates a delirious fable about an authoritarian minister of public development (Charles Denner) who is clearly enamoured of Le Corbusier's plan of razing the historic centre of Paris and covering it with concrete.[15] The minister is set against a band of 'connoisseurs' and historic figures, led by the dandy Gaspard de Montfermeil (Philippe Noiret), all of whom have found refuge underground. *Les*

Gaspards was co-written by René Goscinny, one of the creators of the famous comic-book character Astérix, and the childish Manichaeism implied in the fight between the 'Gaspards' and the minister naturally evokes the fight led by Astérix and the Gauls against the stupid Romans.[16] The film develops a conservative agenda exemplified by a Latin Quarter *bouquiniste* (open-air bookseller) played by Michel Serrault, the author of a nostalgic book entitled *Paris qui s'en va* ('Vanishing Paris'). As he dons the uniform of a World War One soldier, he is fighting a form of modernity envisaged as amnesiac and mutilating: here, the building site evokes the trenches. The rhetoric of war permeates the discourse of both camps, who see a new 'battle for Paris' in this confrontation over the modernisation of the city, as also suggested by the presence of a few German soldiers still roaming the city long after the end of the war. Paris's underground maze becomes a realistic reservoir of cinematographic and literary clichés.

From the credit sequence of *Les Gaspards*, the signage of the building site and its frightful noise are enough to suggest the evil against which the armchair resisters are fighting. In 1967, Jacques Tati had already used this device in *Playtime*: billboards, palisades, zebra crossings, and red and orange lights signal the deviations, dead ends and detours that turn Paris into an obstacle race for its inhabitants. The famous scene at the Royal Garden restaurant is key to understanding the specificity and finesse of Tati's vision. Modernity, barely attained, is already in ruins. Tati captures the dynamic dimension of the motif that he brilliantly brings to light. While customers are already assaulting the brand-new restaurant, the builders and the architect are still putting the final touches, criss-crossing the path of waiters trying to make up for the many design flaws. Sporadic interventions by the protagonist and the crazed customers succeed in bringing the restaurant back to its former state as a building site in just a few hours.

Luis Buñuel devised a crucial sequence of *Le Fantôme de la liberté/The Phantom of Liberty* (1974) from the construction of the Montparnasse tower, the emblematic building of the era. The filmmaker and his scriptwriter, Jean-Claude Carrière, put a sniper atop the building who, to the sound of pneumatic drills, kills passers-by at random and in all directions, from the rue de Rennes to the boulevard Edgar Quinet, and all the way to the avenue de Tourville near the Invalides. This lethal figure embodies the violent controversies sparked off by the tower. We cannot tell if the passers-by collapse as a result of the bullets or the mere sight of the tower. With all the ambiguity and irony that characterises his work, Buñuel paints a picture of murderous modernity.[17]

Realism

The building site of the 1920s and 1930s appeared first and foremost as a space of solidarity between workers and artisans, as well as a space for the valorisation of crafts and skills.[18] Les Trente Glorieuses era marks a turning point in the history of the representation of construction workers. It reveals the degradation of working conditions due, among other factors, to the industrialisation of the means of production. At the beginning of the 1960s, in the middle of decolonisation, southern Europe and the Maghreb became reservoirs of cheap labour. Large-scale techniques of standardisation and prefabrication rendered the know-how of experienced workers obsolete and encouraged recourse to unskilled labour. Thus, the difference between Georges Rouquier short film *Un jour comme les autres/A Day Like Any Other* (1953) and the feature films of the 1960s and 1970s pinpoints the evolution of both the proletariat and its image. While the former reflects the themes and style of pre-war films,[19] in which the worker's dignity was still protected by the strength and prestige of the trade, over the next decades the building site became the locus of unqualified and anonymous labour stuck in the mud, covered in wood dust, splashes of paint and cement, and under constant threat of potentially fatal accidents.

The cinema of the 1960s and 1970s attempted to shed light on the Pompidou-era construction projects[20] by emphasising the space where workers met the marginalised and the immigrants. *Ça va ça vient/It Comes, It Goes* (1972), directed by Pierre Barouh with Areski Belkacem,[21] depicts life in the 1970s around the building site of the place des Fêtes in the 20th *arrondissement*. We follow two workers as they commute to work, and watch as their trajectories are affected by strikes, their relationships with the neighbourhood, their flirtations, meals and work. The main protagonist ends up leaving his job as a builder to go on tour with a band of musicians led by Jérôme Savary. The building site is a transitory space that people simply drift through. It is also an exclusively masculine space; sexual misery is rampant and men surround themselves with a host of pornographic images and objects, as exemplified by *F comme Fairbanks/F as in Fairbanks* (1976), directed by Maurice Dugowson. This film shows the male worker denied access to a social status that might facilitate encounters with women, or foster the possibility of love. The déclassé young engineer played by Patrick Dewaere works a brief stint as a manual worker on a building site. In a metaphoric and heroic scene, he climbs to the top of a crane to unhook an inflatable doll, to the sound of his colleagues cheering.

Les Ambassadeurs/The Ambassadors, directed by Naceur Ktari in 1975, describes the living conditions of Algerian immigrants in the Goutte d'Or area, near Montmartre, and their regular exposure to French racism. Here, the work of the labourer is filmed in great detail. The building site, which seems at first to be a space of possible integration with French workers, slowly reveals itself to be a place of exclusion. The helping hand extended by trade unions is just as conditioned by class conflict; the blue-collar struggle cannot converge with that of the immigrants. The drama culminates with the death of a young man at the hands of a racist concierge and a police raid that deports the protagonist back to Algeria. Ahmed Rachedi's *Ali au pays des mirages/Ali in Wonderland* (1979) depicts the same French post-colonial archetype. Ali, who is employed as a crane operator in an urban renovation project, attempts to escape his proletarian condition through derision. From his perch, adopting an attitude reminiscent of the photojournalist L. B. Jeffries (James Stewart) in Alfred Hitchcock's *Rear Window* (1954), Ali observes and attempts to understand the everyday life of French people. His dreams of integration however wither at the sight of the sordid life below. These militant works of fiction aspire to being realistic reflections of both the hardships experienced by immigrants staying in special hostels such as those run by SONACOTRA[22] and their struggle to defend their rights.

Metaphor for Disaster

At the beginning of Alexandre Astruc's *La Proie pour l'ombre/Shadows of Adultery* (1961), a young woman, Anna (Annie Girardot), crosses a field of rubble to meet her husband, an architect of renown played by Daniel Gélin, at an anonymous building site. The desolate décor stands for the bourgeois couple's relationship undermined by the inability of the husband to listen to his wife's yearning for emancipation. The architect's first appearance on screen is, significantly, on a demolition site, where we measure the extent of his cynicism:

> Him: It's beautiful, isn't it?
> Her: It always breaks my heart to see a home destroyed.
> Him: Typical! These charming old buildings, full of Baudelairian cat piss, always bring out your sentimental side; all the poetry of France!

The confrontation between the two characters against this indeterminate backdrop – made of rubble, collapsed walls and piles of stones – and the slightly low-angle shot that frames a blocked horizon turn the building site into a post-disaster non-place, in which drifting figures cross paths without making contact.

Le Rond-point des impasses/The Roundabout of Dead-ends is a medium-length collective film from 1964[23] whose greatest achievement is to capture the lunar landscapes of the building sites of Belleville, to the north-east of the city; an area then undergoing massive reconstruction. The satirical film, made up of still images, mimics the sentimental *roman-photo* (photo novel) and mocks the sleek image of the capital found in the New Wave films of the 1960s – from the Champs-Elysées of Jean-Luc Godard's *A bout de souffle/Breathless* (1960) to the Montmartre of François Truffaut's *Baisers volés/Stolen Kisses* (1968). The film begins with a parody of shooting on the Champs-Elysées, clearly reminiscent of the emblematic scene in *A bout de souffle*. The filmmakers ridicule the Parisian film milieu of the time, which they depict as populated by brainless starlets, pretentious directors and ambitious producers. The narrative, which ends at the foot of the high-rise blocks under construction in Belleville, surrounded by the razed remains of the area, mischievously recalls the simplistic message of the *roman-photo*, which tends to incite the most humble to accept their lot. The building site takes on an eminently critical dimension here: the desolate décor echoes the absurd pantomime of a gallery of grotesque characters, the decaying products of a city in the process of dereliction. The choice of settings, from the majestic straight lines of the Champs-Elysées to the chaotic, lunar landscape of the Belleville demolitions, is at the heart of the film: cinematic dreams often end up in ruins.

The plundered site of Les Halles, the former food market at the centre of Paris demolished in the 1970s to make way for an underground shopping mall (the Forum des Halles), has caused the most controversy. It is like a wound on the face of the city that has still not healed, as shown by the debates surrounding the inauguration of the latest large-scale renovation of the site on 5 April 2016.[24] But it is the demolition of the 19th-century Baltard pavilions in the 1970s, which left a gaping hole for many years, that has focused filmmakers' attention. Throughout the 1970s, the demolition site of Les

Halles became an ideal terrain for filmmakers to reveal their characters' inner turmoil.[25] For example, in Yannick Bellon's *La Femme de Jean/Jean's Wife* (1974), a woman betrayed by her husband must learn to live after he has left her. As she wanders the capital, notably through the construction site at Les Halles, she comes to terms with her existence and finds the strength to put herself back together. In a scene from *La Marge/The Streetwalker* (1976) using almost the same vantage point, director Walerian Borowczyk plunges us into the troubled mind of a young man (Joe Dallesandro) who leaves his family in the south of France to go to the capital, where he succumbs to the charms of a beautiful prostitute (Sylvia Kristel). While *La Marge* remains anecdotal in relation to this topic, it allows us to understand to what extent the site at Les Halles had become a figurative cliché, a point we will return to shortly.

Towards Abstraction

Impasse des deux anges/Dilemma of Two Angels (1948), directed by Maurice Tourneur, is the film that most vividly captures the metaphorical relationship between character and environment. The then abandoned construction site of the medical school on rue des Saints-Pères[26] in Saint-Germain-des-Prés momentarily becomes the backdrop for a melancholic stroll taken by two ex-lovers who have drifted apart. A successful music-hall singer (Simone Signoret) and a gentleman-thief (Paul Meurisse) walk through a wasteland against the skyline of the city beyond, riddled with gaps where buildings have been torn down. The protagonists are surprised; the place of their first encounter is unrecognisable. A ravaged landscape has replaced the small hotel where they used to meet. 'My God, what happened here? Are you sure this is the right place?' asks Signoret, as if Paris had not escaped the wartime bombings. *Impasse des deux anges* attests to the collective consciousness that Paris is still traumatised by World War Two.[27] By the late 1940s, this building site, started in 1935 and left abandoned

Simone Signoret and Paul Meurisse in *Impasse des deux anges* (Maurice Tourneur, 1948).

for many years, speaks more of ruin and devastation than construction. The couple encounter a child, who evokes the heated arguments around the site and the failures of urban planning: 'There are big buildings they started to build, back there, but they didn't have enough money ... so now the place is ours.' Then, with the help of the little girl, the couple runs from a pair of gangsters and the film slips into film noir mode. The sound of gunshots resounds. Claude Renoir's expressionist and sculptural lighting, evocative of the work of Escher and Piranesi, renders the lovers' increasingly anxious stroll more stylised. The director and cinematographer's inventiveness demonstrate how a reputedly realistic medium such as film can also construct a purely pictorial space. The dramatic depth of field flattens the image to the point that the characters evaporate, backlit against the city. The construction site facilitates the creation of a filmic space that tends towards geometric abstraction: it becomes a network of lines, black-and-white surfaces and contrasts that entrap the human figures and block their escape.

We must at this point make a detour through the educational work of Eric Rohmer, who astutely captures the plastic and formal qualities of the construction site in his film *L'Ere industrielle: métamorphoses du paysage/Changing Landscapes* (1964).[28] Rohmer infuses the film with poetic power and articulates what was left unsaid in Tourneur's film. In this lucid and precise work, the point is not to rehabilitate contemporary ugliness, but to learn how to read and understand the specificity of a particular construction. Rohmer trains our gaze. After reviewing a series of landscapes frozen in the past, he invites us to observe one of the most common spectacles of urban life: a building site in full operation, in which an excavator is in the process of remodelling the space around it:

> Another landscape, another machine. The fascination it exercises, the dreams it incites, the beauty it possesses, even its poetry ... are these so different from those we attribute to an old mill of canvas and wood? [The machine is] monstrous, inhuman and human all at once, since it is made by man and a little bit in his image.[29]

Henceforth, cranes are a part of the skyline. Excavations participate in the spectacle of the modern city and excite the imagination:

> It sometimes takes very little to propel us into the imaginary. In the glow of the setting sun, this landscape at the city gates, where the future *périphérique* ring road is being built, looks for a moment like a mythical El Dorado. Cement mixers rise like towers and flour mills look like enchanted palaces.[30]

Through camerawork, the filmmaker infuses devastated contemporary landscapes with the modern art of Vassily Kandinsky, Fernand Léger and Paul Klee. He reveals the power of abstraction that this reality, once framed, contains: 'Doesn't modern art itself find its foundations, its echo, its origins, in these pared-down or baroque geometrical shapes that could be abundantly harvested by even the briefest walk around a factory and a construction site?'[31] As Rohmer so rightly notes, the construction site's ability to warp and disfigure thus becomes a source of potential formal renewal in post-war cinema.

L'ère industrielle: métamorphoses du paysage/Changing Landscapes (Éric Rohmer, 1964).

The most radical film in this vein is undoubtedly Marco Ferreri's *Touche pas à la femme blanche/Don't Touch the White Woman!* (1974), made in the middle of the 'hole' of Les Halles evoked above.[32] Through Ferreri's brilliant vision, once again we find that fiction is generated by the site itself. Thanks to his meticulous choice of location,[33] Ferreri takes advantage of all available resources, including the events that punctuated the progress of the biggest Parisian construction site. Over the course of the film, the characters witness the deliberate destruction of the surrounding buildings, up until the last scene inside the controversial hole. During the final struggle in the hole (an exuberant parody of the 1876 Battle of Little Bighorn, or 'Custer's Last Stand'), Ferreri substitutes a large stone quarry for Les Halles in order to evoke the vast spaces of the American West – a substitution made possible by his precise editing and subtle use of special effects. The battle is freed from the Parisian setting and therefore finds itself projected into a space akin to Monument Valley, familiar from so many John Ford films. Against a background of horizontal sand strata, ranging from pale yellow to ochre, we see a powerful American army fight weak but numerous Indians. The violent confrontation unfolds in a pictorial space entirely made of lines and slight variations in colour. By relying on the abstract properties of the construction site, this scene gives way to a formal explosion. Ferreri turns this hyperbolic episode into an ode to popular uprisings against oppression and financial power. Of note, this sequence also nods towards the mural from the nearby Bourse de Commerce[34] featured in the film's opening,[35] suggesting that the fiction comes out of it. The work depicts the building of the railways in the American West: Indians, workmen, slaves and cowboys all come to life in this monumental fresco painted by Evariste-Vital Luminais in 1889 in a style typical of late 19th-century historical art. The topic, a recurring motif of the American Western, reminds the spectators of the high financial stakes entailed by the construction of the station at Les Halles, the largest metropolitan interchange in the capital. In turn, it also harks back to the building of the French railways, 150 years earlier, financed by Parisian entrepreneurs and engineers. Through his complex engagement with the Les Halles site – playing on different registers simultaneously (thematic, iconic, visual) and oscillating between parody and the grotesque – Ferreri offers a rereading of both history and the history of cinema and, in turn, ensures his own place in modern cinema.

The topic of the building site in the films of Les Trente Glorieuses era, as we have seen, inspired filmmakers to mine its full potential: thematic, documentary, metaphorical and visual. More often than not, this was associated with an undercurrent of critical discourse. Did Paris, the capital that narrowly escaped destruction during World War Two, generate a taboo around its cultural heritage and identity? The building site certainly generates discomfort, intrusion and aggression for its users as much as for the inhabitants of the city. It is a space of violent exploitation for those who work there, and a symbol of frenetic urban speculation. Does the systematic condemnation of the construction site in feature films speak of conservatism in architecture, even though it is sometimes conjoined with political progressivism and engagement? The brief survey conducted in this chapter allows us to identify the topic of the building site as indubitably *modern* thanks to its dynamic and visual qualities. We might even argue that Les Trente Glorieuses are themselves permanently under construction, a period of deep social and cultural change and instability, a period in which the stages of construction, completion, abandonment and ruin of any given building remain forever unsettled.

Translated from the French by Louise Trueheart.

Notes

1. Friedrich von Raumer, cited in Walter Benjamin, *The Writer of Modern Life: Essays on Charles Baudelaire*, ed. Michael W. Jennings; trans. Howard Eiland, Edmund Jephcott, Rodney Livingston and Harry Zohn (Cambridge, MA, and London: Belknap Press of Harvard University Press, 2006), p. 113.
2. See Jean-Max Colard and Juliette Singer (eds), *Poétique du chantier* (Paris: Association Ligeia, 2010).
3. See Bernard Marrey, *Architecte. Du maître de l'oeuvre au disagneur* (Paris: Editions du Linteau, 2013).
4. Although we may here recall Renzo Piano's fascination for the building site in his work *Chantier ouvert au public* (Paris: Arthaud, 1985) and the experiments led by the architect Patrick Bouchain from 1999 onwards.
5. Alexis de Tocqueville, *L'Ancien régime et la Révolution*, vol. 4, Oeuvres complètes, Alexis de Tocqueville (Paris: Michel Levy Frères, 1866 [1856]).
6. Jean-Sébastien Le Clerc, *Portrayal of the Machines Used to Lift the Large Stones that Cover the Pediment of the Louvre*. Print, 1677.
7. Benjamin, *The Writer of Modern Life*, p. 114.
8. Jean Fourastié, *Les Trente Glorieuses ou la révolution invisible* (Paris: Fayard, 1979).
9. The Forum des Images catalogue is available at: http://collections.forumdesimages.fr/ (accessed 9 September 2017) [Editors' note: for further information, see Jean-Yves de Lépinay's chapter in this volume.]
10. 'Theatre: common name for the places, usually closed, that are assigned by police to large-scale construction entrepreneurs for the depot, scaling and preparation of materials. These theatres are nothing more than closed construction sites,' in Jacques Binet Tarbé de Vauxclairs, *Dictionnaire des travaux publics, civils, militaires et maritimes* (Paris: Carilian-Goeury, 1835).
11. Roofers used to hang a cross while they worked to prevent falling.

12. Nicolas Boileau, *Les Embarras de Paris*, satire VI, 1660, in *Oeuvres de Nicolas Boileau Despréaux*, vol. 1 (Paris: Treuttel & Würtz, 1832), pp. 56–60.
13. This film is not in the Forum des Images collection.
14. Rohmer's episode for *Paris vu par …/Six in Paris* (1965) – alongside episodes directed by Claude Chabrol, Jean Douchet, Jean-Luc Godard, Jean-Daniel Pollet and Jean Rouch.
15. The technocrat's speech is reminiscent of the 'Plan Voisin' presented by Le Corbusier in 1925, which entailed flattening the centre of Paris in order to build two dozen cruciform skyscrapers connected by a network of roads laid out orthogonally.
16. The split image, which shows simultaneously the world above ground and the world below ground, is a visual trick typical of comic-strip aesthetics.
17. The visual play that associates architecture with violence at one point and with pornography at another has several ramifications in the film. In the first scene, the Jean-Claude Brialy and Monica Vitti characters pretend to be shocked while looking at a series of postcards of historical monuments, as if they were erotic images.
18. Jean Epstein's 1938 documentary *Les Bâtisseurs/The Builders*, commissioned by the CGT (Confédération Générale du Travail) trade union, was hailed as a hymn to workers and architectural modernity.
19. This film, commissioned by the Institut National de la Recherche sur la Sécurité and the Organisme Professionnel de Prévention du Bâtiment et des Travaux Publics (two organisations devoted to the prevention of work-related accidents), tells the story of a roofer's daily schedule – his family life, financial worries and commute to work – until he slips while repairing a roof without a safety harness. He catches himself on a gutter and is saved by colleagues who come to his rescue thanks to the fire alarm. But the scene of his near-miss accident plays over and over in his mind. The repetition of this visually powerfully scene suggests an alternative, fatal, ending to the film.
20. Georges Pompidou (1911–74), French president from 1969 to 1974, whose term in office was marked by a series of massive construction projects across Paris.
21. Areski Belkacem was a composer, musician and singer, collaborator and companion of the poet and singer Brigitte Fontaine.
22. La SONACOTRA (Société Nationale de Construction de Logements pour les Travailleurs Algériens, or National Society of Construction of Housing for Algerian Workers) was founded in 1956 to house largely male and single migrants from Algeria. The hostels became the site of important political battles in the 1970s. See Marc Bernardot, *Loger les immigrés. La SONACOTRA 1956–2006* (Bellecombe-en-Bauges: Editions du croquant, 2008).
23. Directed by Bernard Gesbert, Guy Chalon and Gérard Gozlan.
24. David Mangin is the architect in charge of the comprehensive redesign of the underground mall, topped by Patrick Berger and Jacques Anziutti's giant *canopée* (canopy).
25. See Pierre Sorlin, 'Les Fantômes des Halles', in Jean-Louis Robert and Myriam Tsikounas (eds), *Les Halles: images d'un quartier* (Paris: Publications de la Sorbonne, 2004) for a discussion of films documenting the Les Halles construction site.
26. The construction of the new medical school on the rue des Saints-Pères (6th *arrondissement*), which began in 1935, provoked an immediate uproar. It represented, in the eyes of the neighbourhood, a threat not only to the identity of the Saint-Germain-des-Prés area, but also to its heritage.

27. Michael Schmiedel, *'Sous cette pluie de fer': Luftkrieg und Gesellschaft in Frankreich 1940–1944* (Berlin: Humboldt-Universität, 2013).
28. *L'Ere industrielle: métamorphoses du paysage* is a short film made for television as part of a series entitled *Vers l'unité du monde: l'ère industrielle* ('Towards World Unity: The Industrial Era') (Production: Institut Pédagogique National. Distribution: CNDP).
29. Voice-over commentary, *L'Ere industrielle: métamorphoses du paysage*.
30. Ibid.
31. Ibid.
32. Editors' note: for discussions of the demolition of Les Halles's pavilions, see the chapters by Catherine E. Clark, Hélène Jannière and Jean-Yves de Lépinay in this volume.
33. See Jean Gili, 'Marco Ferreri "ambientatore" l'utilisation du décor naturel dans les films de Marco Ferreri', in Jacques Aumont (ed.), *La Mise en scène* (Brussels: De Boeck, 2000), pp. 98–106.
34. The Bourse de Commerce (Commodities Exchange) is situated on the western edge of the Les Halles site.
35. See Nicholas Papayanis and Maïca Sanconie, 'Urbanisme du Paris souterrain: premiers projets de chemin de fer urbain et naissance de l'urbanisme des cités modernes', *Histoire, économie et société*, vol. 17, no. 4 (1998), pp. 745–70.

The Mirror of a City: The 'Parisian Collection' of the Forum des Images

Jean-Yves de Lépinay

The original purpose of the Forum des Images – which was to set up the audiovisual memory of a city – was particularly ambitious because Paris happens to be one of the most often, and best, filmed cities in the world. It has been filmed not only by Parisian and French filmmakers, but also, unusually, by directors from all over the world. The cinema has had a hand in shaping many perceptions of Paris: Americans see it as a city of luxury and freedom (particularly sexual); Russians of the Soviet era regarded it as the scene of popular uprisings such as the 1789 Revolution and the Commune; for Africans, it has been an often tragic Eldorado; in Japanese eyes, it is a wonderful city of great historical interest. And part of the success of the capital as a tourist destination can undoubtedly be explained by the richness of its imagery on film.

But when in 1980 the mayor of Paris, Jacques Chirac, conceived a plan to set up an institution aimed at preserving the audiovisual memory of the city, he was not just thinking in terms of Paris being a tourist attraction. He was also aware that Parisians were keen to keep their memory intact. As Pierre Nora has demonstrated, the need for memory is a need for history: 'Modern memory is first of all archival. [...] The less memory is experienced from within, the greater its need for external props and tangible reminders of that which no longer exists except *qua* memory.'[1] When applied today to France as a whole, and more particularly to cities, does this need for memory reflect an urban crisis? When a sense of history tends to fade away, it is memory that attempts to replace it.

The non-profit-making association Vidéothèque de Paris was set up in 1980 at the initiative of the poet and member of the French Academy, Pierre Emmanuel, who had been the first president of the Institut National de l'Audiovisuel (INA; National Audiovisual Institute) from its creation in 1974 until 1979. He noted that the invention and development of the cinema coincided with a spectacular expansion of cities. He argued that film was the most appropriate medium for recording changes in the world and helping us to understand them. That notion gradually gave rise to the idea of a collection of images which would constitute 'the city's audiovisual memory', and which would be made available to Parisians and visitors, thus helping them to appropriate Paris and providing a basis for their practices as citizens of the city. Opened to the public in 1988, the Vidéothèque de Paris expanded and diversified its activities over the next ten years, at which point it became the Forum des Images.[2]

One of the main aims of the new institution remained the collection, collation and comparison of the considerable and varied corpus of films which had Paris as their theme and setting, as well as the exploration of the many possible interpretations of each of them. That aim, however novel and original it may have seemed when couched in Emmanuel's sensitive terms, in fact formed part of a lengthy historical process.

Cinematographic Archives, Film Archives

'This apparatus will enable everyone to relive the moment when the guests of Mr X and Miss Y's society wedding come out of the church, the finish of a Grand Prix race, the march-past of the armoured cavalry during the Bastille Day celebrations and countless scenes we experience every day in our picturesque city of Paris.'[3] This sentence, which features in one of the very earliest film reviews ever published, shows how the cinema was perceived at its beginnings: if it could not claim to be an art – it took years and the fervent belief of a handful of militant cinephiles for that to be accepted – then it was going to be able to preserve our memory. Another enthusiastic spectator exclaimed, after attending the first projection of the cinematograph: 'Death will cease to be absolute.'[4] The cinema was poised to become 'an archive of life'. Researchers were slow to take possession of that material, either because it was not easily available, or because ignorance and, consequently, mistrust of the codes and conditions surrounding the production of such images meant that their importance tended to be played down. The fact remains, however, that everything that has been captured on film since 1895 now constitutes a considerable corpus of archives and a potentially useful source for historians, sociologists, architects, city planners and others.

As early as 1898, Boleslas Matuszewski, a Polish cameraman, wrote a booklet[5] in which he argued in favour of the creation of a 'repository of historical cinematography'. 'Many lines of vague description in books aimed at young people will become redundant the moment schoolchildren will be able to watch a precise moving representation [...] of the changing and mobile face of their urban landscape.' In passing, Matuszewski said he thought works of fiction should not be included in his project: 'The committee in charge of each deposit should above all engage in a process of elimination, excluding anything which could be described as pure entertainment, and which does not meet the criteria of usefulness that are the concern of the committee.'

In 1906, a Paris city councillor, Henri Turot, suggested that steps should be taken 'to set up cinematographic archives that will make it possible to preserve the memory of all the festivities, ceremonies and important events of interest to the city of Paris'.[6] This idea was taken up again in 1911 by another city councillor, Emile Massard, who pointed out that Vienna already had a 'Museum of Gesture':

> Paris can certainly afford to do as well as Vienna has done and to show how the initiative can be seized by the State, which ought to be the first to set up a library of this kind. What the government does not do in the interests of the nation can be achieved at a reasonable cost by the City Council, in the interests of both France and the city of Paris.[7]

But it was Victor Perrot, a retired solicitor who was president of the Commission for Historical Paris in 1910, and president of the Society for Historical Montmartre, who was no doubt the first to delineate plans for an 'audiovisual memory of the city'. He set up contacts – which unfortunately had no tangible results – with the Historical Library of the City of Paris (Bibliothèque Historique de la Ville de Paris, BHVP), envisaged the purchase of films from their producers, and published various articles and reports. On 7 December 1918, he launched 'an appeal from Historical Montmartre to the authorities, the Paris City Council, the Commission for Historical Paris, all learned societies and the press'[8] and defined the scope of what visual material should be preserved:

> from major public events, official ceremonies and receptions of heads of state to ordinary street scenes and events in everyday life, including portraits of our contemporaries as they go about their daily business; the interiors of public monuments, mansions and houses; in short, all Parisian events ... [9]

In the end, it was on 14 December 1925 that the City Council was presented with a plan for a 'Cinematographic Department of the City of Paris'.[10] One of the aims of the plan was to acquire old collections centred on the history of Paris. Financial restrictions probably prevented that aim from being achieved.[11] The Cinematographic Department of the City of Paris began showing films in schools, thus abandoning its initial remit of creating a local memory. It subsequently became 'the Educational Cinémathèque of the City of Paris', then the 'Robert-Lynen Cinémathèque',[12] which still exists today. It makes a major contribution to the filmic education of pupils at crèches, kindergartens, elementary schools, independent Paris cinemas and leisure centres.

But the large-scale international movement that led to the setting up of modern film archives, first in Stockholm in 1933, then in Berlin, London, New York, Moscow, Milan and Paris in 1936, adopted an approach that was completely different from the one defined by Matuszewski: the aim was no longer to bring together the city's film archive material, but to set up film archives as such. First conceived as a 'documentary' project designed to chart the history of mankind and of cities in particular, film archives became institutions devoted to the history of the cinema.

In other words, the creation of the Vidéothèque de Paris in 1980, then its opening to the public in 1988, had the effect of reviving the practice of the very earliest pioneers of film conservation.

A Directly Accessible Collection

The remit of the Vidéothèque de Paris has an important and original dimension which immediately distinguishes it from most older film archives: it builds up its collection in such a way as to make it immediately, totally and easily available to the general public. When the Vidéothèque de Paris first opened, video production was still very limited, there were fewer television channels than there are today, Video on Demand was not, of course, yet available, and film and audiovisual material could not be found in public libraries either for consultation or on loan.[13] It was an uphill battle for students and researchers to view images they needed for their work. As for members of the general public, it was quite simply impossible for them to watch a film or television programme for a second time, or to discover even a 'classic' movie unless it happened to be shown at the French Cinémathèque or an art-house cinema, or else broadcast on one of the relatively few national television channels.

The first step to be taken in the case of each film chosen for inclusion in the collection was to draw up a contract for the acquisition of non-exclusive and non-commercial rights which authorised the institution:

- To strike prints in the original format when necessary (16 mm or 35 mm silver film),
- To create duplicates on a standard video format (which was initially 1-inch, then digital Beta and nowadays Apple ProRes files or DCP),
- To provide distribution prints (¾-inch BVU, then MPEG-2 and MPEG-4),
- To screen those prints at non-profit showings in its collective viewing theatres,
- To allow them to be consulted in a specialised theatre open to the general public.

In order to identify films suitable for inclusion in the collection, published film histories and filmographies were systematically studied in detail. The main film producers and owners of film archives such as Gaumont, the INA and the collections of several ministries entered into agreements that would make it possible to explore their collections. An appeal was launched in the press and the broadcast media inviting owners of home movies shot in Paris to hand them in to the Vidéothèque.[14] At the same time, an ongoing monitoring unit was set up to scan the programmes of television channels, festival catalogues and suchlike on a regular basis.

The film producers that were identified in this way were then contacted so that viewings of the movies concerned could be organised for the Vidéothèque's archivists. Each year, several hundred companies (both large and small) were contacted in this way by the Forum des Images. A selection committee made up of archivists met regularly to decide which of the films they had been able to view deserved inclusion. Once the go-ahead was given, a purchase contract was negotiated with the producer, after which the medium enabling the film to be included in the collection was manufactured. The selection process was all-inclusive – in other words, blockbusters and family films were just as likely to be included as commercials and industrial or experimental films.

The opening in 1988 of a 'consultation room' totally given over to providing the general public with free access to a sizeable corpus of films of all kinds and of every period was a minor revolution. This quite unique facility combined some novel documentary, computing, audiovisual and robotic technologies which had the sole aim of providing the most direct access to images in the simplest conditions possible.

Each film, whatever its genre or duration, was accompanied by an information folder comprising a catalogue description and a more or less detailed résumé. Such résumés were designed in a specific way that made it possible to describe both the form and the 'content' of the document: themes, people or characters, places filmed, and so on. This method was at the time rather novel, at least as far as fiction films were concerned, and was soon identified as one of the system's strong points. The documentary software was also of a new kind: it was organised around language-processing tools that provided users with a search facility similar to 'normal speech': in other words, considerable freedom to use their own words and syntax without having to resort to a thesaurus, lexicon, dictionary or specific operator – all long before such technologies were implemented by present-day search engines.

The 'consultation room' as it was at the Forum des Images in 1988 (then called the Vidéothèque de Paris).

The catalogue was accessible online: well before the advent of the Internet, users could consult it at home via the public access information system, Minitel. It was possible to prepare a search, choose a programme and reserve online a consultation screen – the Vidéothèque de Paris was at the time probably the first cultural institution in the world to offer that kind of service. In the room, users were able to choose the film they wanted to watch without assistance, handle a videocassette or operate a video recorder. They just needed to press a viewing button. At that point, a spectacular robotic manipulator, visible to the public behind a glass wall in the room, would come into action (for a time, members of the public came simply to watch it in operation!). It would then retrieve the videocassette from the stacks where it was kept and insert it into the player. The 30 viewing stations (at the time of opening) were linked to the series of players by a particularly sophisticated 'lead frame', a 'connection grid' which enabled the system to operate with great flexibility and speed.

The facility was an immediate success, and the number of consultation screens soon had to be increased. Since many researchers wanted to use the collections for their work, a special status needed to be created for them, that of 'associate researcher'. That status was designed to be particularly wide-ranging: it was available to anyone involved in research, whether academic, personal or other, at whatever level. Those who benefited from the facility might include not only undergraduates and research students, but a theatre director, a wardrobe mistress looking for models, a choreographer, a novelist or an illustrator, among others. Many historians used the consultation room to work on their research. They included Christian Delage, Vincent Guigueno, Tangui Perron, Danielle Tartakowsky and Jean-Pierre Bertin-Maghit, among many others. They were all attracted by the rich diversity of the collections. They did however sometimes formulate one or two criticisms. The main one was consubstantial with the institution's role: the selection was restricted to images of Paris, which often resulted in films being regarded independently of their production context and of their directors' oeuvre. As a result, the collection risked being seen as a rather disorganised and incoherent accumulation. To answer that criticism, the archivists did their best to constitute coherent ensembles of works in well-defined areas: the most exhaustive research possible was for instance carried out into the Liberation of Paris in 1944, the events of May 1968 and the area of the central food market, Les Halles.

A Site of Memory

The location of the Forum des Images, as an institution 'of memory', was significant: it was set up in the heart of Paris, in the district of Les Halles, which was then undergoing one of the many transformations that have taken place there since the end of the 1960s.

At the time of its opening in 1988, the new institution formed an integral part of the urban development designed by the City of Paris in an attempt to 'add a touch of soul' to the underground shopping mall whose malfunctions since its opening in the mid-1970s had been symptomatic of botched city planning. A whole series of public and private cultural facilities were then created within a few months, ranging from the Espace Cousteau, the Espace Photographique de Paris, the Maison des Associations and the Musée du Rock to the Musée des Martyrs de Paris, the Médiathèque Musicale de Paris and the Maison des Conservatoires. Many of these have since closed down, either because they failed to attract a sufficient number of visitors, or as a result of a certain degree of insecurity in the underground mall. The Forum des Images was fortunate enough to be able to survive, and even to expand, thanks to support from the Paris City Council.

It is worth noting that, in that problematic urban environment, film probably played a major role in enabling the Les Halles underground complex to escape the downhill spiral to which it had unfortunately seemed doomed in its early years. It was the success of the Forum des Images, and above all the opening, then enlargement, of UGC Cité-Ciné, now Europe's largest multiplex with its 26 screens, that changed the face of the district. It was at the initiative of Michel Reilhac, a former head of the Forum des Images, that in December 2008 the City of Paris inaugurated a 'Rue du Cinéma', which is lined by the Forum des Images, the Bibliothèque du Cinéma François Truffaut and the UGC multiplex. In this way, a whole new cinema quarter came into being in Paris.

But the fact cannot be ignored that an institution partly devoted to the memory of the city stood on the very spot where one of the most serious urban planning crimes of the 20th century took place. Until 1969, this part of central Paris was occupied by the huge Les Halles wholesale food market (which was immortalised by Emile Zola's 1873 novel *Le Ventre de Paris* [*The Belly of Paris*]). It was much loved for its quaintness and its colourful characters, but also notorious for its appalling insalubrity and its traffic jams. The (vital) move of Les Halles to a new and modern market site outside Paris was followed by the demolition of the historic pavilions designed by Victor Baltard[15] and the creation of a huge hole, known as *le trou des Halles*, which had to wait several years before being filled, much to the consternation and anger of Parisians. What eventually occupied the *trou* was an undistinguished and bleak shopping mall. Once the throbbing heart of Paris, the Les Halles quarter became a city centre disliked by Parisians themselves and deliberately shunned by tourists. Ever since then, there have been more or less continuous attempts to heal that wound. From 2010 on, a new and comprehensive plan for the site has been implemented. It is still too early to be sure whether this new undertaking will succeed, more than 45 years later, in drawing a veil over the criminal demolition of the Baltard pavilions and the mediocrity of successive redevelopments.

It may legitimately be assumed, then, that the support by developers and city councillors for a project like the Vidéothèque de Paris could have been some kind of parapraxis or manifestation of a guilty conscience. Significantly enough, when the filmmaker Michel Gondry was asked by the Forum des Images to make a short animated film to mark its reopening in 2008 after improvements, he clearly wanted the venture to be seen as a kind of 'reparation' for the *trou des Halles*.[16] A similar argument is to be found in a remarkable article devoted to the creation of the Vidéothèque de Paris as a 'memory for the future' by Catherine E. Clark, a cultural historian and assistant professor of French studies at MIT.[17]

When we sense that the destruction of a part of our past is imminent or that we are about to lose something dear to us, we strive to save what can still be saved, if only in the form of traces. Surviving traces of the lost quarter of Les Halles can be found in the newsreels that Gaumont started amassing from 1910 on. In 1927, the Russian-born cinematographer Boris Kaufman captured the nocturnal atmosphere of the market in his short *Les Halles centrales*.[18] Jean Gabin played a local restaurateur in Julien Duvivier's *Voici le temps des assassins/Deadlier Than the Male* (1956). Television, institutional cinema and militant films focused in various ways on the move of the market to Rungis in 1969 and the redevelopment of the site. The Italian director Marco Ferreri even used the notorious *trou des Halles* as the location for his Western, *Touche pas à la femme blanche/Don't Touch the White Woman!* (1974).[19] The company in charge of the redevelopment made a series of commercials in 1977 to promote the construction of a 'new heart for Paris'.[20] Today, television crews film both the homeless who doss down in the district's underground freeways and the customers of fashionable hairdressing salons. The major redevelopment currently under way in the district is the subject of promotion campaigns aimed at both passers-by and local residents: films made by specialised advertising agencies vaunting the merits of future construction work are displayed on giant screens located at various busy pedestrian intersections. Video-sharing websites are chock-a-block with clips showing impromptu performances and various incidents shot in the area's streets and underground passages.

The Forum des Images' database, which is available on the Internet,[21] has become a reference tool for images of Paris. It does not simply catalogue the films that can be viewed on site, but offers a reference tool for the image of the City of Paris and the surrounding Ile-de-France area, thus constituting a key element of a possible 'cine-tourism' policy. Tourism is of vital economic importance for Paris and its region. Tourism professionals have realised that foreign tourists' love of the cinema can be exploited as a way of attracting them to the city and ensuring they spend some time there. A selection of 'circuits' is suggested to them[22] and various smartphone applications are also available.[23] The international success of certain films has turned a number of locations into tourist attractions: the Hôtel du Nord, for instance, on the Quai de Jemmapes, has been meticulously maintained so as to resemble as closely as possible its reproduction by Alexandre Trauner in his set designs for Marcel Carné's eponymous film of 1938. Jean-Pierre Jeunet's *Le Fabuleux destin d'Amélie Poulain/Amélie* (2001) attracts scores of visitors to Montmartre every day, thanks to the charm of its star, Audrey Tautou.[24] At the entrance to Saint-Sulpice church, a little guide in several languages is available to tourists on the trail of *The Da Vinci Code* (2006).

The administrative boundaries of Paris have remained virtually unchanged since 1844, and the city has gradually been enclosed within them by an artificial but very real frontier which cuts it off from its suburbs and its region: the *périphérique*, a circular urban motorway built at the end of the 1960s. That encirclement has considerably hampered the expansion of the city. After some typically French political shenanigans, the government and the City of Paris managed to agree on the creation of a new administrative entity, 'Grand Paris' ('Greater Paris'), which includes its suburbs. With its reach now extended beyond the boundaries of the *périphérique*, the Forum des Images' collection can contribute in concrete fashion, and lend a tangible existence, to a new and vital imaginary of the future Greater Paris.

In this respect, Pierre Emmanuel's project has probably never made more sense; and the 'phantom' denizens of Les Halles, who appear in the small hours of the morning, criss-cross the underground galleries of the shopping mall in vast numbers, only to vanish at night, have probably never so needed their traces and those of their predecessors to be preserved. The modern city is constantly being observed by cameras – surveillance cameras, the viewfinders of amateurs, webcams and so on. The city is trapped in a 'sightless' panoptic net. What will all these preserved images tell us tomorrow? The future of cities – and of Paris in particular – could well be in the hands of those who are today creating the archives of the future.

'Re-editing' the World?
Today's Forum des Images is a very different institution from the one imagined at the beginning of the 1980s and from the one opened to the public in 1988. It has broadened its scope well beyond the boundaries of Paris: it has opened up to the world. Every year it attracts 320,000 spectators, who attend 2,000 screenings at its five cinemas (which have between 30 and 444 seats) and its collections room, where more than 5,000 hours of images can be consulted.

But it remains deeply marked by its initial aims and roles, as imagined by Emmanuel. The originality of the Forum des Images resides chiefly in two characteristics of its approach that derive from its initial aim, which was to ignore frontiers between genres, forms and periods, and to regard all moving images as a unique whole and a source of exchanges and emotions; to question the world through the eyes of filmmakers and to imagine it thanks to the profound relationship that develops from spectator to film, as well as from film to film.

The Forum des Images today plays an important role in the cultural life of the city. It has found an original place in the Parisian audiovisual landscape: it offers a focused approach based particularly on the principle of specific topics that makes it possible to suggest interactions between widely differing works by connecting them up with each other and showing how they can together offer new openings on to our world and our society. The Forum des Images not only welcomes all types of images, but is open to members of the public in the broadest sense, whether they visit out of a love of the cinema or mere curiosity, and whether they be children, students, researchers or moving image professionals. Every year, the Forum des Images is visited by almost 60,000 schoolchildren of every educational level.

The 'collections room' at the Forum des Images in 2016.

THE MIRROR OF A CITY

The collections room has been completely reorganised in line with digital technologies. It accommodates visitors in different ways depending on the facility they require, offering comfortable stations for recreational use and work stations for students and researchers, 'saloons' for small groups and a small lecture hall for workshops or classes. At a time when an increasing number of films are easily available online, the Forum des Images works on the principle that there is a greater need than ever for physical locations where individual or semi-collective operations can be carried out simultaneously – meetings, group work, shared discoveries, and both online and face-to-face lessons.

In the firm belief that the cinema can help us to understand our world, the Forum des Images makes a point of not debarring any genres or frontiers in its determination to act as a permanent arena for reflection, debate, lectures and encounters by inviting a wide variety of guests – French and non-French filmmakers, critics, historians, sociologists, philosophers and city planners. In many cases, such events are filmed and available online on the institution's website.[25] It continues to explore all forms of the moving image – from videos made with a mobile phone to previews of *auteur* films, from television series to mash-ups, from experimental documentaries to silent films of the 1920s – by demonstrating that all films, if we put our minds to it, are contemporary with the instant we view them and connect them, through our own sensibility, to the world around us.

To understand the world of today, we need more than ever to track down elements of *meaning* in the avalanche of images that reach us through an ever-increasing number of varied and intrusive screens. The cinema is all about editing, about creating meaning by assembling, comparing and confronting various elements. It is often the case that a particular shot will reveal its full meaning through its interaction with others. Filmmakers and editors attempt, through a lengthy process of trial and error, to create such interactions. Building up a film collection is a somewhat similar process. Each film needs to find its place in an already existing whole, to 'interact' with the rest, to make clear its own characteristics and thus reveal the characteristics of those around it. For example, a very official institutional documentary, made in 1961 to promote the building of large housing estates (Georges Herbuveaux's *Paris gris, Paris rose*/Grey Paris, Pink Paris), affects the way we look at Jacques Tati's comedy *Mon oncle* (1958), a scathing indictment of a type of architecture obsessed by functionalism. Official images of the Liberation of Paris are complemented by films shot by an amateur filmmakers' club. A very recent documentary about a squat in a working-class district harks back to images of demonstrations by people living in poor housing in newsreels around 1910.

This is why the Forum des Images collection can never simply be an accumulation of the 'best films about Paris'. The aim is to enable each user of the collection to exploit all such interactions and 'edits'. Hence, the importance of the work of description and indexing, which opens up numerous possibilities. Hence, too, the importance of programming, which can reveal some remarkable connections. The number of films whose subject or setting is Paris, its monuments, its streets or its inhabitants is impossible to determine. But given that France is a highly centralised country, as well as one whose filmic and audiovisual output is varied and has been continuous from the very start, the number of filmed documents on Paris must certainly run into several hundreds of thousands.

There can be no doubt that Paris is a film star. Since 1895, film has provided us with a constantly changing mirror of the city, one which is not always clear, sometimes idealising it, at other times revealing its flaws and its disruptions. Images have never been as numerous as they are today, and never so widely viewed, sometimes out of context, distorted or misused. The mirror is beginning to cloud over. Building up collections, programming, installing workshops to teach people how to interpret, shoot and edit images, providing an illustrated lecture or simply a screening with a commentary, organising a rational series of screenings – all such activities play a part in the 're-editing of the world' that is so vital and urgent today.

Translated from the French by Peter Graham.

Notes

1. Pierre Nora (ed.), *Realms of Memory: Conflicts and Divisions*, vol. 1: *The Construction of the French Past* (New York: Columbia University Press, 1996), p. 8.
2. For further views on the Forum des Images, see, among others: Josette Naiman, 'La Vidéothèque de Paris', *Vingtième Siècle, revue d'histoire*, no. 18 (April–June 1988), pp. 122–4; Catherine Fournial, 'Vidéothèque et vidéotex. Le système documentaire de la Vidéothèque de Paris', *Documentaliste*, vol. 26, no. 1 (January–March 1989), pp. 3–10; Jean-Yves de Lépinay, 'Le Forum des Images: les collections accessibles et les services associés', *Bulletin des bibliothèques de France*, vol. 52, no. 2 (March–April 2007), pp. 51–4; Evelyne Cohen and Pascale Goetschel, 'Le Forum des Images: un espace dédié au cinéma et à Paris', *Sociétés et représentations*, no. 28 (2009), pp. 187–95.
3. E. H. [probably E. Hospitalier], *La Nature*, no. 1180 (11 November 1896), p. 91. Quoted in Raymond Borde, *Les Cinémathèques* (Paris: Editions Ramsay, 1983).
4. Anonymous text that appeared in *La Poste*, 30 December 1895. Reprinted in Daniel Banda and José Moure (eds), *Le Cinéma: naissance d'un art 1895–1920* (Paris: Flammarion, 2008), pp. 40–1.
5. Bolesłas Matuszewski, *Une nouvelle source de l'histoire. Création d'un dépôt de cinématographie historique* (Paris: Noizette, 1898).
6. Quoted in Borde, *Les Cinémathèques*, p. 35.
7. Paris City Council, 'Propositions-Référence', no. 6 (1911). In Borde, *Les Cinémathèques*, p. 35.
8. Minutes of the Vieux-Montmartre meeting, 7 September 1918. BiFi, Fonds Victor Perrot, VP007.
9. Bolesłas Matuszewski, 'L'Histoire par le film', *Ciné pour tous*, no. 59 (1921), pp. 4–5, 8.
10. Léon Riotor, 'Projet de service cinématographique de la Ville de Paris', *Bulletin municipal officiel de la Ville de Paris* (15 December 1925). BiFi, Fonds Victor Perrot, VP048.
11. See Béatrice de Pastre, 'Une archive dédiée à la pédagogie du cinéma', *1895*, no. 41 (October 2003), pp. 177–86.
12. Editors' note: named after Robert Lynen, a child star of the 1930s who appeared in, among others, *Poil de carotte/The Red Head* (Julien Duvivier, 1932). Lynen joined the Resistance during World War Two; he was arrested and deported to Germany, where he was tortured and shot on 1 April 1944.

13. With the notable exception of the Bibliothèque Publique d'Information (BPI) in the Centre Georges-Pompidou, which has programmed a series of documentary films since 1977.
14. Editors' note: see Roger Odin's chapter in this volume.
15. Translator's note: apart from one pavilion, which was moved to Nogent-sur-Marne in the suburbs.
16. Available at: www.dailymotion.com/video/xtii5n_la-reouverture-du-forum-des-images-par-michel-gondry_shortfilms (accessed 30 August 2017).
17. Catherine E. Clark 'The Vidéothèque de Paris, Memory for the Future', *Contemporary French Civilization*, vol. 40, no. 1 (2015), pp. 1–23.
18. *Les Halles centrales*, a 9-minute black-and-white silent documentary by Boris Kaufman.
19. Editors' note: see the chapters by Catherine E. Clark as well as Marie Gaimard & Marguerite Vappereau in this volume.
20. SEMAH colour commercials, 2'23", 1977.
21. Available at: http://collections.forumdesimages.fr (accessed 30 August 2017).
22. See, for example: www.secretsofparis.com/paris-cinema/ (accessed 30 August 2017); http://cine-balade.com/ (accessed 30 August 2017); www.parisinfo.com/visites-guidees/74438/Cin%C3%A9-Balade (accessed 30 August 2017).
23. In particular, the app designed by Smallbang with the help of Arte. Available at: http://smallbang.fr/cinemacity_fr.html (accessed 30 August 2017).
24. Editors' note: see Isabelle Vanderschelden's interview with Jean-Pierre Jeunet in this volume.
25. Available at: www.forumdesimages.fr (accessed 30 August 2017).

Part IV
INTERVIEW

Filming Paris: An Interview with Jean-Pierre Jeunet

Isabelle Vanderschelden

Since the global success of *Le Fabuleux destin d'Amélie Poulain/Amélie* in 2001, the name of Jean-Pierre Jeunet has become irrevocably associated with the city of Paris. Jeunet has long lived in Montmartre himself and he has therefore partly tried to provide a visual translation of his own experience of Parisian space in his films. Jeunet is certainly a *flâneur*, always walking the city on the lookout for an inspiring Parisian setting that he could use in a future film, but the Parisian sets that he has recreated cinematically also reconcile realism and timeless fantasy through his digital processing of the image. He has the ability to absorb local colour, street life and Parisian architecture and then use his imagination to feed these atmospheric elements into his own personal artistic vision.

This interview seeks to open up new perspectives on the representation of Paris as a cinematic space in some of his films, and investigate the methods used to achieve certain aesthetic effects. The questions were primarily designed to obtain Jeunet's own views on the reasons behind his choices of locations, his motivations for filming narrative fictions set in Paris, and on the actual decisions made during the filming process, including the careful post-production editing.

Jeunet certainly provides some valuable insights into the ways he views Paris as a blend of the real and the imaginary. He demonstrates how the actual world of the city helps to contextualise his idiosyncratic representation of singular Parisian spaces and iconic characters. He also provides clarification on how the different intertextual influences that he has integrated into his cinematic world contribute to the construction of his personal signature. He explains how this conscious recycling has shaped his working method as a filmmaker, before and during filming, as well as at the editing stage in post-production.

The interview confirms that Jeunet is a typical *flâneur* who has spent a great deal of time exploring Paris. Having said this, the Parisian sets of his films also revisit cinephilic and popular cultural sites, some of which have already been identified and commented upon in the critical discourse around the films.[1] Repeated tributes are paid to specific cinema genres and styles that the filmmaker himself admires, as well as to different forms of visual art that range from contemporary painting to cartoon-style drawing, graphic work and *bande dessinée*. In some cases, Jeunet creates fake retro cityscapes with a perfectionist sense of visual detail. He also reconstitutes historical locations that call upon a collective memory of the past.

I have tried to organise the conversation around the three motifs identified to structure the book: representations of Paris as location and space, the links between Paris and the quirky characters of Jeunet's films and the reconstruction of the past. All three elements involve the creation of an original visual and sound style using state-of-the-art digital technology.

Prior to the interview, Jeunet and I selected three of his films related to the motif of Paris: *Le Fabuleux destin d'Amélie Poulain*, *Un long dimanche de fiançailles/A Very Long Engagement* (2004) and *Mic-macs à tire larigot/Micmacs* (2007). Jeunet and Caro's early film *Delicatessen* (1991) was left out of the discussion because it was set in an 'undefined location in a timeless time'.

IV: How would you describe the ways in which your three films represent Paris as a cinematic space? Were your motivations different for each film?

JPJ: *Le Fabuleux destin d'Amélie Poulain* was in fact a reaction to my having just spent 20 months in Los Angeles making my previous film, *Alien: Resurrection* (1997), a typical Hollywood production. L.A. is bizarre. It is not really a city, but rather a series of impersonal suburbs, you can only move around by car, you cannot really go walking about, and if you start walking on a pavement, it's either because you've broken down or it is considered as suspicious, and you are immediately stopped by the police.

For a city-dweller like me, living in Paris, a city that I love, it's really strange, and rather hard to get used to, even if there were lots of pretty houses, nice nature spots and great weather all the time. When I returned to Paris, I rediscovered the city as I had originally seen it when I first came to live there in 1974. On my return from L.A., I was dazzled by the beauty of my city, how lovely everything looked and how lucky Parisians really were. I also realised that we, Parisians, do not notice it anymore, we get used to it and we no longer pay attention.

So I decided to make a film set in Paris, a film that would 'push' the usual representations of the city. I would enhance the sets visually, by creating fake images of Paris in postcard style, and by recreating the Paris atmosphere of Jacques Tati, with a little French flag and accordion music playing in the street, and the small shops: the so-called popular spaces of Paris, and certainly not the 'populist' vision that some people have accused me of promoting. It was a desire to show a fake Paris, a bit like the Paris of [the cartoonist Jean-Jacques] Sempé.[2] I obtained this imagery by modifying images for aesthetic reasons through the colour grading using specific colours, and by removing everything that looked ugly and not visually pleasing. In the 1940s and 1950s, there were not so many cars parked everywhere. I ended up with a bizarre vision of Paris on film and whenever I attended international festivals to present the film, I always started by saying that Paris was not like that, that it rained a lot, there was dog mess and that there were traffic jams all the time ...

IV: Would you say that the Paris that you portray in Le Fabuleux destin d'Amélie Poulain *is a city made for pedestrians?*

JPJ: Not particularly, I did not really think of that. I removed some of the cars because they were traces of modernity, but not all the time. You can see some cars in the film, and Nino (Mathieu Kassovitz) travels round Paris on a 'Solex' moped. It is true that Amélie (Audrey Tautou) walks a lot, but this is because I chose Montmartre as my central location, and her living spaces (the flat, the grocer's and the café) are all geographically close in real life. When the tourists come along, they do a tour of the locations of the film and they can walk from one location to another.

IV: Did your standpoint change for the filming of Paris in **Un long dimanche de fiançailles?**
JPJ: Yes, the film was an adaptation from a novel by [Sébastien] Japrisot, so it was not really my decision, and I had less scope for fiddling with locations. In the novel, the character of Mathilde (Audrey Tautou) comes to Paris to carry out her investigation, but some scenes are set in Brittany, in Corsica, others in the trenches of northern France. It was different, but there were some scenes taking place in Paris.

It was very gratifying for me to reconstruct the Paris of that period [the 1920s], which is a space that I am very fond of and passionate about. I share this passion with [the cartoonist] Jacques Tardi,[3] who is fascinated by World War One and by the imagery of the Paris of that period. So, I made a list of all the places that were of interest to me at the time, including the railway stations, Les Halles, etc.

I have an anecdote for you in this context. During the film's preparation, I was looking for suitable locations in the area of the Gare d'Austerlitz[4] and I took some photos of a bridge opposite. And later, I happened to find a photograph in a Tardi album that was exactly the same as the shot I had made. It was taken from the same angle, which shows that, when you like that sort of iconography, you end up adopting the same artistic approach and spatial positioning.

To give you another example, this is a photo I took of the Pont Neuf [he shows me a large black-and-white print], and I found another photo taken by [Eugène] Atget[5] that had exactly the same focal length, the same angle, the same colouring and lighting and the same shadows, except that it had been made a century and a half before.

For the scene set in the Gare d'Orsay, we cheated a bit because there were no trains running into it at that time, just small electric carriages going to Austerlitz. It was a false station, a great prestige building, just for show, but we cheated and put some trains going in because it made a more interesting shot.

IV: Were you also inspired by period images?
JPJ: Yes it is easy to find period images and to work from them. For the scenes in Les Halles and at L'Opéra Garnier, I used period photographs and images, and also a lot of stock shots. For instance, it gave me great pleasure to reproduce for a short scene, in front of the place de l'Opéra as it was in those days, with all the traffic and the pedestrians. My inspiration came from period stock shots that clearly show how the traffic was organised. It was a time when there were no traffic lights, no zebra crossings. It is quite obvious from the period stock that in those days, pedestrians were walking across in all directions in the street, the square and in front of the Opéra building. It was really fun to film this scene, but at the same time it was a very complex take of the traffic that required substantial technical support. The pedestrians moved without any orderly/organised direction, alongside the horse carriages, and it was all a bit chaotic. It was this type of choreography that we attempted to recreate. First we shot on location

on the square, then on a huge car park where we reconstituted the traffic. We had to introduce a number of special effects. For Les Halles (the belly of Paris), on the contrary – another area of Paris I really love – we used few special effects. The extras were real people, we filmed on location and just added a few digital shots of buildings.

These are different ways to recreate the old visual style of Paris, which were fun to do using the spirit of Tardi's imagery (the scene in the Musée des Sciences with all the skeletons is another example). At the time, I had made up large panels, with period photographs placed alongside modern ones taken during the location scouting, as well as drawings and sketches of what I wanted to arrive at in the film, and these were placed in all the corridors, to inspire everyone, and for the team of set designers to use.

IV: The film Mic-macs *is more modern and shows a more urban side of the city. How did your strategy for choosing locations and filming evolve?*

JPJ: In *Mic-macs*, it's true the settings are more modern, with more cartoon-like visual imagery of traditional Paris and some traces of modernity. So, I used a range of images, such as the tramway, etc. Yes, it is a mixture of both. There are also images of the suburbs of Paris alongside typical Parisian buildings. For example, the building used for the gun manufacture was a building I had found on the old boulevards des Maréchaux[6] while location scouting. I saw a lot of different buildings myself, because I am really interested in that aspect of the film's preparation, and I play an active role in the set selection. I had made a list of buildings that I liked and I would go round on my scooter exploring Paris until I found what I wanted. For example, there was a swimming pool in Pantin with brick walls and porthole windows I had had in mind as a setting for a film scene for a long time. I had even tried to include it in an earlier project with [Marc] Caro. I ended up using it in *Mic-macs*. I also included a scene in the Galeries Lafayette that I had thought of using at the time of *Le Fabuleux destin d'Amélie Poulain* – it would have been perfect, with the dome which would have looked good, but we would probably have found it difficult to recreate the period detail of the shop, so I used it in *Mic-macs*.

IV: Would you say then that you first find a set and try to find a way to integrate it into your script?

JPJ: It varies. That was what I did for the railway stations [in *Le Fabuleux destin d'Amélie Poulain*]. I used the Gare du Nord and the Gare de l'Est from different perspectives, before their hallways were transformed into shopping malls.

IV: Were there any specific challenges when filming on location?

JPJ: I can give you an example from *Mic-macs* at the Pont de Crimée [in the 10th *arrondissement*], a location that I was particularly fond of, because it evokes the Carné/Prévert iconography.[7] We reused exactly the same axes as [Alexandre] Trauner [the set designer] had adopted for *Les Portes de la nuit/Gates of the Night* (1946), except that we used the real locations while he was designing his model sets in a studio.

There is in fact a famous photograph of Prévert taken by [Robert] Doisneau[8] on the bridge, and nearby, there is a Marcel Carné school. So, it is really a typical Prévert/Carné atmosphere. It was really exciting to film this scene on location there. It was supposed to be in early morning, but we needed two days, and the *Le Parisien* newspaper accused me in a provocative title of 'taking the 10th *arrondissement* hostage'. It is true that when you shoot, you have to block the traffic. The Parisians are awkward. The same thing happened when we were shooting another scene in *Mic-macs*. We needed a short take in Montmartre cemetery and we had to stop traffic for a short period. And we had to suffer quite strong verbal reactions from passers-by. The Parisians are a bit grumpy, as we know. It is quite a different mentality in the USA where the public realise that cinema is their second biggest export industry after arms. In France, it is more complicated.

IV: Can you comment on the importance of blending location shooting and high-tech digital special effects added in post-production? Can you say more about the evolution of the use of digital post-production for key scenes set in Paris in your films?

JPJ: We had started using the digital special effect software on the filming of *La Cité des enfants perdus/City of Lost Children* (1995). For *Le Fabuleux destin d'Amélie Poulain*, we were about the first to test out the digital colour grading technology. It was new at the time we made *Le Fabuleux destin d'Amélie Poulain* and it came as a small revolution for cinematography all over the world, and gradually became the method used to grade images. To the point that the magazine *American Cinematographer*, which is the journal of reference for all directors of photography, voted *Le Fabuleux destin d'Amélie Poulain* the most important film of the decade.[9] At the time, it was quite new and we could afford to do things that would have been difficult in optical terms.[10] Using warm colouring and colder hues was something that was quite difficult to achieve before. I am not saying it looked nicer, it opened up new possibilities.

Amélie (Audrey Tautou) walking across the Pont des Arts in *Le Fabuleux destin d'Amélie Poulain/Amélie* (Jean-Pierre Jeunet, 2001).

IV: Did the technology change for the next films?
JPJ: Nowadays, resorting to digital technology is the normal filming procedure. It's a bit like using Photoshop but on moving images. You can do a lot more, create masks, change the colour of clothes, etc. It requires a lot of patience as it is precision work that takes a long time — not everyone wants to go into such detail. Because I am very fond of images, I spend many hours on this aspect of the production. But, there are not really that many differences in the use that I made of it in the three films. It's mainly that the machines and software are always improving, so this is where there is an evolution, but apart from this, there has not been much change in the processes in terms of representing Paris in the films.

And it didn't stop us from using other methods of set design that were not digital but involved the use of real posters as well. My set designer, Aline Bonetto, and I had decided to locate colourful images and we found a German artist living in Grenoble, Michael Sowa, who designed the large posters that we used in the Métro to hide unsightly walls. We were very lucky because they were huge and the graphics were really impressive. We used them a lot.

IV: Was the work of the painter Juarez Machado also used in similar ways?
JPJ: No, Machado[11] was a painter that we used as a visual reference, but for use on the sets, it was more the posters.

IV: Some motifs come back regularly in terms of colours and visual representation. How about the sound design?
JPJ: The sound has nothing to do with Paris. It is an aspect of film production that I take very seriously and I place special emphasis on sound design in all my films, but it is not directly related to the representation of Paris. In *Le Fabuleux destin d'Amélie Poulain*, the work around the sound creates an atmosphere that is cartoon-like, as in a child's world, except that it is real.

IV: How closely are the Paris settings linked to the creation and inclusion of specific characters in the three films?
JPJ: The keyword for cinema in this context is coherence. As soon as the script is a bit different, everything has to fit in well together. If the characters that I create are a bit *décalés* [quirky] then everything has to match to be coherent – the sets, the costumes, the dialogues and the musical soundtrack. For instance, in *Mic-macs*, the characters were more like cartoon characters.

IV: Would you say that your characters are typical Parisians?
JPJ: For *Mic-macs*, not particularly. They are just characters. For *Le Fabuleux destin d'Amélie Poulain*, there are references to people who really existed and lived in Montmartre. For instance, the widow of the *garde champêtre* (a rural police officer)

who wears the uniform of her husband and is mentioned by Amélie as she guides the blind man really existed at the time I made the film. So, I used her as inspiration for the script. At the same time, this can be a bit artificial. The old-fashioned grocer wearing a pencil behind his ear no longer exists in Paris today, so we cheated a little. It's a mixture really.

IV: So you would prefer to say that your characters represent iconic images rather than a realistic representation of the ordinary people living in Paris today?
JPJ: Yes, sometimes they exist. I am sometimes criticised for favouring retro film worlds and atmospheres, and it is true to some extent.

IV: You mention a retro style. Is there any intention behind this strategy?
JPJ: It's a purely aesthetic stand, but this criticism of my style being retro is a bit silly because it is obvious that I also live with the times, and that I use the latest technologies in my films to create state-of-the-art images and sounds.

IV: Are there also elements of nostalgia in the way you envisage Paris?
JPJ: No, I am not driven by nostalgia. I live in the present, not in the past. I love gadgets and technology. The tones were sepia in *Un long dimanche de fiançailles* because I wanted to recreate a 1900s visual style. Of course, I prefer to look at the *colonnes Morris*[12] and the old-fashioned toilets, even if they were dirty, rather than the JCDecaux modern public toilets of today. They are so ugly. This is what I call the syndrome of the Louvre Pyramid: it provoked a scandal because it was a modern building placed in a classical historical setting. But for me there is no debate: it is a glass pyramid, and it looks beautiful. But aestheticism annoys people in France, whereas what is ugly does not seem to bother anyone. Caro and I have always been attacked along the lines of our aesthetic bias. We like beautiful images. It is a French thing. Lots of films are so ugly. I hear similar arguments outside France about the images in my films, but with positive connotations.

IV: Can you comment on the use of colour and black and white in your films?
JPJ: A film in black and white is nearly impossible today. If you make a film in black and white, it's like shooting yourself in the foot. Young people don't want to see black-and-white films. It is a question of education. If they were shown a Buster Keaton film, they would love it. So, I compensate with working on colour, which can also be very interesting. I'd love to make a film in black and white, but it would have to be on a very small budget. [Luc] Besson did it with *Angel A* [in 2004] and drew inspiration for the sets from the aesthetics of *Le Fabuleux destin d'Amélie Poulain*.

IV: Do you recognise your approach to cinema in the post-modern discourse with which your films are often associated? For instance, the intextextual references and the recycling of the Paris of classical cinema in your films?

JPJ: Well, yes, I do since it interests me.

IV: What importance do you attach to the notion of memory when you film Paris?

JPJ: For example, I was rather excited to be shooting where Carné had filmed *Les Portes de la nuit* (in *Mic-macs*). But I have to admit it was more like a wink from a cinephile to that type of cinema. Those classics do not interest anyone today; cinephilia has died and cinephiles are a very small group of marginalised people who go to the Cinémathèque. Young people especially do not have any interest in cinema classics. They show a lack of curiosity. If I include a reference to *Les Portes de la nuit* in my film, it is only noticed by a few people. I do it for my own pleasure.

IV: Would you envisage making another film in Paris?

JPJ: After finishing *Mic-macs*, I felt that I had covered all the spaces of Paris that I wanted to explore cinematically. I now live in Provence part of the year, and when I come back to Paris, I no longer find much pleasure in exploring Paris for ideas. I have already used what I wanted to put on film. I feel less inclined to make another film in Paris. I think I would find it a bit tiresome and embarrassing.

This interview with Jean-Pierre Jeunet was completed on Skype on 25 September 2014.

Notes

1. See, for example, Isabelle Vanderschelden, *Amelie* (London: I. B. Tauris, 2007); Isabelle Vanderschelden, 'Digital Painting: Colour Treatment in the Cinema of Jean-Pierre Jeunet', in Wendy Everett (ed.), *Questions of Colour in Cinema: From Paintbrush to Pixel* (Oxford: Peter Lang, 2007), pp. 67–84; and Elizabeth Ezra, *Jean-Pierre Jeunet* (Urbana and Chicago, IL: University of Illinois Press, 2008).
2. Sempé (1932–) is a French cartoonist known for his gentle, stylised drawing style, his sense of detail and his use of panoramic views. He has illustrated the series of children's books *Le Petit Nicolas*, and draws satirical cartoons for various newspapers including the *New Yorker*.
3. Jacques Tardi (1946–) is an author and *bande dessinée* artist whose iconography of Paris, distinctive attention to photographic detail, and sense of place have become his trademarks. He is known for adapting into comic form the Nestor Burma detective stories of Léo Malet and for the Adèle Blanc-Sec comic-book series (1976–), both set in early 20th-century Paris. Jeunet had long expressed interest in making a film adaptation of the latter, but it was eventually Luc Besson who shot *Les Aventures extraordinaires d'Adèle Blanc-Sec/The Extraordinary Adventures of Adèle Blanc-Sec* in 2010, a lavish production set in Paris of the 1910s that uses settings not dissimilar to those of *Un long dimanche de fiançailles*.
4. The viaduct of Austerlitz station is visited by Nestor Burma in Tardi's album *Brouillard au pont de Tolbiac* (Paris: Casterman, 1982).

5. Eugène Atget (1857–1927) was a *flâneur* and photographer of 19th-century Paris known for his documentary style. He later became identified as an inspiration for the Surrealists.
6. Literally, the 'boulevards of the Marshals'. These are large avenues named after Napoleon's Marshals that form a continuous circular boundary around central Paris.
7. Jeunet here refers to films directed by Marcel Carné in the 1930s and 1940s, many of which were scripted by the poet Jacques Prévert, such as *Le Jour se lève/Daybreak* (1939) and *Les Portes de la nuit*. These films offered a poetic, highly recognisable, reconstruction of the working-class areas of Paris (through set design minutely based on real Parisian buildings). Also important in this respect is *Hôtel du Nord* (1938), directed by Carné, though scripted by Henri Jeanson. The films share a recognisable iconography of canals, factories and rain-covered streets. [Editors' note: for further discussion of *Les Portes de la nuit*, see Thomas Pillard's chapter in this book.]
8. Robert Doisneau (1912–94) was a photographer of Paris who specialised in capturing the popular daily routine of ordinary people and the French *air du temps* of the post-war period.
9. Rachael K. Bosley, 'AC Poll Names 10 Best-Shot Films of 1998–2008', *American Cinematographer*, vol. 91, no. 8 (August 2010), page number unknown.
10. See Benjamin Bergery, 'Cinematic Impressionism: An Interview with Bruno Delbonnel', *American Cinematographer*, vol. 85, no. 12 (December 2004), pp. 58–69.
11. Jeunet has commented elsewhere on the influence of Juarez Machado's paintings. Machado is a Brazilian artist whose work influenced the colour coding of Jeunet's films from *La Cité des enfants perdus* onwards. This fact may explain why Jeunet does not really associate this influence with the visual imagery of Paris specifically.
12. Circular Parisian street furniture used for advertising.

Contributors

The Editors

ALASTAIR PHILLIPS is Associate Professor (Reader) in Film Studies at the University of Warwick, UK. His books include *City of Darkness, City of Light: Emigré Filmmakers in Paris 1929–1939* (2003), *Journeys of Desire. European Actors in Hollywood* (co-edited with Ginette Vincendeau, 2006), *Japanese Cinema: Texts and Contexts* (co-edited with Julian Stringer, 2007), *100 Film Noirs* (co-authored with Jim Hillier, 2009), *Rififi: A French Film Guide* (2009), *A Companion to Jean Renoir* (co-edited with Ginette Vincendeau, 2013) and *The Japanese Cinema Book* (co-edited with Hideaki Fujiki, 2018). He is an editor of *Screen*.

GINETTE VINCENDEAU is Professor of Film Studies at King's College London. She has written widely on popular French cinema and is a regular contributor to *Sight and Sound*. Among her books are *Pépé le Moko* (1998), *Stars and Stardom in French Cinema* (2000), *Jean-Pierre Melville: An American in Paris* (2003), *La Haine* (2005), *Brigitte Bardot* (2013 and 2014). She has edited and co-edited several volumes, including *The French New Wave: Critical Landmarks* (with Peter Graham, 2009), *A Companion to Jean Renoir* (with Alastair Phillips, 2013) and a special issue of *Celebrity Studies* ('The blond issue', vol. 7, no. 1, 2016).

The Contributors

NICOLETA BAZGAN is Associate Professor of French and Intercultural Studies at the University of Maryland, Baltimore County, USA. She has published on cities and women on screen, French female stardom and contemporary European cinema. She is currently writing a book entitled *Parisiennes: City Women in French Cinema*.

JEAN-LOUP BOURGET is Professor of Film Studies at the Ecole Normale Supérieure in Paris and a member of the editorial board of the French film monthly *Positif*. His abiding interest is classical Hollywood cinema, with a special focus on European directors working in Hollywood (Lubitsch, Lang, Sirk, Ophuls, Renoir) and on the relationship between film and other aspects of American culture, such as literature, painting and architecture. He has published and edited 17 books on related subjects, the most recent being devoted to Cecil B. DeMille (2013) and King Vidor (with Françoise Zamour, 2016).

CONTRIBUTORS

CHARLOTTE BRUNSDON is author of *London in Cinema* (2007) and *Television Cities* (2018). She has recently been Principal Investigator on the AHRC-funded 'Projection' Project, based at the University of Warwick, UK, where she holds a Chair in Film and Television Studies.

CATHERINE E. CLARK is Assistant Professor of French Studies in Global Studies and Languages at the Massachusetts Institute of Technology, USA. She has published articles in the *American Historical Review*, *Contemporary French Civilization* and *Etudes photographiques*. She is completing a book about the uses of photographs as historical documents of Paris from 1860 to 1970.

SANDY FLITTERMAN-LEWIS is the author of *To Desire Differently: Feminism and the French Cinema* (1990 and 1996) and co-author, with Robert Stam and Robert Burgoyne, of *New Vocabularies in Film Semiotics* (1992). She is the founding co-editor of *Camera Obscura: A Journal of Feminism and Film Theory* and *Discourse: Journal of Cultural Studies*. Her current work focuses on Jewish families in France under the German Occupation of World War Two, including articles on Alain Resnais, Marguerite Duras and Agnès Varda. She teaches at Rutgers University, New Jersey, USA.

ALISTAIR FOX is Professor Emeritus at the University of Otago, New Zealand. He has written extensively on topics ranging from Renaissance literature to issues of national identity, and in the field of film studies his most recent books are an English translation of Anne Gillain's *François Truffaut: The Lost Secret* (2013), *A Companion to Contemporary French Cinema* (co-edited with Michel Marie, Raphaëlle Moine and Hilary Radner, 2015) *Speaking Pictures: Neuropsychoanalysis and Authorship in Film and Literature* (2016) and an English translation of Anne Gillain's *Truffaut on Cinema* (2017).

MARIE GAIMARD holds a PhD in the history of architecture from the Université Paris 1 Panthéon-Sorbonne. She has been teaching at the Ecoles Nationales Supérieures d'Architecture Paris-La Villette and Normandie since 2011. Her work focuses on the history of architecture and of the architect (*Métier: architecte. Dynamiques et enjeux professionnels au cours du XXème siècle*, co-edited with Claude Massu and Elise Guillerm, 2013). In 2012, she founded, with Marguerite Vappereau, the research group PLAYTIME, dedicated to the history of cinema and architecture. She is currently editing the proceedings of the 2015 seminar 'Architectes cinéastes, cinéastes architectes'.

STEPHEN GUNDLE is Professor of Film and Television Studies at the University of Warwick, UK. His books include *Bellissima: Feminine Beauty and the Idea of Italy* (2007), *Glamour: A History* (2008), *Death and the Dolce Vita: The Dark Side of Rome in the 1950s* (2011) and *Mussolini's Dream Factory: Film Stardom in Fascist Italy* (2013). He also co-edited (with Christopher Duggan and Giuliana Pieri) *The Cult of the Duce: Mussolini and the Italians* (2013). He is currently Principal Investigator on a large AHRC research project on Italian film producers.

MARY HARROD is Assistant Professor in French Studies at the University of Warwick, UK. She has published various book chapters, two prize-winning essays in *Studies in French Cinema* and an article on US and European cinemas in *Screen*. She is the co-editor of *The Europeanness of European Cinema: Identity, Meaning, Globalisation* (with Mariana Liz and Alissa Timoshkina, 2015) and *Women Do Genre in Film and Television* (with Katarzyna Paszkiewicz, 2017). She is the author of *From France with Love: Gender and Identity in French Romantic Comedy* (2015).

HÉLÈNE JANNIÈRE is Professor of History of Contemporary Architecture at the Université Rennes 2, France. Her work focuses on architectural and urban criticism, especially from the 1950s to the 1980s, including, with France Vanlaethem and Alexis Sornin, *Architectural Periodicals in the 1960s and 1970s* (2008); with Kenneth Frampton, issue no. 24/25 of *Les Cahiers de la recherche architecturale et urbaine* ('La Critique en temps et lieux', 2009); and with Richard Leeman, *Michel Ragon, critique d'art et d'architecture* (2013). She has recently coordinated an international research programme (2014–16), funded by the French National Research Agency: *Mapping.Crit.Arch. A Cartography of Architectural Criticism, XXth–XXIst Centuries*.

COLIN JONES CBE is Professor of History at Queen Mary University of London and Fellow of the British Academy. A specialist in French history, he is author or editor of over 20 books. These include: *The Smile Revolution in Eighteenth Century Paris* (2014), *The Saint-Aubin 'Livre de Caricatures': Drawing Satire in Eighteenth-century Paris* (co-editor, with Juliet Carey and Emily Richardson, 2012*)*, *Charles Dickens,* A Tale of Two Cities *and the French Revolution* (co-editor, with Josephine McDonagh and John Mee, 2009), *Twilight Visions: Surrealism and Paris* (co-author, with Therese Lichtenstein, Julia Kelley and Whitney Chadwick, 2009), *Paris: The Biography of a City* (2004) and *The Great Nation: France from Louis XIV to Napoleon* (2002).

ROLAND-FRANÇOIS LACK lectures in French and film at University College London. He is the creator of The Cine-Tourist website (www.thecinetourist.net/), a repository for research into relations between maps and films and between films and places. His research is chiefly centred on early English and French cinema and on the French New Wave. He is the co-editor (with Derek Schilling) of *Screening the Paris Suburbs: From the Silent Era to the 1990s* (forthcoming).

SÉBASTIEN LAYERLE is a Lecturer at the Université Sorbonne Nouvelle-Paris 3 (IRCAV). His research focuses on the relationship between cinema and history, especially within political films of the 1960s and 1970s. He is the author of *Caméras en lutte en mai 68* (2008). He co-edited *Les Producteurs: enjeux financiers, enjeux créatifs* (with Laurent Creton, Yannick Dehée and Caroline Moine, 2011) and more recently, *Voyez comme on chante! Films musicaux et cinéphilies populaires en France, 1945–1958* (with Raphaëlle Moine, *Théorème*, no. 20, 2014).

CONTRIBUTORS

JEAN-YVES DE LÉPINAY was Programme Director at the Forum des Images, Paris. He worked as a production assistant in the audiovisual industry before becoming a librarian specialising in the moving image. He is president of PIAF, an association gathering heads of audiovisual collections and librarians, and of the association Images en Bibliothèques, which works towards the development of film and audiovisual collections within libraries. He has published several articles on Paris in the cinema, in the journal *Urbanisme*, in Thierry Jousse and Thierry Paquot (eds), *La Ville au cinéma* (2005) and in Antoine de Baecque (ed.), *Paris vu par Hollywood* (2012).

MICHEL MARIE is Professor Emeritus at the Université Sorbonne Nouvelle-Paris 3 (IRCAV). He has written widely on the history of French cinema, including silent cinema and the New Wave. His recent work focuses on documentary (Pierre Perrault and the Ateliers Varan). He has been commissioning editor of the Cinema and Visual Arts collection at Armand Colin since 1988. He is co-author of *Esthétique du film* (first published 1983), *L'Analyse des films* (1988) and the *Dictionnaire critique et théorique du cinéma* (2001). He founded the AFECCAV with Geneviève Sellier in 1997 and has been President of the Cinémathèque Universitaire and of the AFRHC.

RAPHAËLLE MOINE is Professor of Film Studies at the Université Sorbonne Nouvelle-Paris 3 (IRCAV). She has published *Les Genres du cinéma* (2002), translated into English as *Cinema Genre* (2008), *Remakes: les films français à Hollywood* (2007), and *Les Femmes d'action au cinéma* (2010). She has edited a number of volumes, including most recently *CINéMAS*, vol. 22, no. 2–3, 'Genre/Gender' special issue (with Geneviève Sellier, 2012), *Voyez comme on chante! Films musicaux et cinéphilies populaires en France, 1945–1958* (with Sébastien Layerle, *Théorème*, no. 20, 2014) and *A Companion to Contemporary French Cinema* (with Alistair Fox, Michel Marie and Hilary Radner, 2015).

ROGER ODIN is Professor Emeritus of Communication at the Université Sorbonne Nouvelle-Paris 3, where he was head of the Film and Audiovisual Institute (IRCAV) from 1983 to 2003. As a theoretician who follows a semio-pragmatic approach (*De la fiction*, 2000; *Les Espaces de communication*, 2011), he has directed an international research group on documentary (*L'Age d'or du cinéma documentaire: Europe années 50*, 2 vols, 1997) and initiated research on home movies (*Le Film de famille*, 1995; 'Le Cinéma en amateur', *Communications*, no. 68, 1999). He has recently worked on the uses of the mobile phone (*Téléphone mobile et création*, with Laurence Allard and Laurent Creton, 2014).

THOMAS PILLARD holds a PhD in Film Studies from the Université Paris Ouest Nanterre La Défense. His research interests include French cinema, film genre and cinephilia. He is the author of two books: *Le Film noir français face aux bouleversements de la France d'après-guerre, 1946–1960* (2014) and *Tavernier – Un dimanche à la campagne* (2015). He is a Lecturer at the Université Sorbonne Nouvelle-Paris 3 (IRCAV).

HILARY RADNER is Professor of Film and Media Studies in the Department of History and Art History at the University of Otago, New Zealand. She has published numerous books and articles in the fields of cinema, visual culture and gender. Her most recent publications include: *Neo-Feminist Cinema: Girly Films, Chick Flicks, and Consumer Culture* (2011), *Feminism at the Movies: Understanding Gender in Contemporary Cinema* (co-edited with Rebecca Stringer, 2011), *A Companion to Contemporary French Cinema* (co-edited with Alistair Fox, Michel Marie and Raphaëlle Moine, 2015) and *The New Woman's Film: Femme-centric Movies for Smart Chicks* (2017).

ISABELLE VANDERSCHELDEN is Senior Lecturer and French Section Lead in the Department of Languages, Information and Communication at Manchester Metropolitan University, UK. Her research focuses on contemporary French cinema and the use of film in education. Her books include: *Amelie* (2007), *France at the Flicks: Issues in Popular French Cinema* (co-edited with Darren Waldron, 2007) and *Studying French Cinema* (2013). She guest-edited a special issue of *Studies in French Cinema* on the French film industry (2016). She is currently completing a history of French screenwriters and their work with Sarah Leahy for Manchester University Press.

MARGUERITE VAPPEREAU holds a PhD in Film Studies and teaches at the Université Paris 1 Panthéon-Sorbonne. She is a member of the research group Théâtre de la Mémoire (Theatre of Memory) and a founding member, with Marie Gaimard in 2012, of the research group PLAYTIME, dedicated to the history of cinema and architecture. She is co-editor, with Sylvie Lindeperg and Myriam Tsikounas, of *Les Histoires de René Allio* (2013), and co-editor, with Claire Deniel, of a book on the Armenian director *Artavazd Péléchian* (2016).

JENNIFER WALLACE holds a PhD from the Film Studies department at King's College London. Her thesis, under the supervision of Professor Ginette Vincendeau, examined the representation of Paris in the films of Agnès Varda. She has given public lectures on the French New Wave and on Jean-Luc Godard as part of the BFI Masterclass season in 2015 and 2016, and she regularly volunteers at the Bechdel Test-Fest in London.

LEILA WIMMER is Senior Lecturer in Film Studies at London Metropolitan University. She is the author of a study of the critical reception of British cinema in post-war France entitled *Cross-Channel Perspectives: The French Reception of British Cinema* (2009). She has published essays on Billy Wilder's *Mauvaise graine*, the critical reception of *Baise-moi*, Jane Birkin as French icon, the cult stardom of Sylvia Kristel, the pairing of Alain Delon and Jean Gabin in the films of Henri Verneuil and women's cinephilia in popular French magazines of the 1930s.

Select Bibliography

Abel, Richard, *French Film Theory and Criticism: 1907–1929* (Princeton, NJ: Princeton University Press, 1988).

Andrew, Dudley, *Mists of Regret: Culture and Sensibility in Classic French Film* (Princeton, NJ: Princeton University Press, 1995).

Andrew, Dudley and Ungar, Steven, *Popular Front Culture and the Poetics of Culture* (Cambridge, MA: Belknap Press, 2005).

Andrew, Dudley and Gillain, Anne (eds), *A Companion to François Truffaut* (Malden, MA: Wiley-Blackwell, 2012).

Ariès, Philippe and Duby, Georges (eds), *Histoire de la vie privée, de la première guerre mondiale à nos jours*, vol. 5 (Paris: Seuil 1987).

Augé, Marc, *Non-places: Introduction to an Anthology of Supermodernity* (London: Verso, 1995).

Augé, Marc, *In the Metro* (Minneapolis: University of Minnesota Press, 2002).

Aumont, Jacques (ed.), *La Mise en scène* (Brussels: De Boeck, 2000).

Austin, Guy, *Contemporary French Cinema: An Introduction* (2nd edn) (Manchester: Manchester University Press, 2008).

Baczko, Bronislaw, *Les Imaginaires sociaux* (Paris: Payot, 1984).

Baecque, Antoine de, *Cahiers du cinéma. Histoire d'une revue 1. A l'assaut du cinéma* (Paris: Editions Cahiers du cinéma, 1991).

Baecque, Antoine de and Toubiana, Serge, *Truffaut: A Biography* (New York: Alfred A. Knopf, 1999).

Baecque, Antoine de, *La cinéphilie. Invention d'un regard, histoire d'une culture 1944–1968* (Paris: Fayard, 2003).

Baecque, Antoine de, *Camera Historica. The Century in Cinema* (New York: Columbia University Press, 2012).

Baecque, Antoine de (ed.), *Paris by Hollywood* (Paris: Flammarion, 2012).

Baecque, Antoine de and Herpe, Noël, *Eric Rohmer* (Paris: Stock, 2014).

Banaji, Ferzina, *France, Film, and the Holocaust: From le génocide to la shoah*, (Basingstoke: Palgrave Macmillan, 2012).

Banda, Daniel and Moure, José (eds), *Le Cinéma: naissance d'un art 1895–1920* (Paris: Flammarion, 2008).

Barber, Stephen, *Projected Cities: Cinema and Urban Space* (London: Reaktion, 2002).

Baron Turk, Edward, *Marcel Carné and the Golden Age of French Cinema* (Cambridge, MA: Harvard University Press, 1989).

Barsacq, Léon, *Le Décor de film: 1895–1969* (Paris: Seghers, 1970).

Barthes, Roland, *The Rustle of Language* (New York: Hill and Wang, 1986).

Barthes, Roland, *The Eiffel Tower and Other Mythologies* (Berkeley and Los Angeles: University of California Press, 1997).

Baudelaire, Charles, *The Painter of Modern Life and Other Essays* (London: Phaidon, 1995).

Benjamin, Walter, *Charles Baudelaire. A Lyric Poet in the Era of High Capitalism* (London and New York: Verso, 1997).

Benjamin, Walter, *The Writer of Modern Life: Essays on Charles Baudelaire*, ed. Michael W. Jennings (Cambridge, MA: Belknap Press, 2006).

Bergala, Alain, *Godard au travail* (Paris: Cahiers du cinéma, 2006).

Bergfelder, Tim, Harris, Sue and Street, Sarah, *Film Architecture and the Transnational Imagination: Set Design in 1930s European Cinema* (Amsterdam: Amsterdam University Press, 2007).

Betz, Mark, *Beyond the Subtitle: Remapping European Art Cinema* (Minneapolis: University of Minnesota Press, 2009).

Binh, N. T., *Paris au cinéma: la vie rêvée de la capitale de Méliès à Amélie Poulain* (Paris: Parigramme, 2003).

Block, Marcelline, *World Film Locations: Paris* (Bristol: Intellect Press, 2011).

Borde, Raymond, *Les Cinémathèques* (Paris: Editions Ramsay, 1983).

Bosseno, Christian-Marc, *La Prochaine séance. Les français et leurs cinés* (Paris: Gallimard, 1996).

Buck-Morss, Susan, *The Dialetics of Seeing. Walter Benjamin and the Arcades Project* (Cambridge, MA: MIT Press, 1991).

Cannon, Steve and Dauncey, Hugh (eds), *Popular Music in France from Chanson to Techno. Culture, Identity and Society* (Aldershot: Ashgate Publishing, 2003).

Canteux, Camille, *Filmer les grands ensembles: villes rêvées, villes introuvables: une histoire des représentations audiovisuelles des grands ensembles, milieu des années 1930 – début des années 1980* (Paris: Créaphis, 2014).

Carly, Michel, *Maigret traversées de Paris: les 120 lieux parisiens du commissaire* (Paris: Omnibus, 2003).

Certeau, Michel de, *The Practice of Everyday Life* (Berkeley and Los Angeles: University of California Press, 1984).

Champion, Virginie, Lemoine, Bertrand and Terraux, Claude, *Les Cinémas de Paris, 1945–1995* (Paris: Délégation à l'action artistique de la ville de Paris, 1995).

Chevalier, Louis, *The Assassination of Paris* (Chicago, IL: University of Chicago Press, 1994).

Chevalier, Louis, *Montmartre du plaisir et du crime* (Paris: Payot & Rivages, 1995).

Chion, Michel, *Audio-Vision: Sound on Screen* (New York: Columbia University Press, 1994).

Clair, René, *Reflections on the Cinema* (London: William Kimber, 1953).

Clarke, David B., *The Cinematic City* (London and New York: Routledge, 1997).

Clarke, David B., Crawford Pfannhauser, Valerie and Doel, Marcus A. (eds), *Moving Pictures/Stopping Places* (Lanham, MD: Lexington Books, 2009).
Clerc, Thomas, *Paris, musée du XXIe siècle* (Paris: Gallimard, 2007).
Clerval, Anne, *Paris sans le peuple* (Paris: La Découverte, 2013).
Cohen, Evelyne, *La Télévision sur la scène du politique: un service public pendant les Trente Glorieuses* (Paris: L'Harmattan, 2009).
Colard, Jean-Max and Singer, Juliette (eds), *Poétique du chantier* (Paris: Association Ligeia, 2010).
Colombat, André Pierre, *The Holocaust in French Film* (Metuchen, NJ: Scarecrow Press, 1993).
Conway, Kelley, *Chanteuse in the City. The Realist Singer in French Film* (Berkeley and Los Angeles: University of California Press, 2004).
Daney, Serge, *L'Exercise a été profitable, Monsieur* (Paris: P.O.L, 1993).
Daney, Serge, *Persévérance* (Paris: P.O.L, 1994).
Debord, Guy, *The Society of the Spectacle* (New York: Zone Books, 1995).
Douchet, Jean, Boujut, Michel and Daney, Serge, *Cités-Cinés* (Paris: Ramsay/La Villette, 1987)
Douchet, Jean, *French New Wave* (New York: D.A.P., 1999).
Douchet, Jean, *L'Homme cinéma, entretiens avec Joël Magny* (Paris: Ecriture, 2013).
D'Souza, Aruna and McDonough, Tom (eds), *Gender, Public Space and Visual Culture in Nineteenth Century Paris* (Manchester: Manchester University Press, 2008).
Dulong, Renaud, *Les Conditions sociales de l'attestation personnelle. Le Témoin oculaire* (Paris: EHSS, 1998).
Dussault, Eric, *L'Invention de Saint-Germain-des-Prés* (Paris: Vendémiaire, 2014).
Evenson, Norma, *Paris: A Century of Change, 1878–1978* (New Haven, CT: Yale University Press, 1979).
Ezra, Elizabeth, *Jean-Pierre Jeunet* (Urbana and Chicago: University of Illinois Press, 2008).
Fermigier, André, *La Bataille de Paris: des Halles à la Pyramide, chroniques d'urbanisme* (Paris: Gallimard, 1991).
Forbes, Jill, *Les Enfants du paradis* (London: BFI, 1997).
Ford, Charles and Jeanne, René, *Paris vu par le cinéma* (Paris: Hachette, 1969).
Fourastié, Jean, *Les Trente glorieuses ou la révolution invisible* (Paris: Fayard, 1979).
Friedberg, Anne, *Window Shopping: Cinema and the Postmodern* (Berkeley and Los Angeles: University of California Press, 1993).
Frodon, Jean-Michel and Iordanova, Dina (eds), *Cinemas of Paris* (St Andrews: St Andrews Film Studies, 2016).
Gaston-Mathé, Catherine, *La Société française au miroir de son cinéma* (Condé-sur-Noireau: Arléa/Corlet, 1996).
Gauthier, Christophe, *La Passion du cinéma. Cinéphiles, ciné-clubs et salles spécialisées à Paris de 1920 à 1929* (Paris: AFRHC/Ecole de Chartres, 1999).
Geffroy, Gustave, *Charles Meryon* (Paris: H. Floury, 1926).
George, Jocelyne, *Paris Province: de la Révolution à la mondialisation* (Paris: Fayard, 1998).

Gheerbrant, Bernard (ed.), *Baudelaire critique d'art* (Paris: Club des Libraires de France, 1956).

Gillain, Anne (ed.), *Le Cinéma selon François Truffaut* (Paris: Flammarion, 1988).

Gillain, Anne, *François Truffaut: The Lost Secret* (Bloomington and Indianapolis: Indiana University Press, 2013).

Gleber, Anke, *The Art of Taking a Walk* (Princeton, NJ: Princeton University Press, 1999).

Goetschel, Pascale, *Imaginaires urbains du Paris romantique à nos jours* (Paris: Le Manuscrit, 2011).

Gumpert, Lynn (ed.), *The Art of the Everyday. The Quotidien in Postwar French Culture* (New York and London: New York University Press, 1997).

Gundle, Stephen, *Glamour: A History* (Oxford: Oxford University Press, 2008).

Haining, Peter, *The Complete Maigret* (London: Boxtree, 1994).

Hancock, Claire, *Paris et Londres au XIXe siècle: représentations dans les guides et récits de voyage* (Paris: Editions CNRS, 2003).

Harrod, Mary, *From France with Love: Gender and Identity in French Romantic Comedy* (London: I. B. Tauris, 2015).

Harvey, David, *Paris, Capital of Modernity* (London and New York: Routledge, 2005).

Hayward, Susan, *French Costume Drama of the 1950s* (Bristol: Intellect Press, 2010).

Henley, Paul, *The Adventure of the Real. Jean Rouch and the Craft of Ethnographic Cinema* (Chicago, IL: Chicago University Press, 2010).

Herpe, Noël (ed.), *Rohmer et les autres* (Rennes: Presses Universitaires de Rennes, 2007).

Hervé, Lucien, *The Eiffel Tower* (New York: Princeton Architectural Press, 2003).

Higonnet, Patrice, *Paris: Capital of the World* (Cambridge, MA: Harvard University Press, 2002).

Hillairet, Jacques, *Connaissance du vieux Paris*, vol. 1, *Rive Droite* (Paris: Editions Princesse, 1956).

Holmes, Diana. *Romance and Readership in Twentieth-Century France: Love Stories* (Oxford: Oxford University Press, 2006).

Ishizuka, Karen L. and Zimmermann, Patricia R. (eds), *Mining the Home Movie: Excavations in Histories and Memories* (Berkeley: University of California Press, 2008).

Jakubowski, Maxim (ed.), *Following the Detectives: Real Locations in Crime Fiction* (London: New Holland, 2010).

Jeanneney, Jean-Noël and Sauvage, Monique (eds), *Télévision, nouvelle mémoire. Les magazines de grands reportage* (Paris: Seuil/INA, 1982).

Jones, Colin, McDonagh, Josephine and Mee, Jon (eds), *Charles Dickens, the French Revolution and* A Tale of Two Cities (London: Palgrave Macmillan, 2009).

Jonnes, Jill, *Eiffel's Tower: The Thrilling Story behind Paris's Beloved Monument and the Extraordinary World's Fair That Introduced It* (New York: Penguin Books, 2010).

Jordan, David P., *Transforming Paris: The Life and Labors of Baron Haussmann* (New York: Free Press, 1995).

Koeck, Richard and Roberts, Les, *The City and the Moving Image: Urban Projections* (Basingstoke: Palgrave Macmillan, 2010).

Koeck, Richard, *Cine-scapes: Cinematic Spaces in Architecture and Cities* (London and New York: Routledge, 2012).

Latour, Geneviève, *Le 'Cabaret-Théâtre' (1945–1965)* (Paris: Bibliothèque de la Ville de Paris, 1996).

Leeman, Richard and Jannière, Hélène (eds), *Michel Ragon, critique d'art et d'architecture* (Rennes: Presses Universitaires de Rennes, 2013).

Lefebvre, Henri, *Writings on Cities* (Cambridge, MA: Blackwell Publishers, 1996).

Liandrat-Guigues, Suzanne, *Modernes flâneries du cinéma* (Saint Vincent de Mercuze: De l'incidence, 2009).

Louguet, Patrick (ed.), *Rohmer ou le jeu des variations* (Paris: PUV, 2012).

Lucan, Jacques (ed.), *Eau et gaz à tous les étages: Paris 100 ans de logement* (Paris: Editions du Pavillon de l'Arsenal/Picard, 1992).

Marcus, Sharon, *Apartment Stories: City and Home in Nineteenth-Century Paris and London* (Berkeley and Los Angeles: University of California Press, 1999).

Marie, Michel, *The French New Wave: An Artistic School* (Malden, MA: Blackwell Publishing, 2003).

Maspero, François, *Roissy-Express: A Journey through the Paris Suburbs* (London: Verso, 1994).

Mennel, Barbara, *Cities and Cinema* (London and New York: Routledge, 2008).

Meryon, Charles, *Old Paris* (Liverpool: Henry Young & Sons, 1914).

Moine, Raphaëlle, Rollet, Brigitte and Sellier, Geneviève (eds), *Policiers et criminals: un genre populaire européen sur grand et petit écrans* (Paris: L'Harmattan, 2009).

Nadeau, Gilles and Douchet, Jean, *Paris cinéma: une ville vue par le cinéma de 1895 à nos jours* (Paris: Editions du May, 1997).

Naumann, Claude and Buache, Freddy (eds), *Jacques Becker* (Locarno: Editions du Festival International du Film de Locarno, 1991).

Naumann, Claude, *Jacques Becker* (Paris and Courbevoie: BiFi/Durante, 2001).

Neupert, Richard, *A History of French New Wave Cinema* (Madison: University of Wisconsin Press, 2002).

Newsome, W. Brian, *French Urban Planning 1940–1968: The Construction and Deconstruction of an Authoritarian System* (New York: Peter Lang, 2009).

Nora, Pierre, *Realms of Memory: The Construction of the French Past*, vol. 3 (New York: Columbia University Press, 1998).

Orpen, Valerie, *Cléo de 5 à 7* (London and New York: I. B. Tauris, 2007).

Paxton, Robert and Marrus, Michael, *Vichy France and the Jews* (Palo Alto, CA: Stanford University Press, 1995).

Peer, Shanny, *France on Display: Peasants, Provincials, and Folklore in the 1937 Paris World's Fair* (Albany: SUNY Press, 1998).

Penz, François, *Urban Cinematics* (Bristol: Intellect Press, 2012).

Penz, François and Koeck, Richard (eds), *Cinematic Urban Geographies* (Basingstoke: Palgrave Macmillan, 2016).

Phillips, Alastair, *City of Darkness, City of Light. Emigré Filmmakers in Paris 1929–1939* (Amsterdam: Amsterdam University Press, 2004).

Pillard, Thomas, *Le Film noir français face aux bouleversements de la France d'après-guerre (1946–1960)* (Nantes: Editions Joseph K, 2014).

Prendergast, Christopher, *Paris and the Nineteenth Century* (Oxford: Blackwell, 1992).

Rascaroli, Laura and Mazierska, Ewa, *Crossing New Europe: Postmodern Travel and the European Road Movie* (London: Wallflower Press, 2006).

Rearick, Charles, *Paris Dreams, Paris Memories: The City and Its Mystique* (Stanford, CA: Stanford University Press, 2011).

Rice, Shelley, *Parisian Views* (London: MIT Press, 1997).

Rifkin, Adrian, *Street Noises. Parisian Pleasure 1900–1940* (Manchester: Manchester University Press, 1995).

Rioux, Jean-Pierre (ed.), *La Vie culturelle sous Vichy* (Brussels: Complexe, 1990).

Robert, Jean-Louis and Tsikounas, Myriam (eds), *Les Halles: images d'un quartier* (Paris: Publications de la Sorbonne, 2004).

Robic, Sylvie and Schifano, Laurence (eds), *Rohmer en perspectives* (Paris: Presses Universitaires de Paris Ouest, 2013).

Rocamora, Agnès, *Fashioning the City: Paris, Fashion and the Media* (London: I. B. Tauris, 2009).

Ross, Kristin, *Fast Cars, Clean Bodies: Decolonization and the Reordering of French Culture* (Cambridge, MA: MIT Press, 1996).

Rousso, Henry, *The Vichy Syndrome: History and Memory in France since 1944* (Cambridge, MA: Harvard University Press, 1991).

Schlesser, Gilles, *Le Cabaret 'rive gauche'. De la Rose rouge au Bateau ivre (1946–1974)* (Paris: L'Archipel, 2006).

Schneiderman, Robert L., *The Catalogue Raisonné of the Prints of Charles Meryon* (London: Garton & Co., 1990).

Schwartz, Vanessa R., *Spectacular Realities: Early Mass Culture in Fin-de-Siècle Paris* (Berkeley and Los Angeles: University of California Press, 1998).

Schwartz, Vanessa R., *It's So French! Hollywood, Paris and the Making of Cosmopolitan Film Culture* (Chicago, IL: Chicago University Press, 2007).

Sheringham, Michael (ed.), *Parisian Fields* (London: Reaktion Books, 1996).

Sheringham, Michael, *Everyday Life. Theories and Practices from Surrealism to the Present* (Oxford: Oxford University Press, 2006).

Shiel, Mark and Fitzmaurice (eds), *Cinema and the City: Film and Urban Societies in a Global Context* (Oxford: Blackwell, 2001).

Shiel, Mark and Fitzmaurice, Tony (eds), *Screening the City* (London and New York: Verso, 2003).

Shonfield, Katherine, *Walls Have Feelings: Architecture, Film and the City* (London and New York: Routledge, 2000).

Simsi, Simon, *Ciné-Passion. Le guide chiffré du cinéma en France* (Paris: Dixit, 2012).

Singer, Ben, *Melodrama and Modernity. Early Sensational Cinema and Its Contexts* (New York: Columbia University Press, 2001).

Steele, Valerie, *Paris Fashion: A Cultural History* (New York: Oxford University Press, 1988).

Stierle, Karlheinz, *Le Mythe de Paris: La Capitale des signes et son discours* (Paris: Editions de la Maison des Sciences de l'Homme, 2001).

Tarr, Carrie, *Reframing Difference, Beur and Banlieue Filmmaking in France* (Manchester: Manchester University Press, 2005).

Tester, Keith, *The Flâneur* (London and New York: Routledge, 1994).

Texier, Simon, *Paris contemporain* (Paris: Parigramme, 2005).

Trihoreau, Michel, *La Chanson de proximité. Caveaux, cabarets et autres petits lieux* (Paris: L'Harmattan, 2010).

Tsikounas, Myriam (ed.), *Imaginaires urbains du Paris romantique à nos jours* (Paris: Editions Le Manuscrit, 2011).

Tweedie, James, *The Age of New Waves: Art Cinema and the Staging of Globalization* (Oxford: Oxford University Press, 2013).

Ungar, Steven, *Cléo de 5 à 7* (London: BFI, 2008).

Uzanne, Octave, *Parisiennes de ce temps en leurs divers milieux, états et conditions* (Paris: Mercure de France, 1910).

Vanderschelden, Isabelle, *Amelie* (London and Chicago, IL: I. B. Tauris, 2007).

Vignaux, Valérie, *Jacques Becker ou l'exercice de la liberté* (Liège: Editions du Céfal, 2000).

Vincendeau, Ginette, *French Cinema in the 1930s. Texts and Contexts of a Popular Entertainment Medium* (UEA: Unpublished PhD thesis, 1985).

Vincendeau, Ginette, *La Haine* (London: I. B. Tauris, 2005).

Vincent, Marie-Christine and de Saint-Exupéry, François, *Paris vu au cinéma* (Paris: Nimrod, 2003).

Wagner, David-Alexandre, *De la banlieue stimatisée à la cité démystifiée: la représentation de la banlieue des grands ensembles dans le cinéma français de 1981 à 2005* (Bern: Peter Lang, 2011).

Wakeman, Rosemary, *The Heroic City: Paris, 1945–1958* (Chicago, IL, and London: University of Chicago Press, 2009).

Wallace, Lee, *Lesbianism, Cinema and Space: The Sexual Life of Apartments* (New York: Routledge/Taylor and Francis, 2008).

Webber, Andrew and Wilson, Emma (eds), *Cities in Transition* (London: Wallflower Press, 2008).

White, Edmund, *The Flâneur: A Stroll through the Paradoxes of Paris* (London: Bloomsbury, 2001).

Willemen, Paul, *Looks and Frictions: Essays in Cultural Studies and Film Theory* (Bloomington: Indiana University Press, 1994).

Wilson, Elizabeth, *The Sphinx in the City: Urban Life, the Control of Disorder, and Women* (London: Virago, 1991).

Wojcik, Pamela Robertson, *The Apartment Plot: Urban Living in American Film and Popular Culture, 1945 to 1975* (Durham, NC: Duke University Press, 2010).

Zuccotti, Susan, *The Holocaust, the French, and the Jews* (New York: Basic Books, 1993).

Index

A bout de souffle/Breathless, 2, 46, 67, 68, 72, 73, 118, 235
A la découverte des Français ('Exploring the French'), 223, 226
Achache, Mona, 147, 152–153
Actualités françaises, Les, 221
Adieu Philippine, 67
Adorables créatures, 169
Agathe Cléry, 150
AJYM Films, 45
Alessandrin, Patrick, 89
Ali au pays des mirages/Ali in Wonderland, 234
Alien: Resurrection, 258
Allégret, Marc, 171
Allen, Woody, 11, 157, 159
Alphaville, 67–68, 71–73
'already said, the', 163
Alves, Ruben, 147
Amants de Bras-Mort, Les/The Lovers of Bras-Mort, 39–40
Amants du Pont-Neuf, Les/The Lovers on the Bridge, 11
Amateur Club of French Filmmakers, 140
Amateur filmmaking, 136–145
Ambassadeurs, Les/The Ambassadors, 234
American Cinematographer magazine, 261
American in Paris, An, 2
Ami de mon amie, L'/Boyfriends and Girlfriends, 88
Amour, 150
Amour à la mer, L'/Love at Sea, 67, 68, 72
Amour en fuite, L'/Love on the Run, 70

Amour existe, L', 68
Amour et turbulences, 160, 161
Amours d'Astrée et de Céladon, Les/The Romance of Astrea and Celadon, 53
anachronisms, 78
ancien régime, 167
Andrew, Dudley, 2, 3
Angel A, 263
Anna Karenina, 39, 153
Année suivante, L', 90
anonymous spaces, 162–164
Antechamber of the Palais de Justice, 189
Antoine et Antoinette, 207–215
Antoine et Colette, 66, 67, 70, 73
Apache, 90
apartments, Parisian, 55–65
Après mai/There's Something in the Air, 93–94
Aragon, Louis, 6
Arc de Triomphe, 91, 133, 141
Archer, Neil, 160
archives, cinematographic/film, 243–244
Arnoux, Alexandre, 31
Arpète, L', 148
arrondissements, 9, 87
Art d'abattre les vieux immeubles, L' ('The Art of Knocking Down Old Buildings'), 221
Arts, 208
ASC (American Society of Cinematographers), 188
Ascenseur pour l'échafaud/Lift to the Scaffold, 131
Assayas, Olivier, 93
Assommoir, L', 30
Astruc, Alexandre, 235

Atget, Eugène, 6, 231, 265n5
Au bonheur des dames, 175n11
Aubert, M., 139
Audiard, Jacques, 11, 89
Audry, Jacqueline, 133
Augé, Marc, 1, 161, 163
Au pan coupé/Wall Engravings, 73
Avengers, The, 110
Aymé, Marcel, 31

Backes, S., 142
Baczko, Bronisław, 31
badaud (bystander), 231
Baecque, Antoine de, 3, 117
Bah, K., 142
Baisers volés/Stolen Kisses, 70, 235
Baltard, Victor, 247
Balzac, Honoré de, 28, 230
Bande à part/Band of Outsiders, 88
Bande de filles/Girlhood, 7, 24, 92–93
Bandera, La, 29
Banlieue, Parisian, 87–99
banlieusard, 87, 89–94
Baratier, Jacques, 35, 71, 88
Bardot, Brigitte, 7, 133, 170–171
Barnaby Rudge, 181
Barouh, Pierre, 234
Barrot, Olivier, 148
Barsacq, Léon, 3
Barthes, Roland, 17, 114
Bas, Frédéric, 42, 44
Bastille Day/The Take, 11
Bastille prison, 183
Baudelaire, Charles, 1, 5–7, 187, 192, 231
Baume, Freddy, 35

INDEX

Bazgan, Nicoleta, 9, 17, 133, 164
Bazin, André, 45, 116–118, 208
Beauregard, Georges de, 53
Beau Serge, Le, 45
Beauvoir, Simone de, 116
Becker, Jacques, 35, 168, 207–217
Bedlam, 189
Bel-Ami, 175n11
Belkacem, Areski, 234
Belle de jour, 171, 172
Belle Epoque, 166–168, 170, 175n16
Belle équipe, La/They Were Five, 88
Bellon, Yannick, 236
Belmondo, Jean-Paul, 67
Bengal Tiger, The, 116
Benjamin, Walter, 1, 56–57, 188
Bensalah, Djamel, 89
Benyamina, Houda, 93
Bérénice, 45
Berlioz, Hector, 192
Bernard, Paul, 89
Bernard-Aubert, Claude, 68
Berne, Édouard, 37
Berthomieu, André, 36
Bertolucci, Bernardo, 160
Besson, Luc, 263
Betz, Mark, 125
Beur sur la ville, 89
Bibliothèque du Cinéma François Truffaut, 247
Bibliothèque Historique de la Ville de Paris (BHVP)/Historical Library of the City of Paris, 243–244
Binh, N. T., 2, 36
Bison (et sa voisine Dorine), Le, 147, 152–153
Blondin, Antoine, 116
Bluebeard, 187–189
Bob le flambeur, 148
Bogdanovich, Peter, 187, 189, 193, 194n2
Boig, Ph., 142
Boileau, Nicolas, 232
Boisrond, Michel, 133
Boîte de nuit/Hotbed of Sin, 40
Bolloré, Vincent, 120
Bonello, Bertrand, 11
Bonheur, Le/Happiness, 88
Bonnes femmes, Les/The Good Time Girls, 132
Borowczyk, Walerian, 236

Bosch, Roselyne, 197, 201
Bosséno, Christian-Marc, 115
Boubat, Edouard, 147
Boudu sauvé des eaux/Boudu Saved from Drowning, 51, 208
Boukhrief, Nicolas, 11
Boulangère de Monceau, La/The Girl at the Monceau Bakery, 50, 53
Boum sur Paris/Rendezvous in Paris, 41
Bourget, Jean-Loup, 8, 9, 187
Boussat, M., 142
Boussinot, Roger, 198
Boyer, Jean, 36
Boyer, P., 142–143
Branque, B., 142
Brassai, 6
Breniaux, F., 142
Bressy, D., 142
Brisseau, Jean-Claude, 89
Brucker, Alex, 120
Brundson, Charlotte, 4, 10, 103, 207
Bruno, Giuliana, 126
Building sites, 230–241
Buñuel, Luis, 172–173, 233
Butte à la Reine, La, 224

Ça va ça vient/It Comes, It Goes, 234
Cabarets, 42. *See also* caves of Saint-Germain-des-Prés
Cacoyannis, Michael, 225
Cage dorée, La, 147, 151
Cahiers du cinéma, 45, 53, 54n13, 74n5, 114–117, 120, 208
Camion, Le/The Lorry, 88
Camus, D., 142
Cannes Film Festival (1959), 45
Canonge, Maurice de, 41
Canudo, Ricciotto, 114
Carax, Leos, 11
Carco, Francis, 30, 33, 43n13
Cargaison clandestine/Alarm in San Juano, 40
Carlyle, Thomas, 181
Carné, Marcel, 2, 9, 26–34, 88, 132, 148, 187–188, 264
Carol, Martine, 169
Caroline chérie/Dear Caroline, 169

Carrefour de la Butte-aux-Cailles, Le ('The Butte-aux-Cailles), 220
Carrière, Jean-Claude, 233
Carrière de Suzanne, La/Suzanne's Career, 53, 70
Casque d'or, 168, 208 Causse, J. P., 140
Cavalier, Alain, 67
caves of Saint-Germain-des-Prés, 35–44
Céline, Louis-Ferdinand, 146
cellars. *See* caves of Saint-Germain-des-Prés
central districts, Rohmer's documentary portrayal of, 45
centralism, French, 231
Certeau, Michel de, 1
C'est la vie...parisienne/It's the Paris Life, 36, 40–41
C'est le bouquet!, 150
Chaban-Delmas, Jacques, 219, 224
Chabrol, Claude, 55, 72, 118, 132, 148
Chacun cherche son chat/When the Cat's Away, 11
Chagall, Marc, 73
Chambre 12, Hôtel de Suède, 67
Champs-Elysées, 138, 158, 235
Le Chanois, Jean-Paul, 88, 149
chanson, disappearance of, 33
Chanteuse in the City, 3
Chapelle, La, 29–30
Chaplin, Charlie, 113
Charef, Mehdi, 89
Charhon, David, 87
Charlet, A., 142
Charlotte et son Jules/Charlotte and Her Boyfriend, 73
Charrier, Jacques, 130
Chartin, L., 142
chase comedy, 41
Chat, Le, 88
Chatiliez, Etienne, 150
Chéret, Jules, posters by, 167
Cherry, Marc, 96
Chevalier, Louis, 29
Chevalier, Maurice, 3
Chibane, Malik, 89
Chirac, Jacques, 242
Chirat, Raymond, 148
Christian-Jacque, 168–169
Chronique d'un été/Chronicle of a Summer, 132

ciné-clubs, 113, 115
Ciné-Latin, 114
Cinéma, 116
cinéma beur, 89
Cinémathèque Française, 113, 115
Cinematographic Department of the City of Paris, 244
Cinéma Vérité, 132
Cinémonde, 37
cinephile culture, 113–124
cinéphobes, 114
'cine-tourism', 248
Cinq colonnes à la une ('Front-page Headlines'), 219, 220
Cirque, Le, 73
Cité des enfants perdus, La/City of Lost Children, 261
City of Light, Paris as, 181
City of Love, Paris as, 156, 157
Clair, René, 2, 17–20, 29, 148
Clara et moi, 161–162
Clark, Catherine E., 1, 8, 10, 13, 76, 228, 241, 248
Cléo de 5 à 7/Cleo from 5 to 7, 4, 7, 67, 125–135
Clockers, 96
Clouzot, Henri-Georges, 133, 148
Cluny-Cinéma, 114
CNRS (National Centre for Scientific Research), 223
Coeur de lilas/Lilac, 32
Cohen, Evelyne, 219, 222
Coing, Henri, 224
Collectionneuse, La/The Collector, 53
Colombier, Pierre, 148
Combat dans l'île, Le, 67
comedies of ethnic integration, 151
Commission for Historical Paris, 243
Companeez, Jacques, 40
concierges, 146–155
Concierge, Le, 147
Conway, Kelley, 3
Côte d'Azur, 53
Cottafavi, Vittorio, 117, 118
couleur du temps, 85n35
Coup du berger, Le/ Checkmate, 55
Cousins, Les, 45, 118, 148

Crime de Monsieur Lange, Le/ The Crime of Monsieur Lange, 2
Critique of Everyday Life, 209
Czajka, Isabelle, 90

Daguerre, Louis-Jacques-Mandé, 28
daguerreotype, invention of, 28
Daguerréotypes, 127
Dame aux camélias, La, 167
Damnation de Faust, La, 192
Daney, Serge, 118
Dans les rues/Song of the Streets, 32
Dans Paris, 11
danse macabre, 198
dark realism, 26
Daumier, Honoré, 146
Davies, Rupert, 110
Da Vinci Code, The, 248
De battre mon coeur s'est arrêté/The Beat That My Heart Skipped, 11
De bruit et de fureur/Sound and Fury, 89
de Gaulle, Charles, 218, 219, 222
De l'autre côté du lit/On the Other Side of the Bed, 94–96
De l'autre côté du périph'/ On the Other Side of the Tracks, 87, 89
Debord, Guy, 1
Décalage horaire/Jet Lag, 161
Défense business district, 231
Delannoy, Jean, 8
Deleyto, Celestino, 156
Delicatessen, 258
Delluc, Louis, 114
Delpy, Julie, 158
DeMille, Cecil B., 113, 117
Deneuve, Catherine, 7, 83n3, 85n35, 170–174
Denis, Claire, 11
Déon, Michel, 116
dépaysement, 163
Derens, Jean, 42
Dernière sortie avant Roissy/ Last Exit before Roissy, 89
Dernier Métro, Le/The Last Metro, 172
Desanges, Chantal, 137
Deshayes, Th., 142
Desperate, 96

Détective, 68
Detour, 187
Deux ou trois choses que je sais d'elle/Two or Three Things I Know about Her, 71–73, 89
Dheepan, 89, 96
Dhibou, Rachid, 89
Dickens, Charles, 179–186
Dieterle, William, 189
Dîner de cons, Le/The Dinner Game, 19
District 13: Ultimatum, 89
Divines, 93
Divorce, Le, 158–160
documentary, 10, 17, 19, 24, 35, 38, 42, 45–46, 49, 67, 87, 88, 125, 127, 130, 132, 133, 136–140, 143, 187, 201, 211, 218–229, 244, 245, 251
Doisneau, Robert, 6, 146, 147
Domicile conjugal/Bed and Board, 57, 67
Donatien, 148
Donen, Stanley, 3, 17, 157
Doniol-Valcroze, Jacques, 55
Douchet, Jean, 1–3, 42, 68
Dragées au poivre/Sweet and Sour, 71
Dragueurs, Les/The Chasers, 130
drowning theme, 191
Dubosc, P., 143
Du côté de chez Swann/ Swann's Way, 193
Du côté de Robinson/Robinson Place, 70
Dugowson, Maurice, 234
Dumas, Alexandre (fils), 167
Durand, A., 141
Durandelle, Louis-Emile, 231
Duras, Marguerite, 88
Dussollier, André, 142
Duvivier, Julien, 21, 29, 88, 248
Dwan, Allan, 117

eastern territories, 29–30
Eaux-fortes sur Paris/Etchings on Paris, 188
Echo des carreaux, L'/The Echo of Windows, 143
Eco, Umberto, 163
Ecole des cocottes, L', 148
Ecole Nationale d'Administration (ENA), 226
Ecran français, L', 37, 208

INDEX

Ecume des jours, L'/Blue Indigo, 82
Educational Cinématheque of the City of Paris, 244
Edwards, Blake, 117
Eiffel Tower, 17–25, 25n8, 141, 157–160, 183, 186n22, 202
Elle court, elle court, la banlieue/The Suburbs Are Everywhere, 89
Elsaesser, Thomas, 163, 165n27
Embarras de Paris, Les, 232
Emmanuel, Pierre, 136, 142, 242, 249
Empreinte/The Mark, 142
Enfants du paradis, Les/ Children of Paradise, 27
Enfer du décor, L' ('Stage-set from Hell'), 226
Enrico, Jérôme, 92
Erdody, Leo, 192
Ere industrielle, L': métamorphoses du paysage/Changing Landscapes, 237
Eric Rohmer, *Le Signe du lion/The Sign of Leo* and, 42–52
Esmery, Alain, 137–138
Espace Cousteau, 247
Espace Photographique de Paris, 247
Espaces verts, Les ('Green Spaces'), 226
Esquive, L'/Games of Love and Chance, 89
Estevez, L., 138
Et Dieu ... créa la femme/And God Created Woman, 170
Etaix, Pierre, 232
Etat des lieux/Inner City, 89
ethnic integration, comedies of, 151
Eustache, Jean, 70
everyday life, 207–217
Evreinoff, Nicolas, 148
existentialism, 35, 37
Exposition coloniale de 1937, L', 139

Fabre, Michel, 114
Fabuleux destin d'Amélie Poulain, Le/Amélie, 9, 146, 150–151, 160–162, 248, 257–258, 260–263
Fairfaix, Danny, 120

Fais pas ci, fais pas ça, 94
Falbalas, 208
Fantôme de la liberté, Le/The Phantom of Liberty, 233
Faucon, Philippe, 90
Faust (Gounod), 188, 192, 193
Faust (Murnau), 192
F comme Fairbanks/F as in Fairbanks, 234
Femme d'à côté, La/The Woman Next Door, 63
Femme de Jean, La/Jean's Wife, 236
Femmes de Paris, 146
Femmes du 6e étage, Les/The Women on the 6th Floor, 151
Ferreri, Marco, 10, 76–86, 238, 248
Fête de l'Humanité 1970, 141
Feu follet, Le/The Fire Within, 71, 73
Fiancés du pont MacDonald, Les, 129
Filliou, Robert, 230
film de banlieue, 88–97. *See also* banlieue
film noir, 26–34
Films du Losange, Les, 53
Finger, Blanche, 202
flânerie, 6, 8, 11, 50, 54n12, 63, 66, 125–126, 128, 131, 163, 165n19, 179, 181
flâneur, 2, 5–7, 10, 74, 103, 125, 126, 161, 163, 188, 207, 213, 214, 257
flâneuse, 2, 125–128, 130, 134
Flitterman-Lewis, Sandy, 9, 125, 127, 129, 196
Florey, Robert, 192
Fontaine, Anne, 90, 150
Forbes, Jill, 30
Ford, John, 117
Forum des Images, 136, 142–144, 231, 240n9, 242–253
Foujita, Leonard Tsuguharu, 65n39
Fourcaut, Annie, 87
Fox, Alistair, 4, 9, 10, 55, 56, 64, 75, 98
France, la vie des soldats allemands/France, the Life of German Soldiers, 141

France défigurée, La ('Disfigured France'), 224
François Truffaut, 142
Franju, Georges, 113
Freda, Riccardo, 117, 118
Frémontier, Jacques, 225–226
French Cancan, 168–169
French centralism, 231
French film noir, 26–34
French Kiss, 157–161, 163
French New Wave, 3–4, 6, 19, 45, 51, 55–56, 59–61, 66–75, 75n5, 125, 208
French Radio and Television Office (ORTF), 219
Frères Jacques, 38
Freund, Karl, 192
Friedberg, Anne, 1, 126
Fromkess, Leon, 187
Fuller, Samuel, 117
Funny Face, 3, 17, 157

Gaimard, Marie, 7, 8, 9, 10, 230, 253
Galeries Lafayette, 260
Garbarz, Franck, 36
Garcia, Nicole, 172
Gare d'Austerlitz, 259
Gare d'Orsay, 259
Gare de l'Est, 143
Gare du Nord, 143
'Gare du Nord', in *Paris vu par.../Six in Paris,* 132
Gaspards, Les/The Down-in-the-Hole Gang, 82, 232–233
Gastambide, Franck, 89
Gaston-Mathé, Catherine, 40
Gauthier, Christophe, 114
Gégauff, Paul, 45
Genestal, Fabrice, 90
Génie de Paris, Le/The Spirit of Paris, 143
Gens de Paris, Les ('the people of Paris'), 208
Ghorab-Volta, Zaida, 90
Gigi, 3
Gilles, Guy, 67, 68
Gilson, René, 208
Girault, Jean, 147
Gleber, Anke, 6
Godard, Jean-Luc, 2, 67, 68, 70, 71, 73, 74, 88, 89, 118, 132, 235
Goetschel, Pascale, 35
Goldenberg, Daniel, 232

Gondry, Michel, 82, 248
Gordan, Michael, 58
Goscinny, René, 233
Gounod, Charles, 188, 192
Grand Café, 1, 113, 114
Grande bouffe, La, 76
Grand partage, Le, 154
Granier-Deferre, Pierre, 88
Grande lessive (!), La, 148
Griffith, D. W., 113
Guadissart, V., 143
Guichets du Louvre, Les/Black Thursday, 197–199
Gundle, Stephen, 7, 8, 166
Gunning, Tom, 6

Habits rouges, Les/Red Outfits, 142
Haine/Hate, La, 19, 87, 89–91, 157
Halal police d'état, 89
Hallam, Julia, 157
Halles, Les, 76–86, 139, 221, 224, 231, 235–236, 238, 247–248, 259–260
Halles centrales, Les, 248
Haneke, Michael, 150
Hanoun, Marcel, 70
Harris, Sue, 3, 173
Harrod, Mary, 8, 98, 156, 164, 165
Haussmann, Georges-Eugène (Baron), 5, 181
Hawks, Howard, 114
Hayward, Susan, 168
Hélian, Jacques, 37
Hepp, Noémi, 167
Herbuveaux, Georges, 251
Herpe, Noël, 117
Hérisson, Le/The Hedgehog, 147, 152–153
Hexagone, 89
Hiroshima mon amour, 46
Histoires d'amour finissent mal … en général, Les/Love Affairs Usually End Badly, 90
historical genre, 170
Historical Library of the City of Paris (Bibliothèque Historique de la Ville de Paris, BHVP), 243–244
Hitchcock, Alfred, 114, 117, 118, 120, 234
'Hitchcocko-Hawksians', 115, 120
Hollande, François, 197

Hollywood, Parisian representation of classical era of, 3
Holy Motors, 11
Homme qui aimait les femmes, L'/The Man Who Loved Women, 62
'Homme qui vendit la tour Eiffel, L', 72
Honoré, Christophe, 11
hotels, in French New Wave films, 66–75
Hôtel Bossuet, 70
Hôtel de l'Europe, 67
Hôtel de l'Observatoire, 70
Hôtel de l'Orient, 71
Hôtel de Senlis, 68
Hôtel de Suède, 67–68
Hôtel des Saisons, 72
Hôtel du Nord, 26, 31, 248
Hôtel du Pas de Calais, 68
Hôtel Scribe, 71
Hôtel Trianon Palace, 72
Huet, A., 141
Hugo, Victor, 28, 90, 189, 191
humanist photography, 147
Humphrey, William, 182
Hunchback of Notre Dame, The, 189
Hunebelle, André, 147
Hunger Games: Mockingjay Part 2, The, 96
Huth, James, 95

Ile de la Cité, 189, 191, 193
Image et son, 116
image-ideas, 31
Impasse des deux anges/Dilemma of Two Angels, 236
Impossible Monsieur Pipelet, L', 147
Impressionist rendering of Paris, 6
Ince, Thomas H., 113
Indian Tomb, The, 116
INHA 'Paris au cinéma' conference, 1
Innocents of Paris, 3
Institut National de l'Audiovisuel (INA; National Audiovisual Institute), 242
intra-muros city, 87
Ionascu, M., 142
Ivory, James, 160

J'ai faim!!!, 147, 152
J'ai pas sommeil/I Can't Sleep, 11
J'irai baver dans votre bière/I Slobber in Your Beer, 37
Janine, 70
Jannière, Hélène, 8, 9, 10, 218, 228, 229, 241
Jardin des Plantes, 212
Jardinier d'Argenteuil, Le/The Gardener of Argenteuil, 88
Jenny, 31
Jermyn, Deborah, 156–157
Jeunesse dorée, 90
Jeunet, Jean-Pierre, 9–11, 146, 151, 160, 248, 257–265
Je vais te manquer, 161–162
Jolivet, Pierre, 148
Jones, Colin, 8, 179, 185
Jost, François, 96
Journal d'un scélérat/Diary of a Scoundrel, 45
Jour se lève, Le/Daybreak, 2, 32, 148
Jouventin, D., 142
Jules et Jim, 70
Julie Lescaut, 94

Kaïras/Porn in the Hood, Les, 89
Kané, Pascal, 120
Karel, William, 202
Kasdan, Lawrence, 157–159
Kassovitz, Mathieu, 19, 87, 89, 157
Kaufman, Boris, 248
Kechiche, Abdellatif, 89
Kessler, S., 142
Kirsanoff, Dimitri, 26
Klapisch, Cédric, 11
Kosma, Joseph, 32
Krakovitch, Olga, 195n19
Krawczyk, Gérard, 17
Krier, Jacques, 223, 226
Krutnik, Frank, 157
Ktari, Naceur, 234

Labrune, Jeanne, 150
Lâches vivent d'espoir, Les/My Baby is Black!, 68
Lack, Roland-François, 4, 9, 10, 48, 49, 66, 74, 75, 97
Lafay Plan, 219
Lagny, Michèle, 212
Landmarks, 9, 130

INDEX

Lang, Fritz, 115, 116, 118, 188
Langlois, Henri, 113
Larkin, Philip, 109
Last Tango in Paris, 160
Latin Quarter, 189
Laurent, Jacques, 116
Lauwe, Paul-Henry Chombart de, 223
La Villette basin, 27, 30
Lawrence, Francis, 96
Layerle, Sébastien, 9, 35, 216
Leclère, Alexandra, 154
Lee, Spike, 96
Lefebvre, Henri, 1, 209
Left Bank, 35–39, 41, 42, 114, 132, 196, 211, 212
Le Guay, Philippe, 151
Legrand, Michel, 88
Leiris, Michel, 208
Lépinay, Jean-Yves de, 1, 9, 10, 144, 228, 239, 241, 242
Lettres françaises, Les, 116
Liandrat-Guigues, Suzanne, 66
Libération of Paris, 140, 251
Liberty Belle, 120
Ligne de mire, La/Line of Sight, 45
Lion volatil, Le, 129
Litvak, Anatole, 32
Locataire, Le/The Tenant, 82
Locataire diabolique, Le/The Devilish Tenant, 148
Logeuse, La, 142
Lorenz, H., 141
Losey, Joseph, 115, 117–118, 197, 199
Lourcelles, Jacques, 114, 117
Louvre Pyramid, 263
Love, Actually, 161
lovers, Parisian. *See* romcom (romantic comedy)
Lubitsch, Ernst, 3, 157
Luce, Maximilien, 231
Lumière Brothers, 17
Lunch on the Eiffel Tower, 19

M, 188
Madhouse, The, 189
Ma nuit chez Maud/My Night with Maud, 53
Ma petite entreprise, 148
Machado, Juarez, 262, 265n11
Mac-Mahon, 113–124
'Mac-Mahoniens', 120
'Mac-Mahonisme', 115
Made in France, 11

Mad Love, 192
Maigret (BBC television), 103–112, 150
Maigret tend un piège/Maigret Sets a Trap, 8
Main, Elizabeth, 148
Maisant, L., 139
Maison des Associations, 247
Maison des Conservatoires, 247
Mandarin et marabout, Le/The Mandarin and the Witch Doctor, 142
Malle, Louis, 19, 22–24, 71, 131
Manet, Édouard, 6
Mankiewicz, Joseph L., 117
Manon Lescaut, 39
Marcus, Sharon, 57
Marge, La/The Streetwalker, 236
Marie, Michel, 4, 8, 9, 10, 42, 45
Marien, Mary Warner, 28
Married to the Eiffel Tower, 24
Marshment, Margaret, 157
Marville, Charles, 6, 231
Masard, Emile, 243
Ma 6-T va crack-er, 89, 97
Matuszewski, Boleslas, 243
Maupassant, Guy de, 167, 175n11
Maurois, André, 146, 147
Médiathèque Musicale de Paris, 247
Méliès, Georges, 148
Mélodie en sous-sol/Any Number Can Win, 88
Melville, Jean-Pierre, 148
memory, 31, 40, 113, 138–139, 143, 144, 167, 174, 196–197, 221, 223–225, 231, 242–253, 257, 263, 264
Ménilmontant district, destruction of, 26, 222–223
Menschen am Sonntag/People on Sunday, 187
Mépris, Le/Contempt, 118
Meryon, Charles, 8, 10, 187–195
Méthode, La, 116
Michell, Roger, 11
Mic-macs à tire larigot/Micmacs, 258, 260–262

'Midi-Minuistes', 115
Midnight in Paris, 11, 158
Mimran, Hervé, 90
Ministère de la marine, Le/The Admiralty, 188
Minnelli, Vincente, 2, 3
Miroir du cinéma, 116
Misérables, Les, 90, 191, 194n15
Mists of Regret, 2
Mitrani, Michel, 197–199
Mitterrand, François, 196–197
Mocky, Jean-Pierre, 130, 148
Modern-Hôtel, 66–67
Mohamed Dubois, 89
Moine, Raphaëlle, 7, 8, 9, 106, 148
Molière, 152
Monde, Le, 1, 77, 149
Mon oncle, 148, 251
Mon pire cauchemar/My Worst Nightmare, 150
Monsieur Klein/Mr. Klein, 197–201, 203
Montmartre, 30, 147, 183, 202, 235, 258–259
'Montmartre, Murder in' (Maigret episode, BBC television), 107–108
Montparnasse tower, 231
Moonfleet, 118
Morel, Pierre, 89
Morgenstern, Madeleine, 60
Morgue, La/The Mortuary, 191
Morin, Ch., 143
Morin, Edgar, 132
Mort à Vignole/Death in Vignole, 138
Moulin Rouge, 169
Mourlet, Michel, 114, 116–118
Moussinac, Léon, 114
Mouton, Janice, 125
'Murder in Montmartre' (*Maigret au Picratt's*), 107–108
Murders in the Rue Morgue, 191–192
Murnau, F. W., 192
Musée des Martyrs de Paris, 247
Musée du Rock, 247
Mystère de la Tour Eiffel, Le/The Mystery of the Eiffel Tower, 21
Mystères des Paris, Les, 146
'Mystery of Marie Rogêt, The', 187, 191, 195n12

Nadeau, Gilles, 1, 2
Nadja à Paris/Nadja in Paris, 53
Nakache, Géraldine, 90
Nana, 169
Nanty, Isabelle, 147
Nathalie Granger, 88
National Centre for Scientific Research (CNRS), 223
Naumann, Claude, 208, 210, 213
neo-noir cinema, 158
Neuville, Charles, 142
newsreels, 139
New Wave. *See* French New Wave
New York, US romcoms in, 157
Nimier, Roger, 116
Ninotchka, 3, 157
Nocturama, 11
Nogent, Eldorado du Dimanche, 88
non-place, in romcom, 162–164
Nora, Pierre, 242
Norman, Barry, 107
Nos oeuvres en 1931/Our Good Works in 1931, 140
Notorious, 120
Notre-Dame cathedral, 47, 183, 189, 191
Notre-Dame de Paris, 28
Nous irons à Paris/We Will All Go to Paris, 36
Nuits de la pleine lune, Les/Full Moon in Paris, 88

Odin, Roger, 1, 10, 136, 145, 253
Offenbach, Jacques, 41
on location, shooting, 56
Ona, Ernesto, 89
162 Avenue d'Italie, 142
Opéra Garnier, 231, 259
Opéra-Mouffe, L'/Diary of a Pregnant Woman, 126, 127, 130
Opération 'Vent Printanier', 202
Ophuls, Marcel, 204
Ophuls, Max, 168, 187, 266
Mac Orlan, Pierre, 29, 30
Orpen, Valerie, 125
ORTF. *See* French Radio and Television Office
Orwell, George, 180
Oskeritzian, Mathilde, 144
Oury, Gérard, 148
Ozon, François, 96, 160

Pagliero, Marcello, 36, 37, 39
Paisan, 42
Panorama pendant l'ascension de la Tour Eiffel/Panorama during the Ascent of the Eiffel Tower, 17
Paris, 11
Paris City Council, 247
Paris des années 30 filmé par des cinéastes amateurs belges, Le/Paris of the 1930s Filmed by Belgian Amateur Filmmakers, 141
Paris gris, Paris rose/Grey Paris, Pink Paris, 251
Paris 1900, 17
Paris nous appartient/Paris Belongs to Us, 3, 45, 55, 68, 69, 73, 131
Paris qui dort/The Crazy Ray, 17, 20–21
Paris Vidéothèque, 136, 137
Paris vu par …/Six in Paris, 42, 50, 132
Paris, je t'aime, 18
Parisian suburbs. *See* banlieue
Parisienne, La, 142–143
Parisienne (female inhabitant of Paris), 7, 8, 10, 143, 166–176
Parisiennes, Les/Tales of Paris, 171–172
Parisiens, 143
Par le trou de la serrure/What Happened: The Inquisitive Janitor, 148
Pas sur la bouche/Not on the Lips, 148, 151
Passy, 59
Paulette, 92, 93, 96
pavillons, 88
Peau douce, La/The Soft Skin, 55, 58–63, 71
Peine de mort pour une prison/Death Penalty for a Prison, 139
Penz, François, 130
Perec, Georges, 138, 146
Père Goriot, Le, 28
périphérique ring road, 9, 87, 231, 249
Perrot, Victor, 243
Peslouan, Hervé de, 37
Petites filles modèles, Les/Good Little Girls, 45
Petit Pont, Le, 189–191

Petits matins, Les/Hitch-Hike, 133, 134
Phillips, Alastair, 1–3, 7, 8, 169, 207
photogénie, 114, 122n8
Pialat, Maurice, 68, 70
Pigalle quartier, 43n10, 58, 158, 197, 215
Pigalle-Saint-Germain-des-Prés, 36–38
Pillard, Thomas, 7, 9, 26, 216, 265
Pillow Talk, 58
Piotrowska, Agnieszka, 24
Pirès, Gérard, 89
'Place de l'Etoile', 232
Place Vendôme, 172
Playtime, 233
Plus belles escroqueries du monde, Les/The World Most Beautiful Swindlers, 72
Plus vieux métier du monde, Le/The Oldest Profession, 71
Poe, Edgar Allan, 187, 191, 195n12
poetic realism, 2, 26, 33, 147, 160, 205n21
Polanski, Roman, 82
politique des auteurs, 114, 115, 117
Pollet, Jean-Daniel, 45, 70
Pompidou, Georges, 219, 220, 240n20
Pompidou Centre, 77, 139
Pont-au-change, Le, 188
Pont Neuf, 212, 259
Pont-Neuf, Le, 189
Portes de la nuit, Les/Gates of the Night, 9, 26–34
Porte des Lilas/The Gates of Paris, 148
Portrait de Marianne/Portrait of Marianne, Le, 232
Positif, 116
post-war noir, 26–34
Pottier, Richard, 169
Pouzadoux, Pascale, 94–95
Powrie, Phil, 35
Preminger, Otto, 116, 118
Présence du cinema, 114, 117, 118, 120
Prévert, Jacques, 26, 27, 30, 32, 260, 261
Proie pour l'ombre, La/Shadows of Adultery, 235
prostitutes, 5, 32, 40, 58, 70–72, 78, 89, 126, 132, 236

INDEX

Proust, Marcel, 193
Punition, La/The Punishment, 74, 132

Quai des brumes, Le/Port of Shadows, 188
Quai d'Orsay/The French Minister, 11
quartiers, 9, 57
Quatorze juillet/July 14, 148
Quatre cents coups, Les/The 400 Blows, 17, 45, 55, 58–59, 61, 70, 73
Queneau, Raymond, 38
Quentin, Florence, 147

Rachedi, Ahmed, 234
Radner, Hilary, 4, 9, 10, 55, 65, 75, 98
Radway, Janice, 161
Rafle, La/The Roundup, 197, 201–203
Ratopolis, 142
Rear Window, 58, 234
Rearick, Charles, 167, 170
Règle du jeu, La/The Rules of the Game, 19, 61, 72
Reichelt, Franz, 19
Reilhac, Michel, 247
Rendez-vous de juillet/Rendezvous in July, 35, 41, 207, 211–215
Renoir, Claude, 237
Renoir, Jean, 2, 19, 51, 61, 72, 168, 208
Rénovation urbaine, La ('Urban Renewal'), 225–226
Réseau Express Régional (RER), 231
Resnais, Alain, 46, 151
Rice, Shelley, 28
Richet, Jean-François, 89
Rimsky, Nicolas, 148
Rissient, Pierre, 114, 118
Rivette, Jacques, 1, 3, 45, 55, 68–69, 74, 131
Robert, Yves, 38
Robert-Lynen Cinémathèque, 244
Robson, Mark, 189
Rocamora, Agnés, 172
Rode, Alfred, 36, 40
Rohmer, Eric, 4, 10, 54n13, 67, 70, 88, 116, 117, 232, 237
Roma città aperta/Rome Open City, 39

Romains, Jules, 31
roman-photo (photo novel), 235
romcom (romantic comedy), 156–165
Rome, Open City, 42
Rome Paris Films, 53
Roméro, N., 143
Rond-point des impasses, Le/The Roundabout of Dead-ends, 235
Ronet, Maurice, 35
Ronis, Willy, 147
Rose rouge, La/The Red Rose, 36–40
Ross, Kristin, 170
Rossellini, Roberto, 39, 42
Roth, L., 139
Roubanovitch, L., 139
Rouch, Jean, 74, 132
Rouquier, Georges, 234
Rozier, Jacques, 67
Rue, La, 30
Rue de l'Estrapade, 208
Rue de l'Evangile, 31
'Rue du Cinéma', 247
Rue du Moulin de la Pointe, 223
Rue et la tour, La ('The Street and the Tower'), 227
Rue Saint-Denis in *Paris vu par…*, 70
Ruthless, 191

Sabrina, 3
Sacré-Coeur, 27, 29, 108, 183, 186n22
Sadoul, Georges, 116
Saint-Etienne Cinémathèque, 144
Saint-Exupéry, François de, 2
Saint-Germain-des-Prés, 35–44, 68, 146, 236
Saint Laurent, Yves, 171
Saint-Sulpice church, 248
Samia, 90
Sang d'un poète, Le/The Poet's Blood, 142
Sans laisser d'adresse, 149
Sartre, Jean-Paul, 35, 37
Scarlet Peony, The, 36
Schlesser, Gilles, 36, 37
Schüfftan, Eugen, 187, 188, 193
Schwartz, Vanessa, 3, 169, 182
Sciamma, Céline, 7, 24, 92
Scipion, Robert, 37
Sebillet, E., 139

Sellier, Genevieve, 40, 93, 94, 168
Selznick, David O., 179–180, 182
Sempé, Jean-Jacques, 258
Sennett, Mack, 113
Serguine, Jacques, 114
Sette contro la morte/The Cavern, 191
Shaller, Y., 139
Sheringham, Michael, 209
Shumway, David R., 157
Signe du lion, Le/The Sign of Leo, 4, 45–52, 67–68, 70
silent film, Eiffel Tower in, 21–22
Simenon, Georges, 10, 104, 107, 108, 150
Singer, Ben, 6
Siodmak, Robert, 40, 187
Siouofi, N., 142
Smithson, Robert, 230
Smolders, Olivier, 138
Société d'Economie Mixte d'Aménagement des Halles (SEMAH), 82
Society for Historical Montmartre, 243
Sonate à Kreutzer, La/The Kreutzer Sonata, 45
Soupault, Philippe, 6
Sous les toits de Paris/Under the Roofs of Paris, 2, 29
Souviens-toi de moi/Remember Me, 90
Soyeux, Jean, 35
Spaak, Charles, 208
Spizza 30, 142
Spleen de Paris, Le (*Little Poems in Prose/Paris Spleen*), 188
Squale, La, 90
Steinlen, Théophile Alexandre, 231
Strange Illusion, 187, 191
Strange Woman, The, 191
street photography, 6
Stryge, Le/The Vampire, 189
Studio des Ursulines, 114
Studio Parnasse, 115
studio-made films, 3
Suard, F., 142
suburbs of Paris. *See banlieue*
Sue, Eugène, 146
Sulfamides 313, 36

Sur les pas d'Henry Miller; Paris 1930–1939/In the Footsteps of Henry Miller; Paris 1930–1939, 142

Tabou jazz club, 35
Taine, Hyppolite, 180
Tale of Two Cities, A, 179–186
Tant qu'on a la santé/As Long as You've Got Health, 232
Tardi, Jacques, 259, 264n3
Tartuffe, 152
Tati, Jacques, 148, 233, 251, 258
Tautou, Audrey, 248, 258, 259, 261
Tavernier, Bertrand, 11, 87
Taxi 2, 17
Tchernia, Pierre, 82, 137, 232
television, 10, 53, 77, 82, 87–88, 90–91, 93–96, 103–104, 114, 137, 218–229, 244, 245, 248. See also Maigret (BBC television)
Tellier, L., 139
terrorism, 11
Tester, Keith, 7
Thé au harem d'Archimède, Le/Tea in the Harem, 89
35 rhums/35 Shots of Rum, 11
Thompson, Danièle, 161
Time without Pity, 118
Tirez sur le pianiste/Shoot the Pianist, 59, 73
Topical Film Company, 19
Touche pas à la femme blanche/Don't Touch the White Woman!, 76–83, 238
Touchez pas au grisbi, 208
Tour, La/The Tower, 18
Tourbillon, 40
tourism, 1, 4, 9, 17, 35, 38, 42, 55, 72, 96, 108, 141, 157–159, 242, 247, 248
Tourneur, Jacques, 117
Tourneur, Maurice, 10, 236
Tout ce qui brille/All That Glitters, 90–93
'Traffic Problems', in *Cinq colonnes à la une*, 220
Trente Glorieuses, Les ('Thirty Glorious Years'), 61, 227, 229n36, 231, 233, 239
Tricheurs, Les/Youthful Sinners, 132
Triet, Justine, 11
Trivas, Victor, 32
Trocadéro, 141, 212
trou des Halles, 76, 83, 247–248

Truffaut, François, 10, 17, 19, 55–67, 70, 172–173, 235
Tirez sur le pianiste/Shoot the Pianist, 73
Turot, Henri, 243
2 Days in Paris, 159

UGC Cité-Ciné (multiplex), 247
Ulmer, Edgar George, 187, 188, 191
Un bonheur n'arrive jamais seul/Happiness Never Comes Alone, 95–96
Un homme marche dans la ville/A Man Walks in the City, 39
Un jour comme les autres/A Day Like Any, 234
Un long dimanche de fiançailles/A Very Long Engagement, 258, 259, 263
Un soleil à Paris/A Sun in Paris, 142
Uncini, Guiseppe, 230
Une femme est une femme/A Woman Is a Woman, 70
Une femme mariée/A Married Woman, 71, 73
Une nouvelle amie/The New Girlfriend, 96
Une Parisienne, 133, 134, 170
Une simple histoire/A Simple Story, 70
Une visite, 55
Ungar, Steven, 3, 125
Union-Hôtel, 69
urban everyday, 207–217
urban renewal, 218–229
Usine, L' ('The Factory'), 226
US romcoms, Paris-set, 157–160
Uzanne, Octave, 166

Vaches maigres chez Juliette Dodu/Lean Times at Juliette Dodu's, 142
Vadim, Roger, 60
Vanderschelden, Isabelle, 9, 10, 13, 253, 257, 264
Vappereau, Marguerite, 7, 8, 9, 10, 228, 230, 253
Varda, Agnès, 4, 7, 10, 67, 74, 88, 125–135, 173
Veber, Francis, 19
Védrès, Nicole, 17
Vel' d'Hiv, 196–206
Venault, Philippe, 137
Vengeance du serpent à plumes, La, 148
Ventura, Claude, 67

Vérité, La/The Truth, 133, 148
Verneuil, Henri, 88
Vian, Boris, 35, 37, 38
Victoria, 11
Vidéothèque de Paris, 242–248. See also Forum des Images
Vie parisienne, La (film) 40
Vie parisienne, La (opera) 41
Vie Parisienne, La (magazine) 167
Vieux-Colombier, 114
'vieux Paris, Le', 181, 183
Ville-Bidon, La, 88
Villion, Emile, 115, 120
Vincendeau, Ginette, 1, 3, 7, 8, 24n2, 87, 105, 109, 171
Vincent, Marie-Christine, 2
Visiteurs du soir, Les, 27
Vivre aujourd'hui ('Life Today'), 226
Vivre sa vie/My Life to Live, 68, 132, 70
Voici le temps des assassins/Deadlier Than the Male, 248
Voyage au bout de la nuit/Journey to the End of the Night, 146
Voyage in Italy, 42

Wagner, Alexandre, 89
Wallace, Jennifer, 7, 8, 10, 75, 98, 125
Wallace, Richard, 3
Walsh, Raoul, 116, 117
Walter Benjamin, 231
Watkins, James, 11
Week-End, Le, 11
Weiss, Don, 117
Whirlpool, 118
Wilder, Billy, 3
Wilson, Elizabeth, 1, 5, 12n15, 126, 166
Wimmer, Leila, 1, 8, 9, 113
Wolff, Janet, 1, 5
women, glamour of Parisienne, 166–176. See also Parisienne
working-class Paris, 26–34
World Cities Culture Report, 11n2
World War Two, 4, 114, 140, 196–206, 231, 236

Z Cars, 109
Zazie dans le métro, 19, 22–24
Zecca, Ferdinand, 148
Zola, Emile, 30, 33, 77, 167, 175n11, 247
zones pavillonnaires, 88, 93
Zorba the Greek, 225